New Philosophies of Learning

Edited by
Ruth Cigman and Andrew Davis

WILEY-BLACKWELL

A John Wiley & Sons, Ltd., Publication

This edition first published 2009
Originally published as Volume 42, Issues 3 & 4 of *The Journal of Philosophy of Education*
Chapters © 2009 The Authors
Editorial organization © 2009 Philosophy of Education Society of Great Britain

Blackwell Publishing was acquired by John Wiley & Sons in February 2007. Blackwell's publishing program has been merged with Wiley's global Scientific, Technical, and Medical business to form Wiley-Blackwell.

Registered Office
John Wiley & Sons Ltd, The Atrium, Southern Gate, Chichester, West Sussex, PO19 8SQ, United Kingdom

Editorial Offices
350 Main Street, Malden, MA 02148-5020, USA
9600 Garsington Road, Oxford, OX4 2DQ, UK
The Atrium, Southern Gate, Chichester, West Sussex, PO19 8SQ, UK

For details of our global editorial offices, for customer services, and for information about how to apply for permission to reuse the copyright material in this book please see our website at www.wiley.com/wiley-blackwell.

Library of Congress Cataloging-in-Publication Data

New philosophies of learning / edited by Ruth Cigman and Andrew Davis.
   p. cm.
"Originally published as volume 42, issues 3 & 4 of The Journal of Philosophy of Education"-T.p. verso.
  Includes bibliographical references and index.
  ISBN 978-1-4051-9564-5 (pbk. : alk. paper)
1. Education—Philosophy. 2. Learning, Psychology of. 3. Cognitive styles. I. Cigman, Ruth, 1951– II. Davis, Andrew, 1948– III. Journal of philosophy of education.
  LB14.7.N49 2009
  370.15'23-dc22
                       2009011980

A catalogue record for this book is available from the British Library.

01   2009

New Philosophies of Learning

Contents

Notes on Contributors

David Bakhurst is Professor of Philosophy and Head of Department at Queen's University, Kingston, Ontario.

Ruth Cigman is Senior Research Fellow in Philosophy of Education at the Institute of Education, University of London.

Michael Connell is Principal at the Institute for Knowledge Design, Cambridge, Massachusetts.

Paul Cooper is Professor of Education at the School of Education, University of Leicester.

Andrew Davis is Research Fellow at the School of Education, University of Durham.

Jan Derry is Senior Lecturer in philosophy of education at the Institute of Education, University of London.

Julian G. Elliott is Professor of Education and Director of Research at the School of Education, University of Durham.

Howard Gardner is Professor of Cognition and Education at the Harvard Graduate School of Education, Cambridge, Massachusetts.

Simon Gibbs is Senior Lecturer in Educational Psychology at the Newcastle University School of ECLS, University of Newcastle.

Usha Goswami is Professor of Education and Director of the Centre of Neuroscience and Education at the University of Cambridge

Paul Howard-Jones is Senior Lecturer in Education at the Graduate School of Education, University of Bristol.

Diana Laurillard is Professor of Learning with Digital Technologies, London Knowledge Lab, at the Institute of Education, University of London.

Jan Masschelein is Full Professor at the Centrum voor Wijsgerige Pedagogiek, K.U.Leuven.

Alistair Miller is doing doctoral research at the Institute of Education, University of London.

Charlotte Moore is a writer and journalist, who lives in Sussex, England with her three sons.

Karin Saskia Murris is Professor of Education at the University of the Witwatersrand, Johannesburg.

Sophie Rietti is Assistant Professor of Philosophy at the University of Ottawa.

Maarten Simons is Assistant Professor at the Centrum voor Onderwijsbeleid en - vernieuwing, K.U.Leuven.

Richard Smith is Professor of Education at the School of Education, University of Durham.

Paul Standish is Professor of Philosophy of Education at the Institute of Education, University of London.

Zachary Stein is Senior Teaching Fellow at the Harvard Graduate School of Education, Cambridge, Massachusetts.

Judith Suissa is Senior Lecturer in Philosophy of Education at the Institute of Education, University of London.

John White is Emeritus Professor of Philosophy of Education at the Institute of Education, University of London.

Christopher Winch is Head of Department and Professor of Educational Philosophy and Policy in the Department of Education & Professional Studies, King's College London.

Preface

Recent work in the philosophy of education has drawn attention to new developments in learning and to the part that these have played in reshaping the idea of education. There has been reason to warn of some dangers in these developments. In a culture of aggressive accountability and credentialism, the promise of new techniques—of teacher-proof teaching method and fail-safe procedures in a data-rich environment, no doubt, but also, in softer focus, of personalisation, learning styles and the holistic proclivities of the right-brain—may lure not only policy-makers and administrators but also teachers and students themselves. For are not teachers inclined, under the pressure of new forms of scrutiny and competition, to find themselves pedagogically challenged? And are not students also, as flexible learners anxious for achievement, eager for the latest educational quick fix? How much better then it surely is to have plain and transparent processes of learning, with clear-cut steps and crisply defined outcomes, sensitively enhanced and suitably tailored to the individual learner's needs. How much better, for the teacher, to know what-to-do-when, without that burden of constantly having to make decisions. How much better for the administrator and the inspector to have clear-cut criteria against which the efficiency of the learning process can be monitored and the performance of institutions accurately assessed. And yet how thin the understanding of education that these innovations breed! And what poor compensation is offered for the eclipse in the teacher's role of practical reason, the loss of trust in the teacher's engaged judgement, by the add-on of reflective practice! what is at stake in these developments is rarely just a matter of the particular technique that they advance but rather the nature of the relationships that they presuppose and reinforce: do these not contribute, each in its own way, to the cumulative disruption of the 'sacred triangle' of teacher, learner and content?

These complaints may seem legitimate enough. Yet this is only to glimpse some examples of what is on offer, when in fact the variety of new methods, and the diversity of the rationales that support them, escapes easy summary. There is always reason to think again about learning. So while it would be easy to dismiss some of these more banal and often gimmicky innovations, this would scarcely be to do justice to those new ideas that have arisen from substantial and serious scholarly work; ideas, it might be said, that respond more assiduously to the challenges of our times. There are, then, changes abroad in learning that deserve more careful and searching consideration: in developmental psychology; in the critical reconsideration of educational categorisations; in the exploitation of the new possibilities offered by ICT; in—most spectacularly—neuroscience; and in the challenge to the curriculum of rethinking what constitutes the good life, especially in terms of happiness and well-being.

The present collection of essays has been devised to answer to the need to take these developments seriously. To do this it undertakes a two-fold task: on the one hand, it exposes and examines the cultural effects of these innovations, especially in their less defensible manifestations; and, on the other, it assesses the cogency of the arguments and research that support their more robust elements. While the majority of the chapters that follow take issue with these new philosophies of learning in one way or another, the views of their advocates are also included, and this is important to our purposes. Hence, there are what we take to be desirable tensions between the chapters that ensue. These invite the reader to face up to the questions these developments raise: they provide a challenge to uncritical champions of the new, but also brusque rebuttal of any complacency on the part of those who take the innovators to task.

As has been indicated above, the matters at issue in these pages are not merely of technical importance—say, concerning which learning method works best. What is really at stake are questions about the nature of knowledge and how we learn, of what constitutes human being and the good life. These are of profound importance for our culture as a whole, and they can scarcely be ignored by anyone who teaches, any more than by the administrator and the policy-maker. We cannot afford to ignore these new philosophies of learning, and there is every reason to think that their careful reappraisal—in this context where advocates and critics meet—should render more legitimate our work as educators.

The editors of this volume, Ruth Cigman and Andrew Davis, have divided the collection into two main parts, each of which contains three suites of chapters that are thematically linked. Part One, entitled 'Neuroscience, Learner Categories and ICT', includes sections on 'Brain-based Learning', 'Learner Categories' and 'ICT and Learning'. Part Two, 'Learning and Human Flourishing', comprises 'The Enhancement Agenda', 'Non-cognitive Intelligences' and 'Learners, Teachers and Reflection'. The editors have provided introductions and commentary to these sections, in a way that draws out salient lines of argument and reveals the coherence of the debate in which the reader is invited to be engaged.

Part One draws attention to the multiple forms of learning innovation, beginning with the empirical and philosophical debates that attach to the idea of brain-based learning. While BrainGym offers what seems to be a handy, low-budget set of practical classroom exercises, the academic prestige of neuroscience, by contrast, seems to thrive in proportion to the considerable sums of money currently invested in it. Can neuroscience help in the practical business of learning, or is biological research largely irrelevant to education? Whether or not this expenditure is justified, the claims made for neuroscience in relation to education, and the research base that is being generated, certainly merit careful examination. Neuroscience appears to be uncovering the 'dysfunctions' that account for a range of learning difficulties, but it is not clear how far these can be understood without reference to the normative and cultural context within which the learner is situated. Does faith in neuroscience, then, ultimately involve a reductionist understanding of what human being is like? In fact, the claims and achievements of the whole psychometric tradition must be judged against the idea that learning is inextricably linked to contexts and situations. If the predominant orientation of the chapters here is one of scepticism, especially regarding neuroscience's grander aspirations, there is evidence also within these pages of the stronger and more substantial case that can be provided.

Under the heading 'Learner Categories', contributors address the thorny problem of how differentiating learners can lead to discrimination. Is it possible to differentiate without comparing and evaluating? The potent effects of such labels as 'dyslexic' and 'ADHD' are considered, as are the consequences of the 'statementing' of children, and the reader is reminded of the scepticism expressed within certain strands of (anti)psychiatry about how far such disorders are real. Relevant here also is the more contemporary movement that identifies such 'deficit thinking' as demeaning and disrespectful, with its commitment to full inclusion and its tendency towards the denial of difference.

ICT's potential to 'transform' learning is the topic of the third set of chapters. While there is no doubt amongst the contributors to these essays about the enhancement to teaching and learning that ICT can offer, there are questions in abundance about the sometimes excessive faith that is placed in the black-box, technical, all-purpose solution it seems sometimes to be held to provide. In particular, there are questions to be raised about the effects of ICT on the way that knowledge is understood. What is the 'information' in 'information technology'? Utterly familiar though this expression has now become, there is reason to wonder how much of the original sense of 'information' is retained—where to inform was to convey the truth about something—when the word is incorporated so effortlessly into 'ICT': information becomes data, with no necessary purchase on truth. New technologies, themselves constantly under development, are progressively shaping not only the way that we think of learning and our understanding of what knowledge is, but also the very nature of the world we live in. All this must be subjected to critical evaluation, and there can be no space for the Luddite. Furthermore, any realistic sense of citizenship and democracy must plainly be attuned to this changing environment, and perhaps this warrants new theorisations of learning in constructivist terms; perhaps it endorses interactive learning. But where does this leave the project of liberal education? Such matters cannot be broached without consideration of the essentially ethical question of what counts as worthwhile learning, whether for liberal or vocational ends. The place of ICT in learning needs to be addressed within this ethical question.

The opening subsection of Part Two, entitled 'The Enhancement Agenda', examines various attempts to incorporate practices into education that purport to foster the well-being and happiness of students. The enormous influence of Richard Layard's 'science of happiness' alone justifies the prominence of this theme in the collection, and our contributors take issue in different ways with the manner in which the idea has assumed a new prominence today. We are encouraged to question specifically the prevailing, somewhat one-tracked conception of happiness, as if happiness and unhappiness necessarily existed in a kind of continuum. More broadly, the approach of 'positive psychology', which has recently gained a higher profile in educational and in therapeutic practice, comes under attack. Do the measures positive psychology promotes amount to an 'emotional habituation' of students to the status quo? And how far do these perceived challenges displace what have commonly been taken to be the higher and more central aspirations of education? These are questions the reader is invited to consider.

Under the heading 'Non-cognitive Intelligences', the collection turns to the highly influential but controversial notions of multiple and emotional intelligences, taking forward debates that have been 'live' for some time and introducing new dimensions to the discussion. Very much at issue is the question of how far intelligence can be understood both as natural (or biological) and as a cultural construction. There is, furthermore, reason to question how far accounts of emotional intelligence, like those of well-being and self-esteem, fight shy of direct consideration of ethical matters, becoming in the process a conceptual muddle and offering no more than a panacea. Once again the importance of questions of naming is emphasised. Where the new learning becomes jargon, appropriate vigilance is called for: categorising people, perhaps especially with such familiar terms as 'intelligent' or 'unintelligent', as 'normal' or 'abnormal', can lead to educational deprivation; so what impoverishments may that new jargon hold in store? Political and moral imperatives are never far from what the close examination of such concepts and language reveals.

In the final suite of chapters, 'Learners, Teachers and Reflection', developments such as learning how to learn, philosophy for children and learning environments are considered. The basis for contemporary assertions that the agenda in education must pass from teaching to learning, apparent as this is especially in the rhetoric of lifelong learning, has never been clearly elaborated, and aspects of the new piety towards learning are examined here in some detail. The section also challenges the assumption that optimum learning involves smooth and relatively stress-free progression towards clearly defined ends, emphasising instead the ways that the experience of puzzlement and disequilibrium, and the practice of making the familiar strange, can figure fruitfully in education. In similar vein, the somewhat modish idea of the learning environment, virtual or otherwise, is here questioned in terms of the kind of construction of the learner it effects.

Emphasis was drawn at the start to the ways that these new innovations in learning are rarely just a matter of technique. Given the essential role of learning in human life, its closeness to the very idea of the human, these reconstructions, piecemeal though some may seem to be, go hand-in-hand with larger changes in the ways we are increasingly required to see ourselves. The new philosophies of learning become philosophies of life, and the close examination of educational techniques in the chapters that follow opens onto the largest questions. This book series is indebted to

Ruth Cigman and Andrew Davis for the imaginative way they have approached the philosophical and educational problems that our topic raises, and for the fine collection of essays they have assembled to address the task. Their enthusiastic engagement with contributors during the writing of the chapters along with the intercalation between sections of their helpful and insightful commentary have produced a combined text that is considerably more than the sum of its parts. The product is indeed a resource to help us to think meaningfully about learning and about its place in the lives of human beings.

Paul Standish

Part I

Neuroscience, Learner Categories and ICT

1

BRAIN-BASED LEARNING

1.1
Introduction

RUTH CIGMAN AND ANDREW DAVIS

Issues surrounding the growing importance of what is sometimes referred to as 'brain-based learning' span both empirical and philosophical debates. All but one of the contributors to this section have a background in empirical research. The exception, David Bakhurst, is first and foremost a philosopher. Nevertheless, all of them offer insights into the complex interrelationships between the sciences of the brain and mind on the one hand, and philosophical accounts of the mind on the other.

Contemporary opinions about the importance of cognitive neuroscience for education vary wildly—from the idea that neuroscience has the potential to solve many important challenges currently faced by educators, to the sceptical view that biological research is largely irrelevant to our understanding of learning.

Usha Goswami sketches some important fundamental facts about neurological development, following this with an illuminating survey of what she sees as current research questions that span cognitive neuroscience and the study of learning. She covers four headings: neural structures for learning, the interconnections between neural structures, studies about the timing of neural activity which help us discover what neural structures are implicated in particular types of cognition and the topic of neural correlation versus causation. She proceeds to note worries about 'neuromyths'—that is, overblown claims made about brain-based learning. Such exaggerated stances are often taken by self-styled educators on the fringe of neuroscience, rather than by academically respectable scientists.

At the heart of her chapter is a summary of learning principles which she feels are robustly supported by empirical research. These, she believes, 'can be incorporated into education and teaching'. She contends that learning is incremental, experienced based, multi-sensory, that brain mechanisms involved in learning 'extract' structure from experience even when that structure is not directly taught, that learning is social, that the crucial importance of emotions in learning is explicable at least in part in evolutionary terms, and that 'it is never too late to learn', given what is now known about the plasticity of brain functioning. She ends by noting that we should be able to identify 'neural markers' to help educators to intervene with pupils especially at risk of encountering learning difficulties. Neuroscience can also help us, she argues, to maximise the efficiency with which the brain learns. She is fully behind the goal of crossing disciplinary boundaries—e.g. of biological and cultural studies in order to develop a 'truly effective discipline of education'.

Paul Howard-Jones, though writing from an empirical research orientation, ventures into the complex intellectual territory that forms the interface between neuroscience and other educational approaches to learning. He examines claims made by some philosophers that certain attempts to draw on neuroscience to further our understanding of learning 'stray beyond the bounds of sense'. Well-known recent proponents of such claims are Bennett and Hacker (2003). Howard-Jones compares accounts of learning offered by neuroscience with those generated from disciplines more traditionally associated with education, following this with a critical discussion of the tensions between these two perspectives. His account of cognitive neuroscience focuses on an effort to understand the interrelations between mind and brain. He argues that there need be no conflict between contemporary neuroscientific thinking about learning, and those social sciences emphasising social and cultural factors. Concerns about the *free will* or otherwise of the learner are the focus of a final section. He concludes by emphasising the importance of attending to the philosophical issues 'within and between' neuroscience and education.

Zachary Stein, Michael Connell and Howard Gardner's chapter covers a wide range of issues, but for the purposes of this section we concentrate on their treatment of neuroscience and education. They emphasise the need for an interdisciplinary synthesis when dealing with key educational issues, and draw attention to what they see as past failures to achieve this. They cite the collaboration of a neuroscientist with a philosopher (Changeux and Ricoeur, 2000). The two participants have, in the view of the authors of this chapter, allegiances to 'two radical distinct viewpoints', namely the scientific perspective on the one hand, and a preoccupation with meaning and value on the other. The result 'is disciplinary ships passing in the epistemological night' (this volume, p. 45).

Their support for an interdisciplinary synthesis is explored further through the example of numeracy. We can study this, the authors tell us, by means of a variety of perspectives, including both neurones in networks, and symbol systems in societies. Developmental dyscalculia is due, on their account, to unusual brain phenomena, which in turn suggest genetic causes. They are also clear that culture impacts significantly on the way such a disability manifests itself. There are 'tensions' between the scientific account and the cultural story. They proceed to speak eloquently of the value issues surrounding the diagnosis and treatment of learning disabilities, pointing out the possibility that 'abnormal' brain states, once postulated, might lead educators to aim at 'normal' states. Such a move arguably sidelines some crucial normative questions.

David Bakhurst draws on his extensive knowledge of Soviet philosophy to reflect upon and illuminate the murky relationships between brain science and notions of mind and person. He evaluates the arguments of Evald Ilyenkov, who fought the influence of 'brainism' in education, a view which links students' capacities to learn with their brain functions, these in turn being strongly associated with genetic factors and the supposition of innate abilities. Bakhurst emphasises that there is much more than mere historical interest in these arguments, urging that 'the problems that exercised Ilyenkov remain with us, and in many respects we are no closer to resolving them' (this volume, p. 59). He contrasts 'brainism' with 'personalism'. According to the latter, it is the *person* who 'sees, hears, imagines, infers, speculates, hopes, intends, wants, reasons' (this volume, p. 56), rather than the brain. Bakhurst devotes much attention to evaluating some arguments for personalism. An educator strongly persuaded by personalism seems unlikely to appeal to neuroscience when seeking to understand the character of learning and how it might best be developed.

Bakhurst notes the relatively cautious claims made about learning by neuroscientists such as Blakemore and Frith, but also the less modest programs suggested by others, using so-called scientific authority. Ilyenkov would have been 'provoked', we are told, by Blakemore and Frith's entertaining the possibility that one day people might pop pills to learn.

Bakhurst defends Ilyenkov up to a point by drawing on John McDowell, and the idea that children learn to inhabit the 'space of reasons'. The thinking of such inhabitants is subject to *normative* rational explanations, which contrast sharply with the causal explanations appropriate to the natural sciences, including neuroscience. Bakhurst contends that brain science need not be restricted to explaining *limitations* in student learning, and opposes Ilyenkov's view that only social factors 'are relevant to the explanation of ability and achievement' (this volume, p. 67). However, he ends by urging that any enthusiasm for contemporary scientific advances should not blind us to the crucial role of *value* in education. This point echoes those made by many other contributors to this volume, including those writing about the enhancement agenda.

1.2

Philosophical Challenges for Researchers at the Interface between Neuroscience and Education

PAUL HOWARD-JONES

INTRODUCTION

In the last decade, there has been a growing educational interest in the brain that reflects an increasing belief amongst some scientists, as well as educators, that education can benefit from neuroscientific insights into how we develop and learn. Initiatives have gone by various names, such as 'Brain, Mind and Education', 'Neuroeducation', 'Educational Neuroscience' and 'Brain and Education'. Although these names may come to represent some differentiation in approach, all these initiatives share a common goal: to combine our educational understanding with our biological understanding of brain function and learning.[1] Several reports have assessed the opportunities offered by this new perspective, and a valuable interdisciplinary dialogue is emerging (Byrnes and Fox, 1998; Geake and Cooper, 2003; Goswami, 2004, 2006). In 2000, Uta Frith and her colleague Sarah-Jayne Blakemore completed a commission by the Teaching and Learning Research Programme (TLRP) to review neuroscientific findings that might be of relevance to educators (Blakemore and Frith, 2000). This review attacked a number of 'neuromyths', including those concerning critical periods for educational development, and highlighted new areas of potential interest to educators such as the role of innate mathematical abilities, visual imagery, implicit processes and sleep in learning. Rather than point out areas where neuroscience could immediately be applied in the classroom, the review sought to highlight neuroscientific research questions that might interest educators, thus making an important initial step towards defining an interdisciplinary area of collaborative research.

In 1999, as the Blakemore and Frith report was being commissioned in the UK, the supranational project on 'Learning Sciences and Brain Research' was being launched by the Centre for Educational Research and Innovation (CERI) at the Organisation for Economic Cooperation and Development (OECD). The first phase of the project (1999–2002) brought together international researchers to review the potential implications of recent research findings in brain research for policy-makers, with a second phase (2002–2006) channelling its activities into three significant areas: Literacy, Numeracy and Lifelong Learning. This OECD project revealed the high level of international interest in developing a dialogue between neuroscience and education, as well as highlighting the diversity of approaches across the world (OECD, 2002, 2007). In April 2005, the TLRP initiated its second initiative in this area, by commissioning the seminar series 'Collaborative Frameworks in Neuroscience and Education'. This produced a commentary, whose popularity (downloading 110,000 copies in the first 6 months after publication) demonstrated the rapidly growing and broadly-based educational interest in the brain (Howard-Jones, 2007). Also in 2007, the specialist journal *Mind, Brain and Education* was launched by Blackwells. In June 2008, a special issue of the educational journal 'Educational Research' was dedicated to neuroscience and education, suggesting that this area is now on its way to becoming an established part of mainstream educational research.

Although interest may be blossoming in this new area, several challenges await those wishing to venture there and some of these are of a fundamental and philosophical nature. Philosophy investigates the 'bounds of sense: that is, the limits of what can coherently be thought and said' (Bennett and Hacker, 2003, p. 399). Those who attempt to work at the interface of neuroscience and education will find themselves straddling at least two, very different, philosophies about learning, each expounding a very different set of concepts. That makes it entirely easy to stray beyond the bounds of sense, at least as interpreted by one or both of these communities. To understand this, and other philosophical challenges faced by researchers within the new field of neuroscience and education, it is first necessary to understand the meaning of 'learning' as it is commonly understood within each community.

1 WHAT IS LEARNING? THE VIEW FROM NEUROSCIENCE
Learning and Memory

In neuroscience, the term 'learning', when used as a noun, is often synonymous with memory. There is now a general acceptance that we have multiple memory systems that can operate both independently and in parallel with each other. It can be useful to classify these broadly in terms of declarative and nondeclarative systems. The declarative memory system is closest to the everyday meaning of 'memory' and perhaps most clearly related to educational concepts of learning. Defined as our capacity to recall consciously everyday facts and events, this system appears most dependent on structures in the medial temporal lobe (e.g. the hippocampus) and the diencephalon (Squire, 2004). The forming and recalling of declarative memories is known to activate a variety of additional areas in the cortex, whose location can appear influenced by other characteristics of these memories, such as whether these are episodic (the re-experiencing of events) or semantic (facts). Nevertheless, it appears semantic and episodic memory arise from essentially the same system, with models now emerging of how the hippocampus operates in facilitating these different types of declarative memory(Shastri, 2002). Whereas declarative memory is representational and provides us with the means to model the world, and to explicitly compare and contrast remembered material, nondeclarative memory is expressed through performance rather than recollection. Declarative memories can be judged as either true or false, whereas nondeclarative memories appear only as changes in behaviour and cannot be judged in terms of their accuracy. 'Nondeclarative memory' is actually an umbrella term for a range of memory abilities arising from a set of other systems. These include the acquisition of skills and habits (related to changes in activity in the striatum) and conditioned emotional responses (associated with activity in the amygdale). Other nonassociative learning responses (such as when a response is diminished by repetitive exposure to a stimulus) can be linked to reflex pathways located chiefly in the spinal cord.

Connectivity

An appreciation of memory as distributed and involving multiple systems is important, but it tells us little about the process by which a memory is achieved. Within the neuroscience community, there is a common acceptance that human learning, in terms of the formation of memory, occurs by changes in the patterns of connectivity between neurons—or 'synaptic plasticity'. There are two key ways in which this can occur, known as long-term potentiation (LTP) and long-term depression (LTD).

LTP refers to an enduring increase (upwards of an hour) of the efficiency by which a neuron relays electrical information, as a result of a temporal pairing (coincidence in time) between the incoming and outgoing signal. Its role within the hippocampus, an area key to formation of memory, has been the subject of particular focus. LTP refers to the ability of a neuron to adjust its connectivity, in response to signals related in time, an ability celebrated in the expression 'neurons that fire together, wire together'.[2] This may seem a modest ability but, as can be seen in simulations involving artificial neurons, it affords even small networks the possibility of organising themselves to produce a type of 'learning' with human-like qualities and a range of cognitive functions (Arhib, 2003; McClelland and Rogers, 2003; Hebb, 1947). Such networks can 'learn' to identify patterns, make useful guesses and exhibit a graded decrease in functionality when connections are lesioned, as do biological neural networks—so called 'graceful degradation'. Long-term depression refers to an enduring decrease in synaptic efficiency. This is a mechanism thought to explain, for example, how neurons in the pererhinal cortex decrease their output as a stimulus is repeatedly presented, underlying our ability to recognise familiarity.

It is not presently possible to directly observe the role of synaptic plasticity in human learning, or the mechanisms thought to facilitate it. Instead, less direct evidence is sought. One example of this type of evidence arises from treating animals with a protein-synthesis inhibitor, known to diminish the retention of memory. Animals treated in this way are shown to suffer a slow (over a period of hours) onset of amnesia, which coincides with decreasing ability to maintain LTP. Such studies are typical in their provision of compelling evidence as opposed to a firm proof of the role of LTP. Present data suggests we can be sure such mechanisms are necessary for learning, but we cannot be sure that the plasticity required for learning rests on these alone (Martin *et al.*, 2000). Or, as warned in a recent review, 'establishing a causal connection between a specific form of synaptic plasticity and the behavioural consequences of specific experiences remains a daunting task' (Citri and Malenka, 2008, p. 30). Indeed, in recent years, there has been increasing criticism within neuroscience of the synaptic plasticity hypothesis. Doubt has been shed upon whether stable declarative memory formation, lasting over decades, is founded on such an unstable phenomenon as synaptic plasticity. This is one of the considerations underlying suggestions for a genomic hypothesis of memory, in which DNA modifications serve as carriers of elementary memory traces (Arshavsky, 2006; Crick, 1984; Davis and Squire, 1984).

Working Memory

There is another, very important, memory ability essential to the type of learning promoted by education. Working memory refers to our ability to temporarily hold information arriving via our senses, or from a longer term store of memory, in order to process it. It is very limited in its capacity. This is demonstrated when, for example, we are writing down a telephone number. Because we can only hold a few unrelated digits in our working memory, we prefer to receive the number in chunks of just 3–4 digits, writing these down before hearing the next few. Activity associated with working memory has been observed in many different parts of the brain, but particularly in an area of the frontal lobes known as the Dorso-Lateral PreFrontal Cortex (DLPFC). Rather than being supported by mechanisms of synaptic plasticity and the production of new connectivity, it would appear that the DLPFC supports working memory by controlling a temporary increase in activity within pre-existing networks that are either within the DLPFC itself or in other areas of the brain where the information is stored (Curtis and D'Esposito, 2003).

Structural Change

In addition to producing changes at the cellular level in terms of connectivity, learning has also been linked to gross structural changes in the brain. Research has shown that learning can produce detectable changes in brain structure over quite short time periods. In a study of adults learning to juggle, the brain areas activated at the beginning of a three-month training period increased in size by the end of it. After three further months of rest, these areas had shrunk back and were closer to their original size (Draganski *et al.*, 2004). It is not presently clear how these structural changes come about and whether, for example, they are due to increased connectivity or the birth of new cells such as glial cells or even neurons.

Functional Correlates

When learning has occurred, it is often possible to observe accompanying changes in biological function. For example, in an fMRI study (Delazer *et al.*, 2003), adults attempting to perform long multiplication generated increased blood flow in the frontal areas associated with working memory load, as these learners worked consciously through new routines step-by-step. However, after practising for a week (25 minutes per day), their performance had improved and imaging showed increased activity in those posterior regions associated with more automatic processing demands. At the same time, frontal activity had decreased in a way indicative of reduced load on working memory. This provides a clear demonstration of how learning is often accompanied by a shift in patterns of activity within brain networks, rather than an increase or decrease *per se* in a single region of the brain. Since we draw on different mental resources when we are first attempting a task, compared with when we are proficient, one may expect a changing relationship between regions of brain activity and learning over time. Thus, any changes in biological activity need to be interpreted in relation to a clear dynamic cognitive model of the learning processes involved and a clear, if often hypothetical, understanding of how different brain networks may be supporting these processes (for discussion see Kaufmann, 2008; Varma and Schwartz, 2008).

2 WHAT IS LEARNING? THE VIEW FROM EDUCATION

Educational ideas about learning are diverse and eclectic in their origins. They are the product of a variety of different processes and forces, including those arising from theoretical educational and psychological traditions, and other culturally transmitted ideas from within and beyond the teaching profession. The lack of consensus and shifting values within the institutions of education also ensure diversity amongst teachers' individual beliefs. Teachers' personal beliefs develop through an accrued professional understanding and do not usually require empirical validation. A teacher's beliefs may not always be reflected in their practise or their justification for it, and neither of these is immune from pragmatism and the pressures of political expediency.

A recent study in the USA (Snider and Roehl, 2007) supported previous research in revealing a generally atheoretical approach amongst teachers (Pinnegar and Carter, 1990), but with beliefs more consistent with the traditions of constructivism than explicit instruction. At the heart of constructivist theories of learning, is the belief that learners construct knowledge based on their own experiences and prior beliefs. Successful learning requires opportunities for meaningful and authentic exploration, engaging activities, interactive group work and student ownership of the learning process.

The executive of Britain's key programme of educational research (Teaching and Learning Research Programme, TLRP) recently published 'Principles into Practice—a teacher's guide to research evidence on teaching and learning'. A review of this text (TLRP, 2007) provides some further indication of the types of ideas about learning that are currently favoured in the UK. The pull-out centre pages list 10 principles. Principles 1 and 6 expand the concept of what learning can achieve beyond factual recall, emphasising that it must 'equip learners for life in the broadest sense', promoting learners' independence and autonomy such that they have 'the will and confidence to become agents of their own learning'. In their indication of how such learning is achieved, Principles 3, 4, 5 and 7 reflect strong constructivist leanings, recognising 'the importance of prior experience and learning', emphasising the need to assess meaningful understanding and to foster 'both individual and social processes and outcomes'. Indeed, Principle 4 states directly that 'effective teaching and learning requires the teacher to scaffold learning'. 'Scaffolding' is a term well known to educators that describes how a teacher can control elements of a task that are initially beyond the learner's capacity, thus permitting him/her to concentrate attention on those elements that are within his/her range of competence (Wood *et al.*, 1976). Principles 2, 8, 9 and 0 encourage an understanding of learning that extends beyond the school pupil, emphasising the importance of teachers' continuous professional development, the significance of informal learning such as that occurring out of school and policy at institutional and system level. The report from which these principles were drawn likens educational innovations to a pebble being thrown into a pond (TLRP, 2006). The first ripple may be a change in classroom processes and outcomes, but this may have implications for teachers' roles, values, knowledge and beliefs. This may require a change in professional development and training that may, in turn, influence school structure and even national policy. The key point here (illustrated in Figure 1) is that changes at any one of these levels may have implications at another level, and that factors influencing learning are distributed and interrelated with each other in complex ways.

The UK and US reports discussed above make no mention of the biological processes involved with learning. Instead, there is an emphasis on social construction, learning within groups and communities, and the importance of context. Additionally, there are issues of meaning, the will to learn, values and how these and other aspects of learning extend beyond the level of the individual.

3 CONCERNS ABOUT THE INCOMPATIBILITY OF NEUROSCIENTIFIC AND EDUCATIONAL PERSPECTIVES ON LEARNING

Some of the concerns in the new discourse between neuroscience and education revolve around some quite old arguments. One of these is an extreme form of dualism: in which the mind and brain are considered as

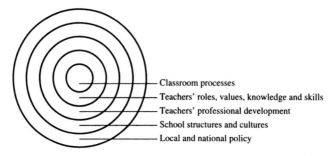

- Classroom processes
- Teachers' roles, values, knowledge and skills
- Teachers' professional development
- School structures and cultures
- Local and national policy

Figure 1 Levels of educational change as proposed in a recent commentary by the Teaching and Learning Research Programme (TLRP, 2006). Adapted from Blakemore and Frith (2000) with permission of the authors.

separate and distinct. The opposite point of view, that they are one and the same, is described here as monism.

Monism: Does Brain = Mind?

Given the very different perspectives on learning within neuroscience and education, it is not surprising that there are concerns about, for example, how helpful neuroscience will be in influencing educational thinking. Some of these concerns have crystallised into objections in principle that have been expressed in terms of basic philosophy. For example, one author has explored the possibility that claims of brain science being relevant to learning involve a 'category mistake' (Davis, 2004). To illustrate this possibility, Davis refers to an article in *Educational Leadership* in which the author discusses learning something new in terms of the brain looking 'for an existing circuit or network into which the information will fit' (Wolfe, 1998, p. 64). In this chapter, the author goes on to discuss how reading about quantum physics cannot make meaningful sense without previously stored information about physics. Davis correctly identifies the author's implicit suggestion that she has empirical evidence for a conceptual truth. Further, Davis suggests this is a typical category mistake, in the sense that connections between psychological items are being confused with neurophysiological connections.

In terming this a category error, Davis suggests that the writer considers the mind, or our 'mental domain', as a category distinct from the brain, and that she has made a mistake in using these two categories—a type of dualism gone wrong. An alternative explanation is that the writer is applying a simplistic brain-mind model that appears to inappropriately conflate the two concepts into one—a type of neurocognitive monism. If we consider the mind and brain as the same thing, we can use terms usually associated with the mind to describe the brain, e.g. 'my brain is confused'. In the instance described by Davis, Wolfe may indeed have made an accidental error in her thinking or expression. Alternatively, she may be deliberately conflating mind and brain in order to provide some provisional truth that is more digestible and more clearly supports the pedagogic advice she wants to promote. Suggesting one-to-one corre-spondences between connections in the mind and synaptic connections in the brain is typical of the type of folk cognitive neuroscience used to market many commercial 'brain-based' educational programmes. But, as is often the case, there is also some grain of truth upon which such explanations are founded. As discussed above, a connection between two concepts in the mind is commonly considered to involve neuronal connections being made, or strengthened, between neurons. As described by Mel (2002): 'pull the average neuroscientist off the street and ask them how learning occurs in the brain, and you're likely to get a reflex response that includes such pat phrases as "activity-dependent changes in synaptic strength, LTP/LTD"'. However, as already described, there are flaws in arguments promoting such mechanisms as a sufficient basis for learning. Therefore, whatever error Wolfe is making, and whether it is deliberate or otherwise, Davis may be correct in suggesting that neuroscience should not presently be used to provide any additional support for promoting concepts of meaning-making that are essentially psychological. Neither might such support be needed, since these psychological concepts are well supported by behavioural studies, even if the neuroscientific search is still on for the biological substrates.

Within neuroscience and psychology, I would argue that scientists are usually quite careful in not conflating mind and brain. I would also argue that neuroscience is well-policed in terms of monism, since there are experts in both the brain and the mind that are defensive of their own territory being misappropriated, as well as peer-reviewed journals where arguments for mind-brain relationships can be thrashed out on the basis of empirical evidence. Others, however, suggest modern neuroscience itself is beset with conceptual confusions arising from attempts to portray our emotional, cognitive and perceptual mental states as states of the brain (Bennett and Hacker, 2003). The claim here is that scientists are prone to their own type of absolute monism, i.e. a belief that the mind can be fully described by states of the brain. In the sense that our mind's contents is influenced by a variety of other external and internal factors beyond the brain itself, Bennett and Hacker suggest that ascribing our mental states to brain states is no more sensible than ascribing them to an immaterial soul. Bennett and Hacker point out that scientists contribute to the impression that our minds are our brains through unrelenting efforts to use metaphors in describing *representations* in the brain (e.g. 'maps', 'symbols, 'images') when these, as commonly understood, cannot exist there. Pointing out that a map is a pictorial representation that follows conventions and is available to be read by a map-reader, Bennett and Hacker accuse neuroscience of using 'old' terms in new ways. However, the fluid use of such metaphors is often essential in formulating hypotheses that may, in one sense, be false (Churchland, 2005). For example, there are no 2-dimensional maps in the brain that use easily understood conventions. And yet, these metaphors can still be meaningful, such that it is sensible to talk of a complex, interactive but essentially topographical mapping of sensory information at different levels of the sensory pathway. The meaning of map in this context is thus contingent and may develop with the conceptual progress made when such hypotheses are scientifically tested. That said, Bennett and Hacker (2003) correctly point out that the 'original' meanings of such words often stem from a folk psychology that is, itself, not policed by the sorts of revisionary pressures within science. Thus, looking also at the range of examples identified by their analysis, it is easy to understand how the meanings ascribed to the same vocabulary within the neuroscientific and other communities, including education, have been rapidly diverging.

This divergence in meaning, the lack of revisionary pressure and scarcity of forums for interdisciplinary communication (Howard-Jones, in press), makes education vulnerable to monist 'non-sense' and presents the first potential challenge for those working to enrich educational thinking with ideas about the brain. Here, as in the case with Wolfe, implicit monism can be used to provide the impression that conclusive biological evidence exists for a psychological idea about how our minds work, or even that a previous biological observation can now be given psychological relevance, when, in fact, no such evidence exists.

Dualism: Are Brain and Mind Distinct Concepts?

If the mind is entirely separate from the brain, then one can make statements about brain-behaviour relationships without considering the mind, or mind-behaviour relationships without considering the brain. If we consider the mind and brain as separate entities, then the mind has no efficacy upon the brain, or vice versa. Indeed, it is difficult to understand how such a view affords any possibility of mind-brain interaction. Again, like monism, few would express a dualistic view explicitly, but it is not hard to find its implicit reference. Partly, this may be because not explicitly mentioning the potential relevance of biological processes to complex cognition, particularly of the types associated with problematic areas such as consciousness, can help neuroscientists publish their work without becoming embroiled with issues that psychologists and philosophers feel more comfortable arguing about. For example, consider the quotation from a scientist that Davis uses to defend his position. This suggests that, to a large extent, mind and brain can be considered as two distinct concepts: 'Our brains do not understand. They do not assign or contemplate meanings. They are only electrical and chemical processes in brain activity which would have no meaning except in so far as they are the working of cognitive tools that *people* use to think with' (Harré, 2002).

Such a statement, suggesting that the brain may reflect the mind but does not contribute to mental meaning, brings us close to a dualistic sense of mind as a theoretical concept that should be considered entirely separately from the physical world, including the brain. It is not difficult to find evidence of a dualist approach existing implicitly in matters connected with the brain, including amongst scientists. Degrandpre conducted a scathing analysis (Degrandpre, 1999) of what he called the 'new scientific dualism' by reviewing studies such as that which claimed differences in brain function between two samples of children, with and without a diagnosis of ADHD, might provide the basis for 'biologically valid criteria' for diagnosis (Vaidya *et al.*, 1998). This study implied such biological differences were causal and led to headlines such as 'Test found to identify attention disorder'. As identified by Degrandpre, however, the results might equally be interpreted as the physiological correlates of a behavioural problem caused by some other factor. This extra factor might be an alternative biological issue, or environmental one, such as their education or their home experiences. The tendency to ignore such factors, as in this confusion between correlation and causation, may arise from an assumption, implicit or otherwise, that the brain can be considered independently of the mind and the external influences upon it.

Another example is also helpful in understanding the dangers of such dualism, covert or otherwise, for education. In a local newspaper, a headteacher discusses the challenge provided by a child suffering from ADHD: 'He is uncontrollable and we do not have the facility or resources at the school to cope with his intolerable behaviour ... this is a medical problem and we need to find a solution that is best for everyone' (Parkinson, 2006). Here, it appears that the biological aspects of ADHD have surfaced as its most salient feature just when all educational efforts to support the child have failed. This may be because medicalisation of a problem effectively shifts the focus of professional responsibility. Once separated from the mind, cause can be attributed freely to the biology of the brain and seen as legitimately leaving the educator's domain of influence.

However, brain processes are clearly more than just a *reflection* of our mind's attempt to assign and contemplate meaning, since the suppression of brain processes (through trauma or experimental techniques such as Transcranial Magnetic Stimulation)[3] can reduce such mental abilities. Biological processes in the brain thus appear intimately bound up with our cognitive abilities, even if they cannot be considered as the same thing. Indeed, our personalities, our values and the recall of what we have learnt and experienced can all be influenced by the biology of our brains. Furthermore, and as discussed above, we know that our mental life, as stimulated by our experiences, can influence our brain development at a number of different levels. Thus, whilst dualism can become, for purely pragmatic reasons, an attractive philosophy for educators and scientists alike, it seems unwise and often nonsensical to consider the mind and brain in separation from each other.

Returning to the example of ADHD, the prevalent use of drugs in its treatment does not mean that this disorder is wholly a medical problem beyond the influence of the school environment. On the contrary, there is growing evidence that teachers following informed strategies can play an important role in improving the well-being and academic performance of students suffering from ADHD (Corkum *et al.*, 2005; Gureasko-Moore *et al.*, 2006; Miranda *et al.*, 2002). Recent successful interventions include the application of cognitive and instructional approaches to managing children's behaviour, the inclusion of parents and teachers in such interventions and the training of students themselves in self-management. Such research emphasises the importance of teachers' understanding of the disorder, its medication and management. It is also reminds us of the practical benefits of avoiding dualist notions, which can be considered as the second fundamental hazard of a philosophical nature faced by workers at the interface between neuroscience and education.

4 MIND AND BRAIN TOGETHER: COGNITIVE NEUROSCIENCE

Understanding the dangers of monism and dualism leads to a desire to understand mind and brain as concepts under construction, used in describing the mental and biological aspects of our behaviour and intimately related in some, mostly still to be determined, way. The interrelation between mind and brain is not straightforward. Indeed, a whole field of scientific research, cognitive neuroscience, has been founded on efforts to achieve such understanding. Cognitive neuroscientists believe that mind and brain must be explained together (Blakemore and Frith, 2000). In this field, the notion of mind is regarded as a theoretical but essential concept in exploring the relationship between our brain and our behaviour, including our learning.

Seen in this way, the study of cognition appears as a vital bridge in linking our knowledge of the brain to our observations of behaviours involving learning. Indeed, it has been pointed out that without sufficient attendance to suitable cognitive psychological models, neuroscience will have little to offer education (Bruer, 1997).

Figure 2 shows a well known model used by cognitive neuroscientists to combine environmental, biological, cognitive and behavioural levels of description (Morton and Frith, 1995). Invisible cognition is portrayed as sandwiched between behaviour (which is usually observable and measurable) and biological processes (which can sometimes be scientifically observed and recorded), with environmental factors influencing outcomes at each level. For example, activity in DLPFC (brain level) can increase with increased working memory load (a cognitive concept), which can occur when an individual carries out a mathematical process (with a behavioural outcome—i.e. producing an answer). In this brain-mind-behaviour model, the term 'environment' must be considered in terms of the level being described. For example, at the brain level, the environment is characterised by biological factors that include oxygen and nutrition. At the level of the mind, the environmental cognitive factors include educational, cultural and social influences whereas behavioural environmental issues include physical opportunities and restrictions.

There are arrows leading from the brain to the mind, and from mind to behaviour. These arrows indicate the directions in which causal connections are most often sought. The issue of cause in cognitive neuroscience, particularly developmental cognitive neuroscience, is very complex and will be returned to again. For the moment, it can be said that

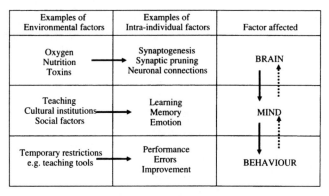

Examples of Environmental factors	Examples of Intra-individual factors	Factor affected
Oxygen Nutrition Toxins	Synaptogenesis Synaptic pruning Neuronal connections	BRAIN
Teaching Cultural institutions Social factors	Learning Memory Emotion	MIND
Temporary restrictions e.g. teaching tools	Performance Errors Improvement	BEHAVIOUR

Figure 2 A model of the brain/mind/behaviour interrelation developed by Morton and Frith (1995) and adapted from Blakemore and Frith (2000) with permission of the authors. The notation in the diagram uses arrows to indicate causal influences. Interactions of external factors with factors that are internal to the individual contribute to causal explanation. 'Facts' are situated at a behavioural and biological level, theories at the cognitive level. The notation can be used to think about links between biology and behaviour via the inferred cognitive level that bridges the gap between them. Adapted from TLRP (2006) with permission of the TLRP.

behaviour is most often explained in terms of the contents of the mind and cognitive neuroscientists usually attempt to understand the mind by drawing upon our understanding of the brain. However, these arrows might also be drawn as bi-directional. For example, environmental influences (such as being able to access new stimulus) can influence our behaviour that also, in turn, influences our mental processes. If these processes produce learning, this learning can be assumed to have some neural correlate at a biological level, such as the making of new synaptic connections in the brain. As discussed above, continual rehearsal of mental processes can even produce changes in the brain in terms of its structure, i.e. the shape and size of its component parts. These directions of influence have traditionally been of less interest to cognitive neuroscientists and this may explain their omission in this diagram. However, they are of considerable interest to educators and so have been added here using dotted lines. This is one way in which the most appropriate model of description for neuro-educational researchers may differ from that currently used in cognitive neuroscience.

5 LEAVING BEHIND BIOLOGICALLY PRIVILEGED LEARNING—A 'LEVELS OF ACTION' MODEL FOR NEUROSCIENCE AND EDUCATION

Another criticism, in principle, of efforts to include the brain in educational understanding is that neuroscience cannot provide the types of explanation required for improving instruction. Schumacher suggests that, whilst neuroscientific studies may be able to inform psychological understanding about learning, its biologically privileged explanations are of no direct interest to educators. Biologically privileged learning is described by Schumacher as occurring if 'biological programmes determine which learning processes are initiated by which environmental influences, at which developmental stage, and taking which way of execution' (Schumacher, 2007, p. 387). In particular, Schumacher (2007) and Davis (2004) emphasise the importance of social and cultural factors in learning that should not be excluded from such explanations. However, there is no conflict here with current neuroscientific thinking. On the contrary, one leading developmental cognitive neuroscientist states clearly 'Cause is not an easy word. Its popular use would be laughable if it was not so dangerous, informing, as it does, government policy on matters that affect us all. There is no single cause of anything and nothing is determined' (John Morton quoted in Howard-Jones, 2007, p. 21). Although cause is a problematic construct, it is a helpful tool in trying to alleviate the difficulties faced by many children. However, an important challenge for those reflecting upon cause may be to resist being seduced by explanations exclusively privileging factors of one type, be it biological, psychological or social. This is particularly true for those involved with research at the interface between brain, mind and education. In this sense, then, the model of individual development depicted in Figure 2 may be unhelpful in its emphasis upon the individual.

Given the emphasis upon social processes, the representation of learning in terms of two individuals interacting (as in Figure 3) becomes more suggestive of the complexity that can arise when including consideration of the brain-mind-behaviour relationship within educational contexts. The two individuals may be two learners or, perhaps, a teacher and learner. In this diagram, the space between the individuals is filled by a sea of symbols representing human communication in all its forms. The lines separating brain, mind, behaviour and this sea of symbols are shown as dotted, to emphasise their somewhat indistinct nature and the difficulty in clearly defining concepts lying close to them.

Travelling Across 'Levels of Action'

It is interesting to take an imaginary journey through Figure 3 to gain some further impression of the philosophical challenges face by researchers attempting to integrate neuroscientific and educational thinking, as they struggle to avoid 'non-sense'. Neither natural nor social science, on its own, presently offers sufficient epistemological traction to travel across all levels of description. Let us take the example of a 'neuro-educational' researcher wishing to integrate neuroscientific perspectives on dyslexia with educational understanding and practice. On Figure 3, the arrows attempt to indicate the most frequently (but not exclusively) travelled pathways of investigation associated with these different perspectives. Cognitive neuroscience is marked by an arrow extending from the brain to

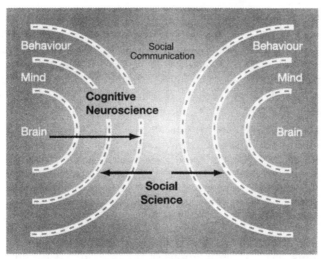

Figure 3 To interrelate the most valuable insights from cognitive neuroscience and the social science perspectives of education (represented by arrows), the brain->mind->behaviour model may need to be socially extended. Even two individuals interacting, as represented here, is suggestive of the complexity that can arise when behaviour becomes socially mediated. Such complexity remains chiefly the realm of social scientists, who often interpret the meaning of such communication in order to understand the underlying behaviour. Cognitive neuroscience has established its importance in understanding behaviour at an individual level but is only just beginning to contemplate the types of complex social domains studied by educational researchers reproduced from Howard-Jones (2007) with permission of the TLRP.

behaviour. Our neuro-educational researcher might access literature from cognitive neuroscience, including studies of reading acquisition using neuroimaging. Turkeltaub *et al.* showed there was gradual disengagement of right hemisphere areas (involved with visual memory) and increased activity in left language areas (involved with phonological processing) as children's reading ability increased (Turkeltaub *et al.*, 2003). This is important, since it supports an existing psychological model of reading in which early readers move from a reliance on visual features of letters to developing a phoneme-grapheme correspondence. When biological and cognitive concepts of development resonate in this way, one can feel more confident about the validity of both. These results might also, for example, help explain how trauma in a particular area of the brain influences reading development. It does not, however, provide an entire explanation of we how come to read, since many other factors, including our education, influence this outcome. Neither can it be said that reading begins as a result of activity shifting from right to left areas, since it could as equally true that the shift occurs because reading has developed. Dyslexic readers show decreased activity in left-hemisphere areas associated with phonological processing. Again, this indicates a potential link between their reading difficulties and their ability to process phonological information, without necessarily proving any causal link (it may, instead, be due to less rehearsal of phonological processing due to some other source of reading difficulty, exacerbating reading problems further). It does, however, help suggest interventions based on improving auditory and oral language skills. Such an intervention, prompted by neuroimaging and behavioural studies, has indeed been shown to help remediate both reading difficulties and the difference in brain activities associated with them (Shaywitz *et al.*, 2004).

Maintaining a careful consideration of the brain-mind relationship allows biological evidence to helpfully augment behavioural evidence and vice-versa, in order to improve outcomes in tractable experimental studies of reading processes and interventions. However, when it comes to a fuller understanding of how such interventions are applied, individual differences in teachers' interactions with children may need to be explored. Here, meaning-based interpretations of the discourse between teacher and pupil are useful in understanding the factors influencing pupils' progress. The meanings ascribed to our actions, including our use of language, are multiple, ambivalent and transitory. The production of language has been a fruitful area for scientific research but the interpretation of meaning within everyday contexts is essentially a problematic area for experimental scientific paradigms. Interpretations of meaning that cannot be judged by the methods of natural science may be considered beyond its jurisdiction (Medawar, 1985). Leaving aside issues of interpretation, the difficulties in using current imaging technology to study everyday social interaction currently provides a barrier for neuroscientists approaching the sea of symbols. The recent flourishing of journals focusing on social cognitive neuroscience demonstrate the beginning of efforts in this area, but interpretation of social complexity remains chiefly the realm of social scientists. Rather than natural science, it is social science, with its own concepts of reliability and validity, that appears most accomplished in interpreting the meaning of such communications in order to understand their fuller significance (Alexander, 2006).

A researcher wishing to carry out a classroom study of an intervention to remediate dyslexia based on neuroscientific research will, therefore, face the task of integrating insights from both perspectives, and in ways that are mindful of the different epistemologies that gave rise to them. Although challenging, this is very different from a wholesale commitment to a biologically privileged approach to learning divorced from all considerations of context, such as that feared by Davis (2004) and Schumacher (2007). It may be true that ideas about the relationship between learning and development have often emphasised the constraining nature of our biology and our biological development upon our learning. Piaget was criticised for suggesting that learning 'merely utilizes the achievements of development rather than providing an impetus for modifying its course' (Vygotsky, 1978, pp. 79–80) and even Bruner, though acknowledging that learning can lead to development, (Bruner, 1974, pp. 417) discussed the psychobiology of pedagogy chiefly in terms of the *constraints* provided by the human nervous system (Bruner, 1972, pp. 118–131). However, in the present model, boundaries with bi-directional permeability emphasise the role of the educational social environment, and to an extent that it influences our biological development. Such a model, compared with notions of biological privilege, also reflects more appropriately the present thinking within developmental cognitive neuroscience.

What About the Free-Will of the Individual?

Educators believe they are striving to produce autonomous learners, personally motivated and able to exercise their own free will when learning. As discussed above, effective teaching and learning is considered by many to depend upon the promotion of learners' independence and autonomy (TLRP, 2007, p. 9). Some researchers within neuroscience, on the other hand, are presently unsure how, and even whether, free-will comes into existence. Studies of apparent mental causation suggest that unperceived causes of action fail to influence our experience of will, suggesting that conscious will is an illusion. For example, when Transcranial Magnetic Stimulation was applied to influence respondents' movements of their fingers, they reported that they were consciously willing their fingers, even though this was clearly not the case (Brasil-Neto *et al.*, 1992). In spontaneous intentional finger movement, another study has shown that electrical brain activity precedes action by at least 550 ms, with awareness that they had made the decision *following* some 350–400 ms after this signal (Gazzaniga, 1995). Some scientists suggest, therefore, that our sense of free will is a trick, just the mind's way of estimating its own *apparent* authorship by drawing causal inferences about relationships between thoughts and actions (Wegner, 2003). Unsurprisingly, this has been identified as another type of biological privilege likely to cause conflict for those working at the interface between neuroscience and education (Giesinger, 2006). However, educators can feel reassured that denying the existence of free will bring neuroscience into conflict not just with education but also with the entire legal system (Burns and Bechara, 2007). Since discussions about the existence of free-will are very bound up with those about consciousness, they are unlikely to be resolved in the near future (Tancredi, 2007). In the meantime, we most of us share, to a greater or lesser extent, some existing construction about free-will as a highly prized causal factor in our behaviour.

Despite the popularity of educational concepts such as the 'independent learner' and the 'autonomous learner', free will has never been a serious focus of educational research, possibly because of the conceptual and methodological difficulties associated with studying it. This fact, together with the ambivalence of neuroscience towards the concept of free will, suggests there may be a danger that the role of free will can be conveniently overlooked by those researching at the interface between neuroscience and education, despite this being antithetical to present educational aims. To understand how such concepts may be included, it may be useful to consider the field of social psychology, where potential conflicts between perspectives historically exist quite similar to some of those already discussed. In the area of personal growth and development, the role of free will is also highly valued and frequently reflected upon by humanitarian psychologists employing experiential perspectives. One such psychologist is Richard Stevens, who has considered how experiential perspectives embracing issues of free will and autonomy may be considered alongside insights from the natural and social sciences. Stevens' 'Trimodal' theory interrelates perspectives in a practical manner based upon 'mode of action' (Stevens, 1998). Although originally intended to describe social behaviour, the trimodal approach will be illustrated here in terms of learning. In trimodal terminology, the *primary* mode of learning arises from the physical embodiment of the learner. This provides a basis for learning that is best described in terms of biological and neurophysiological processes whose scientific study can help explain our thinking and learning mechanisms in terms of causal models that may be informed by, and inform, our understanding of brain function. In trimodal theory, it is these primary mechanisms that support the emergence of symbol systems and the use of language, thus facilitating a *secondary* basis for learning. It is the use of symbol systems that makes it a meaning-based mode of learning that involves interpretation by those participating in it and by those attempting to investigate it. Thus, as discussed above in the context of teacher-pupil interaction, Stevens suggests this basis for learning is often best explored through the perspectives of social science, with a perspective that is appropriately sensitised to the unique and complex nature of meaningful social contexts. According to Stevens, it is our ability to use meaningful symbols that crucially supports our formation and manipulation of concepts, including those that describe ourselves. Thus, from the secondary symbolic mode of action emerges a third basis for action—our reflexive awareness. This *tertiary* mode involves self-awareness and reflective choice. Here, our actions are less determined solely by primary biological and cognitive processes and/ or by secondary meaning-based processes. This is the level at which the learner generates some autonomy through a capacity to reflect upon his/ herself and the events in his/her life. At the tertiary level, investigation becomes something of a moral science. It is concerned with the choices we make and how things, including ourselves, *could* be. Of course, such investigation can still be informed by knowledge of learning processes at the primary and secondary levels, as provided by the natural and social sciences.

At present, and perhaps reflecting our lack of understanding of consciousness, it is not easy to represent such a tertiary level of action in Figure 3. However, given the growing emphasis on learning autonomy in education, perhaps researchers working at the interface between neuroscience and education need to remain mindful that Figure 3 is a poor representation of what is actually a dynamic scenario of change and transformation. Furthermore, free will and reflexive self-determination may be a powerful and essential contribution to learning that requires careful consideration at all the levels (biological, cognitive, behavioural and social) represented here.

In summary, there is presently considerable interest and enthusiasm for the interdisciplinary venture that may be called neuroscience and education, although there are some immense challenges along the way and many of these derive from underlying philosophical issues within and between the two areas. These issues are not fatal in their implications, but initiatives attempting to integrate neuroscience and education would benefit greatly from explicit attendance to them, rather than running the risk of losing what is commonly understood as 'sense' by one or both of the communities involved.[4]

NOTES

1. Although sometimes absent from the name of the enterprise, it is worth noting that an understanding of the mind, as provided by psychology and/or cognitive science, is usually seen as essential in attempts to build conceptual bridges between neuroscience and education.
2. This anonymously derived expression is often used by popular writers about the brain but, for more accurate representations of the Hebbian learning theory it refers to, see Hebb, 1947.
3. Transcranial magnetic stimulation (TMS) is a noninvasive method to excite neurons, and selectively disrupt brain function, by applying rapidly changing magnetic fields.
4. The author would like to thank Paul Standish for his helpful comments on an earlier version of this chapter.

REFERENCES

Alexander, H. A. (2006) A View from Somewhere: Explaining the Paradigms of Educational Research, *Journal of Philosophy of Education*, 40.2, pp. 205–21.

Arhib, M. A. (2003) *The Handbook of Brain Theory and Neural Networks* (Cambridge, MA, MIT Press).

Arshavsky, Y. I. (2006) The 'Seven Sins' of the Hebbian Synapse: Can the Hypothesis of Synaptic Plasticity Explain Long-Term Memory Consolidation?, *Progress in Neurobiology*, 80, pp. 99–113.

Bennett, M. R. and Hacker, P. M. S. (2003) *Philosophical Foundations of Neuroscience* (Oxford, Blackwell).

Blakemore, S. J. and Frith, U. (2000) *The Implications of Recent Developments in Neuroscience for Research on Teaching and Learning* (London, UCL, Institute of Cognitive Neuroscience).

Brasil-Neto, J. P., Pascual-Leone, A., Valls-Sole, J., Cohen, L. G. and Hallett, M. (1992) Focal Transcranial Magnetic Stimulation and Response Bias in a Forced- Choice Task, *Journal of Neurology, Neurosurgery and Psychiatry*, 55, pp. 964–66.

Bruer, J. (1997) Education and the Brain: A Bridge Too Far, *Educational Researcher*, 26.8, pp. 4–16.

Bruner, J. S. (1972) *The Relevance of Education* (London, George Allen and Unwin).

Bruner, J. S. (1974) *Beyond the Information Given: Studies in the Psychology of Knowing*, J. M. Anglin, ed. (London, George Allen and Unwin).

Burns, K. and Bechara, A. (2007) Decision Making and Free Will: A Neuroscience Perspective, *Behavioral Sciences and the Law*, 25.2, pp. 263–80.

Byrnes, J. P. and Fox, N. A. (1998) The Educational Relevance of Research in Cognitive Neuroscience, *Educational Psychology Review*, 10.3, pp. 297–342.

Churchland, P. M. (2005) Cleansing Science, *Inquiry*, 48.5, pp. 464–77.

Citri, A. and Malenka, R. C. (2008) Synaptic Plasticity: Multiple Forms, Functions, and Mechanisms, *Neuropsychopharmacology*, 33, pp. 18–41.

Corkum, P. V., McKinnon, M. M. and Mullane, J. C. (2005) The Effect of Involving Classroom Teachers in a Parent Training Program for Families of Children with ADHD, *Child and Family Behavior Therapy*, 27.4, pp. 29–49.

Crick, F. (1984) Memory and Molecular Turnover, *Nature*, 312, p. 101.

Curtis, C. E. and D'Esposito, M. (2003) Persistent Activity in the Prefrontal Cortex During Working Memory, *Trends in Cognitive Sciences*, 7.9, pp. 455–463.

Davis, A. J. (2004) The Credentials of Brain-Based Learning, *Journal of Philosophy of Education*, 38.1, pp. 21–36.

Davis, H. P. and Squire, L. R. (1984) Protein Synthesis and Memory: A Review, *Psychological Bulletin*, 96, pp. 518–59.

Degrandpre, R. (1999) Just Cause?, *The Sciences*, March/April, pp. 15–18.

Delazer, M., Domahs, F., Bartha, L., Brenneis, C., Lochy, A., Trieb, T and Benke, T. (2003) Learning Complex Arithmetic—an fMRI Study, *Cognitive Brain Research*, 18, pp. 76–88.

Draganski, B., Gaser, C., Busch, V., Schuierer, G., Bogdahn, U. and May, A. (2004) Changes in Grey Matter Induced by Training, *Nature*, 427, pp. 311–12.

Gazzaniga, M. S. (1995) Consciousness and the Cerebral Hemispheres, in: M. S. Gazzaniga (ed.) *The Cognitive Neurosciences* (Cambridge MA, MIT Press), pp. 1391–400.

Geake, J. G. and Cooper, P. W. (2003) Implications of Cognitive Neuroscience for Education, *Westminster Studies in Education*, 26.10, pp. 7–20.

Giesinger, J. (2006) Educating Brains? Free-Will, Brain Research and Pedagogy, *Zeitschrift fur erziehungswissenschaft*, 9.1, pp. 97–109.

Goswami, U. (2004) Neuroscience and Education, *British Journal of Educational Psychology*, 74, pp. 1–14.

Goswami, U. (2006) Neuroscience and Education: From Research to Practice?, *Nature Reviews Neuroscience*, 7, pp. 406–13.

Gureasko-Moore, S., DuPaul, G. J. and White, G. (2006) The Effects of Self-Management in General Education Classrooms on the Organizational Skills of Adolescents with ADHD, *Behavior Modification*, 30.2, pp. 159–83.

Harré, R. (2002) *Cognitive Science: A Philosophical Introduction* (London, Sage).

Hebb, D. O. (1947) *The Organization of Behavior* (New York, Wiley).

Howard-Jones, P. A. (2007) *Neuroscience and Education: Issues and Opportunities, TLRP Commentary* (London, Teaching and Learning Research Programme).

Howard-Jones, P. A.. (in press) Scepticism is Not Enough, *Cortex*.

Kaufmann, L. . (2008) Dyscalculia: Neuroscience and Education, *Educational Research*, 50.2, pp. 163–175.

McClelland, J. L. and Rogers, T. T. (2003) The Parallel Distributed Processing Approach to Semantic Cognition, *Nature Reviews Neuroscience*, 4, pp. 310–22.

Martin, S. J., Grimwood, P. D. and Morris, R. G. (2000) Synaptic Plasticity and Memory: An Evaluation of the Hypothesis, *Annual Review of Neuroscience*, 23, pp. 42303–711.

Medawar, P. (1985) *The Limits of Science* (Oxford, Oxford University Press).

Mel, B. W. (2002) Have We Been Hebbing Down the Wrong Path?, *Neuron*, 34, pp. 175–77.

Miranda, A., Presentacion, M. J. and Soriano, M. (2002) Effectiveness of a School-Based Multicomponent Program for the Treatment of Children with Adhd, *Journal of Learning Disabilities*, 35.6, pp. 546–62.

Morton, J. and Frith, U. (1995) Causal Modelling: A Structural Approach to Developmental Psychopathology, in: D. Cicchetti and D. Cohen (eds) *Manual of Developmental Psychopathology* (New York, Wiley), pp. 357–90.

OECD (2002) *Understanding the Brain:Towards a New Learning Science* (Paris, OECD).

OECD (2007) *Understanding the Brain: Birth of a New Learning Science* (Paris, OECD).

Parkinson, L. (2006) Boy's Behaviour 'Out of Control', *Bristol Evening Post*.

Pinnegar, S. and Carter, K. (1990) Comparing Theories from Textbooks and Practicing Teachers, *Journal of Teacher Education*, 41, pp. 20–27.

Schumacher, R. (2007) The Brain Is Not Enough: Potential and Limits in Integrating Neuroscience and Pedagogy, *Analyse & Kritik*, 29.1, pp. 38–46.

Shastri, L. (2002) Episodic Memory and Cortico-Hippocampal Interactions, *Trends in Cognitive Sciences*, 6.4, pp. 162–68.

Shaywitz, B. A., Shaywitz, S. E., Blachman, B. A., Pugh, K. R., Fullbright, R. K., Skudlarski, P., Mencl, W. E., Constable, R. T., Holahan, J. M., Marchione, K. E., Fletcher, J. M., Lyon, G. R. and Gore, J. C. (2004) Development of Left Occipitotemporal Systems for Skilled Reading in Children after a Phonologically-Based Intervention, *Biological Psychiatry*, 55.9, pp. 926–33.

Snider, V. E. and Roehl, R. (2007) Teachers' Beliefs About Pedagogy and Related Issues, *Psychology in the Schools*, 44, pp. 873–886.

Squire, L. R. (2004) Memory Systems of the Brain: A Brief History and Current Perspective, *eurobiology of Learning and Memory*, 82, pp. 171–77.

Stevens, R. (1998) Trimodal Theory as a Model for Inter-Relating Perspectives in Psychology, in: R. Sapsford, A. Still, D. Miell, R. Stevens and M. Wetherell (eds) *Theory and Social Psychology* (London, Sage and the Open University).

Tancredi, L. R. (2007) The Neuroscience Of 'Free Will', *Behavioral Sciences and the Law*, 25.2, pp. 295–2007.

TLRP (2006) *Improving Teaching and Learning in Schools: A Commentary by the Teaching and Learning Research Programme* (London, TLRP).

TLRP (2007) *Principles into Practice: A Teacher's Guide to Research Evidence on Teaching and Learning* (London, TLRP).

Turkeltaub, P. E., Gareau, L., Flowers, D. L., Zeffiro, T. A. and Eden, G. F. (2003) Development of Neural Mechanisms of Reading, *Nature Neuroscience*, 6.6, pp. 767–73.

Vaidya, C. J., Audtin, G., Kirkorian, G., Ridlehuber, H. W., Desmond, J. E., Glover, G. H. and Gabrieli, J. D. E. (1998) Selective Effects of Methylphenidate in Attention Deficit Hyperactivity Disorder: A Functional Magnetic Resonance Study, *Proceedings of the National Academy of Sciences (USA)*, 95, pp. 14494–99.

Varma, S. and Schwartz, D. L. (2008) How Should Educational Neuroscience Conceptualize the Relation between Cognition and Brain Function? Mathematical Reasoning as a Network Process, *Educational Research*, 50.2, pp. 149–161.

Vygotsky, L. S. (1978) *Mind in Society: The Development of Higher Psychological Processes*, M. Cole, V. John-Steiner, S. Scribner and E. Souberman eds (Cambridge, MA, Harvard University Press).

Wegner, D. M. (2003) The Mind's Best Trick:How We Experience Conscious Will, *Trends in Cognitive Sciences*, 7.2, pp. 65–69.

Wolfe, P. (1998) Revisiting Effective Teaching, *Educational Leadership*, 56.3, pp. 61–64.

Wood, D., Bruner, J. S. and Ross, G. (1976) The Role of Tutoring in Problem Solving, *Journal of Child Psychology & Psychiatry and Allied Disciplines*, 17, pp. 89–100.

1.3

Principles of Learning, Implications for Teaching: A Cognitive Neuroscience Perspective

USHA GOSWAMI

INTRODUCTION

Neuroscience is a large field, and all aspects of neuroscience have some relevance to education. For example, some neuroscientists study how cells grow in the foetal brain, and some neuroscientists study the chemical 'neurotransmitters' that cells use to transmit information to each other. Neither area of study appears *a priori* relevant to education, and yet better knowledge of foetal brain development offers important insights into why children born to alcohol-addicted mothers have particular learning difficulties, for example in numeracy (Kopera-Frye, Dehaene and Streissguth, 1996). Knowledge about neurotransmitters has led to the marketing of drugs that enhance learning ('cognitive enhancers'). As students can take cognitive enhancers before they sit their exams, this aspect of neuroscience has a potentially dramatic impact on educational outcomes (Turner and Sahakian, 2006). Cognitive neuroscience is one sub-field within neuroscience. Cognitive neuroscience takes psychological theories about the mind (e.g. that short-term and long-term memory are distinct systems) or symbolic descriptions of mental processes (e.g. that we can think using images versus 'inner speech') and explores them by measuring electro-chemical activity in the brain. Interpretations of neural activity are constrained by using experimental paradigms drawn from cognitive psychology (see Szücs and Goswami, 2007).

Cognitive neuroscience involves both the direct measurement of electro-chemical activity, and connectionist modelling. Direct measurement of the brain shows the patterns of activity across large networks of neurons (called cell assemblies) that correspond to mental states such as remembering a telephone number. Although this is essentially correlational information, brain imaging also reveals the time course of the activity (e.g. which neural structures are activated, in which order) and interactions and feedback processes within these large networks. Modelling enables in-principle understanding of how synchronised neuronal activity within cell assemblies results in learning and development. I will argue that all of these kinds of information are useful for education, even though the field of cognitive neuroscience is still in its early stages.

COGNITIVE NEUROSCIENCE AND RESEARCH QUESTIONS RELEVANT TO EDUCATION

At birth, considerable brain development has already taken place. Most of the neurons (brain cells) that will comprise the mature brain are already present, and have migrated to the appropriate neural areas. Neural structures such as the temporal cortex (audition) and the occipital cortex (vision) have formed, but will become progressively specialised as the infant and young child experiences environmental stimulation. Neural specialisation depends on the growth of fibre connections between brain cells both within and between different neural structures (called 'synaptogenesis'). Some fibre connections reflect 'experience expectant' processes. These connections are usually in the sensory system, and reflect abundant early growth in response to classes of environmental stimulation (such as visual field information) that the brain 'expects' (via evolution) to receive. Connections that are not used frequently are then aggressively pruned. Experience-expectant plasticity is biologically pre-programmed. Other fibre connections are 'experience dependent'. Here the brain is growing connections in order to encode unique information that is experienced by the individual. Every person has a distinctive environment, even children growing up within the same family, and so experience-dependent connections are the ones that make each brain subtly different. Experience-dependent connections include the connections formed by education. Experience-dependent synaptogenesis enables life-long plasticity with respect to new learning.

The specialisation of neural structures occurs within developmental trajectories that are constrained by both biology and environment. We can study these developmental trajectories by asking questions about structure and function, and some of these questions are relevant to education. Such questions include which neural structures are important for learning different educational inputs (e.g. reading versus arithmetic), which interconnections between structures are important for different educational inputs, what the temporal sequencing looks like, and what can go wrong. We can also try and distinguish cause from effect.

Research Question 1: Neural Structures for Learning

A very active area of cognitive neuroscience is the study of which neural structures are active as the brain learns different inputs or performs different tasks. The method most frequently used is fMRI, or functional magnetic resonance imaging, which measures changes in blood flow in the brain. Blood will flow to neural structures that are active, hence this kind of imaging reveals which parts of the brain are most involved in certain tasks. Such research is essentially correlational, but it is still of value for education.

For example, researchers have measured the main neural structures that are active in novice readers as they perform tasks with print. These studies have found that the neural structures for *spoken* language are those that are most active (Turkeltaub *et al.*, 2003). Such data would appear to rule out theories of reading acquisition that argue that children first learn to read using 'logographic' strategies, going directly from print to meaning without recoding from print to sound (e.g. Frith, 1985). As children are exposed to more and more printed words, brain imaging studies show that a structure in the visual cortex becomes increasingly active (Cohen and Dehaene, 2004). Dubbed the 'visual word form area', this structure appears to store information about letter patterns for words and chunks of words and their connections with sound. It is experience-dependent, storing the learning that results as children are exposed to more and more printed words and recode them into sound. It will therefore respond to 'nonsense words' that have never been seen before, because chunks of these nonsense words will be familiar from prior learning experiences (e.g. 'brate' is a nonsense word, but it is analogous to real words like 'crate' and 'brake').

Therefore, although the brain did not evolve for reading, it is able to develop fibre connections to support reading that encode print experience into the nervous system. This is achieved by recruiting neural structures that already perform very similar functions, such as object recognition. For example, the visual word form area is adjacent to the area in the visual system that is most active during picture naming. One prominent educational neuroscientist calls this feature of experience-dependent plasticity the 'neuronal recycling hypothesis' (Dehaene, 2008). Dehaene argues that our evolutionary history and genetic organisation constrain new cultural acquisitions to some extent, as new learning must be encoded by a brain architecture that evolved to encode at least partially similar functions over primate evolution.

Nevertheless, studies using fMRI have revealed that unexpected neural structures can be involved in educational performance. For example, studies of arithmetic and number processing with adults have shown that an area in parietal cortex is particularly active whenever numerical magnitude must be accessed (Dehaene, 1997). Closely adjacent areas of parietal cortex are activated when judgements about size or weight are required. This has led Dehaene to argue that the parietal cortex is the location of an approximate, analogue magnitude representation in the human brain. However, when Dehaene and his colleagues compared brain activation for two arithmetic tasks, one involving exact addition (e.g. $4+5 = 9$) and one involving approximate addition (e.g. $4+5 = 8$), they found that the parietal structures were only most active in the second case (Dehaene *et al.*, 1999). During exact calculation the greatest relative activation occurred in a left-lateralised area in the inferior frontal lobe, which is traditionally regarded as a language area. Dehaene *et al.* argued that this was because exact arithmetic requires retrieval of over-learned 'number facts', which are stored in the language areas. This implies that part of school mathematical learning is linguistic. The multiplication tables and 'number facts' that children are taught seem to be learned as verbal routines, like the months of the year, rather than as numerical concepts that are coded by the analogue magnitude representation. *A priori*, one might not have expected the brain to develop fibre connections in the language system in order to encode classroom activities assumed to develop neural structures for mathematics.

Research Question 2: The Interconnections Between Neural Structures

Analyses that reveal the interconnections between different neural structures can provide a variety of information relevant to education. Connectivity analyses reveal the white matter tracts formed by bundles of fibre connections, called by neuroscientists 'information highways' in the brain. Connectivity analyses can be informative with respect both to how a child is achieving a particular level of behavioural performance, and with respect to which developmental pathways were important in attaining that particular level of performance. For example, connectivity analyses carried out with children at risk for reading difficulties have revealed two types of neural system supporting reading (Shaywitz and Shaywitz, 2005). One group of children studied longitudinally by Shaywitz and Shaywitz, called persistently poor readers (PPR), had met criteria for poor reading both at the beginning of the study in $2^{nd}/3^{rd}$ Grade, and also later in the study in $9^{th}/10^{th}$ Grade. Another group of children, called accuracy-improved poor readers (AIR), had met the criteria for poor reading in $2^{nd}/3^{rd}$ Grade but no longer met these criteria in $9^{th}/10^{th}$ Grade. Connectivity analyses suggested that reading achievement depended on rote memory for the PPR group, whereas the AIR group were utilising the same neural networks as a control group of children who had never had a reading impairment. Nevertheless, the AIR group were not activating these neural networks as efficiently as the control children. Hence apparently identical performance (in this case, the number of words read correctly) depended on *different* interconnections. The finding that the PPR group had developed fibre connections to right hemisphere systems supporting working memory and memory retrieval rather than between the traditional left-hemisphere language systems that typically support reading is suggestive of different developmental pathways. This kind of information can be useful for education, for example in suggesting the optimal focus for further remediation.

Research Question 3: The Time Course of Neural Activation

Children who are at risk for reading difficulties also show differences in the time course of neural activation in comparison to typically-developing children. One useful imaging method for gaining precise information about neural timing is EEG (electroencephalography). EEG measures the extremely low voltage changes caused by the electro-chemical activity of brain cells by using highly sensitive electrodes that are placed on the scalp. This method yields information precise to the millisecond. EEG studies suggest that the brain has decided whether it is reading a real word or a nonsense word within 160–180 ms of presentation, for children as well as for adults (e.g. Csepe and Szücs, 2003; Sauseng, Bergmann and Wimmer, 2004). When children who are at risk of reading difficulties are shown printed nonsense words (like 'lan') in kindergarten, they are significantly slower to show neural activity (Simos *et al.*, 2005; this study used a variant on EEG that combines information on electrical activity with information on blood flow, called MSI or magnetic source imaging). The researchers found this slowed neural activation even when the children were shown single letters. The at-risk group required almost 100 ms more for neural activity to begin in comparison to kindergartners who were not at risk for reading difficulties. Simos *et al.* (2005) reported that delayed activation actually increased over time for the at-risk group. For example, when providing the sounds for single letters at the end of Grade 1, processing time had increased by around 200 ms for the at-risk children. No increase was found for the children who were not at risk. Such information is important, as it is evidence that the child is not simply disengaged from the task or 'not trying'. Rather, the child has a specific neural processing difficulty.

The time course of neural activation can also be used to test inferences drawn from fMRI studies about the role of different neural structures. For example, in their study of exact and approximate addition, Dehaene and his colleagues tracked the precise time course of brain activation using EEG. They found that the electrical signals to exact versus approximate trial blocks were already different by 400 ms. This was before the possible answers to the additions were displayed. Dehaene *et al.* argued that the time course data supported the idea that exact calculation and approximate calculation relied on different neural structures. If the two types of calculation had relied on the same neural structure, then the time course of activation should not have differed *before* the answers were displayed.

Research Question 4: Neural Correlation versus Causation

Given the current state-of-the-art in brain imaging, most neuroimaging data are correlational and do not provide information about causation. As in all scientific enquiry, therefore, experimental design is crucial to how useful the data will be for contributing to research questions. For example, it is important to control for other factors that might be important for any correlations that are found, and to use control groups. As in all developmental science, longitudinal studies are the most informative, and the studies discussed above taken from the reading literature are a good example (Simos *et al.*, 2005; Shaywitz and Shaywitz, 2005). Intervention studies are also required when reliable correlations are found, in order to manipulate the variables in any association. This enables the study of 'dose-response relationships': if a particular factor is having a particular effect, then receiving more of that factor should increase the effect. A good example of intervention studies in education comes from the extensive literature supporting the importance of phonological awareness for reading development. Interventions to boost phonology show average effect sizes of 0.70, showing that experiencing an intervention makes a large difference to later attainment in reading (Bus and van IJzendoorn, 1999).

AVOIDING THE SEEDING OF NEUROMYTHS

When evaluating neuroscience research, it is important to be vigilant: correlations are still correlations, even when they involve physiological measures. Yet many correlational findings that reach the popular media are given causal interpretations. A good example comes from data sets that have been interpreted to show that fatty acids such as fish oils play a potentially causal role in learning. Unsaturated fatty acids are important in brain development and in neural signal transduction, which has led to the belief that omega-3 and omega-6 highly unsaturated fatty acids may be good for the brain. For example, in a recent paper, Cyhlarova *et al.* claimed that 'the omega-3/omega-6 balance is particularly relevant to dyslexia' (Cyhlarova *et al.*, 2007, p. 116). This claim was based on a study measuring the lipid fatty acid composition of red blood cell membranes in 52 participants, 32 dyslexic adults and 20 control adults. No differences between dyslexics and controls were found in any of the 21 different measures of membrane fatty acid levels taken by the researchers. However, a *correlation* was found between a total measure of omega-3 concentration and overall reading in the whole sample. This correlation by itself does not show that fatty acids have anything to do with dyslexia. The correlation depends on the whole group, potentially relevant variables such as I.Q. have not been controlled, and there is no intervention to test whether the association is a causal one. No plausible mechanism was proposed by the experimenters to explain why omega-3 concentration should have specific effects on reading, rather than general effects on any culturally-acquired skill (for example, arithmetic).

Nevertheless, when physiological variables such as changes in brain activation are involved, it is easy to suspend one's critical faculties. This has been demonstrated empirically by Weisberg and her colleagues (Weisberg *et al.*, 2008). These researchers gave adults bad explanations of psychological phenomena, either with or without accompanying neuroscientific information. The neuroscientific details were completely irrelevant to the explanations given, and yet the adults rated the explanations as far more satisfying when such details were present. The researchers concluded that the neuroscience details were very seductive. These details suggested to the participants that the explanations given were part of a larger explanatory system based on physiology. These seductive details then interfered with participants' ability to judge the quality of the explanations that they were being given. Weisberg *et al.* point out that this propensity to accept explanations that allude to neuroscience makes it all the more important for neuroscientists to think carefully about how neuroscience information is viewed and used outside the laboratory.

PRINCIPLES OF LEARNING FROM COGNITIVE NEUROSCIENCE

Although the field of educational neuroscience is still relatively new, there are a number of principles of learning demonstrated by empirical studies that can safely be incorporated into education and teaching. Some of these are now discussed.

A. *Learning is Incremental and Experience Based*

Although this may seem almost too trivial to note, the fact that the brain develops fibre connections to encode each experience that we have into our nervous systems is fundamental when considering education. The growth of interconnected networks of simple cells distributed across the entire brain eventually results in complex cognitive structures such as 'language' or 'causal knowledge'. The complexity that can be achieved by simple incremental learning has been demonstrated by connectionist modelling, which has shown a number of important 'in principle' effects. For example, complex 'rules' or principles such as the syntactic 'rules' of language can be learned incrementally. There is no need for a specialised 'language acquisition device' (see Chomsky, 1957) that pre-encodes 'innate' knowledge about the general rules that all languages obey, along with innate knowledge of permitted variations. Simple incremental learning also yields 'critical period' effects, originally argued to show that some kinds of learning are particularly effective during a given time window. Connectionist modelling shows that these critical time windows are a natural part of the learning trajectory when learning is incremental. Similarly, incremental learning processes can explain apparent 'gaps' in learning exhibited by children. Learning is distributed across large networks of neurons, and so factors like the number of relevant neurons firing, their firing rates, the coherence of the firing patterns, and how 'clean' they are for signalling the appropriate information will all vary depending on how the current environmental input activates the existing network (see Munakata, 2001). As the fibre connections growing in response to received inputs are strengthened over time, it can also become difficult to reorganise the system when a new learning environment is experienced. This offers one potential mechanism for explaining why it is more difficult to learn a second language later in life (Munakata and McClelland, 2003). The fibre connections representing the phonemes of the first language are already entrenched, so (for example) Japanese speakers who have always encoded 'l' and 'r' as the same sound find it difficult to now encode them as different sounds (the same neural network will be activated by new tokens of both 'l' and 'r'). However, some people can learn to be fluent in a second language later in life, and so entrenchment is not irreversible. In the case of the 'l'/'r' distinction, multi-sensory input appears to be particularly effective (seeing as well as hearing other speakers produce the target sounds, Hardison, 2003).

These demonstrations of the importance of incremental environmental input show that the learning environments created in schools by teachers and other professionals will have important cumulative effects. Clearly, it is important to avoid creating learning environments that support the acquisition of maladaptive connections, for example environments that feel unsafe or stressful. Further, deep understanding of a given educational domain is required in order to present the cumulative information in the optimal sequence for the novice learner (this reflects classic educational concerns for consolidation of learning coupled with progression in curricula). The growth of new fibre connections in the brain always occurs in response to new inputs, and so claims that brain-based learning packages enable 'neuroplasticity' is a redescription of what always occurs for any new learning experience. Perhaps most challengingly, the biological necessity for learning to be incremental questions the notion that we can ever engender 'conceptual change'. Any neural network develops over time, and cannot suddenly be 'restructured' by one learning experience. On the other hand, certain experiences may result in previously distinct parts of the network becoming connected, or in inefficient connections that were impeding understanding being pruned away. Eventually, connectionist models may be able to show how and when this is achieved in a given learning trajectory. Current connectionist modelling is limited by available statistical and mathematical alogorithms, and so the 'in principle' effects discussed above should be taken as suggestive rather than as established fact. Advances in the mathematical modelling of complex networks may reveal other principles of incremental learning.

B. Learning is Multi-Sensory

Different neural structures are specialised to encode different kinds of information, with sensory information being the most obvious example (e.g. visual information is encoded primarily by fibre growth in the visual cortex, auditory information is encoded primarily by fibre growth in the auditory cortex). However, most environmental experiences are multi-sensory, and therefore fibre connections between modalities are ubiquitous. Furthermore, because learning is encoded cumulatively by large networks of neurons, cell assemblies that have been connected because of prior experiences will continue to be activated even when a *particular* aspect of sensory information in a *particular* experience is *absent*. This ability of the brain to respond to *abstracted dependencies* of particular sensory constellations of stimuli enables, for example, a missed word to be filled in when someone coughs across another speaker. Even though our brain received the sensory information about the cough rather than the phonemes in the missed word, prior learning of the statistical regularities between words in connected discourse enables the brain to 'fill in' the missing information (e.g. Pitt and McQueen, 1998, for a related example).

Although this example comes from within a modality (audition), the brain does the same thing across our senses (Noesselt *et al.*, 2007). Again, this principle implies that if children are taught new information using a variety of their senses, learning will be stronger (that is, learning will be represented across a greater network of neurons connecting a greater number of different neural structures, and accessible via a greater number of modalities). A nice example comes from a study by James (2007), who used fMRI to track the neural networks that developed as preschool children learned to recognise letters. Before taking part in the learning activities, the children's brains were imaged as they looked at letters and other familiar visual stimuli (such as cartoon hearts). As might be expected, significant activation of visual neural structures was found. As part of their initial reading activities, the children were then taught to recognise and write the letters. For example, visual letter knowledge was increased by helping children to recognise the target letters in story books, and to pick out target letters from 4 alternative possibilities (including reversed letters). The children were also taught to form and write the letters, thereby using another modality (kinaesthetic) in conjunction with the visual and auditory modalities (recognising and naming the letters). Following the writing training, the children's brains were again imaged while they looked at letters and other familiar visual stimuli. This time, significant activation in motor areas was found for the letters, even though the children were *looking* at the letters and were not making any writing movements. Because their multi-sensory learning experiences had led fibre connections to develop both within the visual system and between the visual system and the motor system, the motor parts of the network were activated even though the current environmental experience was purely visual. Whether this multi-sensory representation can actually be interpreted as showing stronger learning requires further empirical work. Nevertheless, it is clear that information stored in multiple modalities is being activated despite the fact that sensory stimulation is only occurring in one modality (here, vision). This kind of empirical paradigm offers a way of investigating whether children really can be said to have different learning 'styles', for example being 'visual' or 'kinaesthetic' learners. Given the principles of how the brain learns, this seems *a priori* unlikely.

C. Brain Mechanisms of Learning Extract Structure from Input

The fact that incremental learning yields abstracted dependencies is a powerful mechanism for cognitive development (Goswami, 2008a). As the brain experiences particular sensory constellations of stimuli over multiple times, what is common across all these experiences will naturally be represented more strongly than what is different. This is because the fibre connections that encode what is common will become stronger than the fibre connections that encode the novel details. This mechanism effectively yields our 'basic level concepts', such as 'cat', 'dog', 'tree' and 'car' (Rosch, 1978). After 100 'cat' experiences, the strongest fibre connections will represent what has been common across all experienced instances, such as '4 legs', 'whiskers', 'tail', and so on. Therefore, the brain will have developed a generic 'prototype' representation of a cat. Sensory constellations of stimuli are also dynamic in space and time, and so simply by processing features of the input, and correlations and dependencies between these features, the brain will be learning about dynamic spatio-temporal structure and therefore about causal relations (Goswami, 2008c). This means that the child's brain can in principle construct detailed conceptual frameworks from watching and listening to the world. As we learn language and attach labels to concepts, the neural networks become more complex, and as we learn new information via language, fibre connections will form in response that encode more abstract information and therefore more abstract concepts.

I discuss many examples of this in my book (Goswami, 2008a), but to take an example pertinent to education, these learning mechanisms mean that the brain will extract and represent structure that is present in the input *even when it is not taught directly*. An example is the higher-order consistencies in the spelling system of English that I have previously described as 'rhyme analogies' (Goswami, 1986). Spelling-to-sound relations in English can often be more reliable at the larger 'grain size' of the rhyme than at the smaller 'grain size' of the phoneme (Treiman *et al.*, 1995). For example, the pronunciation of a single letter like 'a' differs in words like 'walk' and 'car' from its pronunciation in words like 'cat' and 'cap'. The pronunciation in 'walk' or 'car' can be described as irregular, but it is quite consistent across other rhyming words (like 'talk' and 'star'). One way of exploring whether the brain is sensitive to these higher-level consistencies in letter patterns is to see how children read aloud novel 'nonsense' words that they have not encountered before. For example, children can be asked to read nonsense words matched for pronunciation like *daik, dake, loffi* and *loffee*. Only the rhyme spelling patterns in items like *dake* and *loffee* will have been learned from prior experiences with analogous real words (like 'cake' and 'toffee'). Hence only these 'chunks' of print and their connections with sound should be stored in the neural Visual Word Form Area (VWFA). There are no real English words with letter chunks like '*aik*'. English children indeed show a reliable advantage for reading aloud such analogous nonsense words, despite the fact that the individual letter-sound correspondences in the non-analogous items (e.g. '*d*', '*ai*', '*k*' in *daik*) were matched for orthographic familiarity to those in the analogous items (like *dake*, see Goswami *et al.*, 2003). Such data suggest that orthographic learning, presumably in the VWFA, reflects these higher-level consistencies, even though 'rhyme analogy' reading strategies have not been taught directly to these children (see Ziegler and Goswami, 2005, for converging evidence using other paradigms).

Whether learning (i.e. reading performance) would be even stronger if such strategies *were* taught directly to children remains an open question. In fact, this is an important general question for education. Although it is often noted that learning is 'embedded' in the experiences of the individual, one goal of education is to help all individuals to extract the higher-order structure (or 'principles' or 'rules') that underpin a given body of knowledge. It is generally felt that a combination of 'discovery led' and directly transmitted knowledge provides the best way of doing this, but there are many disagreements over the optimal balance between such teaching methods in different domains and in different views of pedagogy. A deeper understanding of how the brain uses incremental experience to extract underlying structure may help to inform such debates.

D. Learning is Social

We have social brains. The wealth of studies of infant and animal cognition are showing more and more clearly that the complex mammalian brain evolved to flourish in complex social environments. For example, there appear to be specialised neural structures in the human brain for encoding information about agents and their goal-directed actions (the so-called mirror neuron system—see for example Iacoboni *et al.*, 2005). Neurons in this system will respond to a biological agent performing a certain action (e.g. a person lifting a cup), but not to a robot performing an identical action (Tai *et al.*, 2004). In infancy, the attribution of intentionality to the goal-directed actions of others occurs surprisingly early in development. For example, Meltzoff has shown that 14-month-old infants will imitate actions that they have never witnessed, but which they infer to have been intended through watching a particular goal-directed action by a biological agent. If a baby watches an adult carrying a string of beads towards a cylinder, missing the opening and dropping the beads, the watching baby inserts the beads straight into the cylinder (see Meltzoff, 1995). Babies who watch a robot hand modelling an action, even a completed action, do not imitate. Gergely, Bekkering and Kiraly (2002) demonstrated that infants of the same age make very sophisticated inferences about intentional states. They used a different imitation paradigm devised by Meltzoff, in which an experimenter activates a light panel by leaning forwards and pressing it with her forehead. Sixty-nine percent of babies who watched this event also switched on the light panel by using their foreheads. However, in another version of the event, the experimenter said that she felt cold, and she held a blanket around her shoulders with her hands while she illuminated the light panel with her head. Now 79% of watching 14-month-olds used their hand to illuminate the light panel. They appeared to infer that in this latter scenario the experimenter used her forehead because her hands were constrained. She was not using her forehead intentionally because it was necessary to achieve her goal. Hence they no longer copied the 'forehead' action. As Carpenter, Ahktar and Tomasello (1998) have pointed out, infants who selectively imitate only the intentional acts of others will thereby acquire many significant cultural skills.

The social nature of human learning means that learning with others is usually more effective than learning alone, and that language and communication are central to this social process. This was recognised a long time ago in the theory of cognitive development proposed by Vygotsky (1978). Vygotsky argued that cognitive development did not just happen in the brain of the individual child. It also depended on interactions between the child and the cultural tools available for mediating knowledge. A primary cultural tool was language. As well as providing a symbolic system for communication with others, language enabled children to reflect upon and change their own cognitive functioning (in the terminology of modern psychology, by developing 'metacognitive' and 'executive function' skills). Furthermore, Vygotsky proposed the notion of the 'zone of proximal development' (ZPD). In contrast to independent problem solving, the ZPD was the larger area of potential development that was created when learning was supported by others. Most ZPDs are created by the social and cultural contexts created by parents and teachers (although Vygotsky argued that play with other children also creates important ZPDs). This theoretical perspective is reflected in education in socio-cultural theory. Csibra and Gergely (2006) revisited these theoretical ideas, recasting them in the language of brain science. They proposed that human brains have adapted to transfer relevant cultural knowledge to conspecifics, and to *fast-learn* the contents of such teaching via a species-specific social learning system. They called this learning system 'pedagogy'. On my reading, their definition of pedagogy is essentially cultural knowledge transfer via collaborative learning in the zone of proximal development. Gergely, Egyed and Kiraly (2007) have further pointed out that such a system requires a default assumption about other agents, which is that they are trustworthy and benevolent sources of universally shared cultural knowledge.

E. Cortical Learning can be Modulated by Phylogenetically Older Systems

Traditionally, cognitive psychology has separated the study of cognition (thinking and reasoning) from the emotions. Neuroscience has shown that cognitive and emotional processes are integrated in the brain at multiple levels. For example, cortical structures such as orbito-frontal cortex integrate cognitive and emotional information during learning via interactions with phylogenetically older structures that are primarily involved in emotional processing, such as the amygdala. The amygdala controls our response to threat (as in the 'fight-flight' response). A particularly active area of neuroscience with respect to the emotional modulation of cognition is decision making ('neuroeconomics'; Coricelli,

Dolan and Sirigu, 2007). Economics as a discipline has learned that human behaviour cannot be explained solely in rational cognitive terms. Learning based on cumulative emotional experience plays an important role in anticipating the possible future consequences of economic choices, and economic models incorporating emotional measures such as regret appear to be more efficient at modelling human behaviour. Cumulative emotional experience must also play a role in the efficiency of learning. This suggests that models of classroom learning must incorporate the emotions in order to better understand the behaviour of learners.

There is certainly some relevant data from both human and animal cognitive neuroscience. For example, learning in adults is impaired when the impact of punishment relevant to reward is enhanced, and the neurotransmitters that control this process can be identified (Cools *et al.*, 2005). The effect of anxiety on impeding learning can also be increased or reduced pharmacologically (i.e. with drugs). Animal models show that when previously innocuous sensory signals are processed by the amygdala as emotionally salient and aversive, this affects learning in rats (Stutzmann and LeDoux, 1999). The emotional information is prioritised by the brain, and receives privileged access to attention. When experiences are aversive, emotional responding blocks learning. The prioritising of emotional information was presumably evolutionarily adaptive, as emotional stimuli lead to enhanced sensory processing by the brain, enabling better behavioural responding. Such studies may provide a neural framework for explaining why children who are anxious do not learn efficiently. However, the data are suggestive rather than conclusive. Furthermore, there are no comparable animal models exploring the effects of highly rewarding events on attention and learning (rather than aversive events). Emotions seem likely to produce both enhancement and costs to efficient learning, but how this might operate in learning environments like classrooms is currently not well-understood, at least by neuroscience.

F. Learning Shows Life-Long Plasticity and Compensation

Studies of the brain also suggest that it is never too late to learn. Some neural structures are still developing in the mid-twenties (e.g. the frontal cortex), and experience-dependent plasticity means that fibre connections continue to form to represent new learning throughout adulthood. Learning in adulthood often enlarges the relevant neural networks, as in the case of skilled adult pianists, who have enlarged cortical representations in auditory cortex specific to piano tones (Pantev *et al.*, 1998). In London taxi drivers, who need a good 'mental map' of London (called 'The Knowledge'), a small brain area involved in spatial representation and navigation called the hippocampus becomes enlarged. Hippocampal volume is correlated with the amount of time spent as a taxi driver (Maguire *et al.*, 2000). Similarly, the cortical representation of piano tones was found by Pantev and colleagues to be correlated with the amount of time that different individuals spent in piano practice. Greater synaptic density is associated with more learning. When neural networks are lesioned or partially destroyed (for example, by a stroke), connections can re-form. There appear to be differences between neural structures in how effectively this can occur, nevertheless these compensatory mechanisms (which can lead to significant recovery of pre-stroke function) again show that plasticity continues into late adult life. In terms of the brain mechanisms for learning, therefore, there is considerable continuity. This principle of learning provides empirical support for the efficacy of lifelong access to education ('lifelong learning').

Finally, I consider two other aspects of cognitive neuroscience research that are relevant to education.

BIOMARKERS OF LEARNING EFFICIENCY

Neuroscience also offers the promise of biomarkers or neural markers for learning. Cognitive processes are difficult to study directly, because they are theoretical rather than observable. Even processes such as memory have to be inferred from behaviour–we cannot yet pinpoint our memories as linked to particular brain cells, for example, even though the main cell assemblies or neural structures supporting memory are known. Nevertheless, when systematic experimentation enables a meaningful relationship to be identified between hypothetical cognitive processes and neural variables, the neural variables can become physiological markers or biomarkers of these cognitive processes. Therefore, the neural variables can be used to identify those who might be at educational risk. For example, a child may be at risk because aspects of sensory processing are impaired, and biomarkers could show the presence of this processing impairment before any behavioural symptoms have appeared (Goswami, 2008b). The identification of neural markers would thereby enable very early intervention, before a potential learning difficulty has had time to become entrenched. Such interventions are most likely to be environmental, and thereby the provenance of education. Other potential biomarkers include genotypes and blood, plasma and spinal fluid markers, for example based on protein changes.

While the latter biomarkers have been explored most in relation to diseases of the brain such as Alzheimer's disease, neural variables are being explored in relation to learning difficulties. Developmental dyslexia, developmental dyscalculia, specific language impairment, autism and attention deficit hyperactivity disorder are all active areas of research. For example, aspects of language function can be measured very early using EEG. Particular components of the waveform evoked in response to particular aspects of language input (evoked response potentials or ERPs) indicate the integrity of phonological (sound-based) versus semantic (meaning-based) aspects of language processing. These ERP components are already proving to have predictive value in determining who might be at risk of a language impairment (Friedrich and Friederici, 2006). As biomarkers like these can be measured in sleeping babies, they offer opportunities for very early identification of educational risk, without requiring attentive responding. As children with learning difficulties often have attentional difficulties, these methods offer a marked improvement over behavioural indices. However, they do raise potential ethical concerns. For example, early identification may result in benefit, but may also result in harm if the child is then placed in a category that carries stigma. There is also the question of who has the responsibility for detecting and monitoring these biomarkers. The assumption here is that benefits will outweigh harms, as the interventions that can follow early identification should improve learning trajectories over the whole life course. Nevertheless, there is a responsibility to ensure that children do not experience negative discrimination (for example, lowered expectations of their learning abilities) as a result.

MAXIMISING THE LEARNING EFFICIENCY OF THE BRAIN

The brain is an organ of the body, and in terms of efficiency of function it is not distinct from other organs such as the heart with respect to some of the basic factors that affect its ability to work effectively. Nutrition and diet are important for effective function, as are sleep and exercise. The obvious roles of nutrition and exercise have led to various 'brain based learning' claims about particular types of nutrition (e.g. fish oils, water) and particular types of exercise (e.g. Brain Gym[R], see Howard-Jones, 2007, for a useful discussion) and their particular effectiveness for learning by children. When evaluating such claims, it is of course critical to check the quality of the science cited in their support, and to distinguish correlational data from causal data. In terms of underlying physiological mechanisms, there have been some pharmacological insights with respect to sleep, which appears to have an interesting role in consolidating learning. During sleep, there is behavioural inactivity accompanied by distinct electrophysiological changes in brain activity. These changes seem to affect memory, which appears to be consolidated during slow-wave and rapid-eye-movement sleep via the actions of certain neuro-transmitters. Newly encoded memories are stabilised, and are integrated with pre-existing (long term) memories via the action of neurotransmitters like acetylcholine. Low cholinergic activity is associated with slow-wave sleep, and when cholinergic activity is blocked in the brain, there is enhanced consolidation of memory (see Marshall and Born, 2007, for a summary).

One possibility is that we lose consciousness during sleep because the brain needs to use the same neural networks that support conscious activity for the processing and long-term storage of recently-acquired information. Indeed, empirical studies of learning finger tapping sequences show that there is improvement in the learned skill after sleep, with performance levels after sleep that are significantly higher than performance levels at the end of initial training, before sleep occurred (e.g. Fischer *et al.*, 2002). However, sleep has to occur within a certain time window after training in order for benefits to accrue (this time window is approximately within 16 hours of the learning period). Conversely, severe insomnia is associated with decrements in learning. The growing evidence base with respect to sleep shows the importance of these basic aspects of human behaviour to education.

CONCLUSION

Cognitive neuroscience is important for education because it enables a principled understanding of the mechanisms of learning and of the basic components of human performance. It also enables componential understanding of the complex cognitive skills taught by education. Many of the principles of learning uncovered by cognitive neuroscience might appear to support what teachers knew already. For example, aspects of pedagogy such as the value of multi-sensory teaching approaches or of creating safe and secure environments for learning are highly familiar. Nevertheless, cognitive neuroscience offers an empirical foundation for supporting certain insights already present in pedagogy and disputing others. The evidence from neuroscience is not just interesting scientifically. It enables an evidence base for education in which mechanisms of learning can be precisely understood.

Nevertheless, the evidence base that it offers is a challenging one. An interesting analogy is provided by Clark, who was discussing language, but whose analogy also works for the entire cognitive system. Clark's argument is that we can conceptualise the brain as a 'loose-knit, distributed representational economy' (Clark, 2006, p. 373). Some elements in the economy might conflict with other elements in the economy, but this is inevitable, as there is no 'homunculus' or single central overseer who determines learning. Rather, there are many interacting parts of the overall reasoning machinery that the brain is maintaining at the same time. The activity of all of these parts is what the child brings to the classroom, and different parts are more or less affected by different cognitive or emotional experiences. The child brings a 'vast parallel coalition of more-or-less influential forces whose unfolding makes each of us the thinking beings that we are' (ibid.). To borrow from another insightful commentator on the potential of cognitive neuroscience for cognitive development (Diamond, 2007), the truly ambitious goal for education is to cross and integrate the disciplinary boundaries of biology, culture, cognition, emotion, perception and action. Biological, sensory and neurological influences on learning must become equal partners with social, emotional and cultural influences if we are to have a truly effective discipline of education.

REFERENCES

Bus, A. G. and van IJzendoorn, M. H. (1999) Phonological Awareness and Early Reading: A Meta-Analysis of Experimental Training Studies, *Journal of Educational Psychology*, 91.3, pp. 403–414.

Carpenter, M., Akhtar, N. and Tomasello, M. (1998) Fourteen- through 18-month-old Infants Differentially Imitate Intentional and Accidental Actions, *Infant Behavior and Development*, 21, pp. 315–330.

Chomsky, N. (1957) *Syntactic Structures* (The Hague/Paris, Mouton).

Clark, A. (2006) Language, Embodiment, and the Cognitive Niche, *Trends in Cognitive Sciences*, 10.8, pp. 370–374.

Cohen, L. and Dehaene, S. (2004) Specialization within the Ventral Stream: The Case for the Visual Word Form Area, *NeuroImage*, 22, pp. 466–476.

Cools, R., Roberts, A. C. and Robbins, T. W. (2005) Serotoninergic Regulation of Emotional and Behavioural Control Processes, *Trends in Cognitive Sciences*, 12.1, pp. 31–40.

Coricelli, G., Dolan, R. J. and Sirigu, A. (2007) Brain, Emotion and Decision Making: The Paradigmatic Example of Regret, *Trends in Cognitive Sciences*, 11.6, pp. 258–265.

Csibra, G. and Gergely, G. (2006) Social Learning and Social Cognition: The Case for Pedagogy, in: Y. Munakata and M. H. Johnson (eds) *Processes of Change in Brain and Cognitive Development. Attention and Performance XXI* (Oxford, Oxford University Press), pp. 249–274.

Csepe, V. and Szücs, D. (2003) Number Word Reading as a Challenging Task in Dyslexia? An ERP Study, *International Journal of Psychophysiology*, 51, pp. 69–83.

Cyhlarova, E., Bell, J., Dick, J., Mackinlay, E., Stein, J. and Richardson, A. (2007) Membrane Fatty Acids, Reading and Spelling in Dyslexic and Non-Dyslexic Adults, *European Neuropsychopharmacology*, 17, pp. 116–121.

Dehaene, S. (1997) *The Number Sense: How the Mind Creates Mathematics* (New York, Oxford University Press).

Dehaene, S. (2008) Cerebral Constraints in Reading and Arithmetic: Education as a 'Neuronal Recycling' Hypothesis, in: A. M. Battro, K. W. Fischer and P. J. Lena (eds) *The Educated Brain: Essays in Neuroeducation* (Cambridge, Pontifical Academy of Sciences and Cambridge University Press), pp. 232–247.

Dehaene, S., Spelke, E., Pinel, P., Stanescu, R. and Tsivkin, S. (1999) Sources of Mathematical Thinking: Behavioral and Brain-Imaging Evidence, *Science*, 284, pp. 970–974.

Diamond, A. (2007) Interrelated and Interdependent, *Developmental Science*, 10.1, pp. 152–158.

Fischer, S., Hallschmid, M., Elsner, A. and Born, J. (2002) Sleep Forms Memory for Finger Skills, *Proceedings of the National Academy of Sciences*, 99, pp. 11987–11991.

Friedrich, M. and Friederici, A. D. (2006) Early N400 Development and Later Language Acquisition, *Psychophysiology*, 43, pp. 1–12.

Frith, U. (1985) Beneath the Surface of Developmental Dyslexia, in: K. E. Patterson, J. C. Marshall and M. Coltheart (eds) *Surface Dyslexia* (London, Lawrence Erlbaum Associates), pp. 301–330.

Gergely, G., Bekkering, H. and Király, I. (2002) Rational Imitation in Preverbal Infants, *Nature*, 415, p. 755.

Gergely, G., Egyed, K. and Király, I. (2007) On Pedagogy, *Developmental Science*, 10.1, pp. 139–146.

Goswami, U. (1986) Children's Use of Analogy in Learning to Read: A Developmental Study, *Journal of Experimental Child Psychology*, 42, pp. 73–83.

Goswami, U. (2008a) *Cognitive Development: The Learning Brain* (Philadelphia, PA, Psychology Press of Taylor and Francis).

Goswami, U. (2008b) Reading, Complexity and the Brain, *Literacy*, 42.2, pp. 67–72.

Goswami, U. (2008c) Analogy and the Brain: A New Perspective on Relational Primacy, *Behavioural and Brain Sciences*, 31, pp. 387–388.

Goswami, U., Ziegler, J., Dalton, L. and Schneider, W. (2003) Nonword Reading Across Orthographies: How Flexible is the Choice of Reading Units?, *Applied Psycholinguistics*, 24.2, pp. 235–47.

Hardison, D. (2003) Acquisition of second–language speech: effects of visual cues, context and talker variability, *Applied Psycholinguistics*, 24, pp. 495–522.

Howard-Jones, P. (2007) *Neuroscience and Education: Issues and Opportunities*. Commentary by the Teaching and Learning Research Programme (London, TLRP). Available online at: http://www.tlrp.org/pub/commentaries.html

Iacoboni, M., Molnar–Szakacs, I., Gallese, V., Buccino, G., Mazziotta, J. C. and Rizzolatti, G. (2005) Grasping the Intentions of Others with One's Own Mirror Neuron System, *PLOS Biology*, 3, pp. 529–35.

James, K. H. (2007) *Perceptual-Motor Interactions in Letter Recognition: fMRI Evidence*. Paper presented at the Biennial Meeting of the Society for Research in Child Development, Boston, MA, 29 March–1 April 2007.

Kopera-Frye, K., Dehaene, S. and Streissguth, A. P. (1996) Impairments of Number Processing Induced by Prenatal Alcohol Exposure, *Neuropsychologia*, 34, pp. 1187–1196.

Marshall, L. and Born, J. 2007 The Contribution of Sleep to Hippocampus-Dependent Memory Consolidation, *Trends in Cognitive Science*, 11, pp. 442–450.

Maguire, E. A., Gadian, D., Johnsrude, I., Good, C., Ashburner, J., Frackowiak, R. and Frith, C. (2000) Navigation-Related Structural Change in the Hippocampi of Taxi Drivers, *Proceedings of the National Academy of Sciences*, 97.8, pp. 4398–4403.

Meltzoff, A. N. (1995) Understanding the Intentions of Others: Re-Enactment of Intended Acts by 18-Month-Old Children, *Developmental Psychology*, 31, pp. 838–850.

Munakata, Y. (2001) Graded Representations in Behavioral Dissociations, *Trends in Cognitive Sciences*, 5.7, pp. 309–315.

Munakata, Y. and McClelland, J. L. (2003) Connectionist Models of Development, *Developmental Science*, 6, pp. 413–429.

Noesselt, T., Rieger, J., Schoenfeld, M., Kanowski, M., Hinrichs, H. and Driver, J. (2007) Audiovisual Temporal Correspondence Modulates Human Multisensory Superior Temporal Sulcus, Plus Primary Sensory Cortices, *Journal of Neuroscience*, 27.42, pp. 11431–41.

Pantev, C., Oostenveld, R., Engelien, A., Ross, B., Roberts, L. E. and Hike, M. (1998) Increased Auditory Cortical Representation in Musicians, *Nature*, 393, pp. 811–814.

Pitt, M. A. and McQueen, J. M. (1998) Is Compensation for Coarticulation Mediated by the Lexicon? *Journal of Memory and Language*, 39, pp. 347–370.

Price, C. J. and McCrory, E. (2005) Functional Brain Imaging Studies Of Skilled Reading And Developmental Dyslexia, in: M. J. Snowling and C. Hulme (eds) *The Science of Reading: A Handbook* (Oxford, Blackwell Publishing), pp. 473–496.

Rosch, E. (1978) Principles of Categorisation, in: E. Rosch and B. B. Lloyd (eds). *Cognition and Categorisation* (Hillsdale, NJ, Erlbaum).

Sauseng, P., Bergmann, J. and Wimmer, H. (2004) When Does the Brain Register Deviances from Standard Word Spellings? An ERP Study, *Cognitive Brain Research*, 20, pp. 529–532.

Shaywitz, S. E. and Shaywitz, B. A. (2005) Dyslexia (Specific Reading Disability), *Biological Psychiatry*, 57, pp. 1301–1309.

Simos, P. G., Fletcher, J., Sarkari, S., Billingslet, R., Castillo, E., Pataraia, E., Papanicolaou, A., Francis, D. and Denton, C. (2005) Early Development of Neurophysiological Processes Involved in Normal Reading and Reading Disability: A Magnetic Source Imaging Study, *Neuropsychology*, 19.6, pp 787–798.

Snowling, M. J. (2000) *Dyslexia* (Oxford, Blackwell).

Stutzmann, G. E. and LeDoux, J. E. (1999) GABAergic Antagonists Block the Inhibitory Effects of Serotonin in the Lateral Amygdala: A Mechanism for Modulation of Sensory Inputs Related to Fear Conditioning, *Journal of Neuroscience*, 19.RC8, pp. 1–4.

Szücs, D. and Goswami, U. (2007) Educational Neuroscience: Defining a New Discipline for the Study of Mental Representations, *Mind, Brain and Education*, 1, pp. 114–127.

Tai, Y. F., Scherfler, C., Brooks, D. J., Sawamoto, N. and Castiello, U. (2004) The Human Premotor Cortex is 'Mirror' Only for Biological Actions, *Current Biology*, 14, pp. 117–120.

Treiman, R., Mullennix, J., Bijeljac-Babic, R. and Richmond-Welty, E. D. (1995) The Special Role of Rimes in the Description, Use, and Acquisition of English Orthography, *Journal of Experimental Psychology: General*, 124, pp. 107–136.

Turkeltaub, P. E., Gareau, L., Flowers, D. L., Zeffiro, T. A. and Eden, G. F. (2003) Development of Neural Mechanisms for Reading, *Nature Neuroscience*, 6.6, pp. 767–773.

Turner, D. C. and Sahakian, B. J. (2006) Neuroethics of Cognitive Enhancement, *BioSocieties*, 1, pp. 113–123.

Vygotsky, L. (1978) *Mind in Society* (Cambridge, MA, Harvard University Press).

Weisberg, D. S., Keil, F. C., Goodstein, E. R. and Gray, J. R. (2008) The Seductive Allure of Neuroscience Explanations, *Journal of Cognitive Neuroscience*, 20.3, pp. 470–477.

Ziegler, J. C. and Goswami, U. (2005) Reading Acquisition, Developmental Dyslexia, and Skilled Reading Across Languages: A Psycholinguistic Grain Size Theory, *Psychological Bulletin*, 131.1, pp. 3–29.

1.4

Exercising Quality Control in Interdisciplinary Education: Toward an Epistemologically Responsible Approach

ZACHARY STEIN, MICHAEL CONNELL AND HOWARD GARDNER

INTRODUCTION

Most people who are involved in education are aware that educational policies and practices entail weighty ethical and social issues. When it comes to education, conflicts arise because different value systems are in play. What is less apparent is that in the educational domain, different epistemological and metaphysical commitments are also constantly pitted against one another. When we choose to teach scientific accounts of human origins instead of religious ones, for instance, or when we favour inquiry-based curricula over direct instruction, we are expressing our epistemological and metaphysical commitments. Beliefs about the nature of knowledge and the structure of the world have *always* formed the backdrop against which education plays out.

It is not possible, in fact, to insulate education from the broader philosophical trends. Commitments to secularism and science in the West, for example, stand in stark contrast to the religious worldviews that prevail in some other areas, and these differences are reflected in the varying educational aims, methods and institutions. More to the point, educational systems are a major channel through which societies actively *perpetuate*—often unreflectively—the philosophical presuppositions that frame what a culture takes as good, true and beautiful (and, by implication, what is seen as bad, false and/or repugnant).

In all spheres, awareness of one's assumptions is better than ignorance or the belief that assumptions are unimportant. As C. S. Peirce observed, the claim that we do not have philosophical commitments is really a sign that we are doing *bad philosophy*. In our view, the claim that we do not have philosophical commitments underpinning our educational institutions and methods is a sign that we are doing *bad curriculum and/or poor pedagogy*. In this chapter, we focus on an educational issue that has become a hot topic— interdisciplinary curricula and pedagogy. We explicate what it would mean to take an *epistemologically responsible* approach to interdisciplinary education, one in which epistemological commitments are explicitly integrated into the content and structure of the curricula and pedagogy.

In recent years we have seen a proliferation of interdisciplinary institutions, departments and training programmes, all aimed at meeting a global demand for individuals capable of producing high quality syntheses from disparate sources and types of information. To meet this demand, we believe that educators must develop the competencies that will enable them and their students to create high-quality interdisciplinary syntheses and instil the values that will positively dispose them toward that end. As Gardner explains, 'The *synthesizing mind* takes information from disparate sources . . . and puts it together in ways that make sense to the synthesizer and also other persons . . . [This capacity] becomes ever more crucial as information continues to mount at dizzying rates' (Gardner, 2007, p. 3).

Interdisciplinary syntheses are among the most epistemologically complex endeavours that humans can attempt. This complexity arises primarily from the deep differences of perspective that must be bridged in order to carry out interdisciplinary projects. That is, different methods and disciplines frame different perspectives and thus generate different kinds of knowledge. Interdisciplinarity entails integrating more than one of these perspectives to generate a kind of higher-order knowledge that is more than the sum of its parts. These elements cannot simply be tossed together in an interdisciplinary course (or research programme) like so many ingredients in a salad. Rather, successfully carrying out such a process of perspectival integration requires epistemological sophistication.

In what follows we draw on the work of Piaget and Habermas, two expert interdisciplinarians. These authorities aid in characterising the epistemologically significant differences between methodological perspectives that make interdisciplinary synthesis such a complex educational enterprise. In light of these complexities we propose the value of taking a pluralistic attitude toward various methodological perspectives, one that entails a stance of openness toward all relevant methods to insure that no perspectives are unduly highlighted or unduly marginalised. Specifically, we suggest that a kind of *methodological pluralism* (Dawson, Fischer, and Stein, 2006; Stein and Fischer, forthcoming; Wilber, 1999, 2006) is an appealing quality control strategy for interdisciplinary educational endeavours.

To ground our philosophical discussion we focus on how one might teach educators about the complex interdisciplinary topic of *numeracy*. Specifically, we offer several reflections on how to best approach this topic in the field of Mind, Brain and Education (MBE), an emerging area of interdisciplinary research and practice. Our aim is to provide a sense of the advantages of an epistemologically responsible pedagogical approach to interdisciplinarity education.

THE RISING IMPORTANCE OF QUALITY CONTROL FOR INTERDISCIPLINARY EDUCATION

The recent proliferation of high-profile research centres, doctoral programmes and undergraduate majors might seem to suggest that we can simply pursue interdisciplinarity with a 'business as usual' attitude—that is, that interdisciplinary work is simply an extension of disciplinary work that happens to span multiple content domains. The opinion of those who reflect upon and research interdisciplinary endeavours is more guarded, however. There is a growing consensus among analysts that interdisciplinary work gives rise to its own unique 'quality control' challenges (Boix-Mansilla, 2006; Gibbons et al., 1994; Klein, 1990; Weingart, 2001). That is, while disciplines have their own internal standards of quality control, these criteria cannot be automatically applied to interdisciplinary endeavours that transcend the boundaries of the disciplines they subsume. As Klein (1990) observes, 'there are no standards of excellence for interdisciplinary work in general' (p. 94). This fundamental difference between disciplinary and interdisciplinary work applies both to research and to education, and it suggests that interdisciplinary synthesis is a distinct (and relatively new) mode of knowledge production that is not as well understood as disciplinary research. Given the potential power (for good or ill) of the fruits of interdisciplinary research in such domains as genetics, cognitive neuroscience and materials science, quality control in interdisciplinary work is a pressing issue.

The task of characterising the epistemological structure of interdisciplinary problem spaces is not easy, as it requires at a minimum the integration of philosophical and sociological analyses. Most contemporary efforts in this direction have taken up the sociology of knowledge (Boix-Mansilla, 2006; Gibbons et al., 1994; Klein, 1990), offering empirical accounts of how knowledge production tends to proceed at the interdisciplinary level or of how 'successful' interdisciplinary educational efforts achieve their results. To supplement these approaches we pursue a different strategy that is informed by two philosophical characterisations of the epistemological structure of interdisciplinary problem spaces. The result is a set of epistemological distinctions that can be used to organise, compare and contrast perspectives rooted in particular research methods. In the end these epistemological considerations lead us to suggest that interdisciplinary researchers, educators and students should adopt a pluralistic attitude toward different methodological perspectives.

EPISTEMOLOGICAL CHALLENGES IN INTERDISCIPLINARY EDUCATION: FROM NUMBERS TO NEURONS

We frame the discussion that follows with reference to some advanced efforts toward interdisciplinary synthesis that foundered upon the very terrain we are mapping here. Over the past decade the eminent French neuroscientist Jean-Pierre Changeux engaged in two ambitious interdisciplinary conversations, one with a mathematician (Changeux and Connes, 1998) and one with a philosopher (Changeux and Ricoeur, 2000). These conversations were attempts to advance knowledge by bringing together and synthesising diverse and sophisticated perspectives on issues of great importance (from mathematics to morality and from physics to politics). But instead of reading like constructive dialogues, these conversations often read like a set of juxtaposed monologues. In both cases the two experts find it difficult to avoid privileging the methodological perspectives they hold dear. And all too often the result is disciplinary ships passing in the epistemological night.

Specifically, the mathematician and the neuroscientist continually focused on different *levels of analysis* when discussing the nature of numbers and their use. As we will see below, informed by Piaget's reflections on interdisciplinarity, symbol systems and synapses are *both* relevant when looking into the nature of mathematics, but they are understood via distinct methods at different levels of analysis. The conversation between Changeux and Connes (1998), while provocative, is beset by their attempts to establish the primacy of their respective levels of analysis. They both claim some kind of explanatory priority and argue that their own approach is most fundamental. It becomes clear that only courteous 'dissensus' will prevail. Indeed a powerful lesson from the conversation is what it teaches us about the complexity and challenges of attempting synthesis across different levels of analysis.

The philosopher and the neuroscientist fare no better. When Ricoeur and Changeux (2000) debate, they must translate across different *basic viewpoints*. While the neuroscientist directs his gaze to objectify and explain human morality from a scientific perspective, the philosopher is preoccupied with disclosing the meaning and value of our ethical precepts. For Ricoeur and Changeux their allegiance to two radically distinct basic viewpoints ultimately results in a polite and respectful stalemate. Despite their efforts, neither can subsume the other's viewpoint within his own. Ultimately they point longingly to Spinoza and the speculative possibility of some third discourse capable of transcending (and integrating) the epistemologically distinct realms of *mind* and *body*, *fact* and *value*.

The dialogues highlight two epistemological issues, which we characterise as differences between *levels of analysis* and differences between *basic viewpoints*. We now turn to explicating these two types of epistemological issues in the context of interdisciplinary pedagogy, focusing on teaching the topic of *numeracy* in the field of Mind, Brain and Education.

Levels of Analysis

Levels-of-analysis issues are ubiquitous. How do we explain the prevalence of simple but common mathematical fallacies, for instance? Examples of these are the gambler's fallacy (the false belief that the probability of a random event is dependent upon the events preceding it, e.g. that a coin flip is more likely to turn up 'heads' if three prior flips had turned up 'tails') and ignorance of regression to the mean (i.e. ignorance of the fact that those with extreme scores on any measure are, for statistical reasons, unlikely to stay as extreme across repeated re-tests). Why are they common? Well, it depends upon one's level of analysis. A cognitive psychologist will focus on issues such as the cerebral constraints on computation and the built-in tendencies toward the use of heuristics at the level of individual cognition, while a social or cultural theorist will focus on phenomena at a higher level of analysis, such as the legacy of certain symbols systems and the prevalence of certain educational tools (e.g. the errors of those who use an abacus differ from the errors of those who use an electronic calculator). Both explanatory approaches are valid, but they operate at different levels of analysis.

Bringing together constructs from different levels of analysis can certainly provide a more comprehensive view of a phenomenon, but this is easer said than done. As Piaget (1970) notes, for example, we face a kind of chicken-and-egg-problem when looking to combine the individual and social levels of analysis. Clearly the capabilities of individuals determine which mathematical fallacies are likely to be common, yet cultural forms (language, symbols and tools) shape the development of individual capabilities from day one. So how do we integrate these perspectives when neither can necessarily be considered to have some kind of explanatory priority?

Piaget suggests that in cases like this we should focus on the methods associated with each level of analysis. By doing so we call attention to the different perspectives in play and avoid ungrounded speculation about *what is really the case* with the phenomenon in question. We are led to see that we only know the phenomenon in light of certain perspectives, and the validity of each perspective should not be denied in so far as it is the result of inter-subjectively tested methods. Moreover, given the internal validity of each perspective, the respective methods should maintain their autonomy; after all, most researchers can do 'normal science' if left to their own devices. The suggestion for interdisciplinary researchers and educators, therefore, is that they should adopt a kind of multi-perspectival view of a phenomenon, in which they adopt the various views of disciplinary 'insiders'—that is, they ought to view the phenomenon while wearing a set of different methodological or disciplinary 'hats' (Blake and Gardner, 2007; Gardner, 2007).

Some theorists might work towards building synoptic models about *what is really the case out there;* this was, in fact, what Piaget was trying to accomplish with his ambitious models of cognitive development. Such models, Piaget argues, would explicate ways in which different levels of analysis could mutually enrich each other, but he also notes that our ability to validate such models will typically depend upon the emergence of methodological innovations. That is, once we realise that we only know phenomena in light of methodologically grounded perspectives, we must admit that developing new kinds of knowledge—including the kinds that emerge as a result of interdisciplinary synthesis across levels of analysis—often requires new methods. Biochemistry is the classic example of an emergent form of knowledge following upon specific methodological innovations (for example, chromatography and molecular dynamics simulations).

In the absence of such specialised innovations, however, the multi-perspectival strategy of wearing different disciplinary 'hats' seems preferable to both speculation and oversimplification. Specifically, this kind of pluralism toward methods and approaches gives researchers access to diverse types of potentially useful information derived from multiple levels of analysis. Instead of privileging certain levels over others, we should adopt a kind of *methodological pluralism*1 (Dawson, Fischer and Stein, 2006; Stein and Fischer, in prep.) that can be used to assemble a more sensitive, nuanced and complete picture of a phenomenon than would be possible within any single discipline.

EXCURSUS ON LEVELS OF ANALYSIS: MATHEMATICS IN MIND, BRAIN AND EDUCATION

Mind, Brain and Education is an emerging domain of research and practice that aims to bring together biological, psychological and educational perspectives with the goal of improving educational practices. An explicit purpose of the MBE field is to generate, apply and disseminate usable knowledge (Blake and Gardner, 2007; Fischer, Immordino-Yang, and Waber, 2007). Needless to say, this is a highly complex interdisciplinary endeavour, and integrating perspectives across different levels of analysis is an important challenge faced by members of the field. For example, understanding the nature of mathematical competencies requires bringing together a complex set of perspectives (Dehaene, 1997). From neurons in networks to symbol systems in societies, there are many perspectives from which one can study the development, organisation and performance of mathematical competences. If we take seriously the lessons about levels of analysis distilled from Piaget in the previous section, then we should be seeking some kind of multiperspectival (or pluralistic) view concerning different *methods and practices* employed to study mathematical competencies. That is, we should pursue an approach wherein each method is explicitly respected and made the object of considered judgments.

Take a phenomenon like *developmental dyscalculia* (Kosc, 1974; Stanescu-Cosson *et al.*, 2000), which simply cannot be approached from a single level of analysis. The evidence from brain research on this phenomenon suggests that this disability in basic mathematical competence is due to an atypical biological substrate, which points ultimately to causes at the level of genetics (Geary, 1993). But amelioration of the disability through educational intervention requires a focus at a much higher level of analysis – that of behaviour, strategies and motivations. Moreover, it is also clear that certain symbol systems and cultural contexts differentially affect how the disability manifests (Dehaene, 1997). The phenomenon clearly spans multiple levels of analysis, from genetics and brain 'up to' behaviour and culture.

Importantly, understanding dyscalculia *requires* bringing these different perspectives together. For example, studies show that the symbol system used in China for naming the integers 1 through 20 seems naturally to mitigate the effects of the disability, while the symbol system used in

America to name the integers seems to make it worse (Wilson and Dehaene, 2007). If both culture and genes play a role in the manifestation of this learning disability, then anything less than an interdisciplinary approach spanning multiple levels of analysis leaves us missing something. In the light of the epistemological issues raised above, we suggest that a focus on the affordances and limits of different methodological perspectives is preferable to either the presentation of a catalogue of findings (i.e. a survey course) or the development of a speculative synthetic model (i.e. a course driven by a specific theory).

A catalogue of findings about dyscalculia, however synoptic and however well framed, does not properly reveal the complexity of the interdisciplinary problem space. When the science is good, neuroscience finding X, psychology finding Y and educational research finding Z can all be considered valid. But this collection of 'facts' at different levels of analysis conceals the various epistemological systems underlying each method, which is where educative tensions and conflicts lie. In other words, simply covering the topic by surveying the range of findings ignores epistemological issues such as the chicken-and-egg-problem noted above (i.e. that it is not clear which level of analysis should receive explanatory priority). Moreover, while students may come away with a sense of *what* experts believe about the topic, they will lack a sense of *why* and *how* it is that experts have come to hold those beliefs.

The same kind of epistemological naiveté accompanies approaches that offer a speculative explanatory model of dyscalculia in order to synthesise research at different levels of analysis. Syntheses are valuable but premature ones can be misleading. We should hesitate to paint a picture of *what is really the case* with dyscalculia and thus avoid teaching the topic in terms of some explanatory model that *foreshadows* the integration of methods across various level of analysis. As noted above, new knowledge often requires new methods. We oversimplify the process of interdisciplinary knowledge production if we teach an interdisciplinary topic in terms of ideas that cannot be methodologically operationalised. A theory driven class can easily fall prey to what Whitehead (1925) referred to as the *fallacy of misplaced concreteness*. By confusing our constructs with reality, we lose sight of the distinct methods and practices that set different levels of analysis apart.

In contrast, if we approach the research and practice surrounding dyscalculia by focusing on the methods and practices in play, we can get across the same content while preserving the rich texture of epistemological issues that characterise the topic. Exposing students to a plurality of methodological perspectives is just another way of teaching for a kind of deep conceptual understanding (Gardner, 2000). For example, by looking into the methods of behavioural genetics and neuroscience used to research dyscalculia, we can explore the idea that there are individual differences in genetically canalised brain maturation processes, some of which account for certain specific elements of dyscalculia, while at the behavioural level we can focus on the methods of observation and controlled intervention that allow us to make claims about the remedial effects of certain educational initiatives. Crucially, a focus on the methods allows educators to draw attention to the limits and benefits of different *perspectives* as opposed to just the insights afforded by different *findings*.

To summarise, an epistemologically responsible approach to inter-disciplinary topics that span multiple levels of analysis should proceed via some kind of methodological pluralism. The manner in which this is executed is less important than the general approach. Whether it is via the analysis of case studies, the undertaking of individualised projects, or simple didactic instruction, we suggest that the goal of complex interdisciplinary education should be to inculcate a reflective stance toward a plurality of methodological perspectives. By explicitly respecting and considering a variety of methods, we can expose the educative tensions between different perspectives that arise when teaching about topics disclosed at different levels of analysis. We can also call attention to the conflicts and inconsistencies that characterise knowledge production at the highest levels.

BASIC VIEWPOINTS

Alas, differences between levels of analysis are not the only challenges we face when looking at the epistemological structure of interdisciplinary problem spaces. Differences of *basic viewpoint* are also ubiquitous. In contrast to levels of analysis, which tend to differ in obvious ways, basic viewpoints are extremely abstract and differences between them are therefore subtler. Nonetheless, they often point toward deeper epistemo-logical fault lines.

In the case of common mathematical fallacies, for example, there is a clear difference between describing their genesis or prevalence, on the one hand, and evaluating their impact, on the other. When offering descriptions, we appeal to empirical research and theoretical models that address the phenomenon objectively. We might conclude that certain mathematical fallacies, such as the gambler's fallacy, are found in 90% of the population and that their emergence is best explained in terms of certain common psychological processes. When offering evaluations, in contrast, we appeal to the normative frameworks and cultural traditions that provide us with our basic commitments, preferences and values. We might thus conclude that the aforementioned common mathematical fallacies inhibit the general population from properly understanding com-plex scientific and economic issues in the public sphere. This intellectual weakness, in turn, undermines some of the conditions necessary for a truly democratic society, which we value highly. Accordingly we might suggest that common mathematical fallacies be counteracted with certain specific educational initiatives.

Importantly, these two basic viewpoints (description and evaluation) are more often than not connected. Any ameliorative initiatives taken in response to the negative consequences of common mathematical fallacies should be based upon knowledge of the psychological processes in question. By the same token the research providing this usable knowledge has likely been undertaken in the light of evaluative commitments about the value of scientific research and the knowledge it is likely to yield, the importance of the negative social consequences of rampant mathematical ignorance, etc.

Related though they may be, these two basic viewpoints cannot be deduced from one another. The description of a common mathematical fallacy does not come with a label denoting its value. Some such beliefs are benign or even helpful, like certain estimation heuristics that work fine with small numbers in everyday situations. Likewise, knowing something's value does not serve to explain it. Shaking our heads at rampant mathematical fallacies in the public sphere (e.g. misuse of statistical data, etc.) will never help explain them, although it might motivate us to undertake research that will.

These remarks should make clear that relations between basic viewpoints are not the same as relations between levels of analysis. In many areas of inquiry it is the case that knowledge gained at one level of analysis can be used to deduce *the kind of thing* that must be occurring at lower levels. For example, the sociological and historical fact that strategies and techniques for calculation are passed down from generation to generation suggests that there must be some kind of process making this possible, which would be best described at psychological levels of analysis (if not at the physiological, molecular, or even genetic levels). As noted above, these kinds of inferences cannot be made between different basic viewpoints; descriptions do not entail values. Similarly, unlike different levels of analysis, different basic viewpoints are not potentially competing accounts that raise issues of explanatory priority or inter-theoretical reduction. They do not address the same phenomena in terms that are conflicting in scope, scale, or complexity. Rather, different basic viewpoints stand in *supplementary* relations and reflect historically deep-seated and thus seemingly irreplaceable forms of language use and practice (Habermas 1970; 1971; 1984; see also Sellars, 1963).[2]

Reminiscent of Piaget's approach to levels-of-analysis issues, Habermas proposes to handle differences between basic viewpoints by adopting a kind of methodological pluralism. Habermas continually stresses the importance of respecting the differences between basic viewpoints and finding ways to ensure that the dimensions they denote are not overlooked in our pursuit of synoptic interdisciplinary models and usable knowledge.

To avoid these kinds of errors educators should explicate the *distinctness* of different basic perspectives at the same time that they reveal their complex inter-animations.

BASIC VIEWPOINTS IN MIND, BRAIN AND EDUCATION

As noted before, Mind, Brain and Education (MBE) is a complex field of interdisciplinary research and practice and dyscalculia is a complex phenomenon that cuts across multiple levels of analysis. We argue here that the research and practice in MBE also implicates fundamentally different *basic viewpoints*, orthogonally related to the issues about levels of analysis already discussed. Seemingly straightforward shifts between these basic viewpoints can raise subtle yet complex epistemological challenges that require equally careful handling.

Consider, for example, the way that neuroimaging research on learning disabilities is often presented—with fMRI images of 'normal' brain function juxtaposed side-by-side against images of the 'abnormal' activity patterns characteristic of subjects diagnosed with a particular condition such as dyscalculia. Such comparative images might be used simply to support clinical descriptions of group differences and explanations of their underlying causes—when cognitive neuroscientists share their research findings with each other in academic journals or at professional conferences, for instance.

When presented in an educational context, in contrast, these same side-by-side images of 'normal' and 'abnormal' activity patterns can very easily take on a normative edge, inviting educational researchers and practitioners (not to mention the public at large) to think of the 'normal' brain state as the educational objective and the 'abnormal' state as a deviation from that ideal requiring remediation through structured intervention. Pushing the reasoning one step further, it might seem to follow that those dyscalculia interventions are best that tend to produce the most typical brain activation patterns in dyscalculic subjects in the short term. Under this assumption such activities will condition the neural circuitry in ways that will over time make it scan—and behave—in increasingly normal fashion. While this perspective might turn out to be valid, it is also possible that dyscalculic patients can become experts while making use of entirely different neuronal structures and processes.

As soon as we shift from a scientific discussion of dyscalculia and its causes to an educational dialogue about desirable vs. undesirable learning outcomes, we have switched out of a descriptive and explanatory basic viewpoint and into an evaluative and normative one. It is important to be clear about what is at stake here. The basic viewpoints in question mark the difference between what we think *is* the case (e.g. explanations of dyscalculia offered by behavioural genetics) and what we think *ought* to be the case (e.g. educational and cultural norms about mathematical competencies). The viewpoints also mark the difference between what is *possible* (e.g. knowledge from scientists concerning which interventions would be technically effective) and what is *preferable* (e.g. values held by communities that set limits on which interventions would be ethically acceptable).

The same basic viewpoints are implicated in teaching about usable knowledge in genetics (Grigorenko, 2007). Teaching students about the genetic component in disabilities like dyscalculia entails grappling with more than a basic knowledge of the findings and methods in genetics. Fundamental ethical issues are implicated in all discussions of how genetic information can be put to use. When we are discussing usable knowledge in genetics, the basic viewpoints that frame scientific endeavours (e.g. explanation and description) must be supplemented by the basic viewpoints that frame our pursuit of values, justice and self-understanding (Habermas, 2003). As an example, consider the case of teaching about dyscalculia and its increasingly clear genetic aetiology. As soon as we discuss the topic in terms of genetic markers for use in identification and remediation, we have switched out of a descriptive and explanatory basic viewpoint and into an evaluative and moral one.

Despite the great value and promise of scientific approaches to education, it is a grave error to confuse discourses about the technical effectiveness of an intervention with discourses about which interventions are ethically acceptable. Not all knowledge that can be used ought to be used (Stein and Fischer, in prep). That is, to see the full complexity of the interdisciplinary problem space, we must differentiate basic viewpoints in terms of their unique methods and practices before we integrate them in light of our interdisciplinary ambitions. Giving full voice to the basic perspectives in play is an important part of moving towards a more epistemologically responsible approach.[3]

But recognising the full range of basic viewpoints that are in play is not enough. In light of our proposed focus on the *methods and practices* that constitute different basic viewpoints, we can note the liabilities of approaches that offer prefabricated conclusions as a way of covering different basic viewpoints. The complement to offering a catalogue of scientific findings is an approach, equally problematic pedagogically, where we offer a set of ethical guidelines, codes and conclusions as a way of 'covering' that basic viewpoint. A possible university course, like Bio-ethics-of-learning-disabilities-101, is epistemologically naive if the focus is merely on outlining all the positions. Students may come away with a sense of *what* ethicists think, but not a sense of *how* ethicists think. The latter can only be acquired by engaging with the methods and practices that ethicists use when they make complex decisions under conditions of uncertainty. Moreover, by characterising different basic viewpoints as sets of methods and practices instead of as catalogues of findings and conclusions, we give a more accurate view of how knowledge is produced at the cutting edge of inquiry, where models and principles from different basic viewpoints compete for acceptance.

Overall, the foregoing discussion is meant to illustrate how a methodological pluralism should guide approaches to interdisciplinary education. We have sketched the kind of reflections we think are necessary in order to produce epistemologically responsible curricula. The two organising dimensions of *levels of analysis* and *basic viewpoints* provide a basis for a rough taxonomy of interdisciplinary endeavours. Some implicate only level-of-analysis issues, such as efforts at integrating different types of explanatory frameworks that set out from the same basic viewpoint. Others must grapple with both level-of-analysis issues and differences of basic perspectives, such as most efforts in the human sciences that involve biological or materialistic explanations and all efforts that aim to produce applications. We saw this clearly with the example of dyscalculia. Indeed, teaching any complex topic that is socially relevant will almost always entail that we grapple with both levels of analysis and basic viewpoints. We suggest that the contours of the approach we have offered can be useful in a variety of interdisciplinary educational initiatives.

NOTES

1. This approach is comparable to Wilber's *integral methodological pluralism* (Wilber 1999; see also Stein, 2007), which also entails a kind of openness, cooperation, and symbiosis between various methods.
2. This idea is the contemporary expression of certain perennial efforts in philosophy that can be traced from Wilber, Habermas and Sellars, back though C. S. Peirce to Kant, and ultimately to the Greeks. The search for *philosophical categories* has been a search for the most basic or primordial distinctions that frame our knowledge and action in the world. Here we find those indelible distinctions around which philosophical (and scientific) debates still revolve: distinctions like those between the *mental* and the *material* (Chalmers, 1996; see also Changeux and Ricoeur, 2000), the *natural* and the *normative* (Sellars, 2006; see also Damasio, 2003), the *subjective* and the *objective* (Nagel, 1986; see also Damasio, 1999), the Good, the True, and the Beautiful (Gardner, 2000). When we confront differences of basic viewpoint, we confront these types of extremely general and fundamental distinctions.
3. It is worth noting here that discussing basic viewpoints in terms of the difference between *descriptions* and *evaluations* has monopolised our treatment because we think this is the clearest, least controversial, and most important example of a difference between basic viewpoints. The list in the second endnote covers a larger set of basic viewpoints, some of which are relevant to this discussion. For example, an *objective* account of dyscalculia would differ from a *subjective* account. The former would cover the psychology and neuroscience of the learning disability, while the latter would involve the phenomenology of being someone with that learning disability (see: Nagel, 1986; Damasio, 1999; and Thompson, 2007).

REFERENCES

Blake, P. and Gardner, H. (2007) A First Course in Mind, Brain, and Education, *Mind, Brain, and Education*, 1.2, pp. 61–65.

Boix-Mansilla, V. (2006) Interdisciplinary work at the frontier: An empirical examination of expert interdisciplinary epistemologies, *Issues in Integrative Studies*, 24, 1–31.

Chalmers, D. (1996) *The Conscious Mind* (Oxford, Oxford University Press).

Changeux, J. and Connes, A. (1998) *Conversations on Mind, Matter, and Mathematics*, M. B. DeBevoise trans. (Princeton, NJ, Princeton University Press).

Changeux, J. and Ricoeur, P. (2000) *What makes us think?*, M. B. DeBevoise trans. (Princeton, NJ, Princeton University Press).

Dawson, T. L., Fischer, K. W. and Stein, Z. (2006) Reconsidering Qualitative and Quantitative Research Approaches: A Cognitive Developmental Perspective, *New Ideas in Psychology*, 24, pp. 229–239.

Damasio, A. (1999) *The Feeling of What Happens* (New York, Harcourt).

Damasio, A. (2003) *Looking for Spinoza* (New York, Harcourt).

Dehaene, S. (1997) *The Number Sense* (New York, Oxford University Press).

Fischer, K., Immordino-Yang, M. H. and Waber, D. (2007) Toward a Grounded Synthesis of Mind, Brain, and Education for Reading Disorders, in: K. Fischer, J. H. Bernstein and M. H. Immordino-Yang (eds) *Mind, Brain, and Education in Learning Disorders* (Cambridge, Cambridge University Press).

Gardner, H. (2000) *The Disciplined Mind* (New York, Penguin Books).

Gardner, H. (2007) *Five Minds for the Future* (Cambridge, MA, Harvard Business School Press).

Geary, D. C. (1993) Mathematical Disabilities: Cognitive, Neuropsychological and Genetic Components, *Psychological Bulletin*, 114.2, pp. 345–362.

Gibbons, M., Limoges, C., Nowontny, H., Schwartzman, S., Scott, P. and Trow, M. (1994) *The New Production of Knowledge: The Dynamics of Science and Research in Contemporary Societies* (London, SAGE Publications).

Grigorenko, E. (2007) How Can Genomics Inform Education?, *Mind, Brain, and Education*, 1.1, pp. 20–27.

Habermas, J. (1970) *On the Logic of the Social Sciences*, S. Nicholson and J. Stark, trans. (Cambridge, MA, MIT Press).

Habermas, J. (1971) *Knowledge and Human Interests*, J. Shapiro, trans. (Boston, Beacon Press).

Habermas, J. (1984) *The Theory of Communicative Action: Reason and the Rationalization of Society*, T. McCarthy, trans. Vol. 1 (Boston, Beacon Press).

Habermas, J. (1987) *The Theory of Communicative Action: Lifeworld and System, a Critique of Functionalist Reason*, T. McCarthy, trans. Vol. 2 (Boston, Beacon Press).

Habermas, J. (2003) *The Future of Human Nature* (Cambridge, Polity Press).

Kosc, L. (1974) Developmental Dyscalculia, *Journal of Learning Disabilities*, 7.3, pp. 164–177.

Klein, J. T. (1990) *Interdisciplinarity: History, Theory, and Practice* (Detroit, MI, Wayne State University Press).

Nagel, T. (1986) *The View From Nowhere* (Oxford, Oxford University Press).

Piaget, J. (1970) *Main Trends in Psychology* (New York, Harper and Row).

Sellars, W. (2006) *In the Space of Reasons* (Cambridge, MA, Harvard University Press).

Sellars, W. (1963) Philosophy and the Scientific Image of Man, in: *Science, Perception, and Reality* (New York, Humanities Press).

Stanescu-Cosson, R., Pinel, P., Moortele, P-F. v. d., Le Bihan, D., Cohen, L. and Dehaene, S. (2000) Understanding Dissociations in Dyscalculia: A Brain Imaging Study of the Impact of Number Size on the Cerebral Networks for Exact and Approximate Calculation, *Brain*, 123.11, pp. 2240–2255.

Stein, Z. (2007) Modeling the Demands of Interdisciplinarity: Towards a Framework for Evaluating Interdisciplinary Endeavors, *Integral Review*, 4, pp. 91–107.

Stein, Z. and Fischer, K.. (forthcoming) Directions for Mind, Brain, and Education: methods, models, and morality, *Educational Philosophy and Theory*: Special Issue on Educational Neuroscience.

Thompson, E. (2007) *Mind in Life* (Cambridge, MA, Harvard University Press).

Weingart, P. (2001) Interdisciplinarity: The Paradoxical Discourse, in: P. Weingart and N. Stehr (eds) *Practicing Interdisciplinarity* (Toronto, University of Toronto Press), pp. 25–41.

Wilson, A. J. and Dehaene, S. (2007) Number Sense and Developmental Dyslexia, in: D. Koch, G. Dawson and K. W. Fischer (eds.) *Human Behavior, Learning and the Developing Brain: Atypical Development* (New York, Guilford Publications, Inc).

Whitehead, A. (1925) *Science and the Modern World* (New York, Free Press).

Wilber, K. (1999) *Integral Psychology* (Boston, Shambhala).

Wilber, K. (2006) *Integral Spirituality* (Boston, Integral Books).

1.5
Minds, Brains and Education

DAVID BAKHURST

1

From the mid-1960s to the mid-1970s, Soviet philosopher Evald Ilyenkov published a series of writings about the mind-body problem. In these texts, he argued passionately against what I shall call 'brainism', the view (a) that an individual's mental life is constituted by states, events and processes in her brain, and (b) that psychological attributes may legitimately be ascribed to the brain.[1] 'The brain does not think', Ilyenkov maintained, 'a human being thinks with the help of her brain (*s pomoshch'iu mozga*)' (Arsen'ev, Ilyenkov and Davydov, 1966, p. 265; see also Ilyenkov, 1974, p. 183 (1977a, p. 252)).[2] The psychological subject is the person, not the brain, and moreover, the person in unity with nature and society. Human beings are creatures of the natural world, but our mindedness does not consist in the occurrence of a special class of events inside us; rather, it lies in our mode of engagement with the world, a mode of engagement possible only because we are social beings.

Ilyenkov was by no means the only Soviet philosopher to take such a position. In many ways, his views are representative of the generation of Hegelian Marxists who sought to reanimate Soviet philosophical culture in the post-Stalin era. These thinkers typically adopted a strongly socio-historical view of mind that they deemed inconsistent with brainism.[3] But Ilyenkov's contribution was distinctive. He, more than anyone, sought to link philosophical controversies about mind and brain to social and political issues. He was adamant that Soviet fascination with artificial intelligence and cybernetics was a symptom of a growing cult of technology that looked to the development of science to solve socio-economic problems, thereby distracting attention from their true source.[4] He also sought to bring the issues to a wide audience by writing in a lively, accessible style, and publishing not just in philosophical journals, but in popular books and newspapers.[5]

Ilyenkov was especially concerned about the influence of brainism in the domain of education. He thought it would be disastrous for teachers to see education as a matter of training brains. He feared such a view would not only misrepresent the educational process, it would encourage nativist ideas about students' potential to learn. Since the brain's capacities are determined by its physical organisation, and since that organisation is in part determined by genetic considerations, a brain's capacity to learn must be constrained by innate factors. This seems to compel the conclusion that whether someone is intelligent, whether she is talented or 'gifted', how much she can benefit from some or other programme, and so on, is a function of the kind of brain she has. Ilyenkov felt that such reasoning only leads educators to blame children's failure to learn on their supposedly innate abilities, or lack of them, when the real culprit lies in the education system (Ilyenkov, 2002, pp. 76–77). It also encourages the idea that a future brain science might enable us to stream students for specialised programmes in light of their innate abilities, a strategy that, as Ilyenkov was quick to point out, is at odds with Marxism's commitment to abolish the division of labour for the cultivation of 'all-round individuals' (Ilyenkov, 1968b, pp. 147–51). In contrast, Ilyenkov urged that we liberate ourselves from the idea that a normal child's developmental trajectory is significantly predetermined by genetic factors. He embraced a thorough-going 'nurturism', maintaining that a child's capacity to learn has unlimited horizons and that we should educate for people's all-round development. If something goes awry in the learning process, we should look for social, rather than biological, causes.

Especially in his more popular writings, Ilyenkov adopted a strident polemical style and made abundantly clear that he deemed his opponents' views pernicious and reactionary. His opponents, of course, thought that the shoe was on the other foot (see Dubrovskii, 1968; 1990, pp. 6–9). They deemed it inappropriate of Ilyenkov to suggest that brainism was inconsistent with Marxism. After all, Marxists are materialists, and the obvious materialist approach to mind is to recognise that mental processes are brain processes. In any case, it is manifestly unscientific for philosophers to declare that neuroscience and cognate disciplines have nothing to tell us about our mental lives. It is an empirical matter whether, say, the capacity to learn is significantly influenced by genetic factors, so philosophers are in no position to pronounce on the matter. To disregard empirical research and embrace extreme nurturism on *a priori* grounds is not just unscientific; it is utopian, idealistic and patently absurd.

Ilyenkov was undeterred, insisting that: 'The *substance* of mind is always the life-activity [of a person] ... and the brain with its innate structure is only its biological *substrate*. Therefore, studying the brain has as little to do with studying the mind as investigating the nature of money by analyzing the physical composition of the material (gold, silver, paper) in which the monetary form of value is realized' (Ilyenkov, 2002, p. 98).

2

Some forty years have passed since this controversy played out in the Soviet Union. The USSR is no more, and Marxist philosophy is distinctly out of fashion. Ilyenkov is long dead; he committed suicide in 1979. Philosophy of mind, cognitive science, neuroscience and evolutionary biology have been busy—very busy—in the intervening years. So why begin this chapter by describing a thinker so remote from the contemporary scene?

It is striking, however, that for all that has changed, much remains the same. The problems that exercised Ilyenkov remain with us, and in many respects we are no closer to resolving them. Consider, for example, the jointly-authored book *Neuroscience and Philosophy*, published in 2007. In this text, neuroscientist Maxwell Bennett and philosopher Peter Hacker maintain, as Ilyenkov did, that psychological attributes cannot be ascribed to the brain. They argue that it makes no sense to say that a brain thinks or reasons, decides or remembers. Such things are done by people, not brains. In response, the philosophers Daniel Dennett and John Searle argue, in their respective ways, that Bennett and Hacker are wrong. Searle holds that consciousness is a biological phenomenon caused by the brain and that mental states exist in the brain. Dennett argues that attributing psychological predicates to sub-personal brain systems has produced genuinely explanatory cognitive-scientific theories, and if, as Dennett puts it, such a strategy 'lets us see how on earth to get whole wonderful persons out of brute mechanical parts' (Bennett *et al.*, 2007, p. 89), who is the philosopher to say that such attributions make no sense? In response, Bennett and Hacker deny that cognitive science lets us see anything of the kind and disdain Searle's idea that the brain causes consciousness. This discussion would be very familiar to Ilyenkov, as would the acrimonious tone that sometimes creeps into it. Bennett and Hacker write of neuroscientists 'fostering a form of mystification and cultivating a neuro-mythology that is altogether deplorable' (p. 47); Dennett describes their philosophical methods as 'deeply reactionary' (p. 92).[6]

Ilyenkov would also find sadly familiar the burgeoning literature on the relevance of neuroscience to teaching and learning. The most comprehensive summary of how contemporary brain science can inform education is Sarah-Jayne Blakemore and Uta Frith's *The Learning Brain: Lessons for Education*. Although the authors are enthusiasts for their discipline, speculating that 'in the future there will be all sorts of new and radically different ways to increase the brain's potential to learn' (Blakemore and Frith, 2005, p. 167), it must be said that the concrete educational recommendations issuing from the research they review are remarkably modest. Some examples:

> One clear implication for education from this research [on grammatical processing in the brain] is that there *may be* a finite time for the most efficient type of grammar learning. After the age of 13, we will still be able to learn grammar, but we will *probably* be less efficient and use different brain strategies than if we had learned grammar earlier (p. 47, my emphasis).

> [Research on the adolescent brain suggests that if] 0–3 years is seen as a major opportunity for teaching, so should 10–15 years. During both

periods, particularly dramatic brain reorganization is taking place. This *may well be* a signal that learning in certain domains is becoming ultrafast during these periods (p. 121, my emphasis).

[Research on brain mechanisms underlying imitation (specifically mirror neurons) suggests that] [l]earning from observation is *usually* easier than learning from verbal descriptions, however precise and detailed the descriptions may be. This *might be* because, by observing an action, your brain has already prepared to copy it. . . . In education, imitating attitudes, mentalities, and emotions *may be* more important than imitating simple movements (pp. 161–3, my emphasis).

[Research on brain activity during sleep suggests that] it *may be* a good idea to take a nap after learning . . . [and that] learning sessions could also be scheduled in the evening, permitting the beneficial aspects of sleep to improve the performance of the learned tasks (pp. 175–6, my emphasis).

However, notwithstanding the underwhelming character of these conclusions, Blakemore and Frith's book paints an engaging picture of a young science uncovering numerous thought-provoking findings some of which certainly appear to have application to educational matters. This is especially true of research into the neurophysiological basis of conditions that impede learning, such as dyslexia and autism.[7]

As is evident from the claims quoted above, Blakemore and Frith are under no illusions about the need for caution in making educational recommendations on the basis of the present state of research. Such caution, however, is not shown by many proponents of 'brain-based education', who are quick to invoke contemporary neuroscience to recommend 'brain-based curricula' and 'brain-compatible learning programs' (see, e.g., Jensen, 2008). Although Blakemore and Frith ignore this literature, suggesting they give it no credence, others have been unable to suffer in silence. John Bruer, for example, has criticised brain-based education since its inception (see, e.g., Bruer, 1997, 2002). Bruer rightly complains that 'the brain-based education literature is produced not by neuroscientists but by educators and educational consultants'. Though they purport to ground their conclusions and recommendations on science, 'the primary "scientific" sources cited in this literature are popular books written by neuroscientists and journalists' (Bruer, 2002, p. 1031). From these sources, they make cavalier inferences from premises about brain structure to conclusions about brain-functioning. The result is 'at best . . . no more than a folk-theory about the brain and learning' dressed up as science (p. 1032).

Ilyenkov would have applauded Bruer's stand. The worry about brain-based education is that pop-scientific speculation, grounded more in prejudice than science, might significantly influence educational policy, and this is exactly what concerned Ilyenkov, albeit in a very different political context. Of course, Ilyenkov would go further than Bruer. For one thing, Bruer does not question the potential relevance of brain science to education. He just thinks that, as things stand, serious scientific 'research on applications of brain science to general education is non-existent' (ibid.). Moreover, Ilyenkov would fault, not just brain-based education, but the more scholarly work of Frith and Blakemore. He would complain that, when they write that 'the brain has evolved to educate and to be educated'; that it 'acquires and lays down information and skills'; that it 'learns new information and deals with it throughout life'; that it is 'our natural mechanism that places limits on learning', determining 'what can be learned, how much, and how fast', Blakemore and Frith foster the view that the real focus of education is brains, not people (Blakemore and Frith, 2005, p. 1). It is significant that from the very outset, their language is one of *limits* to learning, and that they portray education in terms of an engineering metaphor: education as landscaping (see p. 10). Finally, for all their caution, Blakemore and Frith are not immune from utopian speculation, remarking that '[p]erhaps one day it will be possible to pop a pill to learn!' (p. 167). All this would have provoked Ilyenkov.

No doubt Blakemore and Frith would protest that their view of education does not focus on brains at the expense of learners. On the contrary, the metaphor of landscaping is supposed to evoke the image of gardening, of cultivating the brain's powers so that *learners* should flourish. Their talk of limits is balanced by the desire to exploit neuro-science to maximise everyone's potential to learn. At best, Ilyenkov's complaints are superficial, pertaining to infelicities of language rather than to matters of substance. I suspect, however, that Ilyenkov would have deemed their language indicative of a certain scientistic style of thinking that inevitably influences, perhaps tacitly, the setting of research priorities, the identification of research topics and the categorisation of objects of inquiry. The best way to guard against this influence is to abandon the pretence that studying the brain is studying the mind at all.

As we have seen, Ilyenkov rejects brainism in favour of what we might call 'personalism' about the mental, the view that psychological attributes are properties of persons, not brains. This is a view endorsed by a number of prominent Western thinkers, including Peter Hacker, whom I mentioned above, and John McDowell. In what follows, I examine the case for personalism and consider how its truth might bear on the relevance of brain science to education. It is not difficult to understand what a philosopher takes herself to be claiming when she claims that mental states are brain states or that consciousness is caused by the brain. These claims might turn out to be ultimately incomprehensible, but it is easy to grasp what their advocates are trying to say. It is also not hard to understand why brain-functioning might be thought relevant to question of education. The science described in Blakemore and Frith's book is intellectually demanding, but the book's claims are not conceptually challenging. The kind of view Ilyenkov favours, however, is not as intuitively plausible as his opponents' positions appear to be and it is easily misunderstood and misrepresented.[8] So my aim in this chapter is to do the best for it I can.

3

It is important to underline that personalism is not a form of dualism of the Cartesian variety. When the personalist denies that the brain thinks, or that mental states are in the brain, she is not claiming that thoughts reside in some immaterial substance or non-material organ of thought. The point is that mental states and processes are states of whole persons and persons are material things—human beings—who are inhabitants of the natural world. It is 'I', David Bakhurst, who sees, hears, imagines, infers, speculates, hopes, intends, wants, reasons and so on, not my brain or any other part of me. It is also critical that the personalist does not deny that the proper functioning of a person's brain is a precondition for her having a mental life and that neuroscience may be able to establish significant correlations, perhaps to a high degree of detail, between particular events in the brain and the occurrence of certain mental phenomena, and between activity in certain areas of the brain and the possession or exercise of certain abilities and skills. But to establish a correlation is one thing, to affirm some kind of identity another. Brain functioning enables mind-edness, but is not constitutive of it. Or so the personalist maintains.

What, then, is the *argument* that psychological ascriptions can be made of persons but not brains? According to Bennett and Hacker, whether psychological states can be ascribed to the brain is not a question of fact, but a conceptual issue that precedes empirical enquiry (see Bennett *et al.*, 2007, pp. 15–33, 127–56). They maintain that it is incoherent to use psychological predicates of anything other than persons. Following Wittgenstein, Bennett and Hacker argue that the meaning of an expression is determined by the conditions of its use. But the rules for the use of psychological expressions make no reference whatsoever to what is going on in the brain. You do not have to know anything about what is happening in someone's brain to be able to say of them that they believe it is Tuesday, or that they are deciding what to have for dinner, or that they are day-dreaming about Grenada. Indeed, a person can have an excellent mastery of psychological discourse while knowing nothing about the brain and its relation to our mental lives (this was, after all, true of Aristotle). Psychological predicates are applied to creatures in light of their behaviour as they actively engage with their environment and with each other. Bennett and Hacker write: '[T]he *concept* of consciousness is bound up with the behavioural grounds for ascribing consciousness' to an animal. 'An animal does not have to exhibit such behaviour in order for it *to be* conscious. But only an animal to which such behaviour *can intelligibly be ascribed* can also be said, *either truly or falsely*, to be conscious' (p. 135), and the same goes for other psychological states and processes. Since the brain does not engage in behaviour in the relevant sense, and its processes are unobservable to most speakers, it is simply not a candidate for the possession of psychological attributes. If we apply such terms to the brain, we do so derivatively and in a way parasitic upon ordinary psychological discourse. Of course, nothing prevents scientists from using psychological expressions metaphorically, or from coining novel usages, but as Bennett and Hacker think they can show, neuroscientists and cognitive scientists typically presuppose that they are using psychological expressions literally.

How good is this argument? Bennett and Hacker's critics see it as a futile throwback to ordinary language philosophy. Searle argues that they confuse the criteria for the use of psychological expressions with what these expressions pick out. Although we attribute a psychological state to someone on the basis of behavioural evidence, *what it is* that we are attributing to her is, we now know, a brain state (Bennett *et al.*, 2007, pp. 101–06). Dennett, who is more sympathetic to the view that meaning is tied to criteria for use, argues that if ascribing psychological expressions to the brain yields explanatory theories, then the philosopher is in no position to declare the practice illegitimate. Cognitive science has indeed produced fertile theories by assuming that brains or their parts behave in ways that can usefully be described as 'thinking', 'remembering', etc. If there is a doubt about the coherence of these theories it must be established by close examination of the theories themselves, rather than general considerations about the rules for the use of words. In any case, Dennett comments, what are these rules? As Wittgenstein himself well understood, we are unable to state the rules for the use of most expressions, so philosophers only embarrass themselves by pretending to be the self-appointed guardians of the legitimate use of words (pp. 74–95).

I think Ilyenkov, who was no fan of linguistic philosophy, would agree that personalism cannot be established by appeal to considerations about the meaning of psychological terms. A different style of argument favoured by the Russians starts from the claim that if you open up a person's cranium and look in their brain, you do not find mental images, sensations, beliefs, intentions and so on (e.g., Ilyenkov, 1974, p. 54, and 1977a, p. 73); Mikhailov, 1980, pp. 115–42). At best, all we can observe in the brain are *correlates* of mental processes.[9] What is the basis for this claim? Why deny that brain-imaging techniques allow us to observe mental processes themselves? It might be thought that the personalist is making an argument reminiscent of Thomas Nagel's famous paper 'What is it Like to Be a Bat?' (Nagel, 1979). This is the idea that occurrent mental states have a qualitative dimension. They have a subjective, phenomenological quality. Although we might be able to observe what is going on in a person's brain when she sees a red flag, we cannot observe *what it is like* for her to see it. The subjective dimension, which some claim to be an essential characteristic of conscious mental states, goes missing in any third-personal, physical description of brain states. Hence, we might conclude, all that is observable are the neural correlates of mental activity, not mental activity itself.

The personalist agrees with this conclusion, but I think she takes a different route to it, one that does not depend on considerations of phenomenology. She is more likely to begin from the premise that the human mind is a psychological unity.[10] A person's mental states are not just a rag-bag collection of representations. Any mental state has a place in a network of mental states. They form a unified system. Any new experience, any potential belief, any new intention or desire, must be evaluated in light of its fit with the subject's existing mental states. I can only adopt a new belief if it is consistent with what I already believe, and if it is plausible in light of my existing conceptions. I should only form the intention to do A, if doing A is consistent with my commitments and projects, or if I am willing to revise those commitments in projects to accommodate the action. The possibility of a network of mental states depends on two unifying factors. First, my mental states are unified because they are all states of a particular person, me. Second, they are unified in that they express my orientation to the world, which comprises both a conception of how the world is and commitments to change the world in various ways through action. It follows that if we are to understand the unity of a mental life we have to think of the person, rather than any of her parts, as the legitimate subject of psychological ascription, for it is the person that has an orientation to the world manifest in action, not her brain.[11]

One way to put this argument about psychological unity is to say that brainism struggles to make sense of the first-person perspective. A person does not typically stand to her own mental states as to objects of observation. If I ask myself what I believe about something, I do not determine the answer by observing the contents of my mind and coming across the relevant belief, as if surveying exhibits in a museum. I determine it by making up my mind what to think in light of the evidence as I understand it. The attitude we take to our own mental lives is one of agency: we are the authors of our orientation to the world, responsible for what we think and do and our attitude to our own beliefs is never one of passive observation (see Moran, 2001). Indeed, even in cases where our minds are passive recipients, as they are in perception, we are nevertheless under a standing obligation to evaluate the veracity of what we take ourselves to see, hear and so on. Although we can observe the world, our observing of it is always charged with agency. But although a person does not relate to the contents of her mind as to objects of observation, her relation to her own brain states, as revealed, say, by MRI imaging, *is* one of observation. Thus what she observes when she observes events in her own brain can only be brain events correlated with, and enabling of, her mental life, not her mental life itself.[12]

4

The personalist's objective, as John McDowell puts it, is:

> ... to restore us to a conception of thinking as an exercise of powers possessed, not mysteriously by some part of a thinking being, a part whose internal arrangements are characterizable independently of how the thinking being is placed in its environment, but unmysteriously by a thinking being itself, an animal that lives its life in cognitive and practical relations to the world (McDowell, 1998, p. 289).

Both McDowell and Ilyenkov supplement their personalism with a distinctive view of human development. On this conception, the human child first lives a purely animal mode of existence; that is, her bodily functions, including her psychological functions, answer exclusively to biological imperatives—for food, warmth, comfort, etc. At this stage, we might say that the child's psychological functions are unified by the satisfaction of biological need, rather than by the maintenance of an orientation, cognitive and practical to the world. As the child matures, however, she undergoes a qualitative transformation. She enters a distinctively human, essentially social form of life and acquires distinctively human psychological capacities that enable her to transcend existence in the narrow confines of a biological environment and to hold the world in view. With this, natural-scientific modes of explanation are no longer adequate to explain the character of the child's mindedness.

Exactly what is it about the mature human mind that resists explanation in scientific terms? When Ilyenkov characterises the distinctive character of human thought, his emphasis is always on creativity, universality and unpredictability. Ilyenkov's point is that the human mind is universal in that it is in principle open to *any* subject-matter (Ilyenkov, 1974, pp. 38–39, and 1977a, p. 53). It is able to grapple with and solve hitherto-unencountered problems. The human mind constantly transcends its own limits; it does not simply apply old techniques to new problems. On the contrary, we set ourselves problems precisely to develop the methods to address them, a process that in turn uncovers new questions, creating new problem-spaces demanding further innovation and so on. To understand this dialectical process, we cannot represent the mind as determined by antecedent conditions. If it is determined by anything, it is by the logic of the subject-matter it confronts (Ilyenkov, 2002, pp. 105–06). But if it is to conform itself to an evolving, ever-novel object, the mind must be able to transcend rules and principles that formerly governed its operation. The human mind is not rule-bound. It follows that since the brain is a physical thing operating according to physical laws, its operations cannot be all there is to the life of the mind. A machine, even an astonishingly complex biological machine, can only do what it has been programmed to do by evolution or design. No machine can be truly universal in the way that human minds are universal.

This argument is harder to sustain today than it was in Ilyenkov's time. We are now familiar with computers capable of learning and of forming creative solutions to problems. So the idea that computers are rule-bound in a way that human beings are not lacks the intuitive plausibility it had in the early days of artificial intelligence and cybernetics. So Ilyenkov's opponents will likely dismiss his argument as no more than a misplaced affirmation of humanism.

Ilyenkov's remarks can be redeemed, however, if we bring into play something he largely omits from discussion: rationality. As I observed above, McDowell, like Ilyenkov, argues that human beings 'are born mere animals, and they are transformed into thinkers and intentional agents in the course of coming to maturity' (McDowell, 1994, p. 125). But McDowell makes very clear that human beings' distinctive psychological powers reside in their *responsiveness to reasons*. Human beings think and act in light of the reasons for so doing and their behaviour can be explained only with this perspective in view. Critical to McDowell's view is a distinction, ultimately derived from Kant, between two species of explanation or 'modes of intelligibility'. On the one hand, there is explanation by appeal to scientific law; on the other, there is explanation by appeal to reasons. The explanation of why Harry tripped over the carpet appeals to the physical conditions that were causally sufficient for the accident to occur. In contrast, we explain why Harry opened the door by appeal to his reasons for so doing: we attempt to show the favourable light in which he saw the action. In like manner, we explain what Harry believes by appeal to what it is most reasonable for him to think in light of the evidence, his situation and his existing beliefs, on the assumption that he is rational. These two species of explanation, rational and causal, are fundamentally different in kind.[13] The relations in which rational explanation deals are normative in character. When I decide that Jack must believe that q because he believes (a) that p and (b) that p entails q, I am not making a causal claim. I am assuming that Jack believes what he ought to believe if he is rational.

Earlier, I described the mind as a psychological unity. The relations that unite mental phenomena into a system are precisely normative, rational relations of entailment, probability, plausibility and so on. These are not the sort of relations that are characterised by natural-scientific theories. The language in which we describe and explain mental events and processes, and the constraints that govern those explanations, are fundamentally different in character from the language of natural science. What goes on in the brain is exhaustively open to scientific explanation. The brain is within the realm of scientific law. But mental states and processes occupy a different logical space—the space of reasons. Since there is no possibility of reducing the items that occupy the space of reasons to those that populate the realm of law, it follows that psychological talk represents a fundamentally different discourse from talk of the brain, and these discourses have fundamentally different subjects.[14]

With this view of rationality in place, we can say that the qualitative transformation in the child occurs when it becomes an inhabitant of the space of reasons, a being whose life-activity must be understood by appeal to rational, rather than merely causal-scientific, considerations.[15] For McDowell, what is crucial is the acquisition of conceptual capacities. These enable the child to have perceptual experiences of a kind that have a rational bearing on judgement, and to entertain mental states of a kind that can stand in articulate rational relations with one another. Such a creature is a rational agent, a person. This conception of development consolidates the view that the person is the centrepiece of rational explanation, not her brain. It is persons whose beliefs are consistent or inconsistent, who act reasonably or unreasonably, who argue perceptively or stupidly, who judge carefully or precipitously.

It may seem that these considerations about reason and rationality are at some remove from the Ilyenkovian thoughts about creativity and universality that they were meant to redeem, but they are not. It is a presumption of rational explanation that agents are free and hence responsible for their thoughts and actions. Creatures capable of conceptual thought governed by norms of rationality are able to commune with the universal, first, in the sense that concepts can have universal content and, second, in the sense that there is no limit to what we can entertain in thought (of course there can be empirical limits to what we can entertain in thought, but there is no restriction of subject-matter built into the very nature of thought itself). Finally, rational explanation is tolerant of novelty and creativity: it enables us to see how someone derived a novel solution to a problem without representing its derivation as merely a piecing together of that which was already to hand. Even where judgement is compelled by rational necessity—where a person realises that there is nothing else to think but *p*—creativity may be required to perceive the significance of the considerations that compel judgement. This kind of creative insight can be understood and appreciated; it cannot itself be represented as necessitated by circumstance, or anticipated by substantive rules or procedures. Rational explanation is at ease with this.[16]

It is worth observing that although Ilyenkov and McDowell paint a similar picture of human development, there are marked differences in their views. McDowell links the acquisition of conceptual capacities to the learning of a first language. Ilyenkov, in contrast, argues that language learning is possible only once the child has already entered the human world by learning to interact with artefacts. Ilyenkov holds that the physical form of an artefact embodies the purposes for which it is used. Acquiring facility with artefacts is therefore a matter of coming to respond to a meaningful object, adapting to the 'ideal' form expressed by its physical form. The child inhabits a social world, not just because she constantly interacts with other people (indeed, she is dependent on others for her very survival), but because her world is full of objects created by human beings for human purposes. Learning to negotiate this world is the child's entrance into the space of reasons, for to interact with the artefactual is to engage in activities that are not just elicited by circumstance but mediated by meaning. So the child enters the human world, the world of meaning. Language, for Ilyenkov, is just another artefact, albeit it a supremely complex and sophisticated one.[17]

5

We have now considered some of the central arguments for personalism.[18] In conclusion, I shall examine the bearing of these arguments on the relevance of neuroscience to educational issues.

It is sometimes argued that although there are significant constraints on the extent to which brain science can illuminate learning, it does have a role in the explanation of dysfunction, deficit and disorder (see Davis, 2004, p. 31; Changeux and Ricoeur, 2000, p. 49). Reflecting on the distinction between rational and causal explanation can explain why this position seems attractive. Where learning is proceeding smoothly, we view the child from the perspective of rationality: she is a rational agent gradually taking command of some subject-matter by coming to understand and appreciate the reasons for which she should form certain beliefs, make certain inferences, engage in certain practices and so on. If the child encounters obstacles to learning, we try at first to explain this rationally. So, for example, we might propose that the child cannot see that she should infer that q, because she is missing some vital piece of information. Once she understands that p, then she will quickly realise that q .... But sometimes we decide that such rational considerations cannot explain the child's difficulty. Her problem is not just that she lacks information or understanding in a way that is consistent with our viewing her as a rational agent. Her problem is of a different order. We then look for a causal explanation. Appeal to learning disabilities provides explanations of this kind. Such causal explanations look for underlying mechanisms, and in many cases it makes perfect sense to think that these might be a matter of brain functioning. It is plausible to suppose, for instance, that the particular challenges faced by people with Asperger's Syndrome have their basis in the way their brains work.[19] Once we adopt the causal perspective on the child's problems, we cease to see her as a rational agent, at least in this respect, and absolve her from responsibility, and hence blame, for her failings.

Yet why should we conclude that brain science is only good for explaining obstacles to learning? Why cannot brain science illuminate why someone is especially good at some practice? Admittedly, the explanation of why someone made some inference, or gave some excellent explanation, or solved some problem a certain way, will be a rational one, reconstructing the 'logic' of the achievement. But the explanation of why the person in question is particularly adept at this sort of thing—of her speed of thought, or her talent for seeing unusual connections—need not invoke rational considerations. It will speak to the causal preconditions of her rational powers. Why should we suppose, as Ilyenkov asks us to, that the only relevant neurophysiological fact is that her brain is functioning normally? Surely we can aspire to a fine-grained explanation of exactly what it is about the way her brain functions that enables her to excel as she does.

Ilyenkov insists that only social factors are relevant to the explanation of ability and achievement. Why? Consider the role that the social plays in Ilyenkov's and McDowell's respective accounts of the child's entrance into the space of reasons. McDowell gives pride of place to the child's acquisition of language, but he treats language, not just as a symbolic system, but also as a living embodiment of cultural wisdom, so that the child's acquiring a first language represents her initiation into styles of thinking and reasoning. He writes that 'the language into which a human being is first initiated stands over against her as a prior embodiment of mindedness, of the possibility of an orientation to the world ... [Language is] a repository of tradition, a store of historically accumulated wisdom about what is a reason for what' (McDowell, 1994, pp. 125–26). Acquiring a language, so conceived, is acquiring a form of social life. Ilyenkov, as we observed, stresses that our form of life is embodied, not just in linguistic thought and talk, but in the very form the world takes in virtue of human interaction with nature. Our world is one 'humanized' by our activity, populated by created objects that are embodiments of meaning and purpose. The first step to becoming human is to learn to manipulate such objects in light of the 'ideal form' they have been lent by human agency. And it is not just that initiation into social forms of life kick-starts our mindedness. The life of the mind is lived in social space, mediated by forms of thought and inquiry that are essentially sustained by social practices.

Yet, notwithstanding the prominence both thinkers accord to the social, nothing in their arguments suggests that we should embrace a nurturism as thoroughgoing as Ilyenkov's. They provide no reason to assume *a priori* that causal factors relevant to explaining *this* person's musical ability, or *that* person's proneness to anxiety, are all social. In the absence of real empirical evidence, that assumption can be based only on wishful thinking, on the hope that social factors can be controlled and improved in the way biological factors cannot be. Of course, there is as much reason to avoid crass biological determinism as there is to eschew *a priori* nurturism. It is critical to recognise that even though the acquisition and exercise of an ability (say, to sing a major scale) is enabled by biological factors, some of which may be innate, the ability itself is possessed by the person, not her brain. Moreover, *what* it is an ability to do is intelligible only in light of socio-historical considerations, and its acquisition must be seen as the appropriation of a social practice. Proper appreciation of these points gives the lie to any simple picture of abilities as 'hard-wired'. But there is no reason to claim, as Ilyenkov did, that we can 'divide through' by biological considerations when considering the developmental trajectory of 'normal' brains.

I conclude that, even if personalism is true and psychological attributes cannot be legitimately ascribed to the brain, neuroscience remains relevant to understanding the brain processes that enable and facilitate our mental lives. There are no *a priori* grounds to declare brain science irrelevant to educational issues, or relevant only in 'deficit' cases. What is critical, however, is that interest in the brain should not distract attention from the fact that education is a communicative endeavour, not an engineering problem. Education is not about getting information into students' heads or of implanting skills in them. Learning history, for example, is a matter of acquiring facility with a discipline aspiring to critical self-conscious-ness about our relation to the past. Though a command of facts and skills of analysis are preconditions of historical understanding, they are not what that understanding consists in. This is not true only of high-brow humanities disciplines. When we teach carpentry we are, or ought to be, introducing students to a craft, to a historically-evolving tradition of fashioning wood to make artefacts for various purposes. Once again, information and skills are not all that is at issue. Machines may possess those, or close surrogates, but machines have no practices and crafts. We must never lose sight of the wider communicative endeavour that is the heart of education: the meeting of minds in an encounter with a discipline.

Perhaps these reflections sound old-fashioned and high-minded. But I am amazed at the naiveté of scholars who ponder the possibility of 'popping a pill to learn'. If we object to athletes using performance-enhancing drugs, why should we welcome pharmaceutical ways of enhancing learning? If we stop students taking computers into examinations on which they have downloaded texts, should we look more favourably on the prospect of their downloading material directly into their brains? Such questions, however fanciful, raise ethical issues that force us to confront the issue of what education is and ought to be. My point is a familiar one: we must not let excitement about scientific innovation and technological possibility distort our conception of education and of the values it ought to embody. Above all else, this was the message that Ilyenkov sought to convey in his writings on education. Though many years have passed since he put pen to paper, this message is as relevant today as it ever was. I suspect it will remain so long into the future.

NOTES

1. I owe the term 'brainism' to my colleague E. J. Bond. As I define it in the text, the term serves well to characterise Ilyenkov's target. Ilyenkov himself sometimes describes himself as attacking 'naturalism' about the mind, but even though this is in keeping with how the term subsequently came to be used in Western philosophy of mind, it is not ideal, since there is a clear sense in which Ilyenkov himself embraces a form of naturalism, albeit one more expansive than his opponents'. 'Reductionism' about the mental is too narrow to describe Ilyenkov's target, since he would reject some forms of non-reductive physicalism, as well as eliminative materialism (which, despairing of reducing the mental to the physical, proposes to displace our 'folk psychological' idioms altogether). 'Physicalism' is too broad a term, since there is a huge variety of physicalist views of mind. For example, Ilyenkov would have rejected both traditional identity theory, which holds that for each type of mental state there is a type of physical state with which it is identical, and functionalist theories (the orthodoxy in contemporary cognitive science), according to which mental states are identified with their functional roles, the latter being portrayed as realised by causal processes in the brain. But Ilyenkov might have tolerated *some* versions of non-reductive physicalism. It is important to realise that Ilyenkov did not work at a high level of philosophical resolution, pondering the fine detail of nuanced positions in the philosophy of mind. Rather, he was concerned with our most basic conceptions of the nature of mind and his target was any view that casts the brain as the location of thought. Hence 'brainism' is as good a term as any to describe his *bête noire*.
2. The translation of the quoted remark is not entirely straightforward. First, the Russian '*chelovek*' serves for both 'human beings' and 'person' (the term has rich etymological associations, suggesting a being whose 'face is turned towards the infinite'). However, the potential ambiguity is of no consequence in this context, since Ilyenkov would hold that the paradigm of a person is a living human being. More problematic is the expression '*s pomoshch'iu*'. The literal translation, 'with the help of', is awkward, but so are the alternatives 'by means of', 'with', or 'using', none of which seem wholly appropriate to characterise a person's relation to her brain. This is perhaps only to be expected. If we deny that we can construe the mental in terms of brain functioning, we should not suppose that we will be able to represent the relation of person and brain on the model of some familiar relation, such as a person's relation to a tool. It should not surprise us that the relation is a singular one, in some respects like other relations, and in other ways unique and elusive.
3. Witness Felix Mikhailov's *The Riddle of the Self* (first published in 1964), and the work of psychologists of the Vygotsky school such as A. N. Leontiev and V. V. Davydov (see Levitin, 1982).

4. Of course, in the Soviet political context Ilyenkov had to be extremely cautious in making such points, often casting them as criticisms of *Western* society, but the sub-text would have been clear to many Soviet readers.

5. Ilyenkov's more scholarly treatments of the issue are Ilyenkov, 1974, Chapter 8 (1977a, Chapter 8) and 1984. Ilyenkov, 1968b is a good example of his polemical writing. Writings on education include Ilyenkov, 1964, 1977b/1991 and 2002, the latter containing six previously unpublished papers. Ilyenkov, 1968a is a lively book-length treatment that integrates themes from the philosophies of mind and education. Ilyenkov, 1970, 1975 and 2002 (pp. 95–106) discuss the philosophical significance of Meshcheryakov's work on the education of blind-deaf individuals. I examine Ilyenkov's conception of mind in Bakhurst, 1991: especially, Chapters 6–7, and in a number of subsequent articles, including Bakhurst, 1997 and 2005a. Bakhurst, 2005b, discusses his philosophy of education, and Bakhurst and Padden, 1991, examines his treatment of Meshcheryakov's contribution.

6. *Neuroscience and Philosophy* issued from an 'Author and Critics' session at an American Philosophical Association conference in 2005 that discussed Bennett and Hacker's, *Philosophical Foundations of Neuroscience* (2003), a book that gives a comprehensive statement of their position and includes substantial appendices criticising Dennett and Searle.

7. In these cases, what is contentious is not the potential relevance of brain science but the characterisation of the conditions themselves. For example, although we are now used to thinking in terms of an 'autistic spectrum', it is by no means clear that there is a single spectrum rather than, say, a cluster of related conditions or behaviours. Such questions of typology are profound and neuroscientific data is unquestionably relevant to resolving them.

8. In Ilyenkov's case, his strident polemical tone, and the incautious way he attacks his opponents, positively invite an uncharitable reading. It is important to step back from the heat of the controversy take a sober look at the best of the arguments.

9. Bennett and Hacker make a similar point: 'After all, the only thing neuroscientists *could* discover is that certain neural states are inductively well correlated with, and causal conditions of, an *animal's* being conscious. But *that* discovery cannot show that it is *the brain* that is conscious' (Bennett *et al*., 2007, p.136).

10. It is not that significant psychological disunity is impossible, just that it must be understood as a departure from the norm.

11. It was Kant who brought to prominence the question of the preconditions of psychological unity with his treatment of the transcendental unity of apperception. Kant held that the self that secured such unity was purely formal in nature. This, he believed, was the only alternative to Cartesianism. But Kant failed to see the possibility of taking persons—real living human beings—as genuine psychological subjects. See the excellent discussion in McDowell, 1994, pp. 99–104.

12. It is worth noting an important contrast with Nagel's argument in 'What is it Like to Be a Bat?'. That argument trades on the idea that there is a feature of the mental—namely its subjective phenomenology—that cannot be observed from a third-person perspective. Since physicalist accounts are cast from a third-person perspective, they will always fail to capture a crucial aspect of the mental. The personalist, in contrast, does not depend on the limitations of the third-personal perspective. Indeed, she can hold that much of our mental life is observable from a third-person perspective because it is manifest in the life-activity of the subject. The personalist's point is that the first-person perspective on the mental is not one of observation but agency, and this precludes a person adopting an attitude to her own mental states as if from the third-person (except perhaps in certain unusual circumstances). Our brain states, in contrast, are possible objects of observation.

13. McDowell prefers to cast the distinction as one between rational and scientific explanation because he does not want to make the scientific-naturalist a gift of the concept of causation. He wants to leave open the possibility that rational explanation can be genuinely causal. Conversely, not all scientific explanation is strictly causal in character. However, the rational/causal distinction will do for present purposes, so long as we bear these subtleties in mind.

14. Those who know the work of Donald Davidson may want to resist the final step in this argument. Davidson holds that psychological and physical explanation are fundamentally different in kind, but contends that mental events are physical events (see, e.g., Davidson, 1980). Since an event can be picked out by different modes of description, we can say that any event described

psychologically (e.g. my thinking of Vienna) is identical with some event that can be described physically (e.g. such-and-such neurons firing). Davidson argues that even though this particular (or 'token') mental event is the same as that particular physical event, the fundamental difference between psychological and physical modes of explanation entails that we cannot establish identities between types of mental and physical events or establish psycho-physical laws. He thus arrives at a form of non-reductive physicalism known as 'anomalous monism'. McDowell and others (e.g. Hornsby, 1997) reject anomalous monism on the grounds that we cannot assume that psychological and physical discourses individuate the same events.

15. It is interesting to speculate why Ilyenkov says little about rationality as such. I think he would have taken the rational/causal distinction for granted as a staple of post-Kantian philosophy, but avoided overt talk of reason and rationality for fear of provoking accusations of idealism, Hegelianism, or rationalism—all of which were considered heresies in Soviet philosophy.

16. The concept Ilyenkov deploys to capture the creative movement of thought is *dialectics* (see, e.g. Ilyenkov, 1964, 2002, pp. 26-34).

17. There is an interesting discussion of the significance of artefacts in his writing on the education of the blind-deaf. Reflecting on the importance of the blind-deaf child's learning to eat with a spoon, Ilyenkov writes: 'The first and most fundamental form of human mind is revealed here as the *movement of the hands according to a schema*—according to a trajectory, not defined by biological need, but by the form and situation of objects created by human labour, created by human beings for human beings' (Ilyenkov, 2002, p. 100).

18. But not all. For example, some argue the case for personalism on the basis of 'externalism' about meaning. it is sometimes argued that meaning, and hence mental content, is constituted in part by relations between the speaker/thinker and the external world. So, when I have a thought about tigers, what my thought is a thought about depends on facts about what tigers are. When I have a 'singular thought' about a particular object perceptually present to me (e.g. 'That lampshade is ghastly'), the content of the thought depends upon the existence of the object demonstrated. Such considerations led Putnam to conclude: 'Cut the pie any way you like, "meanings" just ain't in the *head*!' (Putnam, 1975, p. 227). McDowell takes these ideas further, arguing that 'the moral of Putnam's basic thought for the nature of the mental might be, to put it in his terms, that the mind—the locus of our manipulations of meanings—is not in the head either. Meanings are in the mind, but, as [Putnam's] argument establishes, they cannot be in the head; therefore, we ought to conclude, the mind is not in the head' (McDowell, 1998, p. 276). McDowell takes this as an argument for personalism: 'Mental life is an aspect of *our* lives, and the idea that it takes place in the mind can, and should, be detached from the idea that there is a part of us, whether material or (supposing this made sense) immaterial, in which it takes place. Where mental life takes place need not be pinpointed any more precisely than by saying that it takes place where our lives take place. And then its states and occurrences can be no less intrinsically related to our environment than our lives are' (p. 281). (Andrew Davis explicitly discusses the bearing of externalism about meaning on the question of the relevance of brain science to education (Davis, 2004).)

19. Though, in harmony with what I say in note 7 above, I am by no means confident that Asperger's Syndrome is really a single phenomenon, nor am I impressed with the assumption that the deficit is all on the side of the person diagnosed with the syndrome. We are good at describing the respects in which those with the syndrome fail to read other people, but we fail to ask what it is about 'normal' people that makes it difficult for them to read those with Asperger's.

REFERENCES

Arsen'ev, A. S., Ilyenkov, E. V. and Davydov, V. V. (1966) Mashina i chelovek, kibernetika i filosofiya ['Machine and human being, cybernetics and philosophy'], in: *Leninskaya teoriya otrazheniya i sovremennaya nauka [Lenin's Theory of Reflection and Contemporary Science]* (Moscow, Politizdat), pp. 265–285.

Bakhurst, D. (1991) *Consciousness and Revolution in Soviet Philosophy. From the Bolsheviks to Evald Ilyenkov* (Cambridge, Cambridge University Press).

Bakhurst, D. (1997) Meaning, Normativity, and the Life of the Mind, *Language and Communication*, 17.1, pp. 33–51.

Bakhurst, D. (2005a) Strong Culturalism, in: D. M. Johnson and C. Erneling (eds) *The Mind as a Scientific Object: Between Brain and Culture* (New York, Oxford University Press), pp. 413–31.

Bakhurst, D. (2005b) Ilyenkov on Education, *Studies in East European Thought*, 57.3, pp. 261–75.

Bakhurst, D. and Padden, C. (1991) The Meshcheryakov Experiment: Soviet Work on the Education of Blind-Deaf Children, *Learning and Instruction*, 1, pp. 201–215.

Bennett, M. and Hacker, P. (2003) *Philosophical Foundations of Neuroscience* (Oxford, Blackwell).

Bennett, M., Dennett, D., Hacker, P. and Searle, J. (2007) *Neuroscience and Philosophy: Mind, Brain and Language* (New York, Columbia University Press).

Blakemore, S-J. and Frith, U. (2005) *The Learning Brain: Lessons for Education* (Oxford, Blackwell).

Bruer, J. (1997) Education and The Brain: A Bridge Too Far, *Educational Researcher*, November, pp. 1–13.

Bruer, J. (2002) Avoiding the Pediatrician's Error: How Neuroscientists can Help Educators (and Themselves), *Nature. Neuroscience Supplement*, 5, pp. 1031–33.

Changeux, J. and Ricoeur, P. (2000) *What Makes Us Think?* (Princeton, NJ and Oxford, Princeton University Press).

Davidson, D. (1980) Mental Events, in his: *Essays on Action and Events* (Oxford, Oxford University Press), pp. 207–25.

Davis, A. (2004) The Credentials of Brain-Based Learning, *Journal of Philosophy of Education*, 38.1, pp. 21–35.

Dubrovskii, D. I. (1968) Mozg i psikhika [Brain and Mind], *Voprosy filosofii [Questions of Philosophy]*, 8, pp. 125–35.

Dubrovskii, D. I. (1990) Psikhika i mozg: resul'taty i perspektivy issledovanii [Mind and Brain: Results and Perspectives of Research], *Psikhologicheskii zhurnal [Journal of Psychology]*, 11.6, pp. 3–15.

Hornsby, J. (1997) *Simple Mindedness: In Defense of Naive Naturalism in the Philosophy of Mind* (Cambridge, MA, Harvard University Press).

Ilyenkov, E. V. (1964) Shkola dolzhna uchit' myslit'! [Schools Must Teach How to Think!], *Narodnoe obrazovanie [People's Education]*, 4, pp. 2–15.

Ilyenkov, E. V. (1968a) *Ob idolakh i idealakh [Of Idols and Ideals]* (Moscow, Politizdat).

Ilyenkov, E. V. (1968b) Psikhika i mozg [Mind and Brain], *Voprosy filosofii [Questions of Philosophy]*, 11, pp. 145–55.

Ilyenkov, E. V. (1970) Psikhika cheloveka pod 'lupoi vremeni' [The Human Mind Under 'The Looking Glass of Time'], *Priroda [Nature]*, 1, pp. 87–91.

Ilyenkov, E. V. (1974) *Dialekticheskaya logika: Ocherki istorii i teorii [Dialectical Logic: Essays in its History and Theory]* (Moscow, Politizdat).

Ilyenkov, E. V. (1975) Aleksandr Ivanovich Meshcherykov i ego pedagogika [Alexander Ivanovich Meshcheryakov and his Pedagogy], *Molodoi Kommunist [Young Communist]*, 2, pp. 80–84.

Ilyenkov, E. V. (1977a) *Dialectical Logic: Essays in its History and Theory*. Translation of Ilyenkov, 1974, by H. Campbell Creighton (Moscow, Progress).

Ilyenkov, E. V. (1977b) *Uchites' mylit' smolodu [Learn to Think While You Are Young]* (Moscow, Znanie). (The articles comprising this pamphlet are reprinted in Ilyenkov, *Filosofiya i kul'tura* (Moscow, Politizdat, 1991) pp. 18–55.

Ilyenkov, E. V. (1984) Dialektika ideal'nogo [The Dialectic of the Ideal], in his: *Iskusstvo i kommunisticheskii ideal [Art and the Communist Ideal]* (Moscow, Iskusstvo), pp. 8–77. (First published as in two parts as (1979) Problema ideal'nogo [The Problem of the Ideal] in *Voprosy filosofii [Questions of Philosophy]*, 6, pp. 145–58 and 7, pp. 128–40.)).

Ilyenkov, E. V. (2002) *Shkola dolzhna uchit' myslit' [Schools Must Teach How to Think]* (Moscow-Voronezh, Isdatel'stvo NPO 'Modek').

Jensen, E. (2008) A Fresh Look at Brain-Based Education, *Phi Delta Kappan*, February, pp. 409–17.

Levitin, K. (1982) *One is not Born a Personality*, Y. Filippov, trans. (Moscow, Progress).

McDowell, J. (1994) *Mind and World* (Cambridge, MA, Harvard University Press).

McDowell, J. (1998) Putnam on Mind and Meaning, in his: *Meaning, Knowledge and Reality* (Cambridge, MA, Harvard University Press), pp. 275–91.

Mikhailov, F. (1980) *The Riddle of the Self*, R. Daglish, trans. of the 1976 Russian edition (1st Russian edn. 1964) (Moscow, Progress).

Moran, R. (2001) *Authority and Estrangement: An Essay on Self-Knowledge* (Princeton, NJ and Oxford, Princeton University Press).

Nagel, T. (1979) What is it Like to Be a Bat?, in his: *Mortal Questions* (Cambridge, Cambridge University Press).

Putnam, H. (1975) The Meaning of 'Meaning', in his: *Mind, Language, and Reality* (Cambridge, Cambridge University Press), pp. 215–71.

1.6
Commentary

RUTH CIGMAN AND ANDREW DAVIS

The recent report from the Teaching and Learning Research Programme (TLRP) on how brain research might 'contribute to better educational outcomes' seems a good place to begin. Neuroscience has made rapid strides in recent decades, and in its applications to our understanding of learning it enjoys substantial funding and prestige. At the end of this report, it is observed that:

> ... to ignore the relevance of present neuroscientific understanding to education flies in the face of a common-sense connection ... neuroscience has a fundamental and increasing relevance to education ... In the future, neuroscience promises to positively influence the policy, practice and experience of education in a number of important areas, but the full and successful realisation of that promise will require careful educational and scientific scrutiny at all stages (ESRC, 2007, p. 24).

What precisely might be meant by 'relevance', and 'positive influence' in this regard are important and difficult questions. Goswami explores a rich array of examples, affording the lay educator who is pondering possible answers much food for thought.

Evidently the terms concerned are laden with value. They will be infected by their users' judgments about what learning and education *should* be like, and in the developed world there is little consensus to be had here. We must constantly bear this in mind when we ponder the latest triumphs of neuroscience. Arguably we should avoid running together strictly scientific and empirical claims about biology with recommendations about educational aims. The latter are, of course, tied to complex and contested views about ideal societies, these in turn being inextricably linked to visions of what it is to be a person and to flourish as a human being. Scientists have as much right as the rest of us to offer judgments about such things. They have no more right than anyone else, and should not be accorded any special status in this regard by those revering scientific authority. Contributors to this section need no lessons on such a point, but it has to be made over and over again, given the hosts of 'friends' that neuroscience has attracted from some educators. As the old saying goes, with some of these friends, neuroscientists do not need enemies.

Howard-Jones draws attention to the 'dualism' present in discourse about neuroscience and education. He thinks that some neuroscientists subscribe to this. He also notes difficulties arising from privileging explanations *either* in terms of brain functioning *or* in terms of psychological and social factors. In their search to understand and to promote learning, educators should, he believes, combine emerging insights from neuroscience with the more conventional and traditional expertise available in the social sciences.

He refers to ways in which learning may be accompanied by neurological changes, and is careful to point out some of the complexities here: the very idea of 'accompanying' leaves open a verdict on whether the biological events cause the learning, the learning causes the biological events or whether some more complicated interactive relationship obtains. Under the heading 'Avoiding the Seeding of Neuromyths', Goswami comments trenchantly on the dangers of simplistic perspectives in this regard.

The idea that we can fruitfully compare and perhaps combine views of the nature of learning rooted in neuroscience with perspectives located within education and social science seems a constructive one. Stein, Connell and Gardner seem to support it in their drive for a 'methodological pluralism'. Yet such ecumenical aspirations could be problematic. On precisely what basis might neuroscience have any authority to make claims about the nature of learning? It can, of course, tell us a great deal about various *necessary conditions* for learning, but that is a very different matter.

When trying to develop a response to this question it may be instructive to relate it to the research of the eminent psychologist Paul Ekman, who spent several decades studying emotion. He thought that the bodily changes involved in emotions were controlled by 'affect-programs'. The latter were identified as neural circuits that, given appropriate environmental stimulation, would trigger a particular chain of events including facial expression, vocal changes, orienting or flinching, alterations in heart rate and skin temperature. Ekman holds that the relevant neural circuits just are 'basic' emotions. The fact that the programs involve such a rapid onset of these bodily changes, over which agents have little or no control, could, on Ekman's view, be explained by natural selection processes operating between two million and 40,000 years ago. For example, consider the affect program that Ekman identifies with fear. In pre-historic times this neural circuit would have been triggered by the sight of a predator. Once triggered, an immediate flight response would have been initiated, together with other bodily changes which maximised the effectiveness of this response. The fear affect program helped our ancestors to escape their enemies, and hence enhanced evolutionary fitness.

Ekman's critics argued that, however fascinating and robust his research results, he was not entitled to claim that he was investigating our current conception of *emotion*. He might be proposing that we revise it, but that would be a different, and highly contestable proposal.[1] However complicated and even inconsistent our current idea of emotion, this has to be the starting point. The authority for the character of the idea is the actual usage in human societies. In particular, the *language* of emotion would be crucial as a route into our current ideas about these psychological states.

Supporters of Ekman might retort that history is full of cases where science has appropriately led us to revise long-standing ideas. The sun does not go round the earth and the earth is not flat. Why should emotion be any different? So a key issue here is whether, with the ceaseless advance of the natural sciences, we would be *justified* in revising basic psychological concepts. This question in turn rests on how we weigh the authority of science against the 'authority' of facts about the way psychological concepts are bound up with culture and social practices.

Compare the situation with that of money, in an example used by philosopher John Searle (for instance in Searle, 1995) and also credited by Bakhurst (this volume) to Ilyenkov. A £20 note is a piece of paper with a specific chemical make up, physical dimensions, colour pigmentation and so forth. These features, and indeed the very existence of the paper, are necessary conditions for the existence of the currency concerned. However, a great deal more is required for the paper to be money, rather than merely a piece of paper printed in certain ways. It is essential for there to be a range of complex social practices and conventions, some of which involve 'shared intentionality'—that is to say, collective beliefs about how the note is to function. In a sense the relevant community decides that the note is money. We might imagine a scientific money reductionist offering her own view of what money 'really is' in dispute with a financial expert of a different caste with intellectual allegiances to various social sciences. We could suppose further that along comes an intellectual peacemaker who seeks to combine the insights of the two schools.

Surely something would have gone wrong here. Arguably the scientific money reductionist could not contribute to developing an understanding of the nature of money, since money simply is not the type of entity that can be a proper subject of chemical investigation. So any idea of a *synthesis,* or even a dialogue between the money reductionist and the social scientist with the hope of deepening understanding of money, would be an error. The inquiry just is a matter for the economist, the social scientist and others, and the research methods will not include chemical analysis of paper.

To suggest that neurological processes play a similar role in the proper explanation of cognition to that played by paper in the explanation of the functioning of money would be to take several steps too far. Bakhurst urges that the view he attributes to Ilyenkov, that *only* social factors are relevant to the explanation of (cognitive) ability and achievement, is not sustainable. There is incontrovertible evidence, as Goswami and Howard-Jones remind us, that learning can be accompanied by identifiable changes in brain states. Hence there is an intimate relationship or set of relationships concerned. In contrast, all that happens to bank notes is that they wear out, become torn and stained, burned and so on. Until they are utterly destroyed or the regulations change they still have the specific role that they always had. Yet the money example is very important when we ponder the inherent limitations of neuroscience to illuminate the character and development of learning.

Developments in modern philosophy of mind, with roots in the later writings of Wittgenstein, include a family of views about thought and meaning known as externalism. *Content externalism* claims that it is theoretically possible to change the content of a thought, or what someone means when they say something, without changing, for instance, the biological features of the thinker concerned. Hilary Putnam (1975) argued that 'meanings ain't in the head'. On his view, what people meant and thought was *constituted* in part by aspects of their environment. The environmental aspects in which he famously interested himself included 'natural kinds' such as water and gold.

Social externalists concentrate on the thinker's relationships with her social environment, the latter taken to include prevailing social practices and conventions, especially but not exclusively concerning language. 'Relationship' covers a range of features, including facts about the individual's history in the culture concerned, together with aspects of her beliefs and their justification, beliefs whose subject matter covers the relevant social practices and conventions. If, for instance, we are thinking about what medicine we should take for our arthritis, the content of our thoughts depends on a variety of factors. These include conventions in my community about how the term 'arthritis' should be used, who is to be credited with expertise on the kinds of joint problems underlying this condition, and our own beliefs about the nature of these conventions. The word 'depend' does *not* pick out a causal relationship. It is rather that *what it is* for our arthritis thought to have the content that it has is in part constituted by the aspects of our culture referred to above.

Suppose the claims of social externalism could be established. Any neuroscientist who thought that memories could somehow be located *exclusively* 'in' the brain would, on the externalist account, resemble our scientific money reductionist. The latter would seek to uncover the social conventions enabling money to function by examining the molecular structures involved in the paper of which the £20 note is constituted. According to externalism we cannot in principle discover the content of someone's thoughts, or what they mean by, so to speak, looking (exclusively) in their heads. There is at least a hint of externalism in Bakhurst's chapter, for instance in observations such as 'what it is an ability to do is intelligible only in light of socio-historical considerations', though he remains cautious on this issue. Externalists are not merely pointing out that socio-historical considerations are required to make cognition and abilities *intelligible*. They are talking about the inherent constitutions of the latter.

Goswami reports some fascinating research in her section 'Learning is Social', and sees the insights from neuroscience complementing important insights from Vygotsky and those influenced by him. Nevertheless, the claims considered fall short of a full-blooded externalism— they focus on those necessary conditions for learning that relate to social influences.

Moreover this is *not* some kind of dispute between 'monists' and 'dualists'. Social scientists who examine social practices in order to achieve insights into the nature of cognition in general, and learning in particular need not be committed to the existence of 'minds' as somehow separate from bodies.

Defenders of the potential of neuroscience to offer insights into learning can point to the extent to which biological research is beginning to uncover neurological 'dysfunctions' underlying a range of learning difficulties. However, Andrew Davis (this volume, pp. 91–92) tries to show that the notion of a dysfunction cannot be detached from normative and cultural aspects of the context in which the *person* whose brain is in question operates.

David Bakhurst argues that 'There are no *a priori* grounds to declare brain science irrelevant to educational issues, or relevant only in "deficit" cases' (this volume, p. 56). To evaluate such an argument we need, of course, to investigate possible senses of 'relevance' in this context. Bakhurst highlights the possibility that neuroscience explains *success*—briefly referring to examples such as speed of thought and talent for spotting unusual connections.

It is beyond the scope of this commentary to engage with these suggestions. Such examples hint at the idea of broad generic intelligence, about which researchers are divided. Some, sympathetic to the psychometric tradition would have no problems with a whole range of phrases which capture broad aspects of successful cognitive functioning. Others—for instance those favouring the situated cognition approach—suspect that such phrases do not actually identify individual faculties at all, and that the learning and capacities of individuals are inextricably linked to contexts and situations. It is fair to say that the *balance* of Goswami's commentary broadly favours 'deficit' cases. Note, for instance, her idea of biomarkers for learning impairment (this volume, p. 24), where several of the usual suspects are listed, such as developmental dyslexia and ADHD. In contrast Stein, Connell and Gardner want to achieve a 'multi-perspectival view'. This would enable neuroscience to contribute to an account that would *not* be restricted to deficit cases and would avoid 'ungrounded speculation about *what really is the case*' (this volume, p. 43). Now while there are many interpretations of externalism, it must be admitted that at least some of them do appear to involve accounts of what 'really is the case'.

NOTE

We are indebted to Carolyn Price's discussion of revisionary classifications and Ekman in Price, 2005.

REFERENCES

Changeux, J. and Ricoeur, P. (2000) *What Makes Us Think? A Neuroscientist and a Philosopher Argue about Ethics, Human Nature, and the Brain* (Princeton, NJ, Princeton University Press).
Ekman, P. (1992) An Argument for Basic Emotions, *Cognition and Emotion*, 6, pp. 169–200.

Ekman, P. (1994) All Emotions are Basic, in: P. Ekman and R. J. Davidson (eds) *The Nature of Emotion: Fundamental Questions* (Oxford, Oxford University Press), pp. 15–19.

ESRC (2007) Neuroscience and Education: Issues and Opportunities.A Commentary by the Teaching and Learning Research Programme. Available at: http://www.tlrp.org/pub/documents/ Neuroscience%20Commentary%20FINAL.pdf

Price, C. (2005) *Emotion* (Milton Keynes, The Open University).

Putnam, H. (1975) The Meaning of 'Meaning', in his: *Philosophical Papers, Vol. II: Mind, Language, and Reality* (Cambridge, Cambridge University Press).

Searle, J. (1995) *The Construction of Social Reality* (New York, The Free Press).

2
LEARNER CATEGORIES

2.1
Introduction

RUTH CIGMAN AND ANDREW DAVIS

How, if at all, should learners be categorised? Categories differentiate between learners; do they also discriminate? Is it possible to differentiate without comparing and evaluating, giving one group greater priority or respect than another?

There are many reasons why these questions are pressing today. Categories (identified using 'labels') attract resources for children, and many parents are desperate to have these. Charlotte Moore in this section talks about the statements, parking badges and living allowances that ease her life with two autistic children. However, there are many in our society—including large numbers of disabled people—who resist or distrust labels. Differentiation can lead to selective education, with its attendant injustices. It can be exploited by middle-class parents with the power to appeal to tribunals and win disproportionate amounts of resources. It can also be scientifically and logically dubious, as Julian Elliott and Simon Gibbs argue (controversially) of the dyslexia label. They describe the use of this label as 'as tantalising and as forlorn as seeking the philosopher's stone'.

The section opens with philosopher Andrew Davis' discussion of learner categories. He compares the debate about these with the debate about psychiatric disorders which was prominent in the 1960s and 1970s. Are such disorders, asked R. D. Laing and Thomas Szasz, 'real'? Do they have an organic basis or are they ways of classifying individuals that society feels the need to control? This question, Davis observes, is now referred to children. Many argue that the learner categories in common use in schools are social constructions, which preserve the power of those in the medical and psychological professions. It is claimed that they lack a medical or organic basis, and Davis explores this claim by reference to the ideas of Ian Hacking.

There follows a fascinating exploration of what Hacking calls 'indifferent' and 'interactive' kinds. Hydrogen is an example of the first; ADHD an example of the second. The concept of an interactive kind breaks down the medical/social dichotomy so familiar in this area, and involves a notion of a 'moving target' that interacts with, and is changed by, the environment in all sorts of ways. There is a presumed biological basis, which (depending on the condition in question) may or may not be well understood, but the interactive aspect means that conditions like autism and ADHD are also 'made up' concepts, 'ways to be people', 'styles' of living in society.

Paul Cooper would no doubt agree with this. He also spurns the social/medical polarisation, and accuses those who deny the organic basis of ADHD of allowing 'the triumph of ignorance over insight'. Cooper finds no incompatibility between recognition of this basis and careful attention to pedagogy as a vehicle through which children with impulsive or hyper-active dispositions can be helped. He frames the denial of ADHD's organic basis as a catastrophic failure of imagination, akin to that of the po-faced reader from Florida who is mortally wounded by an innocent joke.

Both Davis and Cooper seek to de-polarise the debate about learner categories by emphasising socio-biological interaction. The next two chapters take a different approach. Elliott and Gibbs are resolutely sceptical about the category of dyslexia, and readers may be interested to know that Elliott has the dubious honour of having offended thousands of parents who cleave to this label on behalf of their children. (See http://education.guardian.co.uk/schools/story.) However, the argument of this chapter is not against categories as such. It is against the dyslexia category, which in the view of the authors is attended by 'the mistaken belief that current knowledge in these fields is sufficient to justify a category of dyslexia as a subset of those who encounter reading difficulties'. Elliott and Gibbs contest this, and the reader would do well to consider their argument carefully. More than any other chapter in this volume, perhaps, it provides an object lesson in how we tend to hear the arguments we want or expect to hear, rather than (in Heidegger's words; see this volume, p. 114) '*giving* our mind to what there is to think about'. This is not a denial of reading difficulty, or of a possible genetic foundation for this. It is a frank discussion of the 'interactivity' of the condition known as dyslexia.

Like Elliott and Gibbs, Moore has a view about the interactivity of a category. Hers is 'autism', and she conveys the flavour of a family life over which this casts both light and shadow. In a volume of educational essays, Moore reminds us that homes as well as classrooms are the domains to which our theorising refers. She also reminds us of Wittgenstein's caution about the proper use of examples: essential if we are to avoid losing our way.

2.2

Ian Hacking, Learner Categories and Human Taxonomies

ANDREW DAVIS

INTRODUCTION

The history of psychiatric disorders includes a long-standing debate about their 'existence'. One robust realism about this appeals to biological considerations. Bleuler (1911) is associated with such an approach, assuming that schizophrenia was due to some kind of organic brain disease and that heredity played at least some part in its origins. Those most sharply opposed to this tradition include Szasz (1976) and Laing (1990), the latter a key member of the anti-psychiatry movement. Szasz held that schizophrenia did not exist as a disease, but was a way of classifying individuals that society felt it needed to control.

A notable feature of contemporary education is the proliferation of learner categories, especially those associated with cognitive disabilities. Familiar examples include dyslexia, ADHD, dyspraxia and conduct disorder. Their status is sometimes challenged by researchers, on occasion provoking hostile reactions (see Elliott's chapter in this volume).

Are there any connections between disputes about the 'existence' of psychiatric disorders and the 'reality' of the learner categories in question? To what extent are psychiatric disorder classifications comparable with taxonomies applied to learners? I want to consider these questions in the light of Ian Hacking's approach to the ways in which we categorise people. Hacking offers a thoughtful and subtle account of human types. Examples explored include multiple personality, homosexuality, obesity, autism and criminality.

On a simplistic interpretation of the relevant 'existence' debates we have two opposed positions in respect of psychiatric disorders, expressed as (1) and (2) below. The corresponding verdicts applied to the relevant learner categories are listed as (3) and (4). There are several obviously loaded phrases here to which I return in later discussion.

(1) At least some psychiatric disorders really exist.
(2) No psychiatric disorders really exist: they are merely constructions, involving classifications of people that fail to reflect objective reality.

(3) At least some learner categories reflect 'real' differences between learners.

(4) No learner categories reflect 'real' differences between learners: they are merely constructions, involving classifications of people that fail to reflect objective reality.

In what follows, informed by Hacking's understanding of how we classify people, I draw on both empirical and philosophical literature to argue that neither (1) nor (2) has any kind of simple or straightforward interpretation and that in many construals they represent a false dichotomy. I apply the fruits of this argument to (3) and (4). I argue that biology and neuroscience alone cannot settle whether a number of the most fashionable learner categories reflect 'real differences' between learners even if, for the sake of argument, we suppose that an adequate account of 'real difference' could be provided.

I also show that the 'existence debate' as regards learner categories is far from being merely theoretical or academic. There are several possible verdicts in respect of the issues concerned. Each of these verdicts has important *and distinctive* implications for educational policy and for how learners should be treated. Hence, or so I argue, policy makers and teachers really do need to understand the character of the false dichotomies for which this chapter argues. There are seductive lines of thoughts here that might lead to simplistic or extreme positions if due caution is not exercised. Only in the light of a proper realisation of the complexities can appropriately informed educational decisions be taken.

Claims about the status of psychiatric disorders rehearsed in this chapter are certainly not original (see, for example, Broome, 2006.) If there is anything noteworthy about my contribution in the discussion that follows, it is the attempt to draw comparisons between issues provoked by the status of psychiatric disorders and those arising in connection with certain ways of categorising learners.

THE 'MEDICAL APPROACH' TO HUMAN TAXONOMIES

When discussing the status of learner categories philosophers of education have adopted a range of positions. Recent examples include Ramaekers, who thinks that 'learning disabilities such as dyslexia or non-verbal learning disorder are not just discovered "out there", but are intimately intertwined with a particular kind of society at a particular kind of developmental level, with particular needs and the particular demands it makes of its inhabitants' (Ramaekers, 2006, p. 249).

This 'sociological approach' is contrasted with medical interpretations, characterised by Terzi (2005) as: 'perspectives that causally relate children's difficulties to their individual characteristics ... These ... suggest the adoption of medical categories of disability and concepts of learning difficulties' (Terzi, 2005, p. 446).

So what is this medical approach? Broome (2006) claims that medicine has assumed for a long time that each individual disease has a discrete essence; medical disorders have on this view an autonomous existence and natural history of their own. Medical perspectives seem to be linked to the fundamental goals of classification in the natural sciences. Classifying individual traits in this way is thought to be bound up with the possibility of discovering appropriate scientific laws about their behaviour. Accordingly we should be able to predict, control, and potentially if not actually 'treat' these conditions, whether psychiatric disorders or categories of learner that educators find challenging.

On a medical approach to psychiatric disorders and certain types of learning difficulties, they are thought to resemble diseases such as tuberculosis, measles and cancer. Medicine would think of the latter afflictions as having existed always, though of course doctors did not always classify them or even recognise them as we do now, and for much of human history there were few if any effective treatments. Moreover these diseases are not peculiar to any one culture, either in the ancient or the modern world. A 'medical approach' to psychiatric disorders and a number of learner categories seeks to view them in a similar kind of way. Again, the idea would be that, for instance, bipolar disorder or dyspraxia have always existed, over time and across cultures, though people have not always been classified using these particular labels.

Here are two examples of researchers talking about learning disabilities. I suggest that each of them is adopting some kind of medical approach. First: 'dyslexia, the commonest form of learning disability, is a widespread condition affecting about 5%–7% of school-age children with major impact on their academic and ultimate social achievement' (Joly-Pottuz *et al.*, 2007, p. 2). And again: 'Attention-deficit/hyperactivity disorder is a worldwide and highly prevalent disorder, estimated to affect 5%–10% of children' (noted by Biederman, 2005, p. 1215). Could these contentions simply be read as statistical comments about symptoms, to the effect that up to 7% of school-age children manifest a sufficient number of the prototypical symptoms to be classified as dyslexic, or that up to 10% of children have ADHD?

It is quite clear that this is not what these researchers think. Only a cursory glance at their material reveals discussions of genetic and neurological factors. In addition possibilities such as diet, food additives, mothers smoking in pregnancy, pregnancy complications and so forth are considered as potential factors in the biology of these conditions. It is reasonable, therefore, to credit them with a broadly medical approach to the learning disabilities with which they are concerned.

'MAKING UP PEOPLE', INDIFFERENT KINDS AND INTERACTIVE KINDS

Hacking takes us far beyond any straightforward medical/non-medical contrast in taxonomies. In his writings the term 'human kinds' covers the wide variety of categories of people studied by the human sciences, including child abusers, criminals, teenagers who are pregnant, sufferers from psychiatric disorders and the working classes. At the heart of his perspective is the idea of 'making up' kinds of people. Yet he sympathises with both of two lines of thinking that seem to be in tension with each other. On the one hand, for instance, mental disorders such as autism are increasingly subjected to a biological research program—the thought being very roughly that there is likely to be a 'definite unknown neuropathology P that is the cause of prototypical and most other examples of what we now call childhood autism' (Hacking, 1999, p. 121). On the other hand, autism and many other disorders and disabilities are instances of what he calls interactive kinds.

Interactive kinds and indifferent kinds are compared in his theories: ADHD is an interactive kind; the fact that this classification exists has effects on how those so classified are treated and on the related institutions. ADHD has become a way to be a person, a mode of experiencing the self, and a style of living in society (Hacking, 2006, p. 13). He writes:

> Interactive kinds involve 'looping effects': We think of these kinds of people as given, as definite classes defined by definite properties ... But ... they are moving targets because our investigations interact with the targets themselves, and change them ... That is the looping effect. Sometimes our sciences create kinds of people that in a certain sense did not exist before. That is making up people (Hacking, 2006, p. 2).

By way of contrast, classifying a metal as plutonium is an indifferent kind: the substance cannot be aware of being classified, and nothing about how it is classified can make a difference to its inherent properties.

Hacking's conception of 'kinds' that interact with those using the relevant classifications will prove important when we consider certain ways of categorising learners. But first, a brief exploration of Cooper's (2004) objection to his contrast between interactive and indifferent kinds will help to illuminate his thinking here. She urges that many examples of what Hacking would regard as *indifferent* kinds are in fact *also* affected by feedback mechanisms. Marijuana, a type of soft drug, would seem on the face of it to exemplify an indifferent kind. Yet, quoting Bogen, she discusses marijuana as something also affected by feedback: because some societies classify it as illegal, it is often grown in attics and wardrobes, and hence its appearance is altered (Bogen, 1988, at Cooper, 2004, p. 78).

Now Hacking could respond by conceding that his distinction between indifferent and interactive kinds has not always been supported with the happiest of examples. Thus biological cases expose him unnecessarily to the kind of criticism we have just rehearsed from Cooper. Biological illustrations should be set aside in favour of, for instance, the classification of substances into elements. Hydrogen is truly indifferent to the activities of scientists, related institutions and the efforts of any individuals or groups devising or reviewing taxonomies. Its properties are what they are, independently of societies and cultures, and were always thus.

Cooper feels that Hacking has not sufficiently clarified just what types of interactions between the process of classification and the classified are salient when distinguishing between interactive and indifferent kinds. For instance, Hacking believes that when categories such as multiple personality disorder or autism come into being new ways of *acting* are thereby created. The very existence of the category affords new possibilities for modes of action.

On her view, however, there is a gap in this argument. It implies that a necessary condition of people acting intentionally in a certain way is that they can describe the action in a relevant fashion, and that once a category develops within a society it affords such descriptions. Yet, or so Cooper argues, actions can be intentional even if the actors could not come up with relevant descriptions of their intentions.

For instance, the caveman 'Ug' can intend to make a fire whilst being unable to supply a description of his act. Cooper accepts that certain acts such as marrying *are* tied to descriptions, but contends that these are special, and constitute only a very small proportion of intentional actions.

So, in the light of Cooper's concerns it may be felt that Hacking still owes us an account of how people are affected by and in turn affect the way they are categorised, if we are to make sense of the contrast between indifferent kinds and interactive kinds. Hacking can respond that he *does* offer an account—or rather he offers extensive and detailed accounts that differ from one case to another. Here are just two examples of such accounts.

Hacking (1999) devotes a fair amount of attention to psychiatric disorders such as schizophrenias. He believes that these disorders have both indifferent kind *and* interactive kind characteristics. With reference to the latter, being labelled as schizophrenic affects those who are the victims of this process. Patients are aware of perceptions and attitudes to them in the cultures in which they are situated. They know what sorts of symptoms are fashionable at any one time in the way of diagnosis. They may appreciate what the effects of psychotropic drugs are supposed to be. Patients' approaches to the descriptions of their symptoms may be influenced by all these factors. Sufferers interact with doctors; they react to the questions put to them about their condition, and may change their self-perceptions as a result. What count as key symptoms of the disease shift over time. The classification is a 'moving target'.

Hacking devoted an entire book to the phenomenon of Multiple Personality Disorder. For readers unfamiliar with this phenomenon I quote Hacking's extract from the Diagnostic and Statistical Manual of Mental Disorders third edition (DSM-III), which offers the following diagnostic criteria for multiple personality disorder:

A. The existence within the individual of two or more distinct personalities, each of which is dominant at a particular time.
B. The personality that is dominant at any particular time determines the individual's behaviour.

C. Each individual personality is complex and integrated with its own unique behaviour patterns and social relationships (Hacking, 1995, p. 10).

Hacking claims that there is a sense in which the multiple personalities of the 1980s were 'new'. In the 1950s, 'this was not a way to be a person, people did not experience themselves in this way, they did not interact with their friends, their families, their employers, their counsellors, in this way; but in 1985 this was a way to be a person, to experience oneself, to live in society' (Hacking, 2006, p. 6). Hacking accepts that there were no multiple personalities in 1955 and that there were many of these in 1985, though he also concedes that this way of expressing matters is 'contentious'. Let us label this verdict V. Moreover, 'multiple personality, as a kind of person, did not exist in 1955' (ibid.), but he thinks it did exist in 1985.

LEARNER CATEGORIES AS INTERACTIVE KINDS?

If we applied similar thinking in relation to dyslexia, ADHD and certain other learner categories then, on the face of it at least, the results would be just those that inflame the passions of certain types of learner support groups. Hacking feels that asserting that multiple personalities did not exist in 1955 leads to 'heated but pointless debates' about the reality of multiple personality, which is why he prefers to avoid expressing matters in what I am calling V-type ways. Certainly, if we were to say that there were no dyslexics in, say, 1700 but that there are many now this would be yet another claim that Hacking might acknowledge to be 'contentious'.

It appears to imply that somehow the 'disability' of dyslexia lacks reality and that the phenomenon of dyslexia could have been avoided. Does this mean that we need not have 'made it up'—that this was not, so to speak, forced on us? Could this construction process be reversed?

Hacking is emphatic that a V-type verdict fails to hold for autism. He dislikes discussing the 'reality' of the disorders on which he focuses, yet accepts that autism is 'almost certainly some combination of neurological, biological, and genetic abnormality' (p. 8). At the same time, 'high functioning autism' on his view is something that has been made up. It has become a way of being a person, a way of experiencing and of being in society. The interactions involved in making up this way of being embrace institutions, patterns of behaviour on the part of relevant professionals and much else.

We may concede this much to Hacking without demur: It is not hard to discern, in the developed world, how classifying someone with a learning disability involves a way of being a person, and how those classified interact with the classifying process. One obvious source of evidence for this claim is the World Wide Web. Online searches focusing on specific learning disabilities elicit enormous numbers of responses, including 'scientific' accounts of particular disorders, together with support groups, charities, advice for parents, teachers, dietary advice, recommendations for 'medical' treatment and so on. The claim that those classified in a particular way may well undergo significant changes as a result of the impact of the relevant forces at work in contemporary societies is persuasive.

The thought that in *any* sense we may have 'made up' a learner category such as dyslexia is, as I have already noted, extremely controversial. Hence it is important to explore whether and to what extent it is even possible to conceive of taxonomies of learners as *indifferent kinds*. For being an indifferent kind seems to be one way of earning ontological credentials—of having a 'real existence' in some sense. In the next section I turn to this task.

'INDIFFERENT KINDS', 'NATURAL KINDS' AND ESSENTIALISM

Can any learner taxonomies aspire to the status of indifferent kinds? One way of conceptualising the latter is to draw on the account of natural kinds stemming from Putnam and Kripke. Hacking makes extensive reference to this in *The Social Construction of What?*

A broad-brush approach to the theory of meaning and reference involved in this tradition should suffice. Substances are often classified according to their typical observable properties. In 1750 someone might distinguish water from oil according to taste, colour, viscosity, and so forth. Within the history of natural science, as knowledge of at least some of these substances develops, scientists realise that aspects of the objects' inner structure explain these stereotypical observable properties. They come to understand the character of these substances as natural kinds. For example salt is soluble, has a certain taste, crystalline form and colour; its underlying chemical constitution as sodium chloride explains the surface features. According to Putnam's 'division of linguistic labour' the lay user of relevant terms is usually ignorant of the inner constitution of the substance concerned but assumes its existence and that there are or will be experts who know about it. The reference of natural kind terms is not exhausted by the knowledge, understanding and intentions of the individual user. It involves external factors. Thus people using the term 'water' in 1750 as a matter of fact succeeded in referring to H_2O even though they had no idea at that time of the nature of water's chemical constitution.

To what extent does contemporary research into psychiatric disorders and types of learner think along similar lines? To answer this question it is necessary to do something in the way of interpretation since few if any of the researchers in question would be aware of the relevant philosophical literature. Consider just two examples:

A pathophysiologic profile of ADHD has not been fully characterized, although structural and functional imaging studies consistently implicate dysfunction in the fronto–subcortical pathways and imbalances in the dopaminergic and noradrenergic systems in the origin of core symptoms (Biederman, 2005, p. 1218).

There is more than a hint here that sufferers from ADHD have something in common, namely a specific kind of brain abnormality. The term 'origin' suggests that 'core symptoms' are viewed as being explained by this neural aberration. This explanatory framework is arguably in the same spirit as the natural kind thinking sketched above:

> Difficulty in learning to read is attributable to specific dysfunctions of the brain, which so far remain poorly understood. However, it is recognized that the neurological basis for dyslexia, or reading disability, is caused in large part by genetic factors (Paracchini, Scerri and Monaco, 2007, p. 57).

Similar observations apply to these comments as to those just made about ADHD. This way of thinking certainly is closely related to the medical model for psychiatric disorders, and at least hints at a kind of essentialism—the thought that some types of learner share some kind of neural *essence* that explains their symptoms. There is a strong research tradition identifying widespread tendencies to essentialist thinking *in general* about human functioning and personality traits (see, for instance, Haslam, Bastian and Bissett, 2004). Teachers and policy makers dealing with learners seem unlikely to prove exceptions to this rule.

We should note in passing that a recent study of views about psychiatric disorders suggests that experts are less likely to have 'essentialist' views according to which each disorder has some kind of specific neurological cause, than lay people (Ahn *et al.*, 2006). The researchers in question speculate that one of their results, the verdict that mental health experts were seemingly less 'essentialist' than lay people about psychiatric disorders, might stem from sophisticated views about underlying causes. Some experts may hold that people with the same disorder 'might have different combinations of multiple causes' (p. 765). I am unable to refer to comparable research about learning disabilities such as dyslexia.

All this continues to raise a fundamental question: Can essentialist *intuitions*, either about psychiatric disorders or about types of learner, be turned into coherent beliefs? Essentialism seems most plausible in the case of chemical elements. These can be thought of as possessing essential properties—so gold has an atomic number of 79. The atomic structure that this number represents explains the properties in virtue of which it counts as a metal, melts at such and such a temperature, dissolves in *aqua regia* and so on. The structural features are specific and definitively identifiable. *Either* a substance has the gold-making properties, or it does not.

A search for neurological features that serve to explain *either* psychiatric disorders *or* learning disabilities, where the explanatory role directly corresponds to the atomic structure of gold, bristles with difficulties. What would *count* as a discrete neurological feature in the first place? Each type of atomic structure involved in the chemical elements is 'discrete' in the sense that each type is specific and unique, corresponding to one and only one element. Being 'discrete' is often opposed to being continuous. Elements are 'discrete' in this way—there is no sense in which the atomic structures determining that a substance is gold could *gradually* be changed along a continuum until they became structures determining that the substance was no longer gold. *Either* the substance has a gold-making structure, or it does not.

Neuroscience has a long tradition of 'mapping' the brain, pointing to spatial locations within the brain. However, researchers also emphasise the brain's plasticity and complexity. William Bechtel and Jennifer Mundale (1999) remind us that large portions of the brain are involved in most psychological activities. This surely implies that there could not be discrete types of neurological functioning, if, that is, 'discrete' signified anything like the position of structures in virtue of which a substance is one element rather than another.

Note the situation here in relation to familiar psychiatric disorders. Zachar (2000) reminds us that the DSM does not assume that psychiatric disorders are natural kinds or are even construed as closely resembling paradigm examples of natural kinds. He thinks that psychiatric classifications are 'prototype' categories. No one criterion or group of criteria is necessary and sufficient. Apparently there are 848 ways of meeting borderline personality disorder in DSM-III-R. The categories are pragmatic. Insisting that they might reflect how the world 'really is' has little point or meaning. He also argues that the medical model for these disorders itself fails to point to natural kind conceptualisations, since diseases themselves are not natural kinds either, and makes the point (also to be found in Dupré, 1981, pp. 84 ff.) that even species turn out not to be natural kinds in the strict sense. That is to say, there will frequently be no genetic properties shared by all members of a species.

FUNCTION AND DYSFUNCTION IN THE CLASSIFICATION OF PSYCHIATRIC DISORDER AND LEARNERS

We have already seen that researchers sometimes speak of brain 'dysfunctions'. Such talk requires assumptions about how brains *should* function. Function talk in biology is widespread. On one interpretation, the potentially worrying normative element—worrying, that is to tough-minded scientists who seek to deal in value-free theory and explanation—is cashed respectably in terms of that which contributes to the chances of the relevant organism surviving: 'biological sciences ... use functional analysis, when explaining the structure or behavior of organisms through the benefits for reproduction. This procedure is justified by the theory of natural selection, according to which such beneficial effects tend to maintain their own causes' (Elster, 1982, p. 463). How such evolutionarily backed construals should be applied to the brain is not entirely obvious. In various ways learners with ADHD or dyslexia are certainly disadvantaged, but it is hard to see how this is linked even indirectly to the prospects for their survival, or to the survival of their genes. Were such function discourse to be used in connection with serious psychiatric disorders such as schizophrenia then an evolutionary perspective would seem to have much greater credibility. Debilitating mental illness might well play a significant role in the very 'fitness' of the individuals concerned.

Even if a robust account of function and dysfunction of the brain could be supplied in relation to categorising learners, the analogy with chemical elements fails. If we go down the evolutionary track we will be working with 'fitness' or a related notion. 'Fitness' is supervenient on biological characteristics of the organism concerned and is arguably 'multiply realised'. That is to say, the property of fitness is possessed just because of underlying biological properties; the latter fix the property of fitness. However, that set of biological features in virtue of which one organism is likely to survive need have nothing in common with that in virtue of which another has survival potential. Needless to say the property of being gold, for instance, is *not* multiply realised in this sense.

Suppose then that we abandon Darwinian notions of function in connection with classifying learners. What alternative accounts could be given of function and dysfunction? The normative element—the idea of how brains and individuals *ought* to behave—seems impossible to avoid. We would have to speak of the purposes that brains *should* fulfil, or even the purposes that brains ought to enable their possessors to fulfil. To explain this would involve the values of particular cultures, what counts as important learning, and much else. Arguably we are firmly back in the Hacking territory of 'making up' people. Hacking (2006) emphasises the crucial importance of norms in how we classify people: thus ADHD and dyslexia taxonomies imply what is normal behaviour and language processing in a wide range of contexts.

CAN GENETICS RESCUE ESSENTIALIST INTUITIONS?

Those researchers attracted to essentialist thinking about some categories of learner and to at least some resonances with the chemical element paradigm could respond by acknowledging the complexities here, but claim that we need to look further back in the causal chain. The neurological bases of dyslexia, for instance are held by some scientists to have *genetic* origins. Paracchini, Scerri and Monaco (2007) discuss four candidate genes as implicated in reading disabilities, exploring their role in brain development and hence in the causal origins of dyslexia, though their treatment is explicitly sketchy and to some extent speculative.

I am less than hopeful about the genetic approach as a way of rescuing the *indifferent kind* status of certain ways of classifying learners. My reasons only require some very familiar and basic points to be rehearsed. Let us define the genotype of an organism as the class to which it belongs as determined by the description of the actual physical material made up of DNA that was passed to the organism by its parents at the organism's conception (Lewontin, 2004). The same source characterises the phenotype of an organism as the class to which that organism belongs as determined by its physical and behavioural characteristics. In the context of the discussion here, the physical and behavioural characteristics are at the level of neural descriptions. An elementary point about genetics is that the genotype-phenotype relationship is not one-one but many-many.

Edward Wilson (2006) offers the arrowleaf plant as an example of one genotype expressing many phenotypes. This amphibious plant has evolved to be able to adjust the shape of its leaf in response to the specific environmental conditions in which it grows. On dry land its leaves resemble arrowheads. When it grows in shallow water the leaves at the surface are shaped like lily pads. No known genetic difference between these plants underlies this amazing variation.

A given phenotype can map onto many different genotypes. For instance, consider the redness of a flower or the speed with which an animal can run. Moreover genes interact with each other in very complex ways to produce phenotypes—this underlies the many-many relationship between genotype and phenotype. Hence there will be a many-many mapping between putative genes for specific learning disabilities and neurological states and processes. Any relationship between the genetic origins of an individual and the types of brain states she undergoes seems doomed to a significant degree of complexity and elusiveness.

I am not qualified to comment on the scientific credentials of the search for genetic factors in respect of learning disabilities such as dyslexia. However the upshot of the above elementary points about genetics is as follows: appealing to genes does not produce an obviously healthy essentialist solution to the question of how the status and existence of learner categories such as dyslexia or ADHD should be viewed. Our search for a coherent way of modelling an 'indifferent kind' status for such learner classifications has proved unsuccessful.

THE STATUS OF LEARNER CATEGORIES HAS CONSEQUENCES FOR EDUCATION

Suppose each learner category regarded by educators as a threat to the progress of learners was held to originate in a specific neurological condition distinct from the bases of other categories (assuming for the sake of argument, despite earlier comments, that we can make sense of the notion of 'distinctness' here). It would be at least possible for unique types of treatments to be effective for each type of learner. Researchers might in principle arrive at drug treatments, equipment and guidance for how teachers should handle learners belonging to each of the relevant categories, where no one remedial package resembled any other. Incidentally, these suggestions do not represent mere philosophical speculations. Examples of specific treatments based on such a view of dyslexia, at least include FastForword (FFW) (Merzenich *et al.*, 1996; Tallal *et al.*, 1996). The researchers in question devised a treatment involving video games based on the hypothesis that the brains of dyslexics have a specific problem with brief stimuli that are presented rapidly. (Whether the treatment was successful, or could be known to be successful, *because* the underlying brain condition had been identified correctly are important questions but need not be settled here.)

At the same time, there is no *a priori* reason for asserting that distinct neurological conditions would *necessarily* demand approaches to treatment that did not overlap. Of course, we should also note that, if empirical research failed to uncover any treatments to which there were differentiated responses corresponding to the various categories of learners regarded as problems for education, this would offer at least prima facie evidence against the existence of discrete underlying neurological origins corresponding to each 'condition'.

On the other hand, if it is felt that no such specific and distinct conditions are identifiable but that the causal base of *all* the relevant learner categories can only be characterised far more broadly as some kind of brain abnormality (for authors taking this view see Bonnie Kaplan, Deborah Dewey, Susan Crawford and Brenda Wilson, 2001), then effective treatment based on understanding of underlying causes need not differ from one disorder to another. Indeed, strongly essentialist thinking attributing specific neurological bases for each learner category might interfere with the creation of effective treatment.

If even a broader type of essentialist thinking featuring non-specific neural 'abnormalities' turned out to be mistaken, again this might interfere with the creation of effective treatment, which arguably in this situation should focus directly on the *performances* of learners.

Compare this with the situation arising in connection with two diseases, measles and chicken pox. Certainly the key symptoms here are not 'made up' in any fashion that relates to Hacking's theories about some of his examples. We might treat the irritation linked to spots caused by the measles and chicken pox viruses with the same lotion or we might deal with the high temperatures that can occur in either illness by administering aspirin. But if we wanted to *prevent* these diseases or combat their spread, our methods would generally need to be informed by a thorough understanding of their underlying causes—viz. the characteristics of each virus and how they attack the human body. If this kind of analogy is wide of the mark when seeking an appropriate understanding of dyslexia and other learner categories causing educators concerns, it is very important for teachers and policy makers to know it.

Suppose for the sake of argument we accept the following 'definition' of dyslexia: 'Dyslexia is . . . characterized by difficulties with accurate and/or fluent word recognition and by poor spelling and decoding abilities' (Lyon, Shaywitz and Shaywitz, 2003, p. 2). Evidently such problematic performances can be manifested more or less severely, and are part of a continuum of capacities to be found in the general population. As teachers and researchers we could develop (and of course have developed) strategies to remediate these problems. If we are in the business of dealing with performance rather than underlying causes or conditions, then we need not distinguish between performances produced by 'dyslexics' and performance levels occurring in the general population. Moreover we will be aware of the so-called 'co-morbidity' issue—that is, of the point that the typical indications of a number of learner classifications such as dyslexia, dyspraxia, ADHD and many others *overlap*. Our focus on performance will to that extent seem all the more fruitful. We will be killing several birds with one stone, so to speak.

Concentrating on learner performances places responsibility fairly and squarely in the hands of educators. The notion that some learner categories are indifferent kinds may have allowed educators to claim that they cannot be held fully to account for the poor progress of the students concerned. The latter are viewed as having problematic underlying conditions, the treatment for which requires scientific expertise that the ordinary teacher lacks. I want to argue that the less a learner category can aspire to the status of an indifferent kind, the more the learners concerned should be regarded as belonging on a continuum with their fellow students, and treated accordingly.

CONCLUSION

Obesity is contrasted with autism in Hacking (2006). Merely overweight people are just 'rather plump'—they need not share any other characteristics. Perhaps people actually classified as obese may have a little more in common—such as having below average life expectancy, a greater tendency to diabetes, and so on. However, Hacking also concedes that there might be a subset of the obese that is closer to being a 'real kind'—those with very high Body Mass Indices might be the victims of quite specific biological conditions.

So, despite all that has been said in this chapter, is it not still possible that there are biological bases to the symptoms exhibited at least by subsets of those classified as dyslexic, as sufferers from ADHD and so on? If treatment restricted itself to what educators deemed problematic performance, might it not miss some important tricks?

We have not ruled this out definitively. However, we have not been able to uncover any way of clearly demarcating one set of brain characteristics from another to determine certain currently fashionable ways of classifying learners. Furthermore we have failed to discover just how 'dysfunctioning' brains could be sharply distinguished from normally functioning brains using considerations exclusively drawn from science.

Hacking's treatment does not entirely exclude the possibility that biological and neurological factors may be involved in the origins of at least some of the predicaments associated with the common learning disorders. However, any attempt to base relevant taxonomies *exclusively* on neurophysiology is open to serious objection. These objections have particular force if as part of the construction of such taxonomies we resort to natural kind and essentialist models. In our explorations of the 'reality' of learning disabilities we have also noted Hacking's points about some of the forces at work in 'making up people'. There is no short, simple and coherent route from neuroscience alone to assertions that learner categories such as dyslexics and suffers from ADHD in any sense 'mirror objective reality'. Moreover some of the possible approaches to the status of such learner categories explored in this chapter are significantly different from each other. They vary in their implications for how learners should be treated, so it is really important that educators come to appreciate some of the complexities that I have rehearsed.

REFERENCES

Ahn, W-K., Flanagan, E. H., Marsh, J. K. and Sanislow, C. A. (2006) Beliefs about Essences and the Reality of Mental Disorders, *Psychological Science*, 17.9, pp. 759–766.

Bechtel, W. and Mundale, J. (1999) Multiple Realizability Revisited: Linking Cognitive and Neural States, *Philosophy of Science*, 66.2, pp. 175–207.

Biederman, J. (2005) Advancing the Neuroscience Of ADHD Attention-Deficit/Hyperactivity Disorder: A Selective Overview, *Biological Psychiatry*, 57, pp. 1215–1220.

Bleuler, E. (1911) *Dementia Praecox or the Group of Schizophrenias* (New York, International Universities Press).

Bogen, J. (1988) Comments, *Noüs*, 22, pp. 65–6.

Broome, M. (2006) Taxonomy and Ontology in Psychiatry: A Survey of Recent Literature, *Philosophy, Psychiatry, & Psychology*, 13.4, pp. 303–319.

Cooper, R. (2004) Why Hacking is Wrong about Human Kinds, *British Journal for the Philosophy of Science*, 55.1, pp. 73–85.

Dupré, J. (1981) Natural Kinds and Biological Taxa, *The Philosophical Review*, 90.1, pp. 66–90.

Elster, J. (1982) The Case for Methodological Individualism, *Theory and Society*, 11.4, pp. 453–482.

Hacking, I. (1995) *Rewriting the Soul* (Princeton, NJ, Princeton University Press).

Hacking, I. (1999) *The Social Construction of What?* (Cambridge, MA, Harvard University Press).

Hacking, I. (2006) Kinds of People: Moving Targets. British Academy Lecture. Available at: http://www.britac.ac.uk/pubs/src/_pdf/hacking.pdf

Haslam, N., Bastian, B. and Bissett, M. (2004) Essentialist Beliefs about Personality and their Implications, *Personality And Social Psychology Bulletin*, 30.12, pp. 1661–1673.

Joly-Pottuz, B., Mercier, M., Leynaud, A. and Habib, M. (2007) Combined Auditory and Articulatory Training Improves Phonological Deficit in Children With Dyslexia, *Neuropsychological Rehabilitation*, 18, pp. 1–28.

Kaplan, B., Dewey, D., Crawford, S. and Wilson, B. (2001) The Term Comorbidity is of Questionable Value in Reference to Developmental Disorders, *Journal of Learning Disabilities*, 34.6, pp. 555–565.

Laing, R. (1990) *Sanity, Madness and the Family: Families of Schizophrenics* (Harmonsworth, Penguin Psychology).

Lewontin, R. (2004) The Genotype/Phenotype distinction, *Stanford Encyclopaedia of Philosophy*. Available at: http://plato.stanford.edu/entries/genotype-phenotype/

Lyon, G. R., Shaywitz, S. E. and Shaywitz, B. A. (2003) Defining Dyslexia, Comorbidity, Teachers' Knowledge of Language and Reading, *Annals of Dyslexia*, 53, pp. 1–14.

Merzenich, M. M., Jenkins, W. M., Johnston, P., Schreiner, C., Miller, S. L. and Tallal, P. (1996) Temporal Processing Deficits or Language-Learning Impaired Children Ameliorated by Training, *Science*, 271, pp. 77–81.

Paracchini, S., Scerri, T. and Monaco, A. P. (2007) The Genetic Lexicon of Dyslexia, *Annual Review of Genomics and Human Genetics*, 8, pp. 57–79.

Ramaekers, S. (2006) No Harm Done: The Implications for Educational Research of the Rejection of Truthm, *Journal of Philosophy of Education*, 40.2, pp. 241–257.

Szasz, T. (1976) *Schizophrenia: The Sacred Symbol of Psychiatry* (New York, Basic Books), pp. xiv, 237.

Tallal, P., Miller, S. L., Bedi, G., Byma, G., Wang, X., Nagarajan, S. S., Schreiner, C. J., Jenkins, W. M. and Merzenich, M. M. (1996) Language Comprehension in Language-Learning Impaired Children Improved with Acoustically Modified Speech, *Science*, 271, pp. 81–83.

Terzi, L. (2005) Beyond the Dilemma of Difference: The Capability Approach to Disability and Special Educational Needs, *Journal of Philosophy of Education*, 39.3, pp. 443–459.

Wilson, E. (2006) Discover Interview: E. O. Wilson, *Discover* 25 June. Available at: http://discovermagazine.com/2006/jun/e-o-wilson

Zachar, P. (2000) Psychiatric Disorders are not Natural Kinds, *Philosophy, Psychiatry, & Psychology*, 7.3, pp. 167–182.

2.3

Like Alligators Bobbing for Poodles? A Critical Discussion of Education, ADHD and the Biopsychosocial Perspective

PAUL COOPER

INTRODUCTION

Imagine this page from a book of cartoons. At the top of the page is a cartoon drawing of a domestic sitting room, complete with TV, framed picture on the wall and a curtained window. In the centre of the room there are five, heavily anthropomorphised and rather cuddly looking (though extremely toothsome) alligators. They are all standing on their hind legs around a large tub that is placed on a coffee table. Two of the alligators have their snouts in the tub; the other three stand around in a state of wide-eyed excitement; like little children at a birthday party. We cannot see what is in the tub, but the caption beneath the picture reads:

Bobbing for poodles

Beneath this is the following quotation:

You have offended millions of pet owners with this garbage.
If you can not do better than this, we suggest you seek another occupation.
—Reader, Florida

Beneath this is a further comment. This time it is from the cartoonist, Gary Larson (1992, p. 168):

Thank God I didn't go with my first caption: 'Bobbing for babies'.

You probably have to *see* the cartoon to really 'get' the joke. I would suggest, however, that you don't have to see the cartoon to appreciate the extension of the joke in the two quotations that follow. The offended correspondent from Florida responds to a literal interpretation of the cartoon, and the horrible idea that captive pets might be fed to fierce reptiles. What the correspondent seems to be unwilling or unable to do is to suspend disbelief and enter the strange, surreal and outlandish world of the cartoonist, which demands that we take unusual perspectives on things that we think we understand. On one level, Larson's cartoon is saying that if alligators lived in little houses in suburbia they might well engage in such behaviour. What's more, this would be as innocent to them as 'apple-bobbing' is to us. The style of drawing and the childlike quality of the animals depicted further emphasises the conflicting themes of innocence and horror. As with much subtle humour, the resonances are multiple, and the joke requires us to think about human beings, alligators and suburbia in unexpected ways. Our assumptions are challenged, and maybe we also feel a slight sense of discomfort at the dislocation caused by the juxtaposing of diverse references. In any event, it is unlikely that, in responding to the humour of the cartoon, we are, in any sense, offering our approval of the literal practice of feeding live poodles (or babies) to alligators, or expressing belief in the idea that alligators might watch TV and live in suburbia.

An analysis of Gary Larson's work is not the purpose of this chapter. However, it is my intention to suggest that some of the controversies and conflicts that surround ADHD can be understood as being analogous to those surrounding this cartoon. This chapter also attempts to suggest ways in which apparently opposing positions might be reconciled to produce a genuinely constructive understanding of how best to engage some of our most vulnerable students. This reconciliation, however, will be dependent on willingness to examine and challenge some deeply held assumptions.

DEFINING ADHD

Assessment and Diagnosis

Attention Deficit/Hyperactivity Disorder (ADHD) is a diagnosis of the American Psychiatric Association (APA, 1994). It describes behavioural symptoms of inattention or impulsiveness/hyperactivity that are presented to a degree that significantly interferes with a person's family and peer relations as well as their educational functioning. In addition to the APA criteria, the World Health Organisation offers the diagnostic criteria for 'Hyperkinetic Syndromes' (WHO, 1992), which are similar to the ADHD criteria in many respects, but differ in important ways (Sharkey and Fitzgerald, 2007a): the WHO criteria are less inclusive and therefore produce lower prevalence rates than the ADHD criteria (NICE, 2000).

In the UK ADHD is usually diagnosed by a medical practitioner and sometimes by clinical psychologists. Recommended assessment practice involves a multi-disciplinary assessment (NICE, 2008; BPS, 2000) that focuses on the individual's functioning over the life course to date and requires the in-put of parents and the children themselves, as well the child's teachers and other professionals who may be involved with the child (e.g. social workers, educational psychologists). Appropriate norm-referenced rating scales are also commonly used in the assessment process (Sharkey and Fitzgerald, 2007b). The diagnosis should apply only if the assessment process indicates that symptom thresholds laid down in the diagnostic criteria (APA, 1994) are met. These refer to severity, pervasiveness and longevity.

Prevalence

It is estimated that between 3% and 9% of school-aged children and young people in the UK are affected by ADHD (NICE, 2008), with males outnumbering females by a ratio of 3 or 4:1 (Sharkey and Fitzgerald, 2007b; Tannock, 1998). This makes ADHD the most prevalent of childhood behavioural disorders (Greenhill, 1998). The developmental course of ADHD usually begins between the ages of 3 and 4, though some children show evidence of the disorder in early infancy, and others not until the ages of 5 or 6 years (Anastopoulos, 1999). The APA diagnostic criteria require the presence of symptoms before the age of 7 years.

Co-morbidity and Risk Factors

ADHD commonly co-occurs with other serious behavioural disorders, such as Conduct Disorder and Oppositional Defiant Disorder (McArdle, 2007), emotional disorders (anxiety and depression) (Barkley, 1998), and the developmental disorders, Autistic Spectrum Disorders and Tourette's Syndrome (Gallagher *et al.*, 2007). In the UK, Hayden (1997) found the symptoms of hyperactivity to be one of a range of correlates of formal, 'permanent' exclusion from school among children of primary school age. This is consistent with the findings of prevalence studies carried out in special schools for children with Emotional and Behavioural Difficulties. For example, Place *et al.* (2000) found an ADHD prevalence rate of 70%, whilst Vivian (1994) found a HD rate of 40%. Other studies have found the symptoms of ADHD in adults to be associated with serious relationship problems, marital breakdown, employment difficulties (Hinshaw, 1994) and imprisonment (Farrington, 1990; Weiss and Hechtman, 1993; Young, 2007).

Not surprisingly, school students with ADHD often experience serious educational difficulties and under-perform academically, experiencing greatly reduced opportunities for entry into or success in higher education, and concomitant problems in securing and maintaining employment (Kirley, 2007; Barkley, 1998).

Causes of ADHD

In common with many complex psycho-biological disorders, the causes of ADHD are not fully known. However, ADHD has become one of the most widely researched of all disorders of its type in the psychological and psychiatric literature. Three major areas of theoretical exploration of ADHD have been identified (Tannock, 1998): cognitive research, neurobiological research and genetic research. Evidence from studies in these areas creates a compelling argument for ADHD as a biopsychosocial phenomenon and provides a sound base for a multi-modal approach to intervention that combines medical, psychosocial and educational dimensions.

Cognitive research has increasingly focused on impulsiveness as the central feature of ADHD and on the possibility that the underlying problem is a dysfunctional response inhibition system, a neuropsychological mechanism implicating the physiology of, or relating to, the frontal lobes of the brain (Arnsten, 2007; Bellgrove *et al.*, 2007). This neurobiological explanation is supported by a number of neuroimaging studies (Kelly *et al.*, 2007; Tannock, 1998) as well as neurochemical studies that have detected dysfunctions in certain neurotransmitter systems implicated in the regulation of attention and behaviour (McMullen *et al.*, 1994). That neurobiological factors are implicated in the aetiology of ADHD is further supported by findings from genetic studies that have shown a much greater incidence of ADHD among identical (i.e. monozygotic) twins than among non-identical (dizygotic) twins, and among children who are biologically related as opposed to adopted (ibid.). Molecular genetic research has identified abnormalities in the dopamine system (Arnsten, 2007). Dopamine is a neurotransmitter that is found in systems of the brain concerned with, among other things, the regulation of movement (Thompson, 1993). These findings suggest that children with ADHD are biologically predisposed to experience significantly greater problems than most in inhibiting or delaying a behavioural response. The nature of the dysfunction in this system is described alternatively in terms of a failure of the inhibitory control system to become activated (Barkley, 1997) or as extreme delay in the activation of this system (Sergeant, 1995).

Barkley (1997) proposes an integrated model that suggests that neurologically based problems of response inhibition lead directly to problems in four major 'executive functions' of the brain that are essential to effective self-regulation. The first executive function is working memory, impairment of which makes it difficult for individuals to retain and manipulate information for purposes of appraisal and planning. The second function is that of internalised speech. It is suggested that self-control is exerted through a process of self-talk, during which possible consequences and implications of behaviours are weighed up and internally 'discussed'. The third executive function is that of motivational appraisal. This system enables us to make decisions by providing us with information about the emotional associations generated by an impulse to act and the extent to which the impulse is likely to produce outcomes we find desirable. The final executive function is that of reconstitution or behavioural synthesis. The role of this function is to enable us to plan new and appropriate behaviours as an outcome of analysing past behaviours.

In addition to the cognitive-neuroscientific evidence, there is data from a number of studies to suggest that factors in the family environment may be implicated in the development of ADHD. Family factors include: parenting skills; disorderly home environments (Cantwell, 1996); marital discord between parents (Barkley, 1997), maternal mental health and paternal personality factors (Nigg and Hinshaw, 1998). These findings combined with the neuro-physiological research suggest that ADHD is a biopsychosocial phenomenon—that is, a behavioural manifestation with its origins in a biologically based predisposition. The biological predisposition and the behavioural outcomes, however, are mediated by social, environmental and other experiential factors (Rutter, 2001; Frith, 1992).

Once we move into this biopsychosocial territory the unhelpful polarity that is sometimes stated in terms of biological versus social explanations for learning and behavioural problems (e.g. Booth and Ainscow, 1998; Visser, 1997; Slee, 1995) becomes redundant. It is clear that ADHD is influenced by both biology and the social environment. ADHD is, indeed 'socially constructed' (Purdie *et al.*, 2002; Cooper, 1997a), but certain individuals, by virtue of their biological inheritance and social circumstances, are more prone than others to being constructed as being 'disordered' in this way (Cooper, 1997b). The school is a major setting where this process of social construction takes place, and it is through the patterns of institutional control and pedagogical practices that such construction is implemented. These also provide the means by which deconstruction can take place, as I shall argue later in the chapter.

Common Reactions to ADHD

ADHD has been dismissed by some commentators as a medical construct that individualises educational failure and disruptive behaviour (e.g. Slee, 1995; Lloyd and Norris, 1999; Skidmore, 2004; Visser and Travell, 2006). The effect of such individualisation, it is argued, is to distract attention from the roles that schools and teachers may play (wittingly or unwittingly) in the construction of learning and behavioural problems, and to allow educators to absolve themselves of their responsibility to provide appropriate educational opportunities to certain groups.

This negative reaction is based on a number of erroneous assumptions. The first is that we have to choose between biomedical and environmental explanations for learning difficulties because they are incompatible. This is expressed in an extreme form by Slee: 'The monism of locating the nature of [classroom] disruption in the neurological infrastructure of the child is myopic and convenient' (Slee, 1995, p. 74). Visser (1997) expressed a similar view: 'Rejection of the ADHD label by educationalists is precisely because it offers a view of behaviour which is "nature" without "nurture"' (Visser, 1997, p. 15). More recently, Skidmore, although attempting to offer a faintly conciliatory nod towards what he terms the 'psycho-medical paradigm', recycles the same false oppositions:

> Given its long historical roots, and the undoubted existence of such psychological and medical conditions [as Down's syndrome and autism], it is likely that research into learning difficulties in the psycho-medical paradigm will continue to be conducted, that it will continue to exert an influence on the wider field, and that some of its findings will be found to be of use in the education of pupils who are affected by conditions which

are generally recognised to have an organic basis. The difficulty arises when illicit attempts are made to apply this framework to an infinitely extensible set of putative syndromes or disorders for which reliable evidence of a neurological or organic base is lacking, and where 'diagnosis' rests on value laden, culturally-specific judgements about behavioural or cognitive norms. In the case of ADD [*sic*] it is arguable that the scientistic discourse of positivism and the rhetorical stance of authoritative objectivity which it engenders have been deployed to disseminate a biological determinist hypothesis for which empirical evidence is wanting, and to legitimise the practice of drugging defiant children into docility, using stimulants whose long-term side effects are unknown, in the service of a tacit project of social control (Skidmore, 2004, pp.3–4).

These views reflect longstanding suspicion among some British educationists and educational psychologists of explanations of emotional and behavioural difficulties that cite biological factors as possible causes (e.g. Boreham *et al.*, 1995). The distaste for biological determinism is understandable when we consider the horrors of the eugenics movement that marred the early 20th century in Europe and America. To extend this distaste to ADHD, however, on the grounds that it represents a modern manifestation of an outdated, politically driven and discredited pseudo-science is simply wrong-headed. This view, at best, reflects a profound ignorance of modern understandings of (a) the relationship between biological and environmental factors in human development, and (b) the scientific and educational literature on ADHD. At its worst, this portrayal of ADHD reflects a wilful misrepresentation of the topic that is likely to hinder the development and dissemination of well informed and effective educational interventions that would benefit almost all school students.

It is now necessary to highlight and address the flaws in the arguments presented by Skidmore and others.

DEALING WITH CHALLENGES TO THE VALIDITY OF ADHD DIAGNOSIS

First, it is claimed that the ADHD diagnosis is somehow bogus or 'illicit' because there is an absence of neuro-scientific evidence.

This is patently untrue. As noted above, there is a wealth of evidence from many studies over many years that points to:

- consistency in patterns of symptoms associated with specific clinical impairments of inattentiveness, hyperactivity and impulsiveness;
- genetic pathways being implicated in the distribution of the condition neuro-imaging studies which reveal specific differences between individuals diagnosed with ADHD and those who are not (Sharkey and Fitzgerald, 2007; Tannock, 1998).

The earliest clinical accounts of what we now refer to as ADHD are to be found at the end of the 18th century in the writing of a physician named

Alexander Crichton (Palmer and Finger, 2001), and a paper by George Still, which appeared in *the Lancet* in the early 1900s, is often cited as an early source (e.g. Barkley, 1997). It was during the First World War, and with the opportunity to study extensive numbers of live individuals with serious head injuries, that consistent links were first observed between some of the symptoms of ADHD and damage to the frontal cortex (Barkley, 1997). It was not, however, until the late 20th century and the advent of advanced brain imaging technology that it became possible to study the functioning of the human brain in greater detail. This ongoing research continues to produce findings that enrich our understanding of the relationship between cognitive and neurological functioning (e.g. Kelly *et al.*, 2007). In addition to these sources, both twin studies and advanced molecular genetic studies have produced a wealth of data pointing to specific genetic correlates of ADHD (Arnsten, 2007; Levy and Hay, 2001).

Second, it is claimed that ADHD is an example of biological determinism.

The fear of biological determinism is well founded, partly because it denies the importance of human agency (Rose, 2004) and leads in some cases to an ill founded sense of fatalism in relation to the developmental opportunities available to some individuals. Having said this, there is, at the time of writing, no definitive account of the biological under-pinnings of ADHD. This is hardly surprising, not least because of the complexity of the biological and psychological systems that are implicated. The same would have to be said of other complex conditions, such as Autistic Spectrum Disorders. Another possibly more significant reason for the failure to identify a definitive biological cause is that there may not be one. Not only are there numerous biological pathways implicated in the development of ADHD (Barkley, 1997), but it is also likely to be the case that ADHD is not biologically determined in the simplistic sense suggested by Skidmore and others. On the contrary, as I have indicated, ADHD is widely argued to be the product of a complex interaction between biological and social-environmental factors.

This argument is consistent with current and recent models of gene-environment interaction, such as that presented by Plomin (1988) and, in relation to developmental disorders, Frith (1992). An adaptation of Frith's model of this interaction is represented in Figure 1. The model shows that biologically inherited factors (i.e. genetic endowments) are, from their inception, in constant dynamic inter-action with environmental factors. Gene-environment interaction leads to the development of certain patterns in brain architecture (e.g. lobe development) and functioning (e.g. the neurotransmitter systems), which in turn lead to the development of certain cognitive characteristics (e.g. the efficiency of the executive functions, such as those con-cerned with self talk and working memory). However, the extent to which and the ways in which these cognitive characteristics contribute to presenting behaviours that are functional or dysfunctional is heavily influenced by the environment and experience. For example, an individual

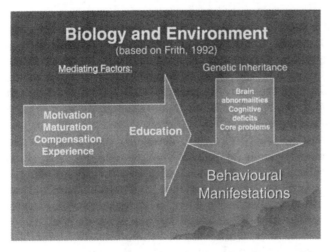

Figure 1 The interaction between biological inheritance and environmental factors in the development of behavioural difficulties

who is prone to memory problems can learn mnemonic strategies that help to compensate for the difficulties. Furthermore, positive, affirming relationships with others may encourage the individual to develop a high level of motivation, which they can deploy in attempting to overcome aspects of their functioning that are potentially problematic in social situations. On the other hand, social and cultural differences will influence the judgements that observers make about the behaviours.

The key implication of this biopsychosocial perspective for education is that the more we understand about the biological and psychological correlates of ADHD (and similar conditions), the better placed we will be to provide educational environments that avoid exacerbating difficulties that children may experience and that promote their optimal educational engagement (see below).

It has been argued here that, whilst biological inheritance plays an important role in the development of the characteristics that are associated with ADHD, whether or not these characteristics lead to problems in the school setting that affect the educational and social engagement of the student is largely determined by characteristics of the school environment. Arguments like that posed by Skidmore (see above), which portray ADHD as an example of biological determinism, simply divert attention from the important process of converting a biopsychosocial account of ADHD into pedagogical and other interventions.

Third, the ADHD 'diagnosis' rests on value-laden, culturally-specific judgements about behavioural or cognitive norms.

This criticism combines paradoxical characteristics of self-evident truth and absurdity. It is self-evidently true that all judgements about the appropriateness or inappropriateness of behaviour or cognitive expression are socially and culturally based. Culture reflects the values, attitudes and beliefs of a social group, and as such it helps to holds the group together. On the other hand, it is absurd to imply that it is possible for human beings to adopt a culture-free stance. Having said this, there are situations where cultural values and assumptions serve to disadvantage members of the social group and require adjustment. The ADHD diagnostic criteria, when considered through a biopsychosocially-informed educational perspective, offers a case in point.

An important point to observe about the ADHD diagnostic criteria is that it harbours taken-for-granted assumptions about the kinds of pupil behaviours that are to be expected in properly functioning *classrooms*. These assumptions include the idea that pupils from an early age are expected to internalise and behave in accordance with a set of rules that derive from constraints imposed by a teacher-centred and curriculum-focused method of teaching pupils in age-related groups. Teacher-pupil ratios create potential problems of social disorder that are met with rules of conduct designed to regulate pupil movement around the classroom and interactions between peers. Externally imposed curricula, as opposed to negotiated curricula, assuming a tight relationship between pupil age and cognitive functioning, tend to be managed by teachers in ways that require pupils to follow a lineal programme of tasks at predetermined times and within strict time limits. It follows from this that teachers often fulfil the role of 'instructors', providing an estimated 80% of the talk that goes on in classrooms (Sage, 2002). Pupils, therefore, are required to be expert in following complex instructions and internalising behavioural and cognitive routines, which, in turn, are intended to establish patterns of self-regulation that become increasingly important as pupils pass through the higher realms of the curriculum and schooling process. It has long been noted that this factory model of education is by no means the only, or even the most desirable, model of schooling. At its worst it rewards conformity and passivity at the expense of intellectual curiosity, critical debate and creativity (Silberman, 1971). At its best it favours pupils whose cognitive styles are orientated towards systematic reflection and abstract lineal thinking. Schools, of course, have always made these kinds of demands. However, it can be argued that there has developed an increasing discontinuity between the demands of school, in these respects, and the behavioural expectations and activities that pupils commonly experience outside of schools. This makes schooling a problematic experience for many contemporary pupils, and it provides a major, relatively new source of stress to pupils with attention and activity problems.

In other words, children who are biologically predisposed to develop ADHD are disadvantaged by culturally based assumptions about what appropriate behaviour in schools and classrooms looks like. This is not the fault of the clinicians who drafted the criteria; on the contrary, the ubiquity and persistence of ADHD and its diagnostic forerunners and equivalents reflect, unintentionally but accurately, one of the most persistent criticisms of Western mass education, namely that it stresses rigid authoritarian values and is relatively unresponsive to individual differences and needs. It follows from this line of argument that schools and teachers (and, indeed, academics and policy-makers) who wish to make our schools and other educational facilities more inclusive should be learning from the lesson that ADHD (for example) teaches us about how we might shape the educational environment in order to improve access to learning opportunities.

Importantly, a biopsychosocial perspective draws a stark picture of the major alternatives facing educators when confronted with students who experience difficulties in engaging effectively in schools: we can either strive to change the educational environment to accommodate the student, or we can attempt to change the student to enable him or her to engage with an unchanging environment. Clearly, in the real world we may often attempt to combine environmental and individual changes. Nevertheless, the use of medication is often best understood as a reflection of the failure of the school to make changes that enable the student with ADHD to engage effectively. This is not the fault of the ADHD diagnosis itself; on the contrary, an understanding of the ADHD diagnosis and the biopsychosocial theories underpinning it can be used to inform the development of effective educational practice that will in some circumstances preclude the need for medication to be used.

Fourth, acceptance of the ADHD diagnosis 'legitimise[s] the practice of drugging defiant children into docility, using stimulants whose long-term side effects are unknown, in the service of a tacit project of social control' (Skidmore, 2004, p. 4).

This is perhaps the most insidious and ill-founded of all the arguments that are posed against the ADHD construct, not least because its acceptance produces the very result that its proponents claim to abhor, namely the over-use of stimulant medication. This is because the failure to admit the validity of ADHD creates a major obstacle to the development of educational interventions for the condition, leaving diagnosed individuals in a situation in which the only source of informed intervention is the medical practitioner. In circumstances where the school is unwilling to cooperate with medics, the likelihood will be that medication will be employed to enable the child to adapt to an unyielding and unresponsive school environment.

In order to avoid this highly negative scenario, it is essential to stress the point that informed opinion on the matter argues strongly that medication for ADHD is by no means an essential treatment, and that when prescribed it should always be within the context of a multi-modal treatment programme that includes psychosocial and educational interventions (Barkley, 1997; NICE, 2000; BPS, 2000). Furthermore, it is argued by some authorities that psychosocial and educational interventions should be the first choice of intervention (e.g. BPS, 2000).

A key feature of the latter approach is that it tends to 'reframe' ADHD as a particular cognitive style, rather than a 'deficit' (Cooper and Ideus, 1996; Cooper and O'Regan, 2001). It involves pedagogical strategies designed to exploit, rather than inhibit, some of the characteristics associated with ADHD (Purdie *et al.*, 2002; DuPaul and Stoner, 1994; Zentall, 1995). Zentall (1995), for example, describes strategies designed to increase the active participation of students with ADHD though the provision of visual motor-tasks. A study by Zentall and Meyer (1987) found that such strategies were associated with improved performance and behaviour of pupils with ADHD, when compared with their performance on tasks requiring more passive engagement of students. Evidence from studies reviewed by DuPaul and Stoner (1994) supports this view, showing that pupils with ADHD respond well to feedback and reinforcement from teachers when the frequency of these interventions is greater than it is for eliciting desired engagement and responses from 'regular' students. Interventions based on the belief that students with ADHD tend to have an active ('kinaesthetic') learning style have been shown to increase levels of attention to task in pupils with ADHD and to reduce disruptive and impulsive behaviours (Hinshaw *et al.*, 1984). Related to this is the insight that pupils with ADHD are particularly prone to the negative consequences of 'recess deprivation' (Zentall, 1995). Zentall and Smith (1992) found that pupils with ADHD self-reported a greater preference for frequent physical activity than pupils without ADHD. Pellegrini and Horvat (1995) found that levels of disruptive behaviour decreased and levels of on-task behaviour increased when periods of 'seatwork' were punctuated by frequent periods in which students were required to engage in structured physical activity. This implies that the redistribution of such time throughout the day at regular intervals will produce positive outcomes.

A major classroom problem associated with ADHD is the tendency of affected pupils to be talkative at inappropriate times. This 'problem' can be exploited for pedagogical purposes by the teacher increasing opportunities for on-task verbal participation by pupils (Zentall, 1995). Studies have found that pupils with ADHD perform better on reading comprehension tasks when they are required to read comprehension passages aloud, rather than silently (Dubey and O'Leary, 1975). Also, the tendency of pupils with ADHD to dominate verbal interactions with peers in negative ways can be modified by training them to use questioning techniques rather than assertion (Zentall, 1995). Zentall found that this technique works best when combined with social skills training. Zentall (1995), drawing on empirical evidence provided by Rosenfeld and colleagues, suggests that seating pupils in a semi-circle around the teacher, or in small groups, produces more on-task verbal participation by pupils with ADHD and more appropriate hand-raising behaviours during whole class teaching episodes. Furthermore, there is evidence to support the conclusion that reducing the teacher-pupil ratio, in situations involving teacher-group verbal interaction, improves the quality of engagement of pupils with ADHD. This effect is enhanced when teachers provide behavioural models for active listening strategies (Carter and Shostak, 1980).

The twin pedagogical strategies of behavioural modelling and teacher-direction are strongly associated with a reduction in pupil inattentiveness and impulsiveness in the classroom and positive academic outcomes. These effects are most powerful when teacher direction involves clear and distinct information about performance, behavioural expectations and expected outcomes. Optimal pupil performance is associated with brevity and clarity of sequences of instruction, the accompaniment of verbal instructions with visual cues and the availability of resources that pupils can refer to for reminders of direction and expectations (DuPaul and Stoner, 1994; Zentall, 1995). The use of pupils as behavioural and academic models through the careful programming of interaction between the pupil with ADHD and preferred role models is also found to be an effective pedagogical tool. It is important, however, that the opportunities for disruption created by such pupil interaction are controlled by the teacher's use of positive reinforcement for task-appropriate and socially desirable behaviour (Zentall, 1995). In accordance with these findings, Cooper and O'Regan (2001) provide case study material indicating that pupils with ADHD can benefit from taking on the role of peer tutors with younger, less competent pupils.

In a classroom environment in which extraneous stimuli such as irrelevant noise and other distractors are limited, and where pedagogical strategies of the type described above are in use, opportunities are created to enable the pupil with ADHD to practise self-pacing. Self-pacing, as opposed to external (i.e. teacher-directed) pacing, is associated with greater accuracy (Zentall, 1995), and pupil self-reported satisfaction (Cooper and Shea, 1999) with learning tasks. This can usefully extend to providing pupils with ADHD with opportunities to remove themselves from classroom situations that they find stressful to a pre-determined quiet area (Zentall, 1995; DuPaul and Stoner, 1994).

In a meta-analysis of interventions for ADHD, Purdie *et al.* (2002) found that, in comparison with clinic-based interventions, educational interventions of the type describe above were most effective in promoting positive cognitive outcomes (defined in terms of non-specified academic performance, language and reading skills, mathematical skills, IQ and memory functions). Although the overall mean effect size was small (.28), it was concluded that educational interventions were the most effective in producing cognitive improvements. School-based cognitive interventions were also more effective than clinic-based cognitive interventions. This highlights the central importance of pedagogical approaches to the amelioration of the negative outcomes of ADHD. Multi-modal approaches (combining medical, psycho-social and educational interventions) were found to be second only to medication in achieving improvements in behaviour, and superior to medication in producing improvements in social functioning.

Fifth, ADHD represents the wrongful medicalisation of defiance in school children.

As noted above, a medical diagnosis does not necessarily require medical treatment. In fact a biopsychosocial perspective enables medical diagnoses, such ADHD, to be used to inform psychosocial and educational interventions that may preclude the need for medical intervention. The development and implementation of such educational interventions, however, depends upon an accurate understanding of the nature of ADHD. The claim, made by Skidmore among others, that ADHD is simply a medical term applied to 'defiant children', if accepted, is guaranteed to produce confusion and inappropriate educational interventions for children with ADHD.

Obviously, children with ADHD are like all children in that sometimes they are deliberately disobedient and defiant. However, ADHD is clearly defined as relating to difficulties in various self-regulatory processes, including sustaining attention, inhibiting responses and controlling motor activity. Crucially, ADHD is non-volitional. Children with ADHD perform differently from other children on tests of vigilance and impulse control (Barkley, 1997). Their failure to comply with the wishes of teachers and parents is theorised as resulting from cognitive deficits, such as problems with executive functions (Barkley, 1997, see above). This helps to explain why ADHD symptoms respond well to pedagogical interventions. Interventions intended to support children whose core problem is that of defiance are quite different.

Defiance, when it reflects a child's dominant style of social engagement, goes beyond appropriate assertiveness and is characterised by an aggressive and uncooperative response to adults or other children in the absence of obvious provocation. Defiance, therefore, is often better understood as a cognitive distortion, rather than as a cognitive deficit. Cognitive distortions require interventions that enable children to examine and reflect on the ways in which they interpret situations and the choices that they make on the basis of these interpretations (Frith, 1992). This is not to say that children may not combine ADHD with conditions associated with defiance. It is widely reported, for instance, that a high proportion of children with the ADHD diagnosis have co-morbid diagnoses of Conduct Disorder or Oppositional Defiance Disorder (McArdle, 2007; Barkley, 1997). Such children will, therefore, benefit from a combination of interventions, some that address deficits and others that address distortions. The crucial thing, however, is for teachers to be able to base interventions on a careful assessment of the specific need in the specific situation.

The key point being made here is that an understanding of the differences between cognitive distortions and deficits can be extremely valuable to teachers, whilst confusion between or the conflation of deficits and distortions are likely to lead to ineffective intervention (Royer, 1999).

CONCLUSION

It has been suggested that some reactions to ADHD among educationists can be likened to those of the pet-loving correspondent from Florida who objected to Gary Larson's cartoon of alligators 'bobbing for poodles'. In short, they impute a range of motives and assumptions to the author of the cartoon (or the educator who sees ADHD as a learning difficulty) that are simply not there. In the case of ADHD, these assumptions are outdated, inaccurate and are easily countered if one takes the trouble to read the scholarly literature underpinning the ADHD concept. What is more, the high moral tone assumed by the detractors masks a poverty of understanding that is positively dangerous; not least, in the case of ADHD, to individuals who may be diagnosed with the condition.

The central argument of this chapter is that ADHD is most usefully understood from a biopsychosocial perspective. Arguments that reject ADHD on the grounds that it reflects a biological determinist view are inaccurate and bogus, in that they fail to acknowledge modern and widely accepted understandings about the ways in which biology and environment interact. Ironically, those who argue for a solely environmentalist explanation for social, emotional and behavioural difficulties (or any other aspect of human functioning) are arguing from a position that owes a great deal to the work of Charles Darwin (Degler, 1994). This, however, is an argument for future work. More worrying is the possibility that an extreme and entrenched position on one side of an argument might lead to a reciprocal entrenchment on the other. In this case, if that were to happen, then we might expect to see even more children being medicated without appropriate educational intervention being provided. In other words, educators who adopt strategies for dealing with properly diagnosed ADHD that ignore the contribution that educational insights based on the biopsychosocial perspective can offer are not only wasting a useful resource, they are failing their students. The problem in this scenario, however, is that the unresponsiveness of the school may be misinterpreted as a problem of the child, leading either to some form of exclusion or to a preference for the option of medication.

The most important implication of this discussion is that educationists, particularly those concerned with issues of inclusion, have a responsibility to update their understanding of how individual factors relate to learning and teaching, to engage constructively with the biopsychosocial perspective, and, through research and scholarship to make best use of this perspective in informing the development of teaching and educational provision (Hernandez and Blazer, 2007). This is a significant point, because an educational perspective is vital to the development and clarification of the biopsychosocial perspective, not least in terms of more research that further explores the power of educational interventions in relation to such issues as ADHD.

Beyond ADHD, however, lie educational issues of a broader nature. The biopsychosocial perspective requires us to acknowledge the richness of human psychological diversity. ADHD is simply one example of how certain widely distributed psychological characteristics are rendered educationally dysfunctional by an education system that is outdated and inflexible. Using biopsychosocial insights in the development of educational provision is likely to lead us closer than we have ever been to a genuinely inclusive education system.

Even though medics, neuroscientists and most psychologists are ill equipped to make judgements about appropriate and effective educational provision, it is not difficult to foresee a situation in which the failure by educationalists to engage constructively with the biopsychosocial paradigm could lead to their marginalisation in favour of these other professions. As it stands, educationalists, particularly those of us who concern ourselves with the most vulnerable of school students, have made little impact on a school system that has consistently failed to provide an adequate service to most of its clients. In the 21st century, those educationalists who would deny that biology has a significant role to play in human development are simply uninformed and, therefore, easy to marginalise. This, some (though not the current author) might think, would not be a bad thing. In my view, this failure to engage constructively with the biopsychosocial perspective will inhibit the development of effective educational provision, to the detriment not only of children with ADHD but of all children.

REFERENCES

American Psychiatric Association (APA) (1994) *Diagnostic and Statistical Manual of Mental Disorders*, 4th edn. (Washington, DC, APA).

Anastopoulos, A. (1999) AD/HD, in: S. Netherton, C Holmes and C. Walker (eds) *Child and Adolescent Psychological Disorders: A Comprehensive Textbook* (Oxford, Oxford University Press).

Arnsten, A. (2007) Catecholamines and the Prefrontal Cortical Regulation of Behaviour and Attention, in: M. Fitzgerald, M. Bellgrove and M. Gill (eds) *Handbook of ADHD* (Chichester, Wiley), pp. 315–329.

Barkley, R. (1997) *AD/HD and the Nature of Self Control* (New York, Guilford).

Bellgrove, M., Robertson, H. and Gill, M. (2007) Genes, Cognition and Brain Activity: The Endophenotype Approach to ADHD, in: M. Fitzgerald, M. Bellgrove and M. Gill (eds) *Handbook of ADHD* (Chichester, Wiley).

Booth, T. and Ainscow, M. (1997) *From Them to Us* (London, Routledge).

Boreham, N., Peers, I., Farrell, P. and Craven, D. (1995) Different Perspectives of Parents and Educational Psychologists when a Child is Referred for Assessment, in P. Farrell (ed.) *Children with EBD: Strategies for Assessment and Intervention* (Lewes, Falmer).

British Psychological Society (BPS) (2000) *AD/HD: Guidelines and Principles for Successful Multi-Agency Working* (Leicester, BPS).

Cantwell, D. (1996) Attention Deficit Disorder: A Review of the Past 10 years, *Journal of Abnormal Child Psychology*, 15, pp. 519–536.

Carter, I. N. and Shostak, D. A. (1980) Imitation in the Treatment of the Hyperkinetic Behaviour Syndrome, *Journal of Clinical Child Psychology*, 9, pp. 63–66.

Cooper, P. (1997a) The Reality and Hyperreality Of AD/HD: An Educational and Cultural Analysis 2nd revd. edn in: P. Cooper and K. Ideus (eds) *Attention Deficit/Hyperactivity Disorder: Medical, Educational and Cultural Issues* (East Sutton, The Association of Workers for Children with Emotional and Behavioural Difficulties).

Cooper, P. (1997b) Biology, Behaviour and Education: AD/HD and the Bio-psycho-social Perspective, *Educational and Child Psychology*, 14.1, pp. 31–38.

Cooper, P. and Ideus, K. (1966) *ADHD: A Practical Guide for Teachers* (London, Fulton).

Cooper, P. and O'Regan, F. (2001) *ADHD: A Manual for Teachers* (London, Routledge).

Cooper, P. and Shea, T. (1999) Pupils' Perceptions of AD/HD, in: P. Cooper and K. Bilton (eds) *ADHD: Research, Opinion and Practice* (London, Whurr).

Degler, C. (1994) *In Search of Human Nature: The Decline and Revival of Darwinism in American Social Thought* (Oxford, Oxford University Press).

Dubey, D. R. and O'Leary, S. G. (1975) Increasing Reading Comprehension of Two Hyperactive Children: Preliminary Investigation, *Perceptual and Motor Skills*, 41, pp. 691–694.

DuPaul, G. and Stoner, G. (1994) *ADHD in the Schools* (New York, Guilford).

Farrington, D. (1990) Implications of Criminal Career Research for the Prevention of Offending, *The Journal of Adolescence*, 13, pp. 93–113.

Frith, U. (1992) Cognitive Development and Cognitive Deficit, *The Psychologist*, 5, pp. 13–19.

Gallagher, L., Bellgrove, M., Hawi, Z., Segurado, R. and Fitzgerald, M. (2007) ADHD, Autistic Spectrum Disorders and Tourette's Syndrome: Investigating the Evidence for Clinical and Genetic Overlap, in: M. Fitzgerald, M. Bellgrove and M. Gill (eds) *Handbook of ADHD* (Chichester, Wiley).

Greenhill, L. (1998) Childhood ADHD: Pharmacological Treatments, in: P. Nathan and M. Gorman (eds), *A Guide to Treatments that Work* (Oxford, Oxford University Press).

Hayden, C. (1997) Exclusion from Primary School: Children in Need and Children with Special Educational Need, *Emotional and Behavioural Difficulties*, 2.3, pp. 36–44.

Hernandez, L. and Blazer, D. (2007) *Genes, Behaviour and the Social Environment: Moving Beyond the Nature/Nurture Debate* (Washington, DC, Institute of Medicine of the National Academies).

Hinshaw, S. (1994) *Attention Deficits and Hyperactivity in Children* (London, Sage).

Hinshaw, S., Henker, B. and Whalen, C. (1984) Self-control in Hyperactive Boys in Anger-induced Situations: Effects Of Cognitive-behavioral Training and Methylphenidate, *Journal of Abnormal Child Psychology*, 12, pp. 55–77.

Kelly, A., Sheres, A., Sonuga Bark, E. and Castellanos, F. (2007) Functional Neuroimaging of Reward and Motivational Pathways in ADHD, in: M. Fitzgerald, M. Bellgrove and M. Gill (eds) *Handbook of ADHD* (Chichester##Wiley).

Kirley, A (2007) Diagnosis and Classification of ADHD in adulthood, in: M. Fitzgerald, M. Bellgrove and M. Gill (eds) *Handbook of ADHD* (Chichester, Wiley).

Larson, G. (1992) *The PreHistory of the Far Side* (London, Warner Books).

Levy, F. and Hay, D. (eds) (2001) *Attention, Genes and ADHD* (London, Brunner-Routledge).

Lloyd, G. and Norris, C. (1999) Including ADHD, *Disability and Society*, 14.4, pp. 505–517.

McArdle, P. (2007) ADHD and Co-morbid Oppositional Defiant and Conduct Disorders, in: M. Fitzgerald, M. Bellgrove and M. Gill (eds) *Handbook of ADHD* (Chichester, Wiley).

McMullen, G., Painter, D. and Casey, T. (1994) Assessment and Treatment of ADHD in Children, in: L. VendeCreek, S. Knapp and T. Jackson (eds) *Innovations in Clinical Practice* (Sarasota, FL, Professional Resource Press).

National Institute of Clinical Excellence (NICE) (2000) *Guidance on the Use of Methyphenidate for AD/HD* (London, NICE).

National Institute of Clinical Excellence (NICE) (2008) *Guidance for ADHD* (London, NICE).

Nigg, J. and Hinshaw, S. (1998) Parent Personality Traits and Psychopathology Associated with Antisocial Behaviors in Childhood AD/HD, *Journal of Child Psychology and Psychiatry*, 39.2, pp. 145–159.

Palmer, E. and Finger, S. (2001) An Early Description of ADHD: Dr Alexander Crichton and 'Mental Restlessness', *Child Psychology and Psychiatry Review*, 6.2, pp. 66–73.

Pellegrini, A. and Horvat, M. (1995) A Developmental Contextualist Critique of AD/HD, *Educational Researcher*, 24.1, pp. 13–20.

Place, M., Wilson, J., Martin, E. and Hulsmeir, J. (2000) The Frequency of Emotional and Behavioural Disturbance in an EBD school, *Child Psychology and Psychiatry Review*, 5.2, pp. 76–80.

Plomin, R (1988) *Nature and Nurture During Infancy and Early Childhood* (Cambridge University Press).

Purdie, N., Hattie, J. and Carroll, A. (2002) A Review of the Research on Interventions for ADHD: What Works Best?, *Review of Educational Research*, 72.1, pp. 61–100.

Rose, S. (2004) The New Brain Sciences, in: D. Rees and S. Rose (eds) *The New Brain Sciences: Perils and Promises* (Cambridge, Cambridge University Press).

Royer, E. (1999) Cognitive Approaches to the Education and Training of Children with ADHD, in: P. Cooper and K. Bilton (eds) *ADHD: Research, Opinion and Practice* (London, Whurr).

Rutter, M. (2001) Child Psychiatry in the Era Following Sequencing the Genome, in: F. Levy and D. Hay (eds) *Attention, Genes and ADHD* (London, Brunner-Routledge).

Sage, R. (2002) Start Talking and Stop Misbehaving: Teaching Pupils to Communicate, Think and Act Appropriately, *Emotional and Behavioral Difficulties*, 7.2, pp. 85–96.

Sergeant, J. (1995) Hyperkinetic Disorder Revisited, in: J. Sergeant (ed.) *Eunythydis: European Approaches to Hyperkinetic Disorder* (Amsterdam, Sergeant).

Sharkey, L. and Fitzgerald, M. (2007a) A History of ADHD, in: M. Fitzgerald, M. Bellgrove and M. Gill (eds) *Handbook of ADHD* (Chichester, Wiley).

Sharkey, L. and Fitzgerald, M (2007b) Diagnosis and Classification of ADHD in Childhood, in: M. Fitzgerald, M. Bellgrove and M. Gill (eds) *Handbook of ADHD* (Chichester, Wiley).

Silberman, C. (1971) *Crisis in the Classroom* (New York, Random House).

Skidmore, D. (2004) *Inclusion* (Buckingham, Open University Press).

Slee, R. (1995) *Changing Theories and Practices of Discipline* (London, Falmer).

Tannock, R. (1998) AD/HD: Advances in Cognitive, Neurobiological and Genetic Research, *Journal of Child Psychology and Psychiatry*, 39.1, pp. 65–99.

Thompson, R. (1993) *The Brain: A Neuroscience Primer*, 2nd edn. (New York, Freeman).

Visser, J. (1997) Response to Cooper. The Myth of the Myth of Attention Deficit/Hyperactivity Disorder: Towards a Constructive Perspective, *British Psychological Society Education Section Review*, 21.1, pp. 15–16.

Visser, J. and Travell, C. (2006) ADHD Does Bad Stuff to You: Young People's and Parents' Experiences and Perceptions of Attention Deficit Hyperactivity Disorder, *Emotional and Behavioural Disorders*, 11.

Vivian, L. (1994) The Changing Pupil Populations of Schools with Emotional and Behavioural Difficulties (A Survey of One County's Schools for Pupils with EBD), *Therapeutic Care and Education*, 3.3, pp. 218–231.

Weiss, G. and Hechtman, L. (1993) *Hyperactive Children Grown Up*, 2nd edn. (New York, Guilford Press).

WHO (1992) *International Classification of Diseases*, 10th edn. (Geneva, WHO).

Young, S. (2007) Cognitive Behavioural Treatment of ADHD, in: M. Fitzgerald, M. Bellgrove and M. Gill (eds) *Handbook of ADHD* (Chichester, Wiley).

Zentall, S. S. (1995) Modifying Classroom Tasks and Environments, in: S Goldstein (ed.) *Understanding and Managing Children's Classroom Behaviour* (New York, John Wiley).

Zentall, S. S. and Meyer, M. J. (1987) Self-regulation of Stimulation for ADD-H Children during the Reading and Vigilance Task Performance, *Journal of Abnormal Child Psychology*, 15, pp. 519–536.

Zentall, S. S. and Smith, Y. N. (1992) Assessment and Validation of the Learning and Behavioural Style Preferences of Hyperactive and Comparison Children, *Learning and Individual Differences*, 4, pp. 25–41.

2.4

Does Dyslexia Exist?

JULIAN G. ELLIOTT AND SIMON GIBBS

INTRODUCTION

> A 22-year-old woman was condemned to 'temporary menial tasks', the
> High Court heard. P.P. claims that she is of average intelligence but
> because her learning difficulty was not discovered until two months before
> she left school, she never learned to read and write properly ... Tests were
> carried out at infant, junior and comprehensive schools. At the age of 10
> she was found to be four years behind in reading and writing skills but the
> reason was never identified (*The Guardian*, 27 July 1997, p. 5).

The Pamela Phelps case, cited above, would seem to provide a perfect
illustration of the key issues that have surfaced in periodic media debates
about the existence and utility of the concept of dyslexia. The case centred
upon the argument that if a diagnosis of dyslexia had been forthcoming at
an earlier stage of her school career her difficulties would more likely have
been overcome. However, in putting forward this position, there was no
suggestion that her reading problems failed to have been noted, or that
there had been no follow up by specialists. An educational psychologist
had seen her at primary school and, on transfer to secondary school,
further assessment indicated that she had a reading accuracy age
equivalent of 7 years and 3 months. She left school with a reading age
equivalent of 8 years.

Although there have been cases of children with severe reading
disabilities failing to receive any specialist attention, this was evidently
not the case here. Miss Phelps had received remedial help in English and
mathematics. The issue was not about the presence or absence of
assessment and support but, rather, the failure to *diagnose* Miss Phelps'
dyslexia. This, it was claimed, would have pointed to the most appropriate
form of intervention, a highly structured, multisensory approach to the
teaching of reading.

In what follows we suggest that the premises and logic of this claim do
not stand scrutiny. We will go further and suggest that the persistence
within educational and clinical settings of the notion of dyslexia as a
discrete, identifiable (*diagnosable*) condition that is held to pertain only
for some, rather than all, with literacy difficulties may obstruct inclusion
and reduce overall educational attainment.

We seek, therefore, to question the meaningfulness, purpose and effect of the dyslexia construct. In arguing that a diagnosis of dyslexia has clinical or educational value, one would anticipate helpful answers to one or more of the following questions:

1. Is dyslexia a clinically or educationally meaningful term for differentiating between children with reading difficulties?
2. To what extent would the dyslexic diagnosis guide the educator in devising appropriate forms of intervention?
3. To what extent should the dyslexic diagnosis result in the differential allocation of resources or other forms of special arrangement?

Following consideration of these questions we conclude by turning to consider some reasons why and how 'dyslexia' might have become a socially constructed term of convenience.

QUESTION 1: IS DYSLEXIA A CLINICALLY OR EDUCATIONALLY MEANINGFUL TERM FOR DIFFERENTIATING BETWEEN CHILDREN WITH READING DIFFICULTIES?

In providing some answers to this question we explore the underlying theoretical and empirical bases in three areas (intelligence testing, biological factors, underlying cognitive processes), used to substantiate a distinct conceptualisation of dyslexia.

From a purely scientific perspective, and to take a Popperian stance (Popper, 1969) with regard to attempts to define dyslexia, it is apparent that it is not possible to set strictly unambiguous criteria of demarcation at either the genetic or the functional boundaries of what is, or what is not, dyslexia. Indeed Stanovich, in cogently demolishing the grounds for identification of dyslexia on the basis of reading-IQ discrepancies, points out that dyslexia, as with many 'developmental disabilities ... carries with it so many empirically unverified [we would suggest *unverifiable*] connotations and assumptions' that the term might be helpfully abandoned (Stanovich, 1994, p. 579). From the perspective of natural science it is evident that on the continuum of highly skilled to less-skilled readers, there is no clear discontinuity that provides an absolute categorical boundary for a diagnostic category of 'dyslexics'. As discussed below, studies that compare dyslexics with non-dyslexics frequently still select participants as representative of 'normal' and 'non-normal' (the latter typically reading at least one standard deviation below the 'norm') groups on the basis of researcher-defined criteria. It is perhaps, then, inevitable that patterns of abilities or functions that discriminate between the two groups may be found, *post hoc*.

It is also perhaps something of a paradox that determined advocates for the value of the label will readily agree that the nature of the underlying difficulties experienced by dyslexics can be highly diverse. The list of possible underlying difficulties typically found in the dyslexia literature is lengthy and it would appear that none of these is essential for the diagnosis (other than literacy difficulties themselves, of course). Thus, dyslexics are often considered to present with such (co-morbid) characteristics as: speech and language difficulties, poor short-term (or working) memory, difficulties in ordering and sequencing, clumsiness, a poor sense of rhythm, limited speed of information processing, poor concentration, inconsistent hand preference, poor verbal fluency, poor phonic skills, frequent use of letter reversals (d for b, for example), a difficulty in undertaking mental calculations, low self-image, and anxiety when being asked to read aloud.

The weakness of such lengthy lists is that they routinely fail to offer meaningful differentiations. Similar items to those listed above are often found in lists of signs of other developmental conditions such as attention deficit hyperactivity disorder or dyspraxia. (For this reason, some prefer to use the term 'specific learning difficulties' to describe those who present with such features.) Furthermore, many features seen as indicative of dyslexia can be found in people who have no significant literacy difficulties, and may be evident in poor readers who are not considered to be dyslexic. Many difficulties that are seen as typical of dyslexics are also found in younger normal readers who read at the same age level, for example, letter reversals (Cassar *et al.*, 2005). This suggests that such problems are more characteristic of a certain stage of reading development, than representing pathological features.

One simple way around this is to take an exclusionary approach that argues that dyslexics are those individuals whose literacy difficulties cannot be explained by low intelligence, socio-economic disadvantage, poor schooling, sensory (auditory or visual) difficulty, emotional and behavioural difficulties, or severe neurological impairment that goes significantly beyond literacy (Lyon, 1995). However, for many educationalists this is likely to prove highly problematic as it might typically exclude from intervention students who attend schools that are seen as poor, who live in disadvantaged neighbourhoods (Rutter, 1978), whose behaviour is problematic (perhaps, in part, because of academic frustrations), or those who score poorly on IQ tests.

Since the use of IQ tests still appears pervasive in many aspects of work in this field, we now address the issue briefly. Before doing so, however, it important to note that the use of IQ tests as valid and equitable tools has been questioned by many psychologists (Cernovsky, 1997; Flanagan and McGrew, 1997; Lopez, 1997).

The Use of IQ in the Assessment of Dyslexia

> Dyslexia ... exists across the whole range of intellectual ability and is identified when there is a characteristic profile of strengths and weaknesses, along with supporting evidence from other sources (Dyslexia Action website: http://www.dyslexiaaction.org.uk).

It is a puzzling phenomenon that, although leading academic researchers and dyslexia support groups now accept that reading difficulties typically encountered by the 'dyslexic' individual apply across the intellectual spectrum (see also Stanovich, 1994), IQ tests are still widely employed as a means for differentiating between dyslexic and poor reading groups (see, for example, a review by Rice and Brooks, 2004). This issue has great importance as the application of an IQ-achievement model can serve to exclude some children from specialised intervention (Catts, Hogan and Fey, 2003).

While a discrepancy between IQ and measured reading ability has long been a key criterion for dyslexia used by clinicians (McNab, 1994; Presland, 1991), more recent research studies have demonstrated that the difficulties encountered by 'dyslexics' are largely independent of intellectual functioning (Fletcher *et al.*, 1994; Stanovich and Stanovich, 1997). While more intellectually able poor readers will be able to use semantic and syntactic knowledge to help them make more sense of passages of text, this is of no help to them when they are asked to read single words—the key task for the study of dyslexia (Grigorenko, 2001; Stanovich, 1991; Vellutino, Fletcher, Snowling and Scanlon, 2004). Despite such understandings, Rice and Brooks (2004) note that IQ/reading test discrepancies continue to be used by many reading research laboratories to identify dyslexic subgroups. Nicolson and Fawcett, for example, define developmental dyslexia as 'unexpected difficulties in learning to read in children of average or above-average intelligence' (Nicolson and Fawcett, 2007, p. 135).

This is rather puzzling, as, with regard to single word reading, the lack of utility of IQ has been clearly demonstrated. As Frith (1997) argues, even if IQ/reading test discrepancies were used to identify a group of dyslexics, the reason for the discrepancies has still to be explained. In reviewing studies that have examined aptitude-achievement discrepancies, Stanovich notes that the information-processing operations underlying word recognition deficits are the same for poor readers with high or low IQ, there is no evidence that these two groups respond differently to treatment, and there is no evidence that any 'neuroanatomical defects that underlie the cognitive deficits of these two groups are different' (Stanovich, 1999, p. 352).

Given this body of research, it is unsurprising that the state of the art review by Vellutino *et al.* (2004), concludes that 'intelligence tests have little utility for diagnosing specific reading disability' (p. 29) and the authors recommend that practitioners should:

> ... shift the focus of their clinical activities away from emphasis on psychometric assessment to detect cognitive and biological causes of a child's reading difficulties for purposes of categorical labelling in favour of assessment that would eventuate in educational and remedial activities tailored to the child's individual needs (p. 31).

Of course, this advice applies to those types of literacy difficulties that are seen as most relevant to dyslexia (decoding and spelling). Some cognitive tests may be helpful in understanding the specific nature of children's higher-order reading comprehension difficulties involving such processes as reasoning, inferencing and logical deduction (Vellutino *et al.*, 2004). Vellutino *et al.* went further, however, recommending that intelligence tests should not be used to identify dyslexia. Snowling (2008) also acknowledges that the use of IQ criteria to differentiate subgroups of failing readers has declined on the grounds that it does not differentiate between groups in terms of underlying phonological difficulties or response to intervention.

However, it is important to recognise that the agendas of researchers and educationalists may be different. Thus, for example, the differentiation used by Snowling (2008) is employed to explore potential differences in underlying cognitive processes. For academic psychologists, differentiating between groups of poor readers on the basis of intelligence *may* help to shed light on mechanisms of reading. However, as indicated above, there can be no theoretical or moral justification for making that an appropriate process for practitioner decision-making.

The Role of Biological Factors

Clearly, the examination of biological factors in reading has yielded many insights and offers great promise for the future (Fischer, Bernstein and Immordino-Yang, 2007). However, it is necessary to remain sceptical about how much has been learned from genetic and brain-based studies that is of significant assistance for making judgements as to whether an individual is or is not 'dyslexic'. It is important to remember that this field of research typically examines populations encountering reading difficulty, not a special subgroup of poor readers that might be labelled 'dyslexic'.

Attempts to isolate the fundamental underlying biological mechanisms that might be 'at fault' in reading disability (dyslexia?) have so far been unsuccessful. Whilst the phenotypic characteristics of dyslexia might seem obvious, it is probably sensible to regard reading generally (and dyslexia specifically) as having a high degree of phenotypic plasticity. Whilst at the level of enquiry into genetic influence it seems likely that there may be some probability of genetic inheritance (Grigorenko, 2001), the indications are that this relates primarily to underlying language processing. However, even if the genotype were discernible (and it is argued that this is unlikely or at least very problematic; see Grigorenko and Naples, in press; Thomas and Karmiloff-Smith, 2002), environmental factors are highly influential on presenting behaviours—as we will illustrate later. Critically, as Grigorenko and Naples (in press) suggest, there is no certainty that hypothesised mechanisms are related only to 'disordered' reading or are involved in reading acquisition generally.

At the level of analysis of neurology and brain structure it also seems that there is no likelihood of discerning structures or mechanisms that are directly and uniquely implicated in reading. While there is much optimism about the potential of functional magnetic resonance imaging (fMRI), there continue to be a number of key methodological difficulties and, at the current time, this technique cannot be used for diagnostic purposes. It is too easily forgotten that brain activation differences are merely correlated with reading disability and these should not be interpreted as proof of causality (Schulte-Körne *et al.*, 2007). At present, the technique's main contributions involve showing which brain regions underlie which reading-related functions (although a neural map of the processes associated with reading and learning to read has yet to be produced), and helping to improve upon existing models and theories (for a detailed discussion of these points, see Paré-Blagoev, 2007). Similarly, work in this area can offer little guidance for intervention for the available knowledge from the fields of neuroscience and genetics is '. . . too basic to draw specific and applicable conclusions for teaching and educational practice' (Schulte-Körne *et al.*, 2007, p. 169).

Any attempt to support the clinical or educational value of the notion of dyslexia on the basis of brain abnormalities would, therefore, represent something of a conceptual sleight of hand (Elliott, 2005a). There is no theoretical justification for using neurology or genetics as the foundations for a clinical differential diagnosis of dyslexia, let alone a practical one. To do so is to leap from exciting work in laboratories that may hold great promise for the future, to making diagnostic decisions about individuals who need help and support now. Some commentators too readily jump from the laboratory to the classroom despite the fact that we are unable to prove a biological origin in respect of a given poor reader; psychologists and educationalists simply lack the measurement tools to make individual distinctions of this nature (Rice and Brooks, 2004). They may even be professionally disabled to some extent by such considerations (as may have been an outcome of the 'Phelps' case). Equally important, whatever their future promise, at the current time, genetic and brain studies currently cannot help us to make decisions about differential forms of intervention.

In summary, the faulty logic here runs as follows:

(a) On the basis of studies of children and adults with reading difficulty (a generic group often described by research scientists as dyslexic), genetic and brain-based factors appear to play an important role (although precise mechanisms are currently unclear). *Comment*: This appears to be incontrovertible.

(b) On the basis of such work we can conclude that dyslexics are those poor readers with some form of underlying biological difficulty. *Comment*: Note the faulty syllogistic reasoning here; the focus moves from research into the biology of reading difficulty that examines poor readers in general, to identification of a category that is seen to represent a subset of the wider group of poor readers who comprised such studies.

(c) On the basis of tests of cognitive functioning and relevant academic skills, and clinical interviews, we can identify from the wider pool of poor readers those who are dyslexic. *Comment*: There is currently no such way in which we can use our knowledge about genetics or brain functioning to make judgements. Of course, there is great promise for the future but it is beliefs about *today's* practice that we are contesting in this chapter.

(d) These children can then be given appropriate intervention that differs from that provided to other children with reading difficulties. *Comment:* At present there is no evidence that biological insights regarding reading difficulty can meaningfully inform the exercise of differentiated forms of intervention.

The Role of Underlying Cognitive Processes

Another argument often put forward to support the clinical value of the concept of dyslexia stems from the work of cognitive psychologists. The rationale here is that key cognitive processes have been identified that can explain a dyslexic profile. Foremost among these is the role of phonological awareness (Bradley and Bryant, 1978, 1983; Snowling and Hulme, 2005), that is, the ability to recognise different sounds in spoken language. The majority of cognitive psychologists see reading as primarily a linguistic, rather than a visual, skill in which phonological factors play a significant role for beginning readers, and semantic and syntactic skills become increasingly important as the reader's expertise increases (Vellutino *et al.*, 2004). Literacy is parasitic on speech and language functions (Mattingly, 1972) and, as Snowling and Hulme (2005) note, given its recent development it is unsurprising that there is no evidence of phylogenetic development of neural or cognitive structures that are uniquely and primarily dedicated to literacy. In fact, there is as yet no agreed overarching account of how reading skills are acquired. It is, however, thought that difficulty with reading is experienced primarily because of difficulties in the process of translating between symbols and speech. While the 'most complete and coherent (across levels of explanation from reading behaviour to neurology) theory in this area' (Torgesen, 2007, p. 249), there is still some debate as to whether phonological awareness is the key explanatory factor of reading difficulty (Vellutino *et al.*, 2004), and even leading proponents of the theory acknowledge that it cannot provide a full account (Snowling, 2008; Torgesen, 2007). Clearly, for some children considered to be dyslexic other mechanisms are responsible. Such differences and doubts render decisions about diagnosis and labelling of a dyslexic subgroup even more problematic. However, internationally there is some evidence that the rate of acquisition of reading skill (or the incidence rate for 'dyslexia') correlates with the nature of the orthography that readers confront, and the relationship that this has with phonological structures in the host language (see Caravolas, 2005; Seymour, 2005). As is readily evident, there is no universally accepted or consistently designed system of representing spoken language in visual symbols. Rather, there are almost as many orthographies as there are oral languages. The systems that there are have largely evolved in a haphazard and unsystematic way dependent to a greater or lesser extent on the whims and vagaries of writers and print setters (for example, in relation to written English, see Crystal, 2004). The task of becoming literate (see Byrne, 2005) is therefore complex, irregular and subservient to other linguistic and cognitive abilities. In short, we have not evolved any natural mechanism that deals specifically with the coding of written language (see also Wolf, 2008). Marvelling or scoffing at the failures of some people confronted with this task is, therefore, perhaps wholly wrong. The marvel is how some achieve success with such an enormous, varied and ill-designed task.

In a systematic review of dyslexia in adults, Rice and Brooks (2004, p.11) conclude that:

- 'There are many definitions of dyslexia but no consensus. Some definitions are purely descriptive while others embody causal theories. It appears that 'dyslexia' is not one thing but many, in so far as it serves a conceptual clearing-house for a number of reading skills deficits and difficulties, with a number of causes.
- There is no consensus either, as to whether dyslexia can be distinguished in practice from other possible causes of adults' literacy difficulties. Many 'signs of dyslexia' are no less character-istic of non-dyslexic people with reading skills deficits. In our present state of knowledge, it does not seem helpful for teachers to think of some literacy learners as 'dyslexics' and others as 'ordinary poor readers'.

QUESTION 2: TO WHAT EXTENT WOULD THE DYSLEXIC DIAGNOSIS GUIDE THE EDUCATOR IN DEVISING APPROPRIATE FORMS OF INTERVENTION?

Typically, we search for a diagnostic label because we believe that this will point towards the most efficacious forms of intervention. Following a medical model, one might assume that a clear diagnosis is necessary in order to know how best to intervene. Thus, behind the rationale for the Pamela Phelps case lay the assumption that if she had been diagnosed as dyslexic a more efficacious intervention could have been put into place. This position would, of course, only be valid if there were clear evidence that differing approaches were suitable for dyslexic and non-dyslexic poor readers. However, this is patently not the case and there continues to be no clear evidence that there exists a particular teaching approach that is more suitable for a dyslexic subgroup than for other poor readers (Stanovich, 1991; Vellutino *et al.*, 2000). Indeed, it is generally considered that the highly structured, phonics-based approach that is widely advocated for dyslexics is equally appropriate for other poor readers (Rice and Brooks, 2004), as are other rather broader intervention programmes (Hatcher and Hulme, 1999; Shaywitz, Fletcher, Holahan and Shaywitz, 1996), although it seems that an intervention that is successful for most is not necessarily effective for all (Hatcher *et al.*, 2006a). In addition, it does not appear that the prognosis for identified dyslexics involved in reading intervention programmes is significantly different from the prognosis for other poor readers (Brooks, Burton, Cole and Szczerbinski, 2007).

In calling for specialist teaching of reading in the UK, the strengths of the British Dyslexia Association's 'Dyslexia Friendly Schools' initiative have been cited as illustrative of good practice (Johnson, 2004; Riddick, 2006). The key areas targeted in this initiative are the development of specialist teaching skills (with an emphasis upon structured, multisensory teaching), close partnership with parents, a resource bank of appropriate 'dyslexia-friendly' materials and a whole school policy for supporting dyslexic children. However, the notion of being 'dyslexia-friendly' is something of a red herring. What these schools are actually seeking to offer are more appropriate educational experiences for all children who struggle with literacy. This is a laudable aim, of course, but one that, in practice, should not be restricted to a dyslexic subgroup.

QUESTION 3: TO WHAT EXTENT SHOULD THE DYSLEXIC DIAGNOSIS RESULT IN THE DIFFERENTIAL ALLOCATION OF RESOURCES OR OTHER FORMS OF SPECIAL ARRANGEMENT?

For many, a diagnosis of dyslexia is seen as a principal means of gaining additional help or support for identified children. It would be naïve to argue that such a label does not put pressure on local authorities, schools and teachers both through formal SEN procedures (SENCO-Forum, 2005) and by placing more subtle pressures upon teachers (Elliott, 2005b). This may explain why it has been suggested that powerful lobby groups have resulted in the over-representation of dyslexic children within the SEN system (Daniels and Porter, 2007).

A more helpful conceptualisation of dyslexia might be one that referred to those individuals who proved resistant to prolonged and systematic reading intervention. Thus, rather than representing some underlying condition, its operationalisation is based upon response to intervention (see Norwich, in press) and would only be applied when it became clear that detailed assessment and intervention were proving insufficient.

The value of such a process of identification is obvious. We would have a clear understanding that the individual would continue to struggle with literacy for the foreseeable future and would be a priority for access to alternative means of communication. Thus, with this scenario, a classification of dyslexia would involve priority access to specialist resources. Already there are a variety of electronic aids that read text aloud and that transform speech into text. The availability of technology that may permit, for instance, instantaneous translation between speech and writing is surely within our grasp.

While recognising this imperative, from the perspective of a parent desperate to secure help for their struggling child, we need to question whether operating in this way serves to prop up a system that most would argue is inefficient and inequitable. It is inefficient because it involves the use of resources for diagnosis and classification that might be better, and earlier, spent upon intervention. It is inequitable because it suggests that other poor readers, without the dyslexia diagnosis, will, in comparison, have less access to resources and support. Such a position is surely morally untenable?

DYSLEXIA AS A CATCH-ALL TERM OF CONVENIENCE

One way to avoid such complexities is to use the term 'dyslexia' in a general way to describe almost all forms of reading decoding and spelling difficulty. For example, the British Psychological Society (1999) provides the following definition:

> Dyslexia is evident when accurate and fluent word reading and/or spelling develops very incompletely or with great difficulty. This focuses on literacy learning at the 'word' level and implies that the problem is severe and persistent despite appropriate learning opportunities (p.64).

While such an all-embracing definition may be attractive both to those who are sceptical about the value of more finely tuned differentiations, and also to those with literacy difficulties who would welcome being given the label, its very broad inclusivity is problematic for educational purposes. Defining dyslexia in such a fashion means that the construct no longer helps us to differentiate between those with reading difficulties in any way that is helpful to those who are seeking specialist insights that can inform intervention.

This is not to deny varying (in)competence in literacy, as perhaps the British Psychological Society's working definition of dyslexia acknowledges. Nor do we wish to suggest that an appreciable number of people do not experience considerable difficulty acquiring skills in literacy. As already noted above there is a substantial body of evidence about the cognitive abilities implicated in literacy or the failure to acquire it (see Grigorenko, 2001; Snowling and Hulme, 2005 for overviews). There is also evidence (Carroll and Iles, 2006; Maughan *et al.*, 2003; Willcutt and Pennington, 2000) of affective states associated with the literacy difficulties that many may experience. However, we wish to argue that the distress that is experienced is at least in part a consequence of societal failure to accept responsibility for the (chaotic) creation of literacy and failure to redirect attention toward solutions not 'cures' (although see Norwich, in press, for discussion of the limitations of the social model of disability). The apparent 'fact' that dyslexia exists, is 'diagnosed' and is 'treated' ignores the artefactual qualities of literacy implicit in any proper consideration of the issues.

But despite the above considerations that, in all modesty, do not seem to us to be original or particularly remarkable, the notion of dyslexia seems to persist almost with a life of its own. Why?

One of the major risks in the continuing debate about dyslexia resides in the failure to acknowledge socio-cultural dimensions. In our view it is possible that dyslexia may be considered as at least partially a social construction. This is in fact relatively uncontentious. As Ferrari notes, 'Psychological development itself cannot be understood as a uniquely individual thing involving only an individual's brain and how that brain interacts with the world. Development depends crucially on the sociocultural context in which (normal and abnormal) children develop' (Ferrari, 2002, p. 756). More specifically Pennington and Olson hold that 'Dyslexia is an interesting example of the intersection between an evolved behaviour (language) and a cultural invention (literacy)' (Pennington and Olson, 2005, p. 453).

Within socio-cultural perspectives the question of distinguishing 'literate' from 'non-literate' becomes a different issue. Cook-Gumpertz (2006), for instance, in exploring the relationship between literacy, education and social power suggests that definitions of 'functional literacy' are hugely problematic. Moreover, attempts at definition persist in subsuming within concepts of illiteracy negative associations with limited ability or social value.

Cook-Gumpertz also provides an important reminder that universal literacy is historically a recently formulated aspiration. Literacy (in Western societies at least) was previously possessed only by a powerful elite; an elite that gained or maintained power through literacy. As Cook-Gumpertz indicates: 'The reversal of position, from seeing a dangerous radicalism inherent in acquiring literacy to the opposite view that the social and political danger was in having illiteracy in the population, began at this time [in the late 19th century]' (p. 32). Thus the social rationale for maintaining a construct of literate/non-literate may be seen as subject to change according to societal priorities and anxieties. Amongst the educational and social consequences of the current positioning of illiteracy as 'dangerous' can be found those with implications for schools. In the UK, for instance, schools are judged on their performance. School performance is largely determined by children's performance against measures that are either explicitly or implicitly dominated by competence in literacy. As Goody and Watt anticipated: 'the literate tradition sets up a basic division that cannot exist in non-literate society: the division between the various shades of literacy and illiteracy. This conflict, of course, is most dramatically focussed in the school, *the key institution of society*' (Goody and Watt, 1968, p. 59, emphasis added). Thus, in order to be seen as successful, schools may find it undesirable to have on roll children with inadequate levels of literacy. They may, therefore, wish to create (or perpetuate) a category of child whose literacy lies outside the school's realm of expertise. The dyslexic child thus not only has to deal with his or her individual perceptions of failure but also bear responsibility for the school's failure. As such s/he becomes disabled from full social and educational inclusion in lessons alongside her or his peers. The American typology of 'reading-disabled' also clearly identifies illiteracy as a disability. This process (of alienating an 'other') denies any acceptance of societal responsibility for causal agency. Here too we may, therefore, find both the social construction of dyslexia *per se* and its social construction as a disability (Brown, 1995; Corker and Shakespeare, 2002; Jones, 1996). We suggest that the key to the answer to the question 'why does the concept of dyslexia persist?' lies here. The concept addresses psycho-social needs. These needs are not founded on testable scientific concepts but on chimera that serve within power struggles and, in psycho-dynamic terms, the need for an 'other'.

Without those who are deemed 'unsuccessful', the successful lose power and position. Although public and political intent may be stated as a determination to 'eradicate illiteracy' (MacKay, 2007), there remains a paradoxical but self-serving need to maintain a group who remain 'illiterate'.

As discussed by Norwich (in press) the above considerations may prove challenging for inclusive interventions within educational domains—and, probably, elsewhere. We would suggest that the infinite regress that follows from attempts to define and isolate dyslexia does not lead directly to interventions that prevent failure occurring. There have been interventions that have shown significant power to overcome difficulties once failure has been identified but not labelled (e.g. Hatcher et al., 2006a, b). An alternative approach—of adjusting literacy learning task require-ments in order to minimise task demands and hence risks of failure—has also shown some interesting results. Findings from this latter perspective (Deavers, Solity and Kerfoot, 2000; Seabrook, Brown and Solity, 2005; Solity *et al.*, 2000) suggest that becoming literate can be constructed as a mediated and inclusive activity compared to the traditional and reactive model in which the learner must struggle to deal with an unmediated and less predictably structured task.

CONCLUSION

In March 2008, widespread media publicity was given to findings from a study of 1,341 children in Years 3 and 7 in 20 schools across three different local authorities (Xtraordinarypeople, 2008). The research, undertaken under the auspices of a dyslexia lobby group, claimed that 55% of students who failed to reach the level expected on national tests (SATS) were found to be at risk of dyslexia/Specific Learning Difficulties (SpLD) (although, in the report, SpLD is described as an umbrella term that also refers to dyspraxia, ADHD and dyscalculia). Unsurprisingly, media reports stressed the first of these two labels with a BBC News website headlining the claim 'Dyslexia link to school failures'.

It is salutary to examine how these figures were arrived at. 'At risk' children were seen as those who scored poorly in measures of reading or spelling (standard scores of 85 or lower) together with (a) problems of phonic decoding, phonological processing and/or verbal memory, or (b) 'other indicators of SpLD such as persistent problems of coordination, attention or visual-perceptual skills' (p. 5). In a telling example of the woolliness involved, the report adds that, 'The pupils' verbal and nonverbal ability was factored into this identification process although it should be noted that a conventional 'discrepancy approach' to identification of at-risk pupils was not explicitly applied' (ibid.). The report fails to explain how, or why, this 'factoring in' process was applied.

While the arbitrariness of the selection procedure would appear to be highly flawed (indeed, we wonder how many poor readers would not meet at least one of the above criteria), an equally misleading argument is put forward that the identified group of dyslexic children requires some form of specialised intervention. In actuality, the teaching approaches recommended are those applicable for all children who struggle to develop literacy skills. Interestingly, while much is made of the high proportion of children in the sample with working memory difficulties, there continues to be no specific educational intervention addressing this problem that is associated with literacy gains (Elliott et al., in prep.). Nevertheless, two months later, the Government announced a review of treatment programmes for dyslexic children with the Secretary of State for Schools, wanting this to provide, 'firm evidence as to the way forward, convince the sceptics dyslexia exists and tell us how best to get these children the help they deserve' (*The Guardian*, 7 May 2008).

While these recent moves are likely to have value in highlighting the need to identify and provide appropriate support to all children with literacy difficulties, we contend that the use of the term dyslexia in such announcements is scientifically flawed and is likely to confuse both teachers and parents. In actuality, it would appear that the true focus of the recent Government initiative is any child at risk of reading failure, not solely those in a given dyslexic subset. However, to take this broader notion and then simultaneously decry those who challenge the utility of the concept of dyslexia as a specific condition ('sceptics' do not deny that many children have great difficulties in acquiring appropriate reading skills and require additional help and support, of course) is to demonstrate a failure to grasp the key issues behind the debate.

We would urge that whilst the curiosity about the nature and causes of reading difficulties (or dyslexia) cannot and should not be curbed, as a scientific endeavour it is probably ultimately as tantalising and as forlorn as seeking the philosopher's stone. The concept is unbounded and unverifiable (Stanovich, 1994). Of course, if dyslexia is taken as a social construct, we can argue that a given set of cognitive or behavioural features (e.g. given levels of IQ and reading scores, a working memory deficit as indicated by a particular centile level), constitutes dyslexia and then *ergo*, it exists. We are, however, currently unable to progress beyond a very long list of possibilities in order to agree upon a requisite set of essential features that would enable reliable and valid identification to be made. Even if that were achieved (and we suggest it is not achievable) we would still be left with the thorny issue as to whether there would be any meaningful clinical or educational implications that follow from such an assessment. Again, this appears unlikely in the short term.

Thus, in summary, we view dyslexia as an arbitrarily and largely socially defined construct. There appears to be no clear-cut scientific basis for differential diagnosis of dyslexia *versus* poor reader *versus* reader. At various times and for various reasons it has been a social convenience to label some people as dyslexic but consequences of the labelling include stigma, disenfranchisement and inequitable use of resources (perhaps this is most disadvantageous for poor readers *not* diagnosed as dyslexic). The social, cognitive and behavioural phenomena associated with the construct remain important and fascinating issues. Proper treatment is, however, hindered by the false dichotomy between dyslexia and non-dyslexia. Let's not ask, 'Does dyslexia exist?' Let's instead concentrate upon ensuring that all children with literacy difficulties are served.

REFERENCES

Bradley, L. and Bryant, P. E. (1978) Difficulties in Auditory Organisation as a Possible Cause of Reading Backwardness, *Nature*, 271, pp. 746–747.

Bradley, L. and Bryant, P. E. (1983) Categorising Sounds and Learning to Read: A Causal Connection, *Nature*, 301, pp. 419–421.

British Psychological Society (1999) *Dyslexia, Literacy and Psychological Assessment*. Report by a Working Party of the Division of Educational and Child Psychology (Leicester, BPS).

Brooks, G., Burton, M., Cole, P. and Szczerbinski, M. (2007) *Effective Teaching and Learning Reading* (London, National Research and Development Centre for Adult Literacy and Numeracy).

Brown, P. (1995) Naming and Framing: The Social Construction of Diagnosis and Illness, *Journal of Health and Social Behaviour.*, 35, pp. 34–52.

Byrne, B. (2005) Theories of Learning to Read, in: M. J. Snowling and C. Hulme (eds) *The Science of Reading: A Handbook* (Oxford, Blackwell), pp. 104–119.

Caravolas, M (2005) The Nature and Causes of Dyslexia in Different Languages, in: M. J. Snowling and C. Hulme (eds) *The Science of Reading: A Handbook* (Oxford, Blackwell), pp. 336–355.

Carroll, J. M. and Iles, J. E. (2006) An Assessment of Anxiety Levels in Dyslexic Students in Higher Education, *British Journal of Educational Psychology*, 76.3, pp. 651–662.

Cassar, M., Treiman, R., Moats, L., Pollo, T. C. and Kessler, B. (2005) How Do the Spellings of Children with Dyslexia Compare with those of Nondyslexic Children?, *Reading and Writing*, 18.1, pp. 27–49.

Catts, H. W., Hogan, T. P. and Fey, M. E. (2003) Subgrouping Poor Readers on the Basis of Individual Differences in Reading-related Abilities, *Journal of Learning Disabilities*, 36, pp. 151–164.

Cernovsky, Z. Z. (1997) A Critical Look at Intelligence Research, in: D. Fox and I. Prilleltensky (eds) *Critical Psychology: An Introduction* (London, Sage).

Cook-Gumpertz, J. (2006) Literacy and Schooling, in: J. Cook-Gumpertz (ed.) *The Social Construction of Literacy*, 2nd edn. (Cambridge, Cambridge University Press), pp. 19–49.

Corker, M. and Shakespeare, T. (2002) *Disability/Postmodernity: Embodying Disability* (London, Continuum).

Crystal, D. (2004) *The Stories of English* (London, Allen Lane).

Daniels, H. and Porter, J. (2007) *Learning Needs and Difficulties among Children of Primary School Age: Definition, Identification, Provision and Issues (Primary Review Research Survey 5/2)* (Cambridge, University of Cambridge Faculty of Education).

Deavers, R., Solity, J. and Kerfoot, S. (2000) The Effect of Instruction of Early Word Reading Strategies, *Journal of Research in Reading*, 23.3, pp. 267–286.

Elliott, J. G. (2005a) The Dyslexia Debate Continues, *The Psychologist*, 18.12, pp. 728–729.

Elliott, J. G. (2005b) Dyslexia: Diagnoses, Debates and Diatribes, *Special Children*, 169, pp. 19–23.

Elliott, J. G., Gathercole, S., Alloway, T. and Kirkwood, H. (in prep) Addressing the Needs of Children with Working Memory Difficulties: From Assessment to Intervention.

Ferrari, M. (2002) Development is also Experienced by a Personal Self who is Shaped by Culture, *Behavioral and Brain Sciences*, 25, pp. 755–756.

Fischer, K. W., Bernstein, J. H. and Immordino-Yang, M.H (eds.) (2007) *Mind, Brain and Education in Reading Disorders* (Cambridge, Cambridge University Press).

Flanagan, D. P. and McGrew, K. S. (1997) A Cross-Battery Approach to Assessing and Interpreting Cognitive Abilities: Narrowing the Gap between Practice and Cognitive Science, in: D. P. Flanagan, J. L. Genshaft and P. L. Harrison (eds) *Contemporary Intellectual Assessment: Theories, Tests and Issues* (New York, Guilford Press).

Fletcher, J. M., Shaywitz, S. E., Shankweiler, D., Katz, L., Liberman, I., Stuebing, K., Francis, D. J., Fowler, A. and Shaywitz, B. A. (1994) Cognitive Profiles of Reading Disability: Comparisons of Discrepancy and Low Achievement Definitions, *Journal of Educational Psychology*, 86, pp. 6–23.

Frith, U. (1997) Brain, Mind and Behaviour in Dyslexia, in: C. Hulme and M. Snowling (eds) *Dyslexia, Biology, Cognition and Intervention* (London, Whurr).

Goody, J. and Watt, I. (1968) The Consequences of Literacy, in: J. Goody (ed.) *Literacy in Traditional Societies* (Cambridge, Cambridge University Press), pp. 27–58.

Grigorenko, E. L. (2001) Developmental Dyslexia: An Update on Genes, Brains and Environments, *Journal of Child Psychology and Psychiatry*, 42.1, pp. 91–125.

Grigorenko, E. L. and Naples, A. J. (in press) The Devil is in the Details: Decoding the Genetics of Reading, in P. McCardle and K. Pugh (eds). *Helping children learn to read: current issues and new directions in the integration of cognition, neurobiology and genetics of reading and dyslexia* (New York, NY: Psychological Press).

Hatcher, P. J. and Hulme, C. (1999) Phonemes, Rhymes and Intelligence as Predictors of Children's Responsiveness to Remedial Reading Instruction: Evidence from a Longitudinal Intervention Study, *Journal of Experimental Child Psychology*, 72, pp. 130–153.

Hatcher, P. J., Hulme, C., Miles, J. N. V., Carroll, J. M., Hatcher, J., Gibbs, S., Smith, G., Bowyer-Crane, C. and Snowling, M. (2006a) Efficacy of Small Group Reading Intervention for Beginning Readers with Reading-Delay: A Randomized Controlled Trial, *Journal of Child Psychology and Psychiatry*, 47.8, pp. 820–827.

Hatcher, P. J., Goetz, K., Snowling, M. J., Hulme, C., Gibbs, S. and Smith, G. (2006b) Evidence for the Effectiveness of the Early Literacy Support Programme, *British Journal of Educational Psychology*, 76, pp. 351–367.

Johnson, M. (2004) Dyslexia Friendly Schools—Policy And Practice, in: G. Reid and A. Fawcett (eds) *Dyslexia in Context* (London, Whurr Publishers), pp. 237–256.

Jones, S. R. (1996) Toward Inclusive Theory: Disability as Social Construction, *NASPA Journal*, 33.4, pp. 347–354.

Lopez, E. C. (1997) The Cognitive Assessment of Limited English Proficient and Bilingual Children, in: D. P. Flanagan, J. L. Genshaft and P. L. Harrison (eds) *Contemporary Intellectual Assessment: Theories, Tests and Issues* (New York, Guilford Press).

Lyon, G. R. (1995) Towards a Definition of Dyslexia, *Annals of Dyslexia*, 45, pp. 2–27.

MacKay, T. (2007) *Achieving the Vision: The Final Research Report of the West Dunbartonshire Literacy Initiative* (Dumbarton, West Dunbartonshire Council).

McNab, I. (1994) *Specific Learning Difficulties: How Severe is Severe? BAS Information Booklet* (Windsor, NFER-Nelson).

Mattingly, I. G. (1972) Reading, the Linguistic Process, and Linguistic Awareness, in: J. F. Kavanagh and I. G. Mattingly (eds) *Language by Ear and by Eye: The Relationship between Speech and Reading* (Cambridge, MA, MIT Press), pp. 3–147.

Maughan, B., Rowe, R., Loeber, R. and Stouthamer-Loeber, M. (2003) Reading Problems and Depressed Mood, *Journal of Abnormal Child Psychology*, 31.2, pp. 219–229.

Nicolson, R. I. and Fawcett, A. J. (2007) Procedural Learning Difficulties: Reuniting the Developmental Disorders?, *TRENDS in Neurosciences*, 30.4, pp. 135–141.

Norwich, B. (in press) Is Recognising Dyslexia Compatible with Inclusive Education?, in: G. Reid, A. Fawcett, F. Manis and L. Siegel (eds) *The Sage Handbook of Dyslexia* (London, Sage).

Paré-Blagoev, J. (2007) The Neural Correlates of Reading Disorder: Functional Magnetic Resonance Imaging, in: K. W. Fischer, J. H. Bernstein and M. H. Immordino-Yang (eds) *Mind, Brain and Education in Reading Disorders* (Cambridge, Cambridge University Press), pp. 148–167.

Pennington, B.F and Olson, R. K. (2005) Genetics of Dyslexia, in: M. J. Snowling and C. Hulme (eds) *The Science of Reading: A Handbook* (Oxford, Blackwell), pp. 296–315.

Popper, K. R. (1969) *Conjectures and Refutations: The Growth of Scientific Knowledge* (London, Routledge and Kegan Paul).

Presland, J. (1991) Explaining Away Dyslexia, *Educational Psychology in Practice*, 6.4, pp. 215–221.

Rice, M. and Brooks, G. (2004) *Developmental Dyslexia in Adults: A Research Review* (London, NRDC).

Riddick, B. (2006) Dyslexia Friendly Schools in the UK, *Topics in Language Disorders*, 26.2, pp. 142–154.

Rutter, M. (1978) Prevalence and Types of Dyslexia, in: A. L. Benton and D. Pearl (eds) *Dyslexia: An Appraisal of Current Knowledge* (New York, Oxford University Press).

Seymour, P. H. K (2005) Early Reading Development in European Orthographies, in: M. J. Snowling and C. Hulme (eds) *The Science of Reading: A Handbook* (Oxford, Blackwell), pp. 296–315.

Seabrook, R., Brown, G. D. A. and olity, J. E. (2005) Distributed and Massed Practice: From Laboratory to Classroom, *Applied Cognitive Psychology*, 19.1, pp. 107–122.

SENCO-Forum (2005) *British Journal of Special Education*, 32.2, p. 165.

Shaywitz, B. A., Fletcher, J. M., Holahan, J. M. and Haywitz, S. E. (1996) Discrepancy Compared to Low Achievement Definitions of Reading Disability: Results from the Connecticut Longitudinal Study, *Journal of Learning Disabilities*, 25, pp. 639–648.

Schulte-Körne, G., Ludwig, K. U., Sharkawy, J., Nöthen, M. M., Müller-Myhsok, B. and Hoffman, P. (2007) Genetics and Neuroscience in Dyslexia: Perspectives for Education and Remediation, *Mind, Brain and Education*, 1.4, pp. 162–172.

Snowling, M. J. (2008) Specific Disorders and Broader Phenotypes: The Case of Dyslexia, *The Quarterly Journal of Experimental Psychology*, 61.1, pp. 142–156.

Snowling, M. J. and Hulme, C. (eds) (2005) *The Science of Reading: A Handbook* (Oxford, Blackwell).

Solity, J., Deavers, R., Kerfoot, S., Crane, G. and Cannon, K. (2000) The Early Reading Research: The Impact of Instructional Psychology, *Educational Psychology in Practice*, 16.2, pp. 109–129.

Stanovich, K. E. (1991) Discrepancy Definitions of Reading Disability: Has Intelligence Led Us Astray?, *Reading Research Quarterly*, 26, pp. 7–29.

Stanovich, K. E. (1994) Annotation: Does Dyslexia Exist?, *Journal of Child Psychology and Psychiatry*, 2.4, pp. 579–595.

Stanovich, K. E. (1999) The Sociopsychometrics of Learning Disabilities, *Journal of Learning Disabilities*, 32.4, pp. 350–361.

Stanovich, K. E. and Stanovich, P. J. (1997) Further Thoughts on Aptitude/Achievement Discrepancy, *Educational Psychology in Practice*, 13.1, pp. 3–8.

Thomas, M. and Karmiloff-Smith, A. (2002) Are Developmental Disorders Like Cases of Adult Brain Damage? Implications from Connectionist Modelling., *Behavioral and Brain Sciences*, 25, pp. 727–788.

Torgesen, J. K. (2007) An Educational/Psychological Perspective on the Behaviours of Three Children with Reading Disabilities, in: K. W. Fischer, J. H. Bernstein and M. H. Immordino-Yang (eds) *Mind, Brain and Education in Reading Disorders* (Cambridge, Cambridge University Press), pp. 243–251.

Vellutino, F. R., Scanlon, D. M. and Lyon, G. R. (2000) Differentiating between Difficult-to-Remediate and Readily Remediated Poor Readers: More Evidence against the IQ Achievement Discrepancy Definition of Reading Disability, *Journal of Learning Disabilities*, 33, pp. 223–238.

Vellutino, F. R., Fletcher, J. M., Snowling, M. J. and Scanlon, D. (2004) Specific Reading Disability (Dyslexia): What Have We Learned in the Past Four Decades?, *Journal of Child Psychology and Psychiatry*, 45, pp. 2–40.

Willcutt, E. G. and Pennington, B. F. (2000) Psychiatric Comorbidity in Children and Adolescents with Reading Disability, *Journal of Child Psychology and Psychiatry*, 41.8, pp. 1039–1048.

Wolf, M. (2008) *Proust and the Squid: The Story of Science and the Reading Brain* (London, Icon).

Xtraordinarypeople (2008) http://www.xtraordinarypeople.com/downloads/No-To-Failure-Interim-Report-(March-2008).pdf Retrieved 17.3.08

2.5

Thoughts About the Autism Label: A Parental View

CHARLOTTE MOORE

How much difference does a label make? Is placing someone 'on the autistic spectrum' a way of ensuring they get the care they need, or does it confine them to a pigeon-hole where they will be viewed as a collection of symptoms, not as an individual?

In the 14 years since my oldest son George was diagnosed, the prevalence of autism has increased dramatically. In 1994 approximately one in a thousand children were labelled autistic. In 2008 the figure is closer to one in a hundred. Most health and education professionals believe that this apparently alarming rise is due to a widening of diagnostic boundaries and to increased awareness and understanding of autism—in other words, that a constant proportion of autists always existed but that in the past they were often unrecognised or differently labelled. In the 1950s and 1960s, for instance, 'childhood schizophrenia' was often used to describe children who would now be regarded as autistic. Autism and schizophrenia are now considered to be in no way connected. In the more able cases, the chances were that the child would be seen as wilful, badly brought up, emotionally disturbed or just plain eccentric, and no diagnosis would be given at all.

Whether recent enthusiasm for applying the autism label wholly accounts for the rise in incidence, or whether environmental factors are causing a 'real' increase, is a matter for debate and investigation. But certainly the concept of a 'spectrum' of autistic disorders, a concept pioneered in the 1980s by Lorna Wing, at least partly accounts for the autism boom. Before the concept of the spectrum, a child had to display the features of Kanner Syndrome ('classic' autism) to be called autistic. Children who were relatively affectionate, sociable and not entirely enslaved to rigid routines would be unlikely to be recognised as having autism.

The broadening of the terms of diagnosis leads one to wonder whether it is fair, helpful or accurate to apply the same term, ASD (Autistic Spectrum Disorder), both to an individual who might have no language, self-injurious behaviour and severe learning difficulty, and to someone who might have high intelligence, fluent speech and considerable self-awareness, but who differs from the 'norm' in terms of social interaction and modes of thinking. The most able people on the spectrum might argue that they do not have a 'disorder' at all. 'People with AS [Asperger

Syndrome] are like salt water fish who are forced to live in fresh water,' said one man, quoted by Simon Baron-Cohen; 'We're fine if you just put us into the right environment. When the person with AS and the environment *match*, the problems go away and we even thrive. When they don't match, we seem disabled' (Baron-Cohen, 2003, p. 180).

It is possible that we are in the process of developing a more tolerant and flexible society, and one in which the so-called 'geek' skills often possessed by high-functioning autists are valued. In such a society an ASD label would almost be a badge of honour. Already, Silicon Valley and major research institutions are heavily populated by people who, arguably, belong on the autistic spectrum. As the autistic author Temple Grandin puts it, NASA is 'the largest sheltered workshop in the world'. For such people, perhaps 'autistic spectrum condition' or 'syndrome' would serve better than 'disorder'.

However, when I look at my household and my two autistic sons, 'disorder' seems accurate in every respect. I'm happy to label my sons as autistic. Even though they are very different from one another, both manifest Lorna Wing's 'triad of impairments' (of imagination, communication and social interaction), which are still the main criteria for diagnosis. George's speech is fairly fluent and almost grammatically correct, but it is over-elaborate and lacks the spontaneity and expressiveness of what is now known as neurotypical communication. Sam's speech is much more limited—he's really only happy with nouns, and he doesn't chat. Both manifest variants of impaired communication. Sam is generally aloof, George is socially 'active but odd'—again, both correspond to the autistic criteria.

I am convinced, then, of the accuracy of their diagnoses. I am also convinced that neither has sufficient self-awareness to care about being 'labelled'. I don't think Sam compares himself to other people at all. I have no evidence that he knows he is younger than George, or older than his little brother Jake. He doesn't even seem certain whether he's male or female. We openly use the word 'autistic' at home, but neither of them react to it. I don't try to sit the boys down and explain autism—they don't respond well to that kind of conversational approach. But I have never hidden it from them, and nor have their teachers. For the purposes of this chapter, I asked George, 'What does autistic mean?'

> 'I'm not sure,' he replied. This is his answer to most questions.
> I persisted. 'Who do you know who is autistic?'
> 'I want a clue!' said George, who always speaks in exclamation marks.
> 'Which of your brothers is autistic?' I asked. (George hates talking about himself.) 'Is it Sam or is it Jake?'
> 'I know! It's Jake!' cried George. Well, no.

Having my boys 'labelled' has many practical advantages. They both have statements of special educational need, with detailed recommendations. When mainstream school proved too much for them, their labels meant that I had no difficulty in placing them in special ASD facilities. We have a disabled parking badge. I receive Direct Payments from Social Services, to help with out-of-school care. Both receive Disability Living Allowance, which I have no qualms about claiming, since looking after my sons as I do and will continue to do for the foreseeable future reduces my earning power by at least half. When I first claimed DLA, years ago, I was told: 'just put "autism" and "incontinence" on the form and you'll get the higher rate.'

None of these sources of help would have been available to me if the boys had not been formally diagnosed. The label also helps me to explain their behaviour to other people—and to myself. When George was diagnosed, my first feeling was relief that it wasn't my fault that my 4-year-old was still in nappies. Now that autism has struggled clear of all those dreadful 1950s and 1960s stigmas associated with 'refrigerator' mothering and has established itself as a *bona fide* genetic condition, no parent needs to feel guilt for having produced such a child. We now know that we do not create, and could not have prevented, our child's autism. Social attitudes towards disability have changed for the better over the last couple of decades in Britain; the days when it was thought shameful to take a disabled child out in public are over. I've never dressed George and Sam in those T-shirts that say, in effect, 'I'm autistic and proud of it', but the very existence of such garments is a measure of how much the climate has changed.

When George was first diagnosed, in January 1994, the expression 'autistic spectrum disorder' was not yet in common use. There was autism, and there was Asperger Syndrome. I was familiar with 'autism', though I had a lot of misconceptions about it, associating it mainly with the 'idiot savant' Rainman stereotype, which didn't fit George. Asperger Syndrome was only just becoming known. Leo Kanner and Hans Asperger both published the results of their ground-breaking research in 1943, but by historical accident Kanner's paper (which was published in English) became widely read, especially in the USA, whereas Asperger's work was only translated from the German in the 1980s. Thus the autism Kanner described (withdrawn, aloof, lower-functioning) came to be perceived as 'classic' autism, while the syndrome to which Asperger gave his name (superior verbal skills, clumsiness, socially eccentric rather than withdrawn) continued to escape general notice until quite recently.

Almost by chance, I came across Asperger Syndrome only a week before George was diagnosed, in an article in the *New Yorker* about Temple Grandin. In those days Asperger Syndrome was seen, rather crudely, as 'mild autism'. (I've come to believe that there's nothing mild about it; the suffering of 'Aspies' seems to me often greater than that of people with 'severe' autism, because they are more painfully aware of their difficulties and differences, and because they are less well tolerated by neurotypicals who feel frustrated that someone with clear speech and signs of good intelligence should behave so bizarrely.) At 4 years old George did, indeed, seem only mildly autistic. He had plenty of speech, though it was very echolalic. He had a prodigious memory for stories, songs and poems; this made him seem more academically able than he really was. Although shy and socially clueless, he showed interest in other people and was affectionate. The doctor said he had Asperger Syndrome, and I think I latched too strongly onto the idea that this was 'mild'. I left the consulting room under the impression that the worst we could have to deal with were some rather charming eccentricities. 'He'll find easy things hard and hard things easy'—that's a phrase that lingers from the diagnostic session. Asperger Syndrome, with its quaint 'little professor' connotations, seemed much more applicable than plain autism. 'Your child has a profound, incurable, lifelong social and cognitive disability'— this was not said to me. Even if it had been, looking at my beautiful, smiley 4-year-old who climbed into my bed and insisted I read him stories, I would not have believed it.

As time went on George's progress plateaued or even went into reverse. His anxieties increased and his behaviour deteriorated. The 'Asperger's' label caused him to be placed in a mainstream school—inappropriately, as I now believe. Despite the school's best efforts, George found the atmosphere overstimulating and overwhelming; and he retreated into rigid rituals and 'stimming' (self-stimulatory behaviour, such as flapping bits of paper or twiddling his fingers in front of his eyes). I do not blame the doctor who diagnosed him for over-estimating his abilities, or rather, for under-estimating his fragility. She made her assessment according to the information available to her, and at the time everyone who dealt with George, myself included, focused on his marked abilities in some— unconnected—areas. We failed to understand how extreme his impairments were in other areas. In George's seventh year, 'Asperger's' no longer seemed correct, and George became simply 'autistic'.

My second son, Sam, is 22 months younger than George. As a baby and toddler he seemed as different from his brother as could be imagined— placid, sturdy, even a little slow, whereas George had been so hyper-alert and highly strung that it had been suggested he might fall into the 'gifted child' category. George had passed most of his milestones very early. He walked alone at 9 months, spoke in sentences by 14 months, sang tunefully by 18 months. Sam seemed more of a plodder. However, for the first 2 years he showed no marked signs of delay. With hindsight I can see that his placidity verged on unresponsiveness, that his calm acceptance of any change of carers, his absence of 'separation anxiety', were early symptoms of autism. But the vast differences between him and George led us to misinterpret his behaviour.

Concerns about Sam grew during his third year. His garbled speech led to an investigation for hearing loss. (His hearing was found to be perfect.) His lack of age-appropriate play was blamed on having the eccentric George as a role model. His obsession with creating pretend washing machines wherever he went was interpreted as the sign of an active imagination. It was when an educational psychologist, noting Sam's gaze-avoidance, said 'You can't copy something as fundamental as eye contact,' that the penny finally dropped. I had come to accept one set of behaviours—George's—as characteristic of autism. Now, I had to broaden my definitions and recognise that Sam's unique set of problems and peculiarities were a different manifestation of the same condition.

The educational psychologist was a perceptive and helpful woman, but when she said, 'We don't need to label Sam. We could just put him down as having language delay,' I disagreed. George's 'label' had proved useful. He only got by at school at all because of the loving attention of Ruby, his designated teaching assistant. Without a label, George would have sunk. I knew that if Sam's condition was formally identified, then he too had a better chance of receiving practical support, and winning sympathy instead of censure.

When Sam was four and a half, he was placed 'on the autistic spectrum'; at the time the phrase was becoming more widely used. Sam had no special gifts, sleight of hand and low cunning excepted, and his speech was limited and incoherent, so there was never any talk of Asperger's. I now had two boys with the same diagnosis who were the opposite of each other in almost every way. It was as if they had looked at the entire range of possible autistic symptoms and agreed to divide them equally between them, George taking high anxiety, echolalia, an extraordinary rote memory, hypersensitive hearing, fixations on certain colours, poor motor skills and complete cluelessness about the correct use of the toilet, while Sam went for delayed speech, a high pain threshold, obsessions with certain machines and buildings, repetitive private play rituals, fearless climbing (on the roof), destructiveness (pulling the roof tiles out and smashing them), self-harming and a refusal to let anyone touch his head. Insomnia, faddy eating and an addiction to Thomas the Tank Engine they agreed to share.

Why do I accept that the same diagnosis is right for two such different boys? Because I believe that their behaviours are their own unique version of the same core problems. For instance, sensory hypersensitivities are common, almost universal in autism, but in George's case his hearing is most affected while Sam is more touch-averse. My third son, Jake, is (as we now say) neurotypical. He's sporty, bright but not studious, highly social, dislikes being on his own. Another child in his class might be dreamy, artistic, indifferent to ball games and reluctant to join in the group activities that Jake loves. Both would be easily recognisable as neurotypical, despite their differences, because both share that innate understanding of the rules of 'normal' social behaviour, the instinct that is absent in an autistic person. Autists are just as intensely individual as anyone else; labelled or not, every person should be treated first and foremost as a unique individual.

It is a measure of the extent of their handicap that George and Sam have no interest in or understanding of their autism, but it makes life easier for me. I have not had to deal with an aware, able child who resents the 'label' and yet still needs the help and support it might provide. There are signs that as autism becomes more widely known, the word is degenerating into a term of playground-style abuse. 'Mongol', 'spastic', 'moron' and 'cretin' all started as non-pejorative descriptive terms. If 'autism' goes down the same route, an alternative will have to be found. A set of initials, such as ASD, or a phrase rather than a single word, may be more resistant to this kind of misappropriation. 'You're such a spastic' has more life in it as an insult than 'you're so like someone who has got cerebral palsy'.

Odd as it may seem, I favour the term 'handicapped' for my sons. I think autism is exactly that—a handicap, a difference that disadvantages you in playing the game of life. The job of the educator or therapist is, of course, to work out strategies whereby the handicaps of autism can be reduced or overcome. I don't like 'disabled', though I use it for convenience; it suggests that a once-able person has suffered some assault that has reduced their powers. I don't like 'retarded', which used to be widely used in describing autists; I dislike it not just because it, too, has become a term of abuse, but because it gives the impression that to be autistic is to develop slowly but with the possibility of one day 'catching up'. In fact, autism is about developing very, very differently, and in fits and starts.

I don't like to read about autism as a 'disease'; this implies that it is catchable and curable, instead of innate. Autistic people are not ill, physically or mentally. They often experience physical peculiarities, such as George's acute hearing, but these can be an advantage as well as a discomfort. Similarly, I don't like to hear the rise in prevalence described as an 'autism epidemic'. I don't like to read of someone 'suffering' from autism. I am not saying suffering isn't involved, but again, the word makes it sound as if autism is something imposed on a potentially 'normal' person. Autistic is what my sons are. To describe them, as 'suffering' from autism is not so different from describing me as 'suffering' from being female.

The way a culture defines or classifies a disability reveals a lot about the prevailing values of that culture. I'm glad I don't live in South Korea, where autism is often described as Reactive Attachment Disorder, a mental illness linked to child neglect. I'm glad I don't live in poor, rural South Africa, where I might be called upon to ask a witch doctor to expel the evil from my children. I'm glad I live in a society that considers the subject of defining autism an important and sensitive business. One may smile at the euphemistic approach to disability behind the phrase 'differently abled', but actually that fits autism rather well. I feel lucky that my sons live in a place and at a time when such a concept can come into being.

REFERENCE

Baron-Cohen, S. (2003) *The Essential Difference: Men, Women and the Extreme Male Brain* (London, Penguin).

2.6
Commentary

RUTH CIGMAN AND ANDREW DAVIS

There is a school of thought that rejects all talk of differences between learners, except insofar as everyone is seen as different from every other. There are no categories or 'nameable' differences: no autistic or dyslexic children, or children with ADHD. There are only Anil and Joe and Rohan and Natalie, each of whom has 'unique' characteristics and needs, and makes 'unique' demands on his or her teachers. Schools which conceptualise differences in this way use the overarching concept of 'diversity', instead of what they see as the discriminatory concept of 'difference'. Labels like 'autistic' and so on, which apply to a minority perceived as abnormal, are said to exemplify what is known as 'deficit thinking', which is demeaning and disrespectful.

This is the philosophy of full inclusion, which seeks the gradual closure of special schools that provide for some learner categories but not for others. The special school debate has been heated over the last few years, and anyone following it in the media will be aware of the intensity of feeling expressed by parents who feel denied a special school education for their children, on the one hand, and a mainstream school education, on the other. What concern us here are the underlying conceptual and ethical/political issues, and these are concisely expressed in what has become known as the dilemma of difference:

> We either treat all children as essentially the same, which means treating them as fairly as possible but with the risk of neglecting individual differences. Or we treat them differently, with the consequence that some are better off than they would otherwise have been, but there is a risk of being unfair by devoting more resources or expertise to some than others (Cigman, 2007).

The denial of difference (except as a universal condition) is motivated by a desire for justice, but is attended by the 'risk of neglecting individual differences'. This can bring about another kind of injustice. When Charlotte Moore's first son was diagnosed with autism, she was glad to be offered mainstream provision, seeing this as evidence that her son was not so 'different' after all. Gradually she discovered that the mainstream could not provide what her son needed—it was too noisy, too crowded, and imported assumptions about children which were grossly inapplicable to her son. She came to see the policy of full inclusion as wrong: 'wrong as in misguided, and in some cases wrong as in immoral' (Moore, 2005, p. 170). In her chapter in this volume, she expresses relief that she lives in a society that 'considers the subject of defining autism an important and sensitive business'.

The chapters in this section are devoted to this business, and they indicate that the issue is not to be ducked. In one sense the dilemma of difference is resolved by treating all children as the 'same', i.e. alike in their diversity. In another it is not resolved at all, as the anguish of many parents who are denied special provision indicates. At the very least, differences need to be taken seriously and discussed sensitively, and Moore suggests that—despite the prominence of the full inclusion movement—this happens in our society. She may be lucky, in a way, that the learner category she has to deal with is widely (though not universally) seen as having an organic basis. More problematic, perhaps, are dyslexia and ADHD, where the 'interactive' issues have a different aspect. A problem with dyslexia is the shame attached to having a child who is a 'poor reader', and the desire on the part of many parents to distinguish their so-called dyslexic children from those who are 'unintelligent'. In this sense, dyslexia is anything but a deficit label; on the contrary, it is sought in order to avoid 'poor reader', which is such a label. If, as Elliott and Gibbs argue, the distinction between 'dyslexia' and 'poor reader' is scientifically unjustified, one may agree that shame is an inadequate basis for a learner category. The issues with ADHD are different again. This category raises questions about physical harm (the ADHD label gains access to powerful medication), as well as issues of oppression and crowd control.

What seems clear is that as a society we need to reflect carefully and communally on our learner categories. The inclusionist who sees children as 'the same' goes too far in the view of this editor, but is right to suggest that passionate attachment to a learner category does not in itself justify its use in our educational system. We need to think about the variety of purposes for which categories are used, and consider them individually and, as Moore says, sensitively. This section demonstrates some ways of doing this.

REFERENCES

Cigman, R. (2007) *Included or Excluded? The Challenge of the Mainstream for Some SEN Children* (Oxford, Routledge).

Moore, C. (2005) *George and Sam* (London, Penguin).

3
ICT AND LEARNING

3.1
Introduction

RUTH CIGMAN AND ANDREW DAVIS

Large claims have been made in recent years about ICT's potential to 'transform' learning, and even to make us revise our basic conceptions of knowledge (e.g. Lankshear, Peters and Knobel, 2000). It appears that less than transparent value judgments about education motivate some of its proponents. We may well sympathise with such judgments but, as always, they need to be made explicit and to be examined on their own merits.

However, at least some of those who think that ICTs are harbingers of fundamental change make highly plausible *empirical* claims about how these new technologies are *actually* shaping the very way in which learning is conceptualised. We should be aware of these transformative processes, since awareness would seem to be at least a necessary condition for keeping them under critical review.

One set of value judgments that sometimes underpin radical claims for ICT's role puts education firmly in the service of industrial economies. It is then argued that employment is being transformed by digital technologies, and that this in turn either actually impacts, or *ought* to impact, in ways to be specified, on curriculum content and style of delivery.

By way of contrast, if we see education as developing citizens for a pluralist liberal democracy, we are also likely to think that the rapid development of ICT ought to transform the liberal curriculum. On this perspective, adults now have to make informed decisions about how to live and about their fundamental value commitments in a world increasingly saturated with digital technologies. An education designed to support flourishing citizenships in such an environment would have to differ in certain respects from liberal education in the 19th century, for instance. Yet it is not immediately obvious that the relevant changes in education would closely resemble those related to the preparation of future employees of a technology-rich world. In theory, at least, a liberal education could offer its participants the possibility of a critical detachment from the advance of technology, this even leading to adult opposition where the associated values and conceptions of knowledge are seen as defective.

The expertise of the two contributors to this section covers both policy issues and empirical research on the one hand, and philosophical concerns on the other.

The explicit focus of Diana Laurillard's chapter is learning in higher education, and the impact of technology on how learning ought to be conceived. She offers a helpful sketch of developments in the 10 years since the National Committee of Inquiry into Higher Education (the Dearing Report). Given economic pressures and other constraints on staffing in higher education, it can be argued that we need to rethink our use of teaching resources. Digital technologies may well be able to help, she urges, despite the fact that they also challenge current ideas about teaching and learning.

She characterises the written word as static and non-interactive, while the computer is an 'interactive medium', offering 'many new ways of representing knowledge'. Technology has the potential to motivate much more powerfully than traditional transmission modes of teaching. She takes from John Dewey onwards the idea that learning is active and that learners are not passive recipients. Note that 'taking' ideas from Dewey arguably involves a commitment to a particular set of values. It looks as though she feels, for instance, that learners *ought not* to be passive recipients. Jan Derry picks up this theme when she observes that such approaches are related to a reaction against the idea that knowledge ought to come from teachers as 'authorities', and also against the thought that learning is the passive acquisition of representations of an objective reality, a thought linked to the correspondence theory of truth. On Derry's view, protagonists of the strong role of digital technologies in education often subscribe to the popular constructivist view of learning, a view whose epistemological credentials are not always clear and robust.

Laurillard feels that technology might be able to simulate small group interactive teaching. On her view, such teaching will no longer be possible in traditional guise, if HE is to reach out to a greater proportion of the population. Policy makers in the UK are pushing this possibility quite hard. Derry might take some convincing that such digital simulation of interactive teaching could be effective—that such an environment could fully support students operating 'within the space of reasons'.

Laurillard argues that technology changes our representations of knowledge. In the light of this we need, on her view, to investigate the very nature of learning and teaching. We ought to become explicit about our knowledge 'of what it takes to learn' so that we can deploy digital technologies appropriately in the cause of learning. The technology also affords rich opportunities to share understanding of these issues as it develops. Laurillard ends on an optimistic note. In the light of appropriate technological applications we might achieve a system 'capable of learning how to teach' (this volume, p. 167).

At one point in her discussion she makes a crucial move. 'Suppose', she says, 'we agree we know what it takes to learn.' She is optimistic that a consensus could be reached. On the view of this editor, such a consensus would have to depend in turn on agreement about *what counts as learning,* or, to be even more explicit, *what counts as worthwhile learning.* We reach a point in any review of the potential of digital technologies which mirrors the situation when we scrutinise the enhancement agenda (see Section 4) and the offerings of neuroscience. This is the point where empirical research comes to a halt, and instead we are in the area of *normative debate.* Evidently we need to be apprised of all the relevant facts when engaging in such a debate, but the issues now relate to what is important for human flourishing, the point of education and the kind of learning that enhances (in some senses to be explained and defended) human existence. (Nothing in Laurillard's chapter implies that she would deny any of this).

Moreover the philosophical scrutiny now required must transcend the normative. When examining what counts as learning, epistemological issues are provoked, together with challenges that can properly be explored by drawing on the philosophy of mind. The situation here arguably mirrors that rehearsed in the section on brain-based learning. There, as here, we are confronted with basic questions about the authority with which a particular perspective might pronounce on the nature of learning, the extent to which a *revisionary* verdict could be justified, and the character of that justification.

Derry is keenly aware that approaches to how technology might be used to support and enhance education make assumptions about both the nature of mind and the fundamental character of learning. One role for philosophy is to examine these presuppositions, having rendered them explicit. There have been high expectations of digital technology in respect of its educational applications. Derry notes that up to now these have not been fulfilled. She feels that in the rush towards technological 'progress' some key historical and social aspects of mind have been overlooked. Moreover, while ICT is very effective in facilitating access to 'information', the link between such a process and the growth of *knowledge* cannot be taken for granted. She devotes significant space to exploring the ideas about mind and world being developed by philosophers such as John McDowell and Robert Brandom, and applies these to the issues raised by the explosion of digital technologies in education. She draws on Nicolas Balacheff to urge that the characteristics of knowledge vary across subjects, disciplines or domains and that technological 'solutions' in education cannot be domain independent. Knowledge itself must be 'brought back in'.

REFERENCES

Lankshear, C., Peters, M. and Knobel, M. (2000) Information, Knowledge and Learning: Some Issues Facing Epistemology and Education in a Digital Age, *Journal of Philosophy of Education,* 34.1, pp. 17–39.

3.2

Technology-Enhanced Learning: A Question of Knowledge

JAN DERRY

Philosophy is set at a distance from concrete questions such as how technologies can be used to enhance learning. Nevertheless there is a significant if not immediate contribution that philosophy can make to technology-enhanced learning. It is widely recognised, for example, that presuppositions involving models of mind and theories of learning underpin attempts to integrate technologies into processes of learning. These presuppositions are also significant in questions concerning the enhancement of learning as they have implications for how technology is designed and applied. It is by making these presuppositions explicit that philosophy can work as an under-labourer, conceptualising attempts to utilise the power of technologies for learning. However, there is a further and more significant aspect to the work that philosophy can do, as it happens that there is a coincidence of pedagogic and philosophic concerns centred on the unique characteristics of the human mind. We owe our distinctive cognitive powers to cumulative cultural evolution (Tomasello, 2000; Bakhurst, 2005), and thus philosophical investigations into the nature of mind and of knowing impinge directly on the question of the development of mind. This question is complicated since the environment in which the human mind develops has a history itself; and this history owes its form to the activities of human beings, which are in turn conditioned by the development of mind. In the light of this one can speak of human beings as both having and inhabiting a *second nature*. This, it is argued here, has implications for epistemology and through epistemology for learning. It is this connection between philosophy and education, and specifically the application of technologies to education, that is traced here.

1

The use of digital technologies in education has so far not fulfilled expectations. Why is this so? Is it the intransigence of teachers? The constraints of schools? Or problems with the hardware and software? These factors are all too often blamed for the failure, and although possibly all bear some responsibility what will be considered here are other issues of an epistemological nature that require philosophical analysis. 'Technology-enhanced learning' (TEL) is a sweeping phrase encompassing an eclectic range of adaptations and usage, and therefore any philosophical points brought to bear run the risk of vagueness. In what follows I shall set up a necessarily simplified characterisation but one that captures many of the assumptions informing practice, even though it may appear at first sight far removed from the issues involved.

In addition to the catch-all nature of the phrase 'technology-enhanced learning', the policy initiatives bringing technologies into education, particularly into mainstream schooling, are in a state of flux. The history of these initiatives shows a change in the focus of attention from an early emphasis on the technology itself towards a greater concern with the details of learning and the learner. In Europe this is illustrated by the recent adoption of the expression 'technology-enhanced learning' in place of 'information technologies'—or, in the case of the UK, 'information communication technologies'. Setting aside the natural emphasis on technologies as such, serious questions can be raised about the way and form in which the human element involved has been recognised. The importance of the primacy of the human element turns out to be much broader than at first appears, for what it involves is nothing less that a recognition of the distinctive quality of human contact with the world. One particularly significant aspect of the ongoing philosophical debate on this subject is the extent to which this human contact with the world is social.

This limited attention given to the role of teachers, in comparison to the volume of research placing emphasis on the technology itself, is understandable. In a period where technology is viewed as educationally indispensable, the authority of the teacher has been questioned, and learners are believed to 'create knowledge'. Against this background it is unsurprising that both policy and research agendas have grown around the issue of how technologies can advance learning, while problems of pedagogy and the acquisition of knowledge, which technologies are intended to resolve, have been neglected. Given the widespread and varied reference to 'pedagogy' in research on technology-enhanced learning, it may appear inappropriate to suggest the issue is neglected. But it is argued here that the pedagogical aspect central to any use of new technologies in education requires much closer examination than it is receiving, and that the unexamined pedagogic presuppositions informing use require spelling out.

So far the project to integrate technologies into education does not have a common research programme. The drive to integrate technologies into education carried all before it. In the rush to achieve results too much has been taken for granted about the way in which students learn. For instance, questions such as that of the social nature of mind have received little attention; and this is so because the pressure to speed up the utilisation of digital technologies has dictated the course of events, even though the human side of the equation is as crucial as the technical specification of technologies—arguably it is far more crucial.

The question of teacher autonomy is another matter requiring careful consideration in this context. Autonomy here means more than the freedom of teachers to exercise their judgment over curricula and pedagogic approaches since it extends to questions about the conditions necessary for the development of teachers as educators in the first place. In practice computers have been introduced into classrooms without taking such matters into account. In a recent Department for Education and Skills policy document, *Harnessing Technology*, government policy appears to give priority to the learners: 'we aim to put learners, young people—and their parents—in the driving seat, shaping the opportunities open to all learners to fit around their needs and preferences' (Department for Education and Skills, 2005); but, although referred to, the issues concerning pedagogy and knowledge are at no point spelt out. Expressions like 'Technology can be mobile. That means e-learning can come to the learner' reveal unexamined suppositions that are still being made. They run as follows: There is such a thing as e-learning that exists in its own right. It can be brought to learners, just as water can be brought down irrigation channels to parched fields. Given the rhetoric that is bound to appear in a widely distributed policy document, it is no surprise that technology is presented as a panacea. The value of greater access to information is not a matter of dispute, but information and knowledge are not the same thing, and the availability of the one does not itself foster the growth of the other. Education involves far more than the acquisition of information and the ability to follow procedures. It also includes the development of capacities of judgment—that is, the capacity not merely to respond passively to events but to make decisions actively in different contexts; and it is here that the distinctive nature of our contact with the world—the distinction between human knowing and mechanical responsiveness—is significant.

2

Philosophy, in particular, has something to offer when questions about knowledge and knowing are central. The discussion of embodied, distributed and situated cognition, and the rise of the learning sciences that have been precipitated in part by the experience of introducing technologies into education, have posed questions about the nature of mind. What is argued in this chapter is that the ideas about mind and world that have been developed by John McDowell and Robert Brandom are relevant to education even though they have not been applied by them in this area. There are three reasons for claiming their relevance: first, that their concern with the nature of knowledge has critical implications for pedagogy; second, that they offer a thorough critique of the conception of experience that by default informs much of the technological work in the area; and third, that they open questions often foreclosed about the distinctive nature of human thought.

It has been noted that 'computers have generally failed teachers and students' and that 'computers only benefit learning when they take into account what we know about how children learn, and when they are designed to be closely integrated with teacher and student interactions in the classroom' (Sawyer, 2006, p. xii). This goes some way towards accounting for the disappointing results of investing in computers in schools (Cuban, 2001). For instance, when some years ago Seymour Papert advocated the replacement of conventional classrooms with computers, it was not his intention to give the teacher a significant role (Papert, 1980). The contrast between 'instructionism' and 'constructionism' has been at the heart of the attempts to use technologies to lever traditional classrooms with poor practices into more active and inclusive learning environments. Difficulties arise from the fact that instructionism is contrasted unfavourably with the more 'active' practices integral to constructivist approaches. For instructionism is characterised in terms of its tendency 'to overvalue abstract reasoning', understood in terms of the isolation of 'pure essential factors from the details of concrete reality' and then attempting to pass these on (Papert, 1993). However, the target here is really the poor teaching practices that treat knowledge as though it were simply a collection of facts and procedures to be conveyed ready-made. But, as these ideas have become generalised beyond specific examples, the idea of knowledge as authority has also been included in the target.

The growth of the Internet has come at a time when the status of knowledge and the integrity of knowledge domains are being called into question. In place of authoritative sources of knowledge, the internet, by providing large quantities of information in a non-authoritative fashion, appears to offer learners the possibility of constructing their own meanings based on their own interests and experiences. Much of the discourse on technologies in education emphasises interactivity, the possibilities for scaffolding learning and the constructive potential for learners to 'make their own meaning'. However, in the case of interactivity, for example, its human side is often not made explicit. What is downplayed is the nature of knowledge and the specific character of knowledge domains. In part the downplaying is a result of the general disenchantment with truth and knowledge as revelation. This idea of knowledge as something to be revealed is forcefully criticised by Richard Rorty (1981) in *Philosophy and the Mirror of Nature*, where he targets the correspondence view of truth, understood in terms of representations mapped on to objects. The wide disenchantment with such a conception of truth and the apparent disintegration of institutional structures that played a pivotal role in the development of knowledge coincided with the growth of a more popular belief that knowledge was a matter of personal construction. But this occurred without a proper regard to the domain within which this construction takes place. As a result, precise questions about knowledge have been pushed to the background, and attention has shifted to the contribution of computers—such as the possibilities they offer for interactivity, scaffolding and dialogue. Even though recent work has concentrated on more detailed questions of learning and pedagogy, the question of knowledge has been neglected. Consequently the weight being attached to the significance of the technology has not been adequately interrogated.

The focus on the learner, without adequate consideration of the nature of the knowledge domain, relies in part on the variety of epistemological assumptions underpinning the popularised idea of learners as constructors. In what Jerome Bruner called 'a policy document in our times' (Bruner, 1996, p. 33), Robert Reich captures the idea of learners as constructors of meaning when he speaks of the need for education to produce 'symbolic analysts', namely learners active in the conceptualisation of the knowledge. His claim in part rests on the idea that we are now part of the 'knowledge age' where 'data . . . will be available . . . at the touch of a computer key' (Reich, 1992, p. 229). Reich uses the contemporary discourse closely associated with new technologies to make a case for the importance of recognising that the specific powers of transformation and synthesis possessed by the 'symbolic analyst' are critical. The counterpart to this idea of the analyst (here a version of constructivism in Reich's thought become apparent) is the concept of the world as devoid of meaning, bearing no particular truth apart from that arising from those constructive interventions imposed on it by humans. Reich writes: 'Consider first the capacity for abstraction. The real world is nothing but a vast jumble of noises, shapes, colours, smells and textures— essentially meaningless until the human mind imposes some order on them' (ibid.). When he writes this, he is giving expression to a dualist default position, common in contemporary thinking, including thinking about technologies in education.

It is precisely this dualism that McDowell takes to task. Once this view of the world is adopted responsibility for meaning is dependent entirely on human construction. The argument here is that this epistemological view goes along with neglect of the fact that at every point in time there is always a body or domain of knowledge about the world already in existence even if it is rejected by later generations as inadequate. Once the existence of these domains of knowledge, embodied in social practices and language, is recognised, questions concerning induction into them come to the fore. By implication, if they are not recognised, these questions have no grounds and thus appear pointless. At stake here is the account of experience that is presupposed.

Two world views can be counterposed at this point. One can be called Humean, a view that envisions a world of determining individuals acting on their desires and that prefigures the modern image of learners as consumers acquiring knowledge from the internet in much the same way as they might shoes from an online shoe store. (Katz *et al.*, 1999, p. 54). The other might be termed 'Aristotelian'. It emphasises virtues of acquiring knowledge and dispositions by pursuing a discipline, where knowledge is acquired by discipline. On this view, the process of acquiring knowledge is as valuable as the knowledge by which it is acquired, as it instils in the learner a way of being in the world and acquiring what Aristotle means by virtue.

An alternative to the epistemological conception underlying the former position, which was originally inspired by Locke and then Hume, is McDowell's account of experience, which has roots in Aristotle, Hegel and Wittgenstein. This account starts by exorcising the anxieties of contemporary philosophy about how thought can be in touch with the world at all. Although it returns us to the position that we take for granted as it unfolds—that is to say, insisting that our thought is in contact with the world from the start, the route it takes to reach this position has fundamental importance for the educationalist, namely that we are not born human but become human in the course of maturity, not by virtue of some realisation of biologically given capacities but socially and culturally by induction into language and tradition (*Bildung*). This concept of human development, where the relation between cognition and the world is different from that envisaged in traditional empiricism, has consequences—in particular, that our contact with the world and thereby that growth in our knowledge can only take place as a moment in a more generalised process of development. This development is not simply due to maturation since this can take place only though initiation into an already humanised world, a process that actualises our second nature. The significance of McDowell's argument is that he resolves the quandary about how thought can get a grip on the world where there is an oscillation between two alternative positions—between a 'coherentism that renounces external constraints on thinking' and 'a vain appeal to the Given, in the sense of bare presences that are supposed to be the ultimate grounds of empirical judgements' (McDowell, 1996, p.24). But in unpacking what is presupposed in both positions—and this is where the force of his argument lies—McDowell shifts attention from what it is mistakenly assumed that we share with animals, to what it is that is distinctive about human beings. This is our responsiveness to reasons—which McDowell calls 'a good gloss on one notion of freedom' (p. xxiii). By shifting the focus to second nature in this way McDowell gives priority to the development of our cognitive capacities by initiation into language and tradition. In initiation far more is involved than simply the acquisition of the means for communication, since initiation into language is nothing less than initiation into the social practices that constitute meaning and establish the conditions within which reasons can be demanded and given. Through initiation into a language children are brought into 'a store of historically accumulated wisdom about what is a reason for what', and they thereby acquire 'the capacity to think and act' (p. 126).

The account of *Bildung* as McDowell sees it may appear esoteric, but since it is relevant to the question of how children make generations of activity in the world their own it has obvious implications for education. McDowell has not explored these implications, and possibly this has left his own project incomplete and under-developed (see Testa, 2007). Cognitive capacities (or what may be called the 'intellectual virtues') are developed through the induction of the child into culture, tradition and so on. These capacities are distinctively human, and it is their distinctiveness that is not taken into account in the epistemological positions that McDowell interrogates. In describing a 'kind of predicament that we tend to fall into when we think about aspects of the human condition', he reminds us that 'we tend to be forgetful of the very idea of second nature' (McDowell, 1996, p. 85). It is claimed here that the work of bringing technology into education, is premised on this same epistemological forgetfulness, which makes proper recognition of the distinctive qualities of the human mind impossible. What makes McDowell's work important in this connection is that the epistemological assumptions involved in the positions he criticises inform much contemporary thinking about the application of technology to education.

3

At the heart of the dualist conception that informs so much of thinking about the use of technologies in education is a conception of experience relying upon what Wilfred Sellars called 'the Myth of the Given' (Sellars, 1997). The idea of the *Given* is the idea that we have immediate awareness of the world from the very start, without either language or reason, and that knowledge results from impressions that, having impinged on our senses, are interpreted by human construction. According to this view of things, concepts come into play late in the day after the world has already, so to speak, been taken in. Coupled to this idea of the *Given* is awareness understood in representational terms. This common sense way of thinking about meaning involves understanding signs or representations as having meaning solely by virtue of the objects they designate. In this commonsense approach accompanying constructivism in many writings on technology, although not obviously consistent with it, objects are believed to be the sole source of meaning, a meaning that is then conveyed to the receptor through their sign or representation. This approach is plausible in certain circumstance—for example, where animal predators see spiky features as unpalatable and respond automatically to them by backing off pursuit of the prey. But are human responses equally automatic in responding to the objects they come across? If so, then we might be correct in assuming that human beings learn in ways not very different from other forms of life. However, as soon as we consider the human infant, it becomes clear that it is responding in an environment where the significance that conditions its response, and thereby its contact with the world, is, in the first place, mediated by other human beings (i.e. it is being initiated into second nature). What is problematic in the picture of the animal and its environment is the idea that the stimulus to which the response is made inheres in the object or representation of the object (i.e. it is a Given). However in the case of the human infant, rather than the event or object being the sole source of the response, it is the parent or other significant actors who provide the active conditions that are decisive in giving meaning for the child's early responses. Vygotsky (1987) captured this process in his concept of a zone of proximal development. Meaning is attributed to the child's utterances and physical movements, and it is to this meaning that the parents respond, regardless of any intention on the part of the child to communicate meaning in the first place. In this sense, meaning is a *product* of a social process, and its significance relies on other actors and their relationships to each other and the world. This is what Vygotsky meant when he argued that what was first external and directed towards others is then exercised on oneself inwardly. This in turn accounts for the shift from external to internal development of the higher capacities of mind. For the use of a word, or the carrying out of an activity before fully understanding the meaning or significance of that activity, is a precursor through inner-directedness of understanding its significance. It might seem that the educational requirements of a social theory of mind must then be satisfied by a transition from classrooms where learners are only drilled in 'facts' to one where they manipulate, investigate, discuss and construct. But if this transition is effected simply by introducing technology into a classroom that itself remains unchanged (i.e. without consideration to human conditions and historically accumulated practices in knowledge domains), little if anything is likely to be achieved. In fact, it is possible that things will simply get worse.

Like McDowell, Robert Brandom (1994) also draws on Wilfred Sellars' critique of this concept of the *Given*, and he similarly takes issue with the idea of immediacy of awareness and its attendant conception of our relation to the world. Sellars' critique involves an attack not just on the idea of impressions as data, but also on the entire 'framework of givenness' or what Hegel would call *immediacy* (Sellars, 1997)—that is, on the idea that our relation to the world is one of direct awareness. This may seem identical to common versions of the constructivist approach— that is, that what we see is dependent on our construction of it and not *given* to us by data. But what is really at stake here is not construction as such but the way this construction is effected: the question is at what point concepts enter the picture and how these concepts are acquired. Whereas the picture of mind and world that appears to inform Reich's view sees construction as arising from the ability of the analyst to construct meaning out of raw data, the alternative view, associated with Sellars, McDowell and Brandom, sees construction as originating through induction into what Sellars calls *the space of reasons*. It may be useful to point out that, in this context, the space of reasons contains both objects as well as subjects; it contains mind as well as world. The process that, on the one side, establishes humans in terms of second nature has its corollary, on the other, in the constitution of the world as data.

Contrary to the idea of immediate awareness of the world as data impinging on our senses, Sellars' states in his attack on the myth of the given: 'In characterising an episode or a state as that of *knowing*, we are not giving a . . . description of that episode or state; we are placing it in the . . . space of reasons, of justifying and being able to justify what one says' (Sellars, 1997, p. 76). Responsiveness to the world does not start with our causal relation with raw data. It is immediately social in virtue of the development of our second nature, and this involves the actualisation of our cognitive capacities. So rather than our responses comprising merely causal relations with our environment, they take place, from the very start, within the space of reasons. This has consequences for how we think about the nature of experience since, according to McDowell, a normative context is necessary for being in touch with the world at all, whether knowledgeably or not.

In alerting us to the fact that knowing is not something that can arise by direct (unmediated) contact with the world, that it involves not just concepts but concepts in systematic relation to one another, Sellars introduces the Kantian conception of representation, a conception where judgments play an integral role. Our contact with the world as human beings with a second nature entails that our responses are governed by reasons as well as causes. In other words our responses are essentially normative in the sense that they depend upon the significance that human activities have given to objects, phenomena and events in the course of their activity in the world. Since Descartes and the development of modern science, epistemology has relied on a representational paradigm in which experience is understood in terms of perceiving minds making sense of a brute *Given*—what McDowell (1996) calls a disenchanted world. This epistemological picture results in the problem of the nature of our contact with the world, a problem that has pre-occupied modern philosophy and that McDowell sets out to address. Without understanding that *experience is already conceptual*, we are left with an anxiety about how thoughts can be in touch with the world at all. The argument that experience is already conceptual goes against our common-sense intuition, yet these developments in philosophy provide rich resources for understanding the issues raised by the use of technologies to enhance learning.

The Cartesian epistemological picture criticised here forms a background to educational thought, including those relativistic forms of constructivism that argue that there is no way of ruling between one position and another and no convincing grounds for seeing progress in science or exercising any criteria of truth (Gergen, 1999). More importantly, it has led to a neglect of the question of knowledge and of the full extent of what is involved in bringing a learner into a knowledge domain. For philosophy it has led to an oscillation between a thoroughgoing coherentism—the position that only beliefs can justify beliefs, which takes away external constraints on our thinking—and the counter position where the external constraints on thinking are seen as absolute. Neither position provides a satisfying account of the relations of mind to world: each misses the active, productive character of our contact with the world; that is, each misinterprets experience as being outside of thought rather than containing thought itself, indeed as intricately entwined with the very possibility and constitution of thought.

McDowell's exorcism of the Cartesian picture results in an account of experience as already conceptual. Humans inhabit not nature but second nature, and they are not subject to this in the way that animals are subject to nature. The world of second nature is already infused with meaning as a result of the practices and modifications of nature through which it has been brought about. McDowell's argument that human beings are 'born mere animals and they are transformed into thinkers and intentional agents in the course of coming to maturity' (McDowell, 1996, p. 125) has great significance for how we think about learning. Thought connects with reality only because to be a thinker is to inhabit the space of reasons, and powers of thought develop by being initiated into a language, into the 'putatively rational linkages that constitute the space of reasons' (p. 186). This idea that experience is already conceptual is very different from any view that takes humans to be constructing meaning out of raw data.

And yet the idea that human beings do construct meaning out of raw data still forms the background to much educational thought. Hence, insufficient attention is given to the interrelation of knowledge and learning—or, to put it another way, to the importance of epistemology for education. The philosophical innovations touched on here draw a different line between mind and world, or in McDowell's terms between reason and nature, than that drawn in the Cartesian picture. In this alternative to what McDowell calls 'bald naturalism', nature includes second nature since human thoughts are as much a part of nature as the activities of animals. In this respect the modification of nature, which this capacity to think has made possible, also counts as natural. Drawing the line between mind and world differently, this view places far greater weight not just on knowledge and its constitution but on the activity of coming to know.

If we accept the idea that when we respond to an environment, we do so within a space of reasons, we can appreciate what distinguishes human knowing from animal or mechanical responsiveness. Brandom (2000) illustrates this idea with a simple example when he asks us to consider what distinguishes human responsiveness from that of a machine or animal. He takes an example of the contrast between a fire alarm and a human being shouting the warning 'Fire!'. Fire alarms may well respond more effectively and reliably to the stimuli of fire than the human being. Their sensors are probably more sensitive than human organs, the sounds they make more compelling of attention. But Brandom asks us to contrast a child shouting 'Fire' with the mechanical alarm and consider what initiates the response. With the alarm the response is the end point of a causal chain in which smoke hits sensors and activates a process resulting in a siren sound. However, for the child reasons are involved from the very start, even if initially only as background to her response, before she becomes fully aware of them. Unlike an alarm, which responds mechanically to temperature and smoke, etc., the child has a concept of fire and therefore an appreciation of its consequences, though this appreciation may be limited and developing. In other words the response of the child is not a reflex. Even though it may be automatic and in this sense not entail conscious thought, it nonetheless involves responsiveness to reasons; that is, it involves *thought*. This the machine lacks. For the child the fire is the *reason* for the alarm and not merely the cause, because the child perceives the fire as fire; unlike a machine, the child has a concept of fire as part of a system of concepts. For Brandom, making a report as a human being is not 'responding differentially' since it involves inferring rather than merely representing. Brandom's argument rests on a critique of the dominant representational paradigm and on the claim that, insofar as human contact with the world is concerned, we need to privilege inference over representation; our awareness should not be understood primarily in representational terms but in terms of the inferential space that we inhabit as thinking creatures. Awareness of any one concept is dependent on awareness of a range of other concepts that constitute its meaning in the first place.

This distinction that Brandom draws between reacting differentially and responding to reasons, a distinction already drawn in German idealist thought at the end of the 18th century, has a contribution to make to the problems that arise with the application of technology to education. For, once the idea of immediacy is rejected and it is recognised that the awareness of human beings operates within a space of reasons, it is clearly the task for educators not only to provide learners with rich data from which they can construct meanings but also to move them from the space of reason within which they start to that of the knowledge domain they are studying. The knowledge to which learners *qua* learners are introduced is different from the knowledge that arises from everyday experience. Education as the means by which hard-won knowledge is passed from one generation to the next involves practices and objects that are not the content of everyday lives, however important they may be for it. The knowledge with which education is concerned cannot be acquired without conscious and purposeful involvement by both teachers and learners regardless of the setting (Young, 2008).

As far as pedagogy is concerned, the priority of inference over reference means that the grasping of a concept involves the learner's committing to the inferences implicit in its use in social practices of giving and asking for reasons. Effective teaching involves providing the opportunity for learners to operate with a concept in the space of reasons within which it falls and through which its meaning is constituted. Participation in such a space does not require an immediate and full grasp of the concept from the start, but rather only the ability to inhabit the space in which reasons constituting the concept operate.

4

Technology offers the possibility of engaging with the world before fully knowing it (Noss and Hoyles, 1996); it enables us to gain access to inferential relations between concepts before fully acquiring the concepts involved. Digital technologies make it possible to bring changes in the relationships between concepts and hence their meanings into plain view. However, this requires not only a high level of pedagogic design but also active participation by both teacher and learners. It is not the concepts themselves and their referents that are the object of learning, but their meaning as governed by their systemic relation to one another. Through being inducted into the inferential relations between concepts, learners begin to understand what it is to *do* mathematics and history and so on. Giving inference priority over representation means that pedagogic design must focus not on individual concepts but on the knowledge domains that constitute them. This is a more exacting task for design than dealing with concepts alone. This pedagogic strategy that recognises inferential systems requires much more time and effort than the more common approach that treats concepts as representations.

An example of the way in which a technology facilitates the use of concepts before they are fully grasped is the programming language Logo. This, as is widely known, allows children to explore mathematical relations concretely before they have any idea of what explains them in abstract terms. But while a technology like Logo can make visible the inferential relations that constitute concepts, as for instance when the making of a triangle reveals the specifications of the figure, the advantages of this will only be properly realised when the technology is used as an element in a programme in which priority is given to knowledge domains. To make it work effectively not only do teachers need to be there when they guide the learner, but they need to have a clear understanding of the priority of the particular knowledge domain in mind. However, the lack of recognition of what is involved in teaching, in terms of the development of cognitive capacities, has meant that the time and resources required by such a way of teaching are well beyond what is available for teachers preparing for lessons in most contemporary classrooms.

The application of technology without adequate attention to the knowledge domain runs into problems that can be traced back to the way that learning is based on the weak and narrow conception of *experience* criticised here. Certainly it is true that, as far as the application of technology to education is concerned, it is generally recognised that the exposure of learners to rich information is insufficient by itself. But there is far from full agreement about what steps are needed to augment it. In this connection the argument made by Nicolas Balacheff, who acted as scientific manager for the Kaleidoscope European research network on technology-enhanced learning, is particularly relevant.

A concentration on learning with little or no attention paid to the question of knowledge as such is criticised by Balacheff, who argues for 'design supported by a deep epistemological analysis of the domain considered' (Balacheff, 2004). Noting that the project to bring technologies into education started with the push of technology and only later, at the close of the 20th century, turned to the learner-driven principle of design, Balacheff argues that the project will not be soundly based until knowledge is placed at the centre of learning: 'The agreement we might reach on a "learning driven" principle of design of technology-enhanced learning (TEL) environments would in the end prove as disappointing as the naïve and initial focus on technology per se and the subsequent reaction by the focus on the learner' (ibid.). He goes on to argue that the term learning has no meaning unless it is concerned with knowledge. In other words focus on the learners without recognition of knowledge domains offers no way forward: 'After sixty years of research . . . in the field of TEL we are sent back to the understanding of knowledge [and] that understanding knowledge is a strategic condition for the development of TEL from a theoretical as well as from an operational perspective' (ibid.).

There is then what appears to be a mundane but is in fact the central, on-going problem in the classroom: how those learners who are least engaged in contemporary classrooms can become engaged by the use of technology. Even where learners are motivated, their orientation towards what it is that they are to make sense of cannot necessarily be assumed to be adequate (Arnseth and Säljö, 2007). To underline this argument, it must be stated that adequacy is not the serial learning of concepts on a scale of growing complexity, what is required is entry into a knowledge domain, with all that is implied by this. Moreover the approach must vary from domain to domain, for as Balacheff points out:

> The characteristics of the milieu for the learning of mathematics, of surgery or of foreign languages are fundamentally different . . . [O]ne may say that the milieu for surgery is part of the 'material world' (here, the human body), for foreign languages it includes human beings, for mathematics already a theoretical system. Although these observations seem obvious most of the ICT projects claim they contribute to TEL research at a general level and they pretend to be domain independent (ibid.).

Recognising the provocative nature of what he is saying, he continues 'A devil's advocate may say that ICT research does not see itself being accountable beyond the coherency and robustness of the software it produces, not to mention the constraint of re-usability often mentioned to justify the search or claim for domain independence' (ibid.). In fact, it is possible that the proper design of technology-enhanced learning environments is an even more complicated matter than Balacheff believes since not only do knowledge domains vary as regards content but so also do conceptual frameworks and what counts as a reason for what. In fact matters are even more complicated when one moves from the sciences and mathematics to the humanities and the arts.

If Balacheff's claim about knowledge were taken seriously, many of the projects to implement technology-enhanced learning would have to be radically restructured. For the conclusion to which his work points would demand a turning of attention away from the technology to the knowledge domain, from here to questions of pedagogy and from there one step further, back to epistemology.

REFERENCES

Arnseth, H. C. and Säljö, R. (2007) Making Sense of Epistemic Categories. Analysing Students' Use of Categories of Progressive Inquiry in Computer Mediated Collaborative Activities, *Journal of Computer Assisted Learning*, 23.5, pp. 425–439.

Bakhurst, D. (2005) Il'enkov on Education, *Studies in East European Thought*, 57.3, pp. 261–275.

Balacheff, N. (2004) *Knowledge the Keystone of TEL Design*. Proceedings of the 4th Hellenic conference Information and communication technologies in education, Athens, Greece (2004). Available at: TeLearn at http://telearn.noe-kaleidoscope.org/

Brandom, R. (1994) *Making it Explicit: Reasoning, Representing, and Discursive Commitment* (Cambridge, MA, Harvard University Press).

Brandom, R. (2000) *Articulating Reasons: An Introduction to Inferentialism* (Cambridge, MA, Harvard University Press).

Bruner, J. S. (1996) *The Culture of Education* (Cambridge, MA, Harvard University Press).

Cuban, L. (2001) *Oversold and Underused: Computers in the Classroom* (Cambridge, MA, Harvard University Press).

Department for Education and Skills (2005) *Harnessing Technology: Transforming Learning and Children's Services*, Reference: DFES-1437-2005 (London, DfeS).

Gergen, K. J. (1999) *An Invitation to Social Construction* (London, Sage Publications).

Katz, R. N.and Associates (1999) *Dancing with the Devil: Information Technology and the New Competition in Higher Education* (San Francisco, CA, Jossey-Bass Higher and Adult Education Series).

Noss, R. and Hoyles, C. (1996) *Windows on Mathematical Meanings: Learning Cultures and Computers* (Dordrecht, Kluwer).

McDowell, J. (1996) *Mind and World* (Cambridge, MA, Harvard University Press).

Papert, S. (1980) *Mindstorms: Children, Computers and Powerful Ideas* (New York, Basic Books).

Papert, S. (1993) *The Children's Machine: Rethinking School in the Age of the Computer* (New York, Basic Books).

Reich, R. (1992) *The Work of Nations: Preparing Ourselves for 21st Century Capitalism* (New York, Vintage Books, A Division of Random House, Inc).

Rorty, R. (1981) *Philosophy and the Mirror of Nature* (Princeton, NJ, Princeton University Press).

Sawyer, R. K. (ed.) (2006) *The Cambridge Handbook of the Learning Sciences* (Cambridge, Cambridge University Press).

Sellars, W. (1997) *Empiricism and the Philosophy of Mind*, R. Rorty, intro.; R. Brandom, study guide (Cambridge, MA, Harvard University Press).

Testa, I. (2007) Criticisms from Within Nature: The Dialectic between First and Second Nature from McDowell to Adorno, *Philosophy and Social Criticism*, 33.4, pp. 473–497.

Tomasello, M. (2000) *The Cultural Origins of Human Cognition* (Cambridge, MA, Harvard University Press).

Vygotsky, L. S. (1987) *The Collected Works of L.S. Vygotsky, Volume 1 Problems of General Psychology*, (including the Volume *Thinking and Speech*). N. Minick, trans.; R. W. Reiber and A. S. Carton, eds (New York, Plenum Press).

Young, M. F. D. (2008) *Bringing Knowledge Back In: From Social Constructivism to Social Realism in the Sociology of Education* (London, Routledge).

3.3

Technology-Enhanced Learning as a Tool for Pedagogical Innovation

DIANA LAURILLARD

1. INTRODUCTION

This chapter argues that the nature of learning and teaching in a higher education (HE) system is an indicator of how adaptable a country is likely to be in response to global change.[1] In the UK we have a system that does change, and has recently updated itself more successfully than many in the western world. It is just over 10 years since the National Committee of Inquiry into HE (the Dearing Report) proposed significant changes to the way teaching and learning is carried out in the sector. The intervening years have seen developments that are indicative of an energetic sector interested in self-improvement in the way it supports learning. Is this degree of adaptability sufficient?

There are powerful forces converging on HE. Worldwide demand is increasing beyond the capability to supply. Business demands of HE remain unsatisfied. And knowledge and communication technologies have made education a global enterprise. All these trends affect the nature of learning and teaching. What would it mean to ensure that we are able to adapt to such forces while retaining fundamental academic values that should not change?

The chapter proposes that lecturers need to understand what it takes to learn their subject in the context of the environment their learners inhabit. Only they can be responsible for the nature of the pedagogic innovation that is needed if the sector is to be adaptive to this environment. This is the unchanging core at the heart of all the pressures on the sector. The argument here is that technology, although it is part of the problem, can also contribute to the solutions.

2. RECENT DEVELOPMENTS IN LEARNING AND TEACHING IN HE IN THE UK

The learning and teaching recommendations from the National Committee of Inquiry were ambitious, aiming to enable a rapidly expanding and diversifying sector to prepare itself for the adaptation it would need. Five main areas were identified as needing immediate action: accreditation of teaching for staff; research and development funding in learning and teaching; funding for innovation; a requirement that institutions develop learning and teaching strategies; and better support for academic staff in the use of ICT in their teaching. In the 10 years since, by Watson's analysis of these recommendations (Watson, 2007), the last two in particular made a difference. On both counts, there has been a great deal of activity, making use of a variety of strategic and funding mechanisms. Table 1 summarises the main developments in terms of these five principal areas where action was recommended.

Table 1 shows a range of initiatives, mechanisms and activities that have helped to strengthen the capacity of UK HE to be responsive to new pressures on learning and teaching. In the 10-year period, only one activity failed: the UK e-Universities initiative. It had diverse origins, from the ambition to capitalise on UK HE as a global business, to a recognition of the need for substantial central support for institutions struggling to innovate with new technology. It did not learn the lessons of previous commercial failures to create e-universities, nor from the successes of those universities already making the shift towards blended approaches (Laurillard, 2001). With no central support or coordination of e-learning effort, the HE sector continued to make small gains in localised projects, but not to achieve mastery of the technology in service of its learning and teaching ambitions. The sector still suffers from this failure, and we return to this point below.

By 2007, 10 years on from the National Committee of Inquiry, UK HE was in a much stronger position to operate *as a sector* to improve the quality of its learning and teaching. With a secure set of funding, reward, research, and support mechanisms established, it is now well placed to maintain and improve the quality of students' learning experience in HE.

Does it succeed? Academic staff appear to believe it does: more than 60% say the sector is improving overall in terms of its performance in teaching (Amoah, 2007, p. 114). The figures are even better for the assessment of their own institution (p. 118). As far as students are concerned, we have no earlier benchmark for comparison, but at least we know from the National Student Survey that over 80% of universities score 4 or more out of 5 on a 5-point scale of overall satisfaction. That is a good score. There is room for improvement, but there are now well-established mechanisms to help with that. Are they enough, if the sector is to withstand the forces affecting a 21st century system?

3. FORCES AFFECTING LEARNING AND TEACHING IN HE

Higher Education operates in a complex environment of conflicting demands from stakeholders, public (government, taxpayers), private (business, public sector) and personal (individuals and families). If we consider just the demand from Government, students, and employers, there is a considerable potential impact on learning and teaching. If we add in the challenges being presented by new technologies, the impact is even greater.

Table 1 Principal developments in the improvement of learning and teaching, in terms of the Dearing recommendations on where action was needed.

1997	Accreditation	R&D	Innovation	Inst'l L&T	ICT support
1998				TQEF	
1999	ILTHE		LTSN	NTFS	LTSN
2000		TLRP (14)			
2001					
2002					UKeU
2003	HEA			HEA	
2004					
2005		NSS	CETLs	CETLs	TEL strategies
2006		TLRP/TEL			
2007					

Key: TQEF: Teaching Quality Enhancement Fund; ILTHE: Institute for Learning and Teaching in HE; HEA: Higher Education Academy; TLRP: Teaching and Learning Research Programme; NSS: National Student Survey; TLRP/TEL: TLRP research call on Technology Enhanced Learning' LTSN: Learning and Teaching Support Network; CETL: Centre for Excellence in Teaching and Learning; NTFS: National Teaching Fellowship Scheme; UKeU: UK e-Universities initiative; TEL strategies: strategies for e-learning from DfES, HEFCE, JISC.

3.1. The Pressure from Policy

The pressures on the sector from Government are all expansionist—more and better, both quality and scale (see, for example, DfES, 2005), but without a commensurate increase in funding. There is more funding now through the introduction of graduate contributions to HE, but this does not match the drop in public funding to 63% of its value in 1980 (Watson, 2007, p. 37). The ambitions are right, but they set a demanding challenge on a sector that has to cope also with the expectations of delivering world-class research.

3.2. The Pressure from Demand

Within the UK, student demand for HE remains buoyant, and this seems set to continue, despite the rise in fees. Internationally, the demand for higher education is increasing, and can only increase further. Simply to keep pace with world population growth, there would need to be one university being created each week somewhere in the world (Daniel, 1996). In many countries, demand already far exceeds supply, and perpetuates elitism when high quality HE is only available to the rich (Bates, 2001).

We can expect that the demand for good value higher education will continue to grow, and there will be many competitors willing to offer HE for a low price. The UK HE system will not be able to compete on price, although it should be able to compete on quality and value for money. In fact, UK market share dropped from 16% in 1998 to 11% in 2004, but in a growing market this still means a significant rise in the numbers of international students, by 50% to 350,000, over the same period (HEPI, 2007). Maintaining our place in the global HE market is important for HE, and as a recent survey shows, universities' international strategies focus particularly on the economic rationale (Middlehurst and Woodfield, 2007). Competing on value for money means that as volumes expand, there is a potential problem in how we maintain quality. With demand at its current level, even if we could afford a commensurate increase in teaching staff, we cannot train lecturers fast enough to maintain our current teaching model, which relies on a staff:student ratio of, approximately, 1:20. Therefore, in order to maintain quality the unit cost of teaching must decrease as volumes expand, which suggests the need to consider how to achieve a different teaching resource model.

3.3. The Pressure from Technology

Technology creates another important pressure for change. It is changing both what we need to know, and how we come to know it. As the workplace diversifies, graduates need to keep renewing and developing their high-level skills, e.g. for information-handling, independent learning, critical thinking, reflective innovation, project management, resource modelling, knowledge management, communication, networking, inter-personal negotiation, design, creativity, time management, and enterprise, and they need ICT skills to support all these. In particular, there are new skills and patterns of knowledge that employees increasingly need in the workplace where technology is ubiquitous (Kent *et al.*, 2005).

Foundational knowledge is important, but will need to be continually updated. The curriculum in HE therefore has to differentiate between building foundational knowledge, and using this knowledge-building process as the vehicle for the acquisition of all the high-level cognitive skills they need. The mismatch between the predominant HE focus on discipline knowledge, and the workplace requirement for high-level cognitive, or 'knowledge', skills, is probably the main reason for the absence of HE from the provision of 'workforce development', even though much of this is now high-level and post-graduate (Connor, 2005). As a result, some businesses have turned to the 'corporate university' solution, not always successfully. Eventually, it is likely that the private sector will learn how to innovate in learning and teaching for itself, and respond to these increasing demands, as HE is not stepping forward to supply.

The three pressures on learning and teaching in HE outlined here suggest that we need to rethink the way we do this. I suggest that digital technologies themselves, while they challenge, can also support.

4. TECHNOLOGY AS A CATALYST FOR CHANGE

Digital technologies take many forms, and create opportunities for change, and support for new ways of working. However, few universities have gone far beyond the provision of technology for information, communication, and organisational transactions, to use its wider capabilities to improve the quality of the learning experience itself.

Digital technologies present education with a range of opportunities that is hard to comprehend, and even harder to address. There is a sense that they provide something akin to the Gutenberg revolution, as the new technology of the printing press brought the technology of the written word to a much wider audience than was previously possible. This is a good analogy for the Internet, but the Internet alone seriously under-represents the diversity of the technology opportunities now available (Laurillard, 2006). An interactive computational model in itself provides a form of knowledge representation as radically different from the book as the mode of writing was from the oral mode of representation. The written medium changed the way an individual could study and reflect on the knowledge being communicated. Prior to that, it was essential to memorise the knowledge that could only be delivered orally. The act of learning could go beyond sitting at the feet of the master, and become an act of private study and reflection. Similarly, in the shift from the static, non-interactive medium of the written word to the interactive medium of the computer, there is a comparably radical effect on the act of learning. Digital technologies offer many new ways of representing knowledge, such as computational models of human or natural systems, animated diagrams of theories and concepts, role-play models of events and processes. Every discipline area finds new ways of using the technology to understand or illuminate its knowledge. And new forms of representation offer new forms of engagement with, and ownership of knowledge and the individual's developing understanding.

The historical shift from listening, through reading, to interacting with ideas is mirrored in the way the learner is able to express their own thinking. There is a move from talking to writing, and with the advent of digital technologies a rich variety of possibilities become available.

All the forms of representation accessible to the teacher can be open also to the learner. The teacher can build a model of climate change in a spreadsheet to enable learners to explore the effects of changes in one parameter; the learner can also build a model, and check its behaviour against known data. Building a model, a 'constructionist' ideal, is a fundamentally different kind of learning experience from writing an essay.

The technology opportunities for new kinds of teaching and learning will continue to develop, and HE will find it difficult to keep up with them. There is the potential for technology to offer a higher level of engagement with learning about difficult ideas, in a way that is far more motivating than the conventional 'transmission' mode of teaching. What is critically important, however, is that education should not be led by the technology, but should be imagining its own desirable future, and harnessing the development of learning technology to that.

There is often, in the e-learning literature, a certain breathless expectation of how things will need to change. For example: 'As our students enter the workforce, the ability to deal with complex and often ambiguous information will be more important than simply knowing a lot of facts ... We need to think in terms of transforming the educational experience so that it's meaningful to the information-age learner' (Frand, 2000). But is this the right contrast? The conventional educational experience is not, or should not be, 'knowing a lot of facts'. University students set out to develop a fundamental understanding of a discipline, which is not the same. 'Knowing a lot of facts' would be a poor description of a university education. And while we certainly have to make learning intelligible and meaningful, is it really the case that what it takes to learn is so different in 'the information age'? The next section considers this question.

5. DESIRABLE FUTURES?

To think through the future of learning in the context of new technology, it is important to begin from an analysis of 'what it takes to learn'. Without a clear understanding of pedagogy, predictions for the future of learning and teaching will tend to be driven by what the technology makes possible, rather than what learners need.

The analysis of 'what it takes to learn' has been widely discussed and researched in education, across all sectors, over many decades. There is a common thread running through the writings of the great educators, not always shared by learning theorists from behaviourist psychology, cognitive psychology, and cognitive science, but common at least to the great majority of educators. From John Dewey onwards, through Piaget, Vygotsky, Freire, Bruner, Papert, Marton, Lave, the common thread is that learning is *active*. Therefore, the role of the teacher is not to transmit knowledge to a passive recipient, but to structure the learner's engagement with the knowledge, practising the high-level cognitive skills that enable them to make that knowledge their own. The collective analysis of what it takes to learn, combined from all these educators, identifies learning, in the context of formal education, as involving 'cognitive motivation', 'meta-cognition', 'problem-oriented', 'inquiry-oriented', 'goal-oriented action', 'repeated practice', 'feedback', 'reflection', and 'social communication'—i.e. it sees learning not as something that happens to the learner, but as an activity they *do*. With this general degree of consensus it is unlikely that learning will be found to require something radically different in the near future. Learning complex concepts and mastering difficult procedures and processes, will always require effortful thinking. Technology will probably not change what it takes to learn, therefore, but it may change how the process of learning is facilitated.

In order to see what kinds of contribution technology could make to learning, the research community itself is a valuable indicator of the potential. An analysis of the successful applications to the 2007 ESRC-EPSRC funded Technology-Enhanced Learning research call demonstrated a rich variety of learning activities and forms, as in the following quotes from proposals:

Inquiry-based; Construction; Conceptual understanding; Taking tests; Problem-solving; Narrative; Literacy; Game authoring; Techno-computing skill-learning; Fieldwork; Communication; Collaboration; Learning identities; Conceptual networks; Manipulation skills; Informal interests; Self-worth; Modelling; Scenarios; Evaluating evidence.

These descriptors reflect many of the concerns of the educational theorists who want to make learning an active process. But what do they see as the role of digital technologies? The research proposals identified a wide range of applications:

Games; Tools; Cultural tools; Adaptive intelligent tutoring systems; Avatars; Embodied interaction; Augmented cognition; Personal learning environments; Learner models; Portable devices; Conversation agents; Editable digital artefacts; Digital data tracking; Haptic devices; Virtual objects; Online communities; Adaptive support; Simulation; Collaborative technology.

We talk about 'technology' or 'e-learning', as if it is a unitary concept, but the terms listed above cover an immensely wide range of artefacts, offering many different ways of enhancing learning. In the research proposals, these included ways of making the provision of education more flexible, making the learning process more active, improving assessment, scaling up high quality interactions, and giving teachers interactive frameworks for designing lesson plans and learning activities.

Education can pose some testing challenges to new technologies, as we have seen. Suppose we agree we know what it takes to learn? A consensus could probably form around something like the ideal conditions of the small group practice-based tutorial, of well-matched learners, and a teacher able to inspire, encourage and guide the learners individually and collectively to a shared understanding of a negotiated goal. The ideal conditions are very difficult to achieve in a mass education system, and higher education is becoming a mass system with few prospects of providing this ideal very often for many of its students. In the future conditions of an ever-expanding system it will probably be impossible.

So this defines our challenge to the technology: make it possible to emulate the ideal conditions of the small group practice-based tutorial in a large-scale non-elite HE system.

Could it be possible? We know it is possible for the technology to:

- emulate small group tutorial discussions through virtual communications;
- provide realistic feedback on actions in a virtual environment;
- track learner performance to predict the optimal next task;

and many other aspects of good teaching. We know this capability is possible, but its use is not widespread, it is not available in most curriculum topics, and it is not widely understood how to exploit it in the service of good pedagogy and an inspiring learning experience.

The challenge of providing high quality HE on the larger scale is critical. We have seen that the demand can only increase. It is clear that we cannot possibly maintain the effectiveness of higher education through conventional methods. The 1:10 or even 1:20 staff-student ratio is not viable on the large scale. With a falling unit of resource for teaching, down 63% on 1980 figures (Watson, 2007), not compensated by the increase in fees, there is no hope of improving that ratio in future. Worse, within that reduced resource we have to manage not just expansion of numbers, but also much greater diversity of need, interest, motivation, and capability in our student population.

Against this rather pessimistic analysis we have the promise of new technology. In addition to the emulation of aspects of the ideal teaching conditions above, it can also sometimes achieve economies of scale. In the context of education, for example:

- the tutor's answer to one student's question is accessible and preserved in the online discussion for a very large number of others;
- the interactive simulation that works for introducing a difficult idea could work the same way for the many, not just the few it was originally created for;
- the small group discussions reporting back to a plenary can be many hundreds of small groups, merging into smaller numbers of large groups, with the few key questions being inherited by a very large plenary.

In such ways, the technology can handle scale in terms of both access to ideas, and the 'inter-connectedness' that enables meaningful discussions.

Equally, it can handle diversity of content. The digital resource demonstrating the application of theory to a case-study can be reused in many different locations by replacing the link to the case-study with a locally defined link to a local study. Similarly, students generating their own digital data from local research can contribute their findings online to generate a multi-cultural community-owned resource for all to share. In these examples we can see the germ of a future in which the academy operates in a very different way, to achieve its traditional ends. But plotting the course by which we get there is complex. We are currently in the very early stages of learning how to make best use of these multi-functional technologies.

If technology is to be the key to enabling higher education to achieve its ambitions for both expansion and quality, then we need a theory of change that tells us how that is to be achieved. We have a tiny proportion of academic staff engaged in research on teaching. Teacher education, as an academic subject, struggles to lead. As the only major subject with decreasing numbers (Watson, 2007), despite an education system that has expansion and improvement in all its aims and policies, there is little room for radical innovation. In the next section we look at how the teaching profession might tackle this dilemma.

6. MECHANISMS FOR INNOVATION IN LEARNING AND TEACHING

If we were to pose the question 'who will lead innovation in learning and teaching?' there is really only one legitimate answer. No academic could countenance a solution other than to put this responsibility with the academic profession itself. The interrelationship between what is taught, and how it is taught, is too close for it to be otherwise. The occasional fantasy of policy-makers and consultants, that 'content' could be generated by the commercial world on behalf of education, has not yet borne fruit, and certainly would not be shared by academics who care about their field. Academics do not separate 'content' from the process of learning. The 'what' and 'how' and 'why' of learning are internally related, which is what makes learning technologies exciting. As we shift to different representations of knowledge, offered in ways that are as different from books as the written word was from the spoken word, we necessarily change our relationship to knowledge. There is no viable alternative therefore. We have to discover for ourselves how to harness the capability of digital technologies to extend and enhance learning and teaching. Is this feasible?

I would argue that it is feasible, but on one necessary (though not sufficient) condition: if we properly acknowledge that discovery requires something akin to a scientific approach; that we need to problematise learning and teaching, subjecting it to the same level of investigation as we would bring to any academic research topic.

Our knowledge and understanding of 'technology enhanced learning' will develop faster in an academic teaching community that acts like a learning system, in the same way as knowledge develops fast in peer-reviewed collaborative research. Innovation and discovery, which are peer reviewed and quality assured, will need the same conditions in the context of learning and teaching as they need in any other field. It would involve making explicit our knowledge of *what it takes to learn*, so that we can instantiate it in the digital technology, just as we did with the older technology of the textbook. Once developed, it must be possible to test it, adapt it, refine the design, reflect on the process, rearticulate what it takes to learn, and share that new knowledge. All the characteristics of 'learning', present in the way scientists learn about our natural and social worlds, must be there too, in the way we learn how to improve learning and teaching.

If teaching were to become problematised in this way, then lecturers would conduct the process of teaching as rigorously as they conduct their research. And certain expectations would follow. They would expect:

(i) support for some personal development in how to teach;
(ii) the means to build on the work of others to design their approach;

(iii) the means to experiment and reflect on what the results imply for their design and their understanding, and

(iv) the means to articulate and disseminate their contribution.

Those four characteristics together define the essentials of what we might call 'open teaching'—what James Dalziel has called 'open source teaching', i.e. an environment in which 'educators can freely and openly share best practice teaching' (Dalziel, 2005). This communitarian approach would reflect the ideals of the research community in general, and the scholarship of teaching in particular (Kreber and Cranton, 2000). Specifically, it would enable the academic teaching community, throughout higher education, to learn how to adapt to the new challenges for HE, and to exploit technology in the process.

It sounds infeasible in a system under so much pressure simply to deal with the requirements of expansion and diversity. But from the arguments above it is clear that this situation will not improve, and yet, without harnessing the advantages of learning technologies, higher education will not meet demand. Happily, the technology itself embodies the means to provide the support academics will need:

(i) Support for some personal development in how to teach—there are online learning design tools under development, which are explicitly designed to help teachers gradually bring learning technologies into their work, and link to repositories of existing digital resources in their field;[2]

(ii) the means to build on the work of others to design their approach— online communities of practice can offer access to existing learning designs, case studies, lessons learned;

(iii) the means to experiment and reflect on what the results imply for their design and their understanding—an interactive learning activity management system can offer a simple authoring environment for the lecturer to sequence a set of learning activities, run it for student groups collaborating online, monitor student progress, offer a simple editing environment to improve it in the light of practice (see Figure 1);[3]

(iv) the means to articulate and disseminate their contribution— creating a learning activity sequence is one form of articulation of what the lecturer thinks it takes to learn a particular topic, or achieve a particular learning outcome, and the online community is the means to disseminate that idea, once proven.

Perhaps it is not an impossible dream, to imagine an academic teaching community connected in exploration and discovery of what it takes to learn, and what it takes to enable learners to learn, not just within our conventional teaching environments, but in ways that address the scale and diversity of the HE system of the future. Technology can be a solution to the pressures and demands on HE, but only if pedagogy is the driver, and only if the academic community is doing the driving.

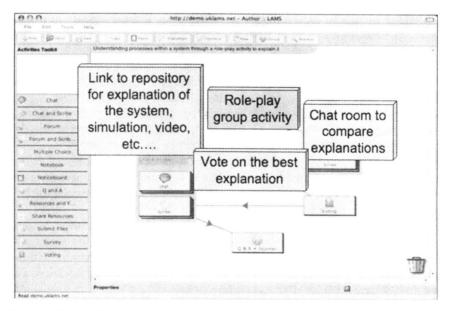

Figure 1 The LAMS authoring environment enables the academic to drag and drop a sequence of generic learning activities onto the panel and link them together. Within each one they can then specify, e.g. the simulation or website to link to, the roles for the groups, the issues to vote on, etc.

7. SUMMARY

The HE sector has moved a long way in the 10 years since the Dearing Report, and has developed the capability to continue to develop the quality of teaching and learning. There are now several enduring mechanisms and agencies for improving teaching and learning, as outlined in Table 1. Technology is forcing the pace of change, but also offers intriguing potential ways of contributing to the adaptability of the sector, in its response to change. From the arguments outlined above, if HE is to make the best of this opportunity, then we should aim for:

> Innovation in teaching and learning focused on educational ambitions;
> A clear strategy to link research, teaching and innovation;
> Academics leading innovation in learning and teaching with technology.
> And we should avoid:
> Innovation in teaching left to specialists;
> Efforts to innovate that are non-strategic;
> Technology used as a driver of innovation in teaching.

It is essential that we do not devolve responsibility for innovation to specialists, or publishers, or software houses. But it is unsurprising that academics find little kudos in teaching innovation when by far the most impressive rewards are for research. It is essential, therefore, if academics are to lead the discovery of new pedagogies, that innovation in learning and teaching be linked to educational values, and institutional strategies. However, we lack the leadership we need to ensure either that teaching innovation is linked to strategic needs, or that it is accorded the time and status of research. If we could achieve these two changes, then perhaps we could avoid the awful prospect of forever using technology as a solution in search of a problem.

Even so, the successive developments in HE teaching and learning since the Dearing Report put the UK in a much better position than most other countries to be the world leader in innovation in learning and teaching in HE. With better use of digital technologies, we could be on the point of a breakthrough to a system capable of learning how to teach. This fits very well with the values articulated in the original Dearing report, which saw the aim of HE as being 'to enable society to make progress through an independent understanding of itself and its world: in short, to sustain a learning society' (NCIHE, 1997). If this is important for society as a whole, how much more important it must be for HE to be 'a learning sector', able to develop an understanding of technology-enhanced learning as a tool for pedagogic innovation.

NOTES

1. This is adapted from the text version of a presentation given at the conference *The Dearing Report: Ten Years On*, held at the Institute of Education, London, 25 July 2007.
2. See the JISC Design for Learning Programme, http://www.lkl.ac.uk/research/d4l/
3. See, for example, the Learning Activity Management System (LAMS), http://www.lamsinter-national.com/

REFERENCES

Amoah, M. (2007) '100 Voices': The State of the HE Nation, in D. Watson and M. Amoah (eds) *The Dearing Report: Ten Years On* (London, Institute of Education).

Bates, A. W. (2001) *National Strategies for E-learning in Post-secondary Education and Training (Fundamentals in Educational Planning)* (Paris, UNESCO, International Institute for Educational Planning).

Connor, H. (2005) *Workforce Development and Higher Education* (London, Council for Industry and Higher Education).

Dalziel, J. (2005) LAMS Community Launch, *LAMS Foundation News*. Available at: http://www.lamsfoundation.org/news/

Daniel, J. S. (1996) *Mega-Universities and Knowledge Media: Technology Strategies for Higher Education* (London, Kogan Page).

Frand, J. L. (2000) The Information-Age Mindset: Changes in Students and Implications for Higher Education, *Educause Review*, (September/October), pp. 14–24.

HEPI (2007) The Economic Costs and Benefits of International Students, *HEPI Report Summary* (Oxford, Higher Education Policy Institute).

Kent, P., Bakker, A., Hoyles, C. and Noss, R. (2005) Techno-mathematical Literacies in the Workplace, *Mathematics Statistics and Operational Research*, 5.1, pp. 5–9.

Kreber, C. and Cranton, P. A. (2000) Exploring the Scholarship of Teaching, *The Journal of Higher Education*, 71.4, pp. 476–495.

Laurillard, D. (2001) The E-University: What Have We Learned?, *International Journal of Management Education*, 1.2, pp. 3–7.

Laurillard, D. (2006) E-Learning in Higher Education, in: P. Ashwin (ed.) *Changing Higher Education: The Development of Learning and Teaching* (London, RoutledgeFalmer).

Middlehurst, R. and Woodfield, S. (2007) *Responding to the Internationalisation Agenda: Implications for Institutional Policy and Practice* (Research Project Report) (Kingston, Surrey, Higher Education Academy).

NCIHE (1997) *Higher Education in the Learning Society* [The Dearing Report] (London, HMSO).

Watson, D. (2007) The Fate of the Dearing Recommendations: Policy and Performance in UK HE, 1997–2007, in: D. Watson and M. Amoah (eds) *The Dearing Report: Ten Years On* (London, Institute of Education).

Part II

Neuroscience, Learner Categories and ICT

4
THE ENHANCEMENT AGENDA

4.1
Introduction

RUTH CIGMAN AND ANDREW DAVIS

Recent educational policy has broadened its aims. No longer are mere 'standards' to be achieved, conceptualised as cognitive achievements and skills relevant to the economy. Now educators are to be concerned with aspects of personal flourishing. In this section, dubbed 'The Enhancement Agenda' three contributors raise critical questions about some of the assumptions that underpin such a program. Each of the writers is very concerned to show that, among other things, fundamental questions about the value of human existence are involved. This point takes the 'Agenda' well beyond mere empirical considerations, and represents a salutary warning to any policy makers who believe that improving personal flourishing might be treated as though it was an engineering challenge.

Judith Suissa explores the idea of teaching happiness in schools. She questions the very possibility of 'measuring' happiness, an option canvassed by 'positive psychologists' such as Martin Seligman. On her view, the role of happiness in education cannot be settled on the basis of empirical research alone. If happiness is something to do with living a worthwhile life then those seeking such a life need to understand what it is to be human and the justification for associated value judgments. Suissa points to the tensions and complexities inherent in these issues through an illuminating discussion of the character of Levin in Tolstoy's *Anna Karenina*. Levin in some senses is happy, yet is sometimes near to suicide. Suissa acknowledges that there are basic conditions such as freedom from hunger without which any kind of meaningful well-being is impossible. However, she points to the importance of the realms of interpretation, meaning and value involved in happiness, realms on which education should operate. Simplistic packages of 'skills' cannot be the answer here.

Ruth Cigman investigates a selection of what she sees as the ethical and conceptual questions surrounding the project of enhancing feelings. Important issues are provoked here, *both* about the very idea of enhancement, *and* about what it is that is supposed to be enhanced. She draws on Aristotle's account of moral education and emotion to support her explorations, and worries about the artificial separation of the cognitive from the non-cognitive in the enhancement agenda. Moreover she feels that this agenda exaggerates the non-cognitive aspects of 'enhancement'. If *emotions* are elements in what is being enhanced, then we need to remember that emotions have a cognitive component, involving 'thoughts, beliefs and judgments' (this volume, p. 174).

It would be surprising if the fashionable idea of promoting self-esteem did not figure in this volume's critical reflections on the enhancement agenda. Accordingly Cigman devotes significant attention to this. She argues that people need to feel worthy to aspire as a condition of healthy self-esteem. The 'real concept' of self-esteem on her account is effectively explained by salient examples of its absence in individuals who become 'trapped in the circular logic of failure' (this volume, p. 173). Teachers should be supported by empirical work on how we can work with others appropriately so that they believe themselves more worthy to aspire to a 'better kind of life' (this volume, p. 189).

Richard Smith explores a selection of those desires and values which are important to human existence and yet do not make us especially happy. He appeals to J. S. Mill's classic distinction between 'higher' and 'lower' pleasures, and reminds us that we may prefer at times to be one of Mill's 'dissatisfied pigs'. Smith argues that we value many 'conditions' in addition to happiness. Some art moves us to tears; we value activities that frustrate and puzzle us. Smith offers us the always important Wittgensteinian 'assembly of reminders', illuminating his discussion with helpful literary examples. Human existence includes an exhilarating diversity of pursuits and experiences. In the face of Smith's vivid portrayal of this fact, the idea put forward by Layard and others that 'happiness and unhappiness ... are simply different points along a continuum' looks wildly implausible.

Alistair Miller's chapter takes on the whole project of 'positive psychology' and offers an explicit critique of what he sees as some of its central ideas and arguments. He relates his discussion to selected contemporary philosophical work in the theory of emotions, to empirical writings on happiness by Seligman and others and to empirical explorations of trait theory. He attacks the conception of life as the attempt to follow a series of goals, a key assumption that he attributes to positive psychology. In passages that reinforce points also made by Cigman, he opposes the idea that one legitimate goal for positive psychology is to turn pessimists into optimists. This is wrong because we must, *of course* consider *why* someone is pessimistic, and that it is wholly facile to seek to identify 'learned helplessness', or lack of confidence and self-belief with pessimism *per se*. Sophie Rietti (this volume, p. 271) also has concerns about any suggestion that education might aim at the 'emotional habituation' of students without the underlying value assumptions being properly transparent and open to critical review by those subjected to the educational processes concerned. Miller defends the thought that the wise person appreciates the complexities and ironies in life, and would rarely 'respond unambiguously positively or negatively'.

4.2
Enhancing Children

RUTH CIGMAN

1 INTRODUCTION

Educational policy in the UK has taken an interesting turn. The preoccupation with standards in schools, which has been with us for many years, has given rise to a set of aims that policy-makers would hardly have recognised two decades ago. Not only should educators pursue the traditional aims of imparting knowledge, understanding and skills to children. They should set the scene for such aims by getting children into an 'appropriate condition' from which to learn. This can mean anything from eating a good breakfast to playing outdoors or developing good 'social and emotional skills'. Schools should promote these 'conditions for learning' as seriously as they have always promoted learning itself. This idea has spawned an abundance of social research, policy initiatives, business ventures and public debate. But does it make sense?

The idea emerged in the highly politicised educational climate of the 1990s, in which the alleged failures of mass education were giving rise to an obsession with standards in schools. The ills of under-achievement, disaffection and violence would dissipate, it was thought, if only standards could be raised. But a difficulty emerged. A standards agenda involves identifying and possibly shaming children and schools that fail. The social consequences of educational failure include disaffection, delinquency, violence and so on: the very problems that the standards agenda set out to address. Such an agenda may help some children, but for others, arguably, it makes matters worse by drawing attention to their failures and making them feel unworthy and excluded.

It was this concern that led to a supplementary agenda focusing on so-called non-cognitive traits like confidence, motivation, resilience, well-being and self-esteem. Such traits are thought to be possessed by individuals to a greater or lesser degree, and to play a crucial part in learning. Children with low confidence levels or poor self-esteem, for example, are seen as more easily frustrated and defeated by challenges than children who have high levels of these. The idea emerged that there are necessary *affective* conditions for successful learning, and that these can be usefully boosted, heightened or enhanced.

I shall call this the enhancement agenda in education. It may be pointed out, rightly, that educationalists sometimes talk about enhancing attainment or achievement, as though the enhancement agenda is not distinct from the standards agenda after all. But the typical use of the term 'enhancement' is not this. More frequently, its object is some sort of affective disposition, or a condition like 'well-being' that presupposes certain affective dispositions. The enhancement agenda is not simply about getting children to perform better. It is about getting them to *feel* better—more motivated, more confident, happier—and about the idea that feeling good in these ways leads to success at school and in life generally.

The upshot of these ideas is that schools have a duty to enhance certain feelings, and recent policy documents like the Children's Plan (DCSF, 2007a,b) and the Social and Emotional Aspects of Learning (SEAL) (DfES, 2005) programme are full of exhortations to schools to fulfil this duty, and guidance about how to go about it. The former identifies as one of its 'goals for 2020': 'to enhance children and young people's well-being, particularly at transition points in their lives' (Children's Plan Executive Summary, DCSF, 2007b, p. 19). It goes on to describe the 'positive activities' that 'develop social and personal skills' and 'promote well-being' (p. 20). The SEAL Guidance goes into greater detail, and includes a section called 'Managing Feelings', in which children are taught to say things like: 'I know what makes me feel good and know how to enhance these comfortable feelings.' Another section from the SEAL Guidance called 'Going for Goals!' talks about an inspection framework that will assess outcomes like 'enjoyment', rather than focusing simply on attainment.

As with many policy ideas, much of this is laudable. The Children's Plan in particular takes a practical approach to well-being, accepting the responsibility of the government to put real money into the support of families, the provision of safe play areas, health promotion, housing, etc. (It remains to be seen whether these worthy intentions will be realised.) More problematic is the idea that schools should undertake to enhance children's feelings directly, through a variety of expertly devised strategies. It is not obvious, in the first place, that one can identify particular feelings as unconditionally good, so that more is necessarily better. In general, confidence is a beneficial feeling to have, but it can be excessive and associated with risky behaviour. Some important empirical research (Emler, 2001) has prompted questions about the benefits of feelings (and attitudes) that are assumed to be positively linked to effective learning.

There are also ethical and conceptual questions about the project of enhancing feelings. Philosopher Richard Smith (2002) has expressed concerns about the 'inward turn' in education, and Ecclestone (2004) talks about the recent 'therapeutic ethos' as emphasising 'fragile identities', turning children into victims. More fundamentally, one needs to raise the conceptual question: what exactly is it that educators and policy-makers are seeking to enhance? The Centre for the Wider Benefits of Learning at the Institute of Education in London (2008a and b) has usefully documented the bewildering variety of terms associated with the concept of enhancement in current educational policy. Many of these employ the term 'self': for example, self-esteem, self-discipline, self-awareness, self-concept, self-efficacy and self-regulation. There are several 'umbrella' terms that are thought to embrace a variety of 'skills' or 'qualities': non-cognitive skills, socio-emotional abilities, well-being, emotional intelligence etc. And there are some familiar terms that already have a secure place in the home and classroom, like perseverance, resilience and motivation. An enhancement agenda that is worth its salt needs to rationalise this assortment of terms and clarify its basic aims.

In Section 2, I explore what I call an ordinary concept of enhancement as a component of moral education. I suggest that the primary object of enhancement in this context is feeling, emotion or passion. We try, for example, to enhance children's confidence and hope, and conversely to inhibit feelings like fear, shame and despair. We try to do this appropriately rather than indiscriminately, for the context is all-important. There are times, we feel, when children should be encouraged to experience more rather than less shame or fear. However, there are loose connections between emotion and learning that educators need to be aware of. In general, children do not learn well when they experience high levels of shame or fear.

This brief introduction to the concept of enhancement is based on the philosophy of Aristotle, and it leads to a discussion in section 3 of the enhancement agenda in current educational policy. This involves measuring and then enhancing 'something' that is believed to cause children to learn. The indeterminacy of this 'something', the concept of measurement and some empirical disagreements about causality will occupy us here. I shall question the shift from an informal enhancement agenda (in the classroom and the home) to a more formal version of this in the domain of public policy.

Finally, I explore the concept of self-esteem, and present an account of this concept that in my view deserves a place in education. Concepts go in and out of fashion, and this one has passed its peak. This is partly because outrageous claims have been made on its behalf, and partly because of an empirical study that claimed to overturn our cherished assumptions about self-esteem. When Polly Toynbee (2001) hailed this study in an article headed 'At Last We Can Abandon that Tosh about Low Self-Esteem', some of us knew that the matter deserved a closer look.

2 ENHANCEMENT AND ITS OBJECTS

What does 'enhancement' mean? Dictionaries are not always useful philosophically, but in this case the Shorter Oxford Dictionary gets us off to a good start. 'Enhancement' (the dictionary tells us) comes from the Latin root 'altus', meaning 'high'. To enhance is to 'lift, raise or set up'. It generally means raising or increasing 'the price, value, importance or attractiveness' of something.

The concept of enhancement thus has a spatial aspect and a normative dimension. It is not used literally in a spatial sense (we do not 'enhance' the pictures on our walls when we raise them), but there is an analogue to the spatial aspect that the dictionary fails to mention. This is the notion of 'heightening' (or intensifying) a property, quality or sensation. Your graphics software allows you to enhance the colours on your screen; in a similar sense, a beauty therapist may enhance your tan. An audio technician may enhance the sound on your hi-fi, and a meal or sexual experience or afternoon in the sun may enhance your sensations of pleasure. I shall call this the intensity dimension.

Both the intensity and normative dimensions are relevant to the enhancement agenda in education. This agenda is based on the idea that successful learning presupposes certain ways of feeling. This suggests at least two things: 1) that there is greater value in some feelings than in others (the normative dimension); and 2) that it is possible for educators to 'heighten' the feelings that are valuable, and inhibit feelings that are less so (the intensity dimension). There is generally greater value, for example, in remaining calm before difficult learning challenges than in getting agitated and frustrated by them. 'Calming children down', i.e. enhancing pleasant, hopeful feelings at the expense of painful, hopeless ones, is therefore the business of educators.

However this suggestion may worry us in various ways:

1. Although we can imagine contexts in which 'calming a child down' seems like the right thing to do, we can also imagine contexts in which this would be wrong. Particular children may be better off agitated; it may be their way of getting down to some serious, creative work, or thinking through a problem. In this case the ambition to calm them down may seem patronising and misconceived.
2. There is arguably a sinister aspect to the notion of enhancement, associated with notions like manipulation and control. If enhancing a child's confidence is like intensifying the colour saturation on a computer, this sounds intrusive and even tyrannical. The opposite idea of 'inhibiting' children's feelings may also sound warning bells. There is a fine line between inhibition and repression, and most of us would worry about educators who seek to do the latter.

Such concerns may be alleviated by a brief look at Aristotle's theory of moral education, which is the background for this discussion. Though not universally accepted in every detail, Aristotle's theory of moral education as the cultivation of 'sentimental dispositions' is, many feel, a fundamentally correct account. It captures the basic principles of thought and practice in this area, and provides strong answers to the concerns set out above. Aristotle did not use a term corresponding exactly to the English term 'enhance', but he was concerned, as we are, with ways in which (as I should like to put it) adults 'prevail upon' children morally. In particular, he was concerned about the responsibility to regulate, cultivate or moderate children's feelings. All these concepts have a causal implication, which we will examine more closely when we look at the enhancement agenda in a policy context.

Whatever word we use, the basic idea is that adults should promote some feelings rather than others. The first concern above was that what is right in one context might be wrong in another; and this no one need deny. The Aristotelian position is expressed in this well-known passage:

> ... fear and confidence and appetite and anger and pity and in general pleasure and pain may be felt both too much and too little, and in both cases not well; but to feel them at the right times, with reference to the right objects, towards the right people, with the right motive, and in the right way, is what is intermediate and best, and this is characteristic of virtue (Aristotle, 1972, 1106b19).

This passage employs the distinctive Aristotelian concept of rightness. Aristotle does not say, as some do: it is never right for children to experience anger or agitation. He says that that there is a right time and a wrong time for these emotions, depending on the context. In this regard, he was opposed to philosophers like Seneca the Stoic, who thought that anger and agitation are always indicators of moral weakness.

However, Aristotle was conspicuously silent on the general question of which emotions should be experienced when. He believed that adults should regulate the feelings of children 'appropriately', rather than according to a rulebook. This raises the question of how we know which feelings are appropriate and inappropriate, and Aristotle's answer is considered by many unsatisfactory. We should aim, he said, for the mean, that is, for what is 'intermediate and best'. We know what this is by exercising good judgement about the basic needs and interests—the 'flourishing'—of the child. Whether Sally feels too fearful or too confident as she approaches her maths GCSE exam depends on what is best for Sally as an individual. If she is a timid child, a confidence-boost may do her good. If she is arrogant and conceited, it may be appropriate to instil a little fear.

For Aristotle there are objectively right and wrong ways to feel in particular circumstances, but no general account (nor is a general account possible in principle) of what these are. On the one hand this is unsatisfactory; on the other, one may argue, it reflects the true relationship between language, value and reality. That there are *real values*—i.e. objectively better and worse ways to feel in particular circumstances—is compatible with the impossibility of specifying in a general way what these are.

If this is correct, an enhancement agenda had better face up to the fact. It implies that the regulation of emotions belongs first and foremost in intimate contexts, like the classroom and home, in which adults know and care about children and try to make sound judgements about their interests. This perspective on the matter addresses the second concern above: that enhancement means manipulation and intrusion. The difference between enhancing a child's feelings of hope or confidence and enhancing the colour saturation on a screen is that the first has a crucial moral reference whereas latter has none. There is and must be a normative dimension to enhancement: otherwise we are right to have serious concerns. What this means in practice is that we *hope* that teachers and parents will 'prevail upon' children in ways that are, if not wise, at least benign. We *hope* that they have children's interests at heart, and make sound judgements about what these are. This has implications for teacher selection and training, but it marks (regrettably, in some ways) the end of the road for philosophy. Aristotle's insight was that philosophy, or indeed any *general* discourse, takes us only a certain way towards the situations and happenings of everyday life. This sounds a cautionary note not only for philosophers, but also for policy-makers.

In the next section, I shall examine the policy perspective on enhancement, but first I want to bring out a dimension of emotion-regulation that can easily go missing. This is the cognitive dimension. We have seen that emotions have varying levels of intensity, and this is why we can talk about enhancing them rather as we talk about enhancing colour. It seems a small step from here to the thought that emotions are non-cognitive states, and indeed the term 'non-cognitive' is peppered confusingly throughout many policy documents in relation to the concept of enhancement. However emotions are both non-cognitive *and* cognitive, for they crucially involve thoughts, beliefs and judgements in addition to levels of intensity. The emotion of anger, for example, in addition to a feeling of pain, involves a belief about having been slighted or wronged. The regulation of anger, in this respect, is not at all like the regulation of colour saturation, for in some circumstances it can be tempered or eliminated simply by showing a person that she made a mistake. What she thought was a slight was no such thing. In short, she misunderstood the situation, and when she understands it properly her anger should fade. Her new understanding and the ebbing pain should (if she is rational) be one. Certain beliefs or judgements simply *are* pleasurable or painful, and this is part of what it means to have an emotional life.

This point has important implications for an enhancement agenda. I said that there is and must be a normative dimension to enhancement if we are to allay concerns about manipulation. The cognitive dimension of emotion means that, in our regulation of other people's emotions, we are or should be concerned about their interest in *understanding* themselves and the situations they are in. If we simply wanted to 'tone down' an angry person's pain, we might tell a lie, assuming the person has been grievously wronged. However we cannot, and normally do not, systematically ignore considerations of understanding and truth when we seek to enhance or inhibit people's feelings. We believe that people have an *interest* in understanding the situations they are in, even though this can sometimes conflict with their interest in not experiencing too much pain. It would be an unprincipled adult who tried indiscriminately to enhance children's pleasure, irrespective of the extent to which they understood themselves or the situations they were in.

This brings me to the policy agenda. The project of enhancing children's self-esteem often sounds like a project that has drawn a firm line between cognitive and so-called non-cognitive skills. It suggests that the tendency to feel good about oneself should be promoted independently of the *truth* about one's virtues, efforts or achievements. It siphons off understanding and insight—the cognitive aspects of emotion—in favour of heightened positive feelings. In some respects, this is not unreasonable. I have argued that childhood is a time during which feelings about one's worth develop through attachments to adults, and these can have lifelong importance (Cigman, 2004). There is nothing original about this idea, which I called 'basic self-esteem', and which is derived from Freud's theory of narcissism. However, reality needs to set in, and children need to develop an ability to discriminate between true and false claims about themselves, and to experience, without being crushed by, pain.

The policy agenda plucks the idea of regulating children's feelings from the realm of individual encounters, and sets it down—apparently unaltered—in the realm of public policy. It is not unaltered, however, for the concerns are different and the pressure on key concepts has changed. The policy concerns include 'system reform' and lists of goals on the strength of which political careers will stand or fall. There are 'high expectations . . . for children's trusts to deliver measurable improvements for all children and young people' (DCSF, 2007a, pp. 18–19), and there is guidance for schools on their 'duty to promote well-being' (Centre for the Wider Benefits of Learning, 2008b). There are promises to schools that they will be assessed on the fulfilment or non-fulfilment of this duty, rather than simply on the basis of attainment. The focus is strongly on measurable outcomes, for there is no point (it would seem) in trying to enhance social and emotional skills nationally if one cannot determine objectively whether, and to what extent, one has succeeded.

All this takes us a million miles from the home or classroom. On an Aristotelian view, what need to be regulated are our familiar friends, the emotions. On the policy view, what need to be enhanced are things that we find much harder to grasp, like well-being and social and emotional skills. The need to measure these amounts to an inducement to exaggerate the non-cognitive dimensions of enhancement at the expense of the cognitive dimensions, with a serious cost to the integrity of the agenda. We now need to look into this further.

3 THE ENHANCEMENT AGENDA IN EDUCATIONAL POLICY

The enhancement agenda has several requirements. It needs to identify 'something' that is believed to support and improve learning. It needs to show that this 'something' does in fact support and improve learning. It needs to measure this 'something', and then enhance it. Finally, it needs to prove that this 'something' has in fact been enhanced, through further measuring.

An initial difficulty is that the commitment to measurable outcomes means that the *nature* of what is being enhanced is not the first priority. The first priority is to measure *something* that can be correlated with behavioural and other variables. Although Emler says that test scores should 'behave in a manner that is consistent with what is known or believed to be the nature of the phenomenon' (Emler, 2001, p. 9), he does not treat this as a crucial aspect of the investigation. His relative indifference to the 'nature of the phenomenon' is echoed in the social science literature, and I shall express this by saying that the enhancement agenda is committed to measuring quality Q, without necessarily knowing what Q is.

Ignorance about the nature of Q is evident is many ways. Emler admits: 'Knowing that one has measured something with a reasonable degree of accuracy is not the same as knowing *what* one has measured or whether it is what one intended to measure ... Despite imperfect agreement about its nature, levels of self-esteem can be reliably and easily measured' (Emler, 2001, Summary). So on the one hand, test scores should be 'consistent with what is known or believed to be the nature of the phenomenon', and on the other, we have 'imperfect agreement about [self-esteem's] nature'. This is deeply puzzling. Imagine someone saying: I have measured *something*, but I'm not sure whether it is heat, weight, height or light. To measure something is to claim to *know* something rather precise about that thing, and it is hard to see how one can do this without knowing what 'it' is. One may not understand the physical properties of heat, but measuring the temperature of something means at least knowing that one is measuring heat rather than weight. We can imagine a child who gets this wrong. She has learned to use a thermometer in the sense that she can get a correct reading, without understanding that the highest reading has something to do with the painful sensation of being burnt. She needs to know this. For a measurement to be meaningful, it must yield precise knowledge, not only of a numerical value but also of the 'nature of the thing' that is measured.

Not only is the nature of Q (or, for Emler, self-esteem) problematic. The nature of measurement is equally so. Emler writes:

> It is good practice in psychological measurement to demonstrate that one can obtain similar results using different methods of measurement. With respect to self-esteem, this has yet to be demonstrated. But this should not discourage us from looking for patterns of evidence within the methods of measurement that are available (p. 12).

This sounds to me like an admission that self-esteem measurement is not 'good practice', but my more fundamental concern is that it is not even measurement. Wittgenstein has a telling comment about what it means to measure something: 'Imagine someone saying: "But I know how tall I am!" and laying his hand on top of his head to prove it' (Wittgenstein, 1953, para. 279). This remark is funny (philosophical humour was a serious business for Wittgenstein) precisely because a knowledge claim is being made that cannot be tested in any shape or form. I do not 'know' how tall I am when I place my hand on top of my head, because I have done nothing to suggest that I have measured the spatial dimension that we call 'height'. I am (perhaps) going through *some* of the routine of measuring height, but I am crucially missing out the rest. What I am missing is the possibility of alternative yardsticks (I am not only taller as measured by a slide-rule, but my clothes are too small, my bed is too short ...) and this is a non-optional dimension of what Wittgenstein would have called the language game of measurement.

The enhancement agenda has two clear aims. These are the aims of (a) measuring and (b) raising or enhancing *something*. More cynically, I would say that the aims of the agenda are to produce the *appearance* of doing these things. One cannot appear to raise something in a way that will satisfy a sceptical electorate without appearing to measure that thing. And one cannot appear to measure something without appearing to do this with precision, for the concept of precision is embodied in the concept of measurement. What is required, therefore, is an instrument of measurement that commands general approval and assent.

Self-esteem questionnaires are the instrument of choice, and it must be said that they are widely accepted. They assign numerical values to ticks in boxes, and what policy-makers want almost more than anything else is to get children to tick higher-scoring boxes. I say: they *almost* want this. It satisfies one of their goals, which is to improve 'measurable outcomes'. However there are armies of researchers who are not necessarily friends of the government, ready to expose a flaw in this process. This is what Nicholas Emler did. He claimed to show that the high self-esteem that we had assumed was the key to a teenager's sunny future was nothing of the kind. On the contrary, high self-esteem is a risk factor for drug and alcohol abuse, racism, child abuse and an assortment of other ills. Conversely the low self-esteem that we had blamed for society's ills had little if nothing to answer for, for 'the evidence was about as clear as it could be' in ruling out a causal connection between low self-esteem and crime, racism and so on.

Emler's study changed the landscape of self-esteem research, and I shall look at it more closely in the following section. In particular, I shall be concerned about the use of self-esteem questionnaires as instruments of measurement. One consequence of the study was that it led to some careful re-marketing. Well-being and social and emotional skills overtook their discredited cousin, self-esteem, in the public domain. Except that the *ideas* refused to go away. What we had was still a policy agenda with a bent towards measurable outcomes, and assumptions about 'something' that would cure social ills. We still had little if any idea what this 'something' was, and some of us had a nagging suspicion that low self-esteem had been let off too lightly. The recent debate reflects a more sophisticated view of the alleged trajectory from low to high self-esteem. Emler's discovery that high self-esteem causes drug and alcohol abuse, racism, child abuse and so on reminded us of those famous megalomaniacs whose unalloyed approval of themselves led to horrific atrocities. Psychologist Roy Baumeister *et al.* (2003) called high self-esteem a 'heterogeneous category', observing that it encompasses 'people who frankly accept their good qualities along with narcissistic, defensive and conceited individuals'. Several philosophers, including myself, have written about the excessive or *too*-high self-esteem that presents as bravado, arrogance, big-headedness (Cigman, 2004).

So what did Emler's study show? It is important to see that the thrust of his research was negative: he set out to demonstrate the *absence* of a causal link between low self-esteem and under-achievement, disaffection and violence, contrary to popular assumptions about, and public investment in, such a link. Despite his acknowledgement that it is harder to disprove than prove causal linkages, he claimed success in this ambition. But was he successful? Did he really overturn a 'popular view'? In the next section, I try to answer this question.

4 SELF-ESTEEM: THE POPULAR VIEW

Emler introduces his study with a short quotation: 'Violent children hold other lives cheap because they believe their own lives to be worthless' (Melanie Phillips, quoted in Emler, 2001, p. 1). This, he says, will strike a chord with readers because it 'mirrors many widely accepted views'. He is right: many people agree with this, and would add that they see under-achieving children, teenage mothers, criminals, drug addicts as in this position because they 'believe their own lives to be worthless'.

This is an explanatory theory. It says that people who manifest certain sorts of behaviour do so because they have low self-esteem. 'Because' in this context signals a necessary condition; if you are violent or under-achieving, you *must* have a self-esteem problem. People who believe this often believe that it works in the other direction too. If you have low self-esteem (they think) you will inevitably (or almost inevitably) become a violent person, a person who does badly at school, a girl who gets pregnant at fifteen. This is a predictive theory, and it merges with the explanatory theory in the view that low self-esteem is *necessary and sufficient* for educational failure and anti-social behaviour.

These ideas are simplistic and implausible. There *are* no necessary or sufficient conditions for anti-social behaviour or educational failure, though journalists, self-help therapists and positive psychologists would like to think there are. At most, there are loose causal connections, though it is exceedingly hard to specify what these are, especially if self-esteem or Q are poorly understood. It would be wrong, in my view, to equate the explanatory/predictive theory with the 'everyday' understanding of self-esteem in a more functional sense. The former is the absurd social vaccine view: inject a population with Q or self-esteem or whatever it is, and we all become happier, safer and more productive overnight. Teachers and parents who worry about the self-esteem of the children in their care do not think this way; yet their concerns may have features in common with the explanatory/predictive theory in the sense that they *worry* about the educational futures of children with low self-esteem, and *look beyond* the bravado of disruptive or violent children to see if they are covering a sense of low self-worth.

The explanatory/predictive theory is in essence the self-help conception of self-esteem. According to this conception, we may not know what self-esteem is, but we know that it needs to be enhanced in as many individuals as possible because it is the source of, and prerequisite for, all things good. The challenge for anyone who is looking for a serious conception of self-esteem is to distinguish between this vapid, implausible idea and the ordinary, functional view of teachers and parents in the classroom and the home. This Emler conspicuously fails to do. Having quoted Phillips disparagingly, he goes on:

> [Phillips'] observation will have struck a chord with many readers because it mirrors many widely accepted views. These include the ideas that many children, rather too many, are now growing up with a sense that they have no value, and that their damaged sense of their own worth in turn causes them to do violence to themselves and others (p. 1).

Here Phillips' claim is linked to the ideas: (1) that many children are growing up with low self-esteem, and (2) that this causes them to be violent (one could add: to under-achieve). It seems to me quite wrong to conflate (1) and (2), as Emler does, with Phillips' claim that all violent children believe their lives to be worthless. The latter is indeed speculative hype. (1), on the other hand, far from being hype, is almost certainly true. Of course its truth needs to be confirmed (although the term 'many' is so vague that it could hardly be false), and this can only be done if we establish that we all mean the same thing by the 'low self-esteem' and agree about the methods by which its presence in greater and lesser (but not necessarily measurable) quantities and absence are assessed. But as a simple claim, based on ordinary observations to the effect that *this* child has low self-esteem, and *these* children and *those* children, it is surely sensible enough to take seriously. (2) is less convincing, because it has the ring of a sufficient condition: if C has low-self-esteem, she *will be* violent (will under-achieve). On the other hand, I would suggest that many parents and teachers are justified in being concerned that *particular* children with low self-esteem may under-achieve or behave disruptively or violently *as a consequence* of their low self-esteem. They would need good reasons for thinking this about the children in question, rather than a causal hypothesis about self-esteem and its effects, but I see no reason in principle why such reasons should not exist. On the contrary, the idea that Mary or Joe, who are always saying 'I'm stupid' or 'I'm hopeless' in class, might *as a consequence of their feelings* under-achieve, seems like a perfectly reasonable one.

Discussing the analysis of difficult concepts like self-esteem, philosopher Kristján Kristjánsson writes: 'Sometimes, as in the case of self-esteem, a clearly specified meaning may even be missing in ordinary language (it is not as though we could go into the field and ask the real self-esteem to please stand up); and in such cases, more radical conceptual regimentation may be required' (Kristjánsson, 2007). I disagree. I believe that we can and should ask the real self-esteem to please stand up, just as we ask the real knowledge, the real justice or the real beauty to stand up when, as philosophers, we enquire into the 'real' uses and purposes of such words, as opposed to their corruptions in various theoretical contexts. The concept of self-esteem is what we are concerned about when we notice that Mary or Joe is always putting her/himself down, and worry about how this will affect her/his future. Self-esteem is an ethical concept, bound up with the notions of 'too little' and 'too much', and these crucially refer us to an individual's flourishing. Despite being hugely influential, Emler's work misses all this, because it is locked into precisely the conceptual framework that it purports to overturn. He concludes that, not *low* self-esteem but *high* self-esteem is causally linked to alcohol and drug abuse, and risky sexual behaviour. Moreover low self-esteem, *like* high self-esteem, has no effect on educational achievement. The conclusions are different from those of the self-helpers, but the basic assumptions are the same. It is assumed that self-esteem is incorrigibly known by self-report, so the absence of yardsticks by which to test these is not a serious difficulty. It is assumed that the motives for filling in self-esteem questionnaires are transparent, so when a person ticks a box that says 'strongly agree' alongside the statement 'I feel I have a number of good qualities', this means that she feels she has a number of good qualities, end of story. It is assumed that 'more' self-esteem can be quantitatively distinguished from 'less' self-esteem, and that this can be done meaningfully without asking: how truthful are these feelings? However, these are only assumptions, products of thinking. We now need to go into the field.

5 WILL THE REAL SELF-ESTEEM PLEASE STAND UP?

What *concerns* does the preoccupation with self-esteem try to address? I see this as the fundamental question.

This is different from the questions raised by most researchers in this area. The usual starting point is a brief discussion about the meaning or definition of self-esteem in which the key question is whether this is a set of feelings or a set of beliefs, attitudes, judgements. *Why* one answer or another is preferred (given that, as I argue, self-esteem involves them all) is never entirely clear. To elect for one or another definition is not to do what I have been arguing needs to be done, which is enquire about the *nature* of self-esteem and the concerns that brought this concept to our attention in the first place.

The most popular definition is that of psychologist William James (1890/1950, chapter 10), who says that self-esteem is the ratio of people's successes to their pretensions or aspirations. For James, the basic question we need to ask when enquiring into a person's self-esteem is: to what extent do you see yourself as having met your own standards and aspirations? The many questionnaires that have been devised to measure self-esteem depart from this basic idea. But here is a difficulty. The easiest way to meet one's standards and aspirations is to have none at all. The child who feels so bad about herself that she feels unworthy to aspire to anything may have the highest ratio of successes to aspirations, i.e. in *this* sense, a very high level of self-esteem. However, part of what people are concerned about when they are concerned about self-esteem is precisely the inability, failure or reluctance to aspire *because one feels unworthy to aspire*. This idea—that in order to flourish, human beings need to feel 'worthy to aspire'—is, I would argue, a crucial component of our ordinary concern about self-esteem.

A good way to explore this is through a fictional character. In good fiction, thought, beliefs, motives and actions are integral and highly transparent. Assuming that the author is doing her job well, our role as readers is not to be sceptical (imagine someone saying, no, it didn't really happen that way), but to be, as Henry James put it, 'finely aware and richly responsible' (quoted by Nussbaum, 1990). There is no place for doubt, as such; there is only a place for obtuseness, that is, for a failure to see, feel, be 'finely aware'. This is a great advantage in a discussion like this. I can question the motives of children who tick boxes in one way or another, and even if I know the children well, this question may remain unresolved. I cannot question the motives of a fictional character in the same way, for such motives are (assuming that the fiction is good) *there* for me to find or fail to find in the text. Novels create windows into human hearts and minds that may be interpreted differently, but cannot be in an ordinary sense opaque or hidden from view.

The novel I shall look at is *Untouchable*, by Mulk Raj Anand, and the main character is a young man called Bakha. Bakha is not only an 'untouchable', i.e. an outcaste from Hindu society. He is a sweeper, which means that his role in life is to clear away other people's excrement, and he belongs to the bottom rung of the untouchable group socially. His status compels him to shout warnings of his approach as he walks on the streets, so he can be avoided by people who believe they will be defiled by touching him. Bakha has few aspirations the author tells us: 'He had begun to work at the latrines at the age of six and resigned himself to the hereditary life of the craft ...' (p. 39). He knows his place in society, and frankly accepts his extremely low status. On one occasion he is walking along a street, and a Hindu man touches him accidentally. He starts hurling abuse at Bakha, calling him a 'low caste vermin' and complaining that he will have to take a bath to purify himself. This is Bakha's response:

Bakha stood amazed, embarrassed. He was deaf and dumb. His senses were paralyzed. Only fear gripped his soul, fear and humility and servility. He was used to being spoken to roughly. But he had seldom been taken so unawares. The curious smile of humility which always hovered on his lips in the presence of high-caste men now became more pronounced. He lifted his face to the man opposite him, though his eyes were bent down. Then he shot a hurried glance at the man. The fellow's eyes were flaming and red-hot (p. 46).

Bakha cannot read, but if he were somehow able to fill in a self-esteem questionnaire, we would not expect a high result. In particular, we would expect him to 'strongly disagree' with the statement on the well-known Rosenberg self-esteem scale: 'I feel that I'm a person of worth, at least on an equal plane with others.'

However, Bakha is a human being, and the picture is more complex than this. The idea of placing him on a trajectory from low to high self-esteem—i.e. of *measuring* his self-esteem—begins to looks absurd when we consider aspects of his life and personality. We are told that, though Bakha had 'resigned himself to the hereditary life of the craft', he could not 'consciously accept' the fact that he was a sweeper, and indeed 'dreamed of becoming a sahib'. He was resigned to a bleak existence, but felt worthy of a great deal more.

Shortly after his self-deprecating response to the bullying Hindu, he is walking along the street, and there develops:

> a smouldering rage in his soul. His feelings would rise like spurts of smoke from a half-smothered fire, in fitful, unbalanced jerks when the recollection of some abuse or rebuke he had suffered kindled a spark in the ashes of remorse inside him. ....'Why was all this fuss? Why was I so humble? I could have struck him!' (p. 51).

The reader is relieved. Thank goodness, one thinks; Bakha has some pride. He was *appropriately* enraged by a terrible insult, and we see this, together with the fact that Bakha could not 'consciously accept' that he was a sweeper, as evidence that he has a modicum of self-esteem after all[1].

This impression is strengthened by another brief incident. One day Bakha has the bright idea of asking a higher caste child to teach him to read, and he cleverly bribes both the boy and his younger brother to give him lessons. He needs to do this in order to prevent the younger child from feeling jealous and ratting on the older child to their mother; if she were to find out, that would be the end of lessons. The deal is done and Bakha feels elated. The author tells us that he: 'headed towards the gates of the town, his basket under one arm, his broom under another, and in his heart a song as happy as a lark's (p. 41).

There is, in my view, much to be learned from this story. First, the story calls into question the idea that self-esteem and similar questionnaires are (as IQ tests were once wrongly thought to be) culture-independent. On the improbable supposition that an individual like Bakha would complete such a questionnaire, we cannot ignore the way his responses would reflect how he has been taught to think and talk about himself by people he has been conditioned to see as in every way superior. According to the picture we have of Bakha, the idea about talking well of himself in the company of literate people would be unthinkable.

However the author of *Untouchable* encourages his readers to experience a tension between the 'official' sense of low self-worth that would no doubt manifest on a self-esteem test, and something that is equally if not more important. Bakha's eventual anger towards the Hindu bully, his sense of pride as he refuses to 'consciously accept' that he is a sweeper, and his confidence and joy in the face of an educational opportunity: these are crucial indicators of *good* self-esteem, and they make the book a richly rewarding, rather than an agonising and in some sense pointless read. We know that people can be crushed by abuse and denigration. Far more interesting are the ways in which they can be both crushed and uncrushable: both succumb to and rise above misfortune.

I do not believe most teachers would have concerns about Bakha, were he miraculously to walk into their classrooms. Yes, he might grovel and fawn for a while, but the crucial thing is that he would learn. He would quickly learn to read (we are led to suppose), and one expects him to learn to look people in the eye, to stand tall if they bully him, and much else besides. Bakha seems *capable* of learning all this because he has what we see in an everyday sense as 'good-enough' self-esteem. What this means, to repeat, is that he has 'appropriate' emotional tendencies. He feels pride and anger rather than shame when bullied, and confidence and joy rather than fear at the prospect of learning.

Consider another child called Emily. Emily makes a cameo but unforgettable appearance in John Holt's 1964 classic *How Children Fail*. We do not know her age, but she is old enough to be expected to spell, or learn to spell, the word 'microscope'. Emily fails to do this in a test. She bizarrely writes MINCOPERT, which indicates not only that she cannot spell 'microscope', but also that she cannot properly *attempt* to spell this word. As Holt puts it: 'She obviously made a wild grab at the answer, and having written it down, never looked at it, never checked to see if it looked right. I see a lot of this one-way, don't-look-back-it's-too-awful strategy among students' (Holt, 1964, pp. 19–20). It does not seem to have occurred to Holt, as it would occur to most of us nowadays, that Emily might belong to the group of individuals that are known as 'dyslexic'. The readiness to label children this way belongs to an area of controversy that I do not want to engage with here. (Section II of this book—Julian Elliott's and Simon Gibbs' chapter in particular—is devoted to this topic.) I am interested in the strategy that Holt vividly describes as 'don't-look-back-it's-too-awful', suggesting that it is employed by children who are *too* afraid of learning, *too* ashamed of their performances. I am not suggesting that it is appropriate for children to feel fear or shame in the context of learning, so long as it is not 'too much', as I hope I have made clear. The point is that some children experience these emotions in an extreme and debilitating excess. Such children, I believe, are encountered not infrequently in the classroom, and the expression 'low self-esteem' naturally arises in this connection.

We do not know, obviously, how Emily would fare on a self-esteem test, but I see no reason to assume that a child who tackles a spelling challenge this way would necessarily disagree with a statement like 'I feel that I am a person of worth, at least on an equal plane with others'. Perhaps she is attractive and has a lot of friends; perhaps her looks and popularity enable her to present in many situations as a person with good self-esteem. However I suggest that this performance in a spelling test calls into question her self-esteem, in an important and widely accepted use of that term. Emily didn't merely fail to meet a standard; she demonstrated (at that moment, at least) that she lacked the emotional resources to remedy that failure. She ducked rather than faced the challenge. If she were to adopt the 'don't-look-back-it's-too-awful strategy' in her education generally, she would no doubt fail at many things and be in danger of developing a sense of 'unworthiness to aspire'. (On the lack of 'confidence to fail', see Cigman, 2001).

The child who cannot or will not make an effort to learn is of great educational concern, and it is this, I believe, that the enhancement agenda sets out to address. The Social and Emotional Aspects of Learning (SEAL) programme says that it:

> ... will be used by schools who have identified the social and emotional aspects of learning as a key focus for their work with the children. These will be schools who know that the *factors holding back learning* in their setting include children's difficulties in understanding and managing their feelings, working co-operatively in groups, motivating themselves and demonstrating resilience in the face of setbacks (my italics).

The enhancement agenda is about certain 'factors holding back learning'. These are not primarily physical, cognitive, social or cultural, but emotional. We all know that such factors exist and can be hard to overcome. What we have not succeeded in doing is understanding their nature, though expressions like 'low self-esteem', 'poor social and emotional skills', 'poor motivation' and 'poor resilience' hint at this. I would now like to venture a more detailed suggestion about the 'nature of the phenomenon' that these terms attempt to capture.

Emily, I suspect, is caught in a trap. *First*, she fails, and the 'don't-look-back-it's-too-awful strategy' used on the spelling test suggests that she may have a habit of failing. Let us assume for the sake of argument that Emily fails often. As regular occurrences in a person's life, failures tend to lead to a sense of worthlessness, as least in the competitive environments of schools. This is not an empirical generalisation, but a comment on the expectations that are generated by our society. *Second*, as a 'worthless person' in this sense, Emily is repeatedly confronted by educational challenges. (She is a schoolchild, and schoolchildren face constant challenges.) Emily has failed in the past—she has learnt to see herself as ineffective in the face of challenges—*therefore*, she expects to fail in the future. The 'don't-look-back-it's-too-awful strategy' expresses a sense of the inevitability of failure, given repeated failures of the past.

This, I submit, is the circular logic of failure, though the negative sequence of thinking is not inevitable, and indeed the aim of the enhancement agenda as I understand it is precisely to interrupt or overturn it. The circular thought is this: I am worthless because/therefore I fail. *Because* I have failed to achieve certain standards, *therefore* I will do so in the future. The educator's priority must be to stop such thinking in its tracks, and notions like resilience, persistence, motivation etc present themselves as possible ways to do this. *We must make children more motivated, more resilient* ... The concept of self-esteem plays a crucial role here. There is a curious debate amongst philosophers about whether self-esteem has a motivational aspect; we have seen that some, like William James, see self-esteem as essentially backward-looking, a matter of rating one's achievements relative to one's aspirations. Kristján Kristjánsson argues in this vein that self-esteem is conceptually independent of confidence, which is forward-looking. This misses the vital point that our *concern* about self-esteem is a concern about creatures that live inescapably in time, and are *integrally* backward-looking and forward-looking. The circular logic of failure, as I described it, is low self-esteem on a temporal stage, in which negative self-appraisals feed into, and in some cases tragically undermine, executive, forward-looking behaviour. We do not want this for children, and the recent intense interest in enhancement obscurely acknowledges this fact.

6 CONCLUSION

The enhancement agenda in education involves multiple errors. It has based around a property to which a variety of terms have been appended; I called it simply Q. It is assumed that Q is rather like blood pressure, quantifiably higher or lower. It is supposed that Q belongs on a moral trajectory, where 'more' is always better than 'less'. Finally, it is supposed that Q is reliably measured by 'tick behaviour', as though it has never occurred to anyone to attribute ambivalent or complex motives to human actions.

Some useful work has borne in on these fictions. Baumeister's observation that high self-esteem is a 'heterogeneous category' has aroused suspicions about the idea of the moral trajectory. However the criticisms have not in my view gone far enough, for the interest in measurable outcomes persists. There is still a tendency to attribute self-esteem or well-being 'quotients' to entire populations, so that educators can get to work on boosting these and news can hopefully be broken that they have risen. However, the *real* concept of self-esteem has nothing to do with quotients; indeed, I would say that it has a fairly limited application. The 'real concept' expresses a concern about individuals who experience certain inappropriate emotions and get trapped in the circular logic of failure. Of course, the emotions and the logic are inextricable; the latter involves a tendency to experience too much fear and shame, too little confidence and joy.

There is a great deal of talk nowadays about 'barriers to learning', particularly for children who are seen as having difficulties and disabilities. I have argued that low self-esteem can be a significant barrier to learning, though human beings are (as I have said several times) sufficiently complex that it would be wrong to see this as a sufficient condition for educational failure. Some children succeed precisely *because* they feel bad about themselves; they work hard (sometimes obsessively) to overturn this view of themselves. Others, however, need help, and this should come in the form, first, of acknowledgement of the problem; second, of identification of particular children who suffer from the problem; third, of empirical work—particularly, I would think, by teachers—on the question: how can children be helped to escape from the circular logic of failure? This is a question on which philosophers and empirical researchers can usefully converge, for it is about our ability to 'prevail upon' other people's wills to aspire towards a better kind of life.

NOTE

1. Critics may argue that this example illustrates not self-esteem, but self-respect. It is true that these are independent in some cases, but I am working here with the assumption that a tendency to one is psychologically and conceptually coincident with a tendency to the other.

REFERENCES

Anand, M. R. (1986) *Untouchable* (London, Penguin).

Aristotle (1972) *Nichomachean Ethics*, D. Ross, trans. (London, Oxford University Press).

Baumeister, R., Campbell, J., Krueger, J. and Vohs, K. D. (2003) Does High Self-Esteem Cause Better Performance, Interpersonal Success, Happiness or Healthier Lifestyles?, *Psychological Science in the Public Interest*, 4.1, pp. 1–44.

Centre for the Wider Benefits of Learning (2008a) *Non-Cognitive Skills: What Are They? How Do They Support Life Chances? Briefing paper 1: Aims and Scope* (London, Institute of Education, University of London).

Centre for the Wider Benefits of Learning (2008b) *Non-Cognitive Skills: What Are They? How Do They Support Life Chances? Briefing paper 2: Policy Context* (London, Institute of Education, University of London).

Cigman, R. (2001) Self-esteem and the Confidence to Fail, *Journal of Philosophy of Education*, 35.4, pp. 561–575.

Cigman, R. (2004) Situated Self-esteem, *Journal of Philosophy of Education*, 38.(1), pp. 91–105.

Department for Children, Schools and Families (2007a) The Children's Plan: Building Brighter Futures. Available at: http://www.dcsf.gov.uk/publications/childrensplan/downloads/ The_Childrens_Plan.pdf

Department for Children, Schools and Families (2007b) The Children's Plan: Executive Summary. Available at: http://www.dcsf.gov.uk/publications/childrensplan/downloads/Chi ldrens_Plan_Executive_Summary.pdf

Department for Education and Skills (2005) Excellence and learning: Social and Emotional Aspects of Learning. Available at: http://www.standards.dfes.gov.uk/primary/publications/ banda/seal/

Ecclestone, K. (2004) The Rise of Low Self-Esteem and the Lowering of Educational Expectations, in: D. Hayes (ed.) *The Routledge Guide to Key Debates in Education* (Oxford, Routledge).

Emler, N. (2001) Self-Esteem: The Costs and Causes of Low Self-Worth. Summary. Available at: http://www.jrf.org.uk. Full text of the article is available at: http://www.jrf.org.uk/bookshop/ eBooks/1859352510.pdf

Holt, J. (1964) *How Children Fail* (London, Penguin).

James, W. (1890/1950) *The Principles of Psychology*, Vol. 1 (New York, Dover).

Kristjánsson, K. (2007) Justified Self-esteem, *Journal of Philosophy of Education*, 41.2, pp. 247–261.

Smith, R. (2002) Self-Esteem: The Kindly Apocalypse, *Journal of Philosophy of Education*, 36.1, pp. 87–100.

Nussbaum, M. C. (1990) 'Finely Aware and Richly Responsible': Literature and the Moral Imagination, in her: *Love's Knowledge: Essays on Philosophy and Literature* (Oxford, Oxford University Press).

Toynbee, P. (2001) At Last We Can Abandon that Tosh about Low Self-Esteem, *Guardian*, 28.December.

Wittgenstein, L. (1953) *Philosophical Investigations* (Oxford, Blackwell).

4.3
The Long Slide to Happiness

RICHARD SMITH

> When I see a couple of kids
> And guess he's fucking her and she's
> Taking pills or wearing a diaphragm,
> I know this is paradise
>
> Everyone old has dreamed of all their lives—
> Bonds and gestures pushed to one side
> Like an outdated combine harvester,
> And everyone young going down the long slide
>
> To happiness, endlessly.
>
> (Philip Larkin, *High Windows*)

> People in the West have got no happier in the last 50 years. They have
> become much richer, they work much less, they have longer holidays,
> they travel more, they live longer, and they are healthier. But they are
> no happier. This shocking fact should be the starting point for much of
> our social science.
>
> (Richard Layard, 2003, p. 14)

The concern that children in the UK are significantly less happy than their
counterparts in other countries, and the responses to this concern that take
the form of proposals to 'teach happiness' in schools, are discussed
elsewhere in this volume (by Ruth Cigman and Judith Suissa). They have
come from, among others, Anthony Seldon, Master (i.e. Headmaster) of
Wellington College and biographer of Tony Blair, Tal D. Ben-Shahar,
who teaches 'Positive Psychology' at Harvard, and Richard (Lord)
Layard, author of *Happiness: Lessons from a New Science* (2005). If any
further illustration of such concern is needed, the publisher's blurb for
Layard's book supplies it:

> Richard Layard shows that there is a paradox at the heart of our lives.
> Most people want more income. Yet as societies become richer, they do
> not become happier. This is not just anecdotally true, it is the story told by
> countless pieces of scientific research. We now have sophisticated ways
> of measuring how happy people are, and all the evidence shows that on
> average, people have grown no happier in the last fifty years, even as
> average incomes have more than doubled. In fact, the First World has
> more depression, more alcoholism and more crime than fifty years ago.

This paradox is true of Britain, the United States, continental Europe and Japan. What is going on?

These ideas and the proposals to which they have led echo to a remarkable degree the 'self-esteem movement' which has been vigorous in the USA and has been influential in the UK. This movement emphasises the widespread incidence of psychological harm caused by damage to the child's sense of self-worth, including damage done by formal education itself, and looks to education, suitably reconceived, as a site where such damage can be repaired.

Like the self-esteem movement, the focus on happiness promises a more sensitive culture, and one more aware of the casual injustices and indignities that education can inflict. In particular—to take a matter that I have written about before (Smith, 2006) and that exercises me because I see its effects almost daily in my work with university students—it might make us more capable of noticing the obsession with a kind of perfection on the part of young people whose schooling has persuaded them that anything other than a series of top marks and grades means complete academic and personal failure. The focus on happiness is kindly, and unquestionably well-intentioned, but also potentially cataclysmic in two of its tendencies especially. It contains the seeds of a worrying emphasis on the self as opposed to the world that the individual benefits from engaging with, and treats happiness as an achievement on the part of individuals. I have written about this before in the context of self-esteem (Smith, 2002) and will not repeat the argument here. In this chapter I shall focus on the point that the focus on happiness cannot account for the fact that we want and value all sorts of things that do not make us particularly happy. Above all, it overlooks the diversity of goods that we value in education and in life more broadly, as if anything that we found worth pursuing must be understood in terms of the common currency of happiness.

1 PARADISE CONFUSED

Claims that we now know what makes for happiness, and can proceed to 'teach happiness' in schools, tend on closer inspection not always to be versions of the same claim but to be various different claims. In the new literature on teaching happiness can be found the following:

1. Claims about the need to teach 'the whole child', which generally seem to turn on a concern that education has become (i) narrowly academic and (ii) dominated by regimes of assessment;
2. Claims that instead of learning all kinds of 'facts out there', which by implication are inert, fusty and irrelevant, children ought to 'know themselves';
3. Claims that there are different areas of experience or understanding, of which education has focused on far too few;
4. Claims that children need exercise—for instance, along the lines that twenty minutes of exercise a week does as much good as Prozac, if not more;

5. Claims that we know what causes happiness and unhappiness (divorce, bereavement, misuse of drugs) and that children would benefit from this knowledge;
6. Claims that children would benefit (i.e. be made happier) by yoga-style exercises designed to help them to relax, focus and concentrate;
7. Claims that children need to learn that other people's happiness can be damaged by thoughtlessness, bullying, racism, etc.

Naturally rather different claims are made by different writers, but confusion often reigns even in the ideas of any one writer. Since this provides an *a fortiori* element to the discussion I shall focus briefly on the claims made by Anthony Seldon in a debate with Frank Furedi titled 'Can we Teach People to be Happy?' in *The Guardian* (19 February 2008). Seldon begins:

> There is only one important question: what is the purpose of education? Is it to cram students with facts to maximise their test performances, so that whole institutions become exam factories, tensing and stretching every sinew to achieve five A*s-Cs at GCSE, and comparable results at A-level and beyond?
>
> Or is there a wider vision? One that involves developing the whole student, so that we help them know who they are and what they want to do in life. On leaving full-time education, not only will they be able to wave certificates with pass marks written on them, they will also be fully prepared to embrace life in all its fullness.

Here, clearly, is a vigorous version of (1), but an element of (2) enters with the aspiration to 'help them know who they are'. After noting that schooling is too much subject to the 'top-down' drivers from government, universities and employers (the demand, essentially, for academic results) Seldon claims that these 'drivers' should be 'balanced with "bottom-up" factors: what makes up each child, and how they can make the most of their linguistic and logical, social and personal, spiritual and moral, creative and physical faculties. Every school should be developing these eight aptitudes'. Thus claim (3): and while it is the kind of claim with which one can easily nod along—who would not agree that education should attend to the spiritual and creative dimensions, for example, and that they are too easily squeezed out of the curriculum?—it is important to note that a great deal is assumed here. Are the personal and the social distinct 'faculties', for instance, or the spiritual and moral? If someone produces some creative writing, are they using their linguistic or creative faculties, or both? And what if the writing is in some sense personal? These questions become pressing ones when there are proposals to re-shape the curriculum on the basis of the existence of such 'faculties'. Seldon continues:

> ... depression, self-harming and anxiety among students are reaching epidemic proportions. So are drinking and drug-taking. Teaching

schoolchildren how to live autonomous lives increases the chances of avoiding depression, mental illness and dependency when they are older.

This is claim (5), here apparently consisting of the argument that there is factual evidence about, say, the harm done by cannabis use or alcohol dependency, and children ought to know it. Some further point is being made here about autonomy, but it is not easy to see quite what it is. Is the value of living an autonomous life here being assumed, so that it can be invoked as a motivator in persuading children of the evils of drugs? Or is the claim that people who live autonomous lives (a life which is apparently exclusive of inappropriate drinking and drug use) do as a matter of fact tend to avoid depression and mental illness? No evidence is offered for this, and it seems on the face of it unlikely.

After some unexceptionable remarks about the sensible use of technology, about keeping one's room tidy and having good personal relationships, Seldon writes:

> Most important of all is the relationships with oneself. Students learn how to manage their minds, their emotions and their bodies. Bit by bit, they learn what makes them distinctive. They learn to recognise and manage their negative and positive emotions. They learn the value of accepting themselves as they are and appreciating others. They are taught to calm themselves by deep breathing and other techniques, and discover that three 20-minute bouts of exercise a week have the same effect on raising the spirit and avoiding depression as a standard dose of Prozac.

Here (4), the simple point that exercise is good for you, and (6), the 'deep breathing and other techniques', sit uncomfortably with echoes of (2), the focus on the self, and a suggestion of (7), the appreciation of others that will include an understanding of the effects of our actions on *their* happiness.

The fact that there are very different kinds of claims being made here is not a trivial matter, since the variety of claims undermines the possibility that it is just one thing, happiness, which is being talked about in every case. The feeling of well-being that comes from brisk exercise, for example, is very different from the sense that you are to some degree in control of your own destiny and know what you want to do with your life. The former brings exhilaration, a feeling of cares dropping away: the latter may bring a vertiginous and unsettling feeling—frightening, even—as a young person realises that all along they have wanted to be a creative artist, for instance, and begins to recognise the rocky and uncertain path along which they will have to go, or sets their sights on the long journey to qualifying as a doctor. These conditions in turn are different from the calm that comes through 'deep breathing and other techniques', or from whatever satisfaction is supposed to result from 'knowing who you are' or what makes you distinctive (not forgetting of course that you might find that you are a rather unpleasant person who has inherited various undesirable but highly distinctive traits from your parents).

2 STANDARDISING HAPPINESS

Since it seems so very clear that an unhelpfully wide range of states and emotions are here being recruited under the banner of 'happiness' it is worth enquiring how this state of affairs has come about. The line of thought in its modern form—though it can be traced without difficulty to the utilitarian philosophers of the nineteenth century—is set out by Richard Layard in his 2002/3 Lionel Robbins Memorial Lectures (Layard, 2003). Happiness means 'feeling good—enjoying life and feeling it is wonderful'. Unhappiness, by contrast, means 'feeling bad and wishing things were different' (p. 4). Layard agrees that there are innumerable sorts of things that make us happy or unhappy, but claims that at root there is always this element of feeling good or bad. And it is this, of course, that makes it possible to compare experiences in terms of how much happiness they produce, and then to measure and rank them.

> I want to stress the point about a single dimension. Happiness is just like noise. There are many qualities of noise, from a trombone to a caterwaul. But they can all be compared in terms of decibels. In the same way different kinds of pain, like toothache and tummy ache, can be compared, and so can different kinds of enjoyment . . . happiness and unhappiness are not separate dimensions; they are simply different points along a continuum . . . they are all part of the same phenomenon (ibid.).

In support of this way of thinking of happiness Layard cites a study of women in Texas. They were asked to divide the previous day into a number of episodes, and they came up with roughly 15 such episodes. They were asked to describe each episode, and who was involved in it with them. 'Finally they were also asked how they felt in each episode, along twelve dimensions *which were then combined into a single state of feeling*' (p. 5, my italics). In other words, whatever subtleties were there in the original responses were systematically flattened out so that every episode could be fitted somewhere onto one standard scale: that of happiness.

As a way of getting to grips with what is going wrong here we might try an experiment, substituting 'response to art' for 'happiness'. In same way, then, as we can compare noise in terms of decibels, so different kinds of response to art, like our impatience at a self-indulgent poem and our sense that there is something (like a low-level toothache) naggingly not right about the structure of *Macbeth*, can be compared. So too with our positive responses. It may sound odd to compare listening to a Beethoven quartet with contemplating Anthony Gormley's *Field for the British Isles*, but at root there is always the dimension of feeling good or bad. Let us propose a measure of response to art, AR. Now we can survey various experiences of art. Please come up with about 15 AR episodes, and say how you felt in each episode. You were stunned by that painting, intrigued by the poem, left speechless by that memorial to the Holocaust. And so on. We can then divide these into twelve dimensions, *and then combine them into a single state of feeling*, AR.

One of the many things going wrong here is that it is impossible to understand a response to art independently of understanding the work of art itself. My response to Gormley's *Field for the British Isles* is different from my response to Barbara Hepworth's *Oval Sculpture (No. 2)* because those responses are bound up with what they respond to: you will not be able to grasp my response unless you have some familiarity with those art works themselves. It cannot be a matter of comparing the responses and situating them on a common standard or scale. This is, I hope, clear enough in the case of response to art. But is it so very different in the case of the study that Layard reports, and other studies like it? The Texas women appear to have enjoyed sex most: it comes top of the ratings, with a measure of 4.7 in the Happiness Index. And surely we know what they are responding to: we know what sex, of all things, is.

However, a well-publicised recent piece of research casts doubt even—or perhaps particularly—on this. Drawing on replies from nearly 1,900 people, Meston and Buss (2007) distinguished 237 categories of reasons why people have sex. They include, among the reasons we might expect, such as 'I wanted to express my love for the person' and 'I was sexually aroused and wanted the release', a great range of other reasons, for instance: 'I wanted to feel closer to God', 'to get rid of a headache', 'help me fall asleep', 'make my partner feel powerful', 'burn calories', 'keep warm', 'hurt an enemy', 'It would allow me to "get sex out of my system" so that I could focus on other things', 'It was the only way my partner would spend time with me', 'I wanted to even the score with a cheating partner'.[1] What this research reminds us is that we do not know what 'having sex' is all about, until we know what it *means*. When sex scored 4.7 in the Texas Happiness index it is not just that we do not know exactly what was causing the women to be 'happy': we do not know what their 'happiness' was. Was it the religious ecstasy of feeling closer to God, the comfort of keeping warm, the vindictive thrill of hurting an enemy, the relief of *not* enjoying sex ('It would allow me to "get sex out of my system" so that I could focus on other things'), an escape from loneliness? Even where sex is the expression of love for a person, we need to understand the kind of love for the particular person involved before we can imagine we know anything about what the sexual act means, just as we need to appreciate the art work before we can understand the response.

The same argument applies to other items on the Texas list. 'Dinner' scored high. Again it might seem that this is a simple physical pleasure, a matter of relishing the flavour and texture of the food, and of course it might be just this. But for one woman the pleasure might be to a large extent that of having her family together and seeing them enjoy the food she has devotedly prepared for them; for another the meal might be an integral part of an evening with her lover. One woman may take particular pleasure in eating fast food, effortlessly microwaved, in front of the television, while for another the rhythms of unhurried preparation and cooking are part of what distinguishes this part of the day from the rest of it. The important general point here is made by Alasdair MacIntyre with the example of a man digging his garden (MacIntyre, 1981, Chapter 15). Is he doing it to please his wife, or for the sake of exercise (or both), is it part of a competition with his neighbour to see who can grow the biggest marrow? We do not know what he is doing until we know what the digging means, and this is often a matter of knowing the narrative or story of which it is part: the story here of the man's relationship with his wife or neighbour, or in the example of eating a meal the story of the woman's relationship with family, lover and food in general.

These considerations weigh heavily against the possibility of measuring and comparing happiness in the way that Layard argues for and that is presupposed by most programmes for the teaching of happiness. Layard knows this and attempts to dismiss the counterargument briskly by referring to the work of John Stuart Mill. Mill, he notes, made a distinction between quantity and quality in his account of happiness. Layard writes:

> However psychologists have not been able to identify a separate qualitative dimension. Mill was surely onto something, but what he should have said is that there are different causes of happiness—those that produce enduring effects on happiness and those whose effects are transient (Layard, 2003, pp. 4–5).

This, though, is not enough to refute the kind of point that Mill was making. Mill was concerned with the difficulty of distinguishing between what he called the higher and lower pleasures, and with justifying the higher ones. Mill memorably uses as his example a satisfied pig and Socrates dissatisfied: the pig enjoying the lower pleasures of eating and generally snuffling around, and Socrates exercising his higher faculties and engaging in the 'higher pleasure' of philosophy which may involve being puzzled, not content with the answers you have reached, obsessed with a particular problem, and so on. Mill insists that we do as a matter of empirical fact value the higher pleasures:

> Now it is an unquestionable fact that those who are equally acquainted with, and equally capable of appreciating and enjoying, both, do give a most marked preference to the manner of existence which employs their higher faculties (*Utilitarianism*, Chapter 2, para. 6).

The problem however is more difficult for any version of utilitarianism to cope with than Mill acknowledges. First, we do not in fact always markedly prefer using these higher faculties. We know that reading a demanding novel is more satisfying than doing the crossword, but often we settle for the crossword. Bach's *Brandenburg Concertos* are infinitely complex and rewarding, and we would certainly put them at the top of our desert island list, yet it is surprising how seldom we actually listen to them at all, let alone listen to them carefully and with concentration. Second— and this is the major difficulty for any kind of utilitarian theory such as Mill's or Layard's—it simply is not obvious that many of those 'manners of existence which employ the higher faculties', which we clearly value and aspire towards, actually bring us anything that can simply and helpfully be described as happiness. In Mill's own example, an individual may feel she has some talent for philosophy, may feel drawn to it and pursue it, but at the same time be made thoroughly miserable by it (this seems to have been the experience of the philosopher Ludwig Wittgenstein for much of the time). In short, we value activities and ways of life that do not bring us happiness.

This point is of the highest importance and is explored further in the next section. Before moving on, however, there is one oddity that should be noted. The proponents of the teaching of happiness invariably complain of the damage done to education by the culture of high-stakes testing and league-tables. Seldon, for instance, writes that the government's vision of education extends no further than trying to 'show, year on year, a quantifiable improvement in results . . . . It has little incentive to concern itself with holistic and non-measurable aspects of learning'. Yet the research Seldon and others draw upon, and Layard's in particular, is precisely an attempt to measure and quantify. Is the teaching of happiness, to paraphrase Mill, to concern itself only with the measurable aspects of the enterprise?

3 THE DIVERSITY OF VALUE

Layard concludes his first Lecture with the assertion that we know that 'happiness is basic to human motivation' (Layard, 2003, p. 21). Since I am about to argue that we value a great variety of conditions other than happiness, it is important to counter a version of Layard's claim that is usually known as 'motivational hedonism'. This is the idea that everything we do we do for the sake of pleasure or happiness: and to the objection that people have all sorts of other motives, the motivational hedonist may respond that, perhaps deep down, people really find pleasure, albeit sometimes of a strange kind, in what they do, otherwise they would not do it. The self-sacrifice of the individual who rushes into a burning house to save a child, for example, then becomes reinterpreted in term of his or her brief but intense enjoyment of their own nobleness. (We suppose here for the sake of simplicity that the heroic individual has no belief whatever that they will get their reward in heaven.) Other examples can be found easily enough: the person who risked their life and endured years of fear rescuing Jews from the Nazis, the doctor who works in a leper colony, people who face torture and death because of their principled opposition to their own government.

Though these examples and others like them appear to demolish his case, the motivational hedonist often responds to the effect that 'they *must* be doing it for the sake of happiness': of course this is to take the theory of motivational hedonism as proven, and demonstrates the extent to which the person who makes this response is in the grip of a theory and unwilling to consider inconvenient counter-examples. In cases like the ones sketched above it seems very implausible to suggest that people are 'really' acting for the sake of happiness or pleasure, especially since more persuasive explanations are available. The rescuer says 'I just couldn't do otherwise'; the doctor explains that her patients will suffer without medical help, and we sense the demand on her that she feel this makes; the opposition leader says that someone has to make a stand. These ordinary and diverse explanations only invite scepticism if there is a reason for scepticism. Otherwise there is simply no requirement for any further explanation; and there is something rather insulting in the idea that people of courage, compassion and principle—and perhaps a combination of all three—are in truth only motivated by a kind of self-indulgence.

With this theoretical obstacle removed, it becomes easier to see that we value other conditions than those that involve pleasure or happiness or, to put it differently, that Layard's notion of happiness as 'feeling good—enjoying life and feeling it is wonderful' (Layard, 2003, p. 4) does no kind of justice to the variety of what we pursue, value and find worthwhile. As is often the case, philosophy can do valuable work here by assembling reminders, in Wittgenstein's phrase (*Philosophical Investigations*, §127), of what we know perfectly well if we are not in the grip of theory. A fuller and different kind of essay would consist largely of such reminders, set out at sufficient length to demonstrate their richness. For reasons of space I shall indicate some examples briefly and then develop two more fully.

First, it seems evident that we engage in all sorts of puzzles—crossword puzzles, sudoku, Rubik's Cube and so on—where we may encounter difficulty and frustration rather than the pleasure or happiness of 'feeling good'. Of course it may be said that we relish the difficulty, but this involves being thwarted, baffled, coming up against the limitations of one's knowledge, following blind alleys. These can hardly be called states of happiness, and to suggest that we endure the frustration for the sake of the happiness of getting the puzzle out simply does not feel true to the experience, which is of a few moment's satisfaction in having, say, completed the crossword after what may be hours of working through it.

A child playing may be engaging with difficulties in much the same way. Building the sandcastle or the house of cards involves many failures before the brief moment of success, and it is interesting how the child often immediately begins on a still more elaborate attempt which she must know will be equally taxing and bring similar failures. We talk rather too easily of children 'happily playing' almost as if the phrase were a tautology, but from the home to the school yard play brings with it as much pain as pleasure—the disappointment of losing the competitive game, anger when other children dominate the longed-for toys and equipment, the sense that what one was trying to make was a sorry thing in the end. Of course this is one reason that play is valuable, because it is partly through play that we learn to cope with negative emotions. As with puzzles we certainly relish play, but we play for the sake of play itself, and to say that we do it for the sake of the happiness it brings seems to get something wrong.

It is hard to explain why we value art—reading a demanding novel, for instance—in terms of happiness. (This reminds us of the problem John

Stuart Mill had in justifying what he called the 'higher pleasures'.) It is one thing to read a comic novel: here there are moments of laughing out loud, and the longer pleasure of seeing a scene building up to the comic *dénouement* and the unlovable character getting his just and entertaining deserts. But complex and often bleak novels (like those of Brian Moore, for example, some of whose titles convey the flavour: *The Lonely Passion of Judith Hearne, Cold Heaven*) can hardly be thought of in the same way. There is a sense of some of the darker aspects of life being observed with honesty and compassion. Even to say one *enjoys* such novels is misleading, yet the reader returns to them, recommends them to friends, looks forward to the writer's next one. They are perhaps to be thought of as moving and absorbing, and we value art that has these qualities even if it does not make us happy, often valuing it more than art that does straightforwardly make us happy, such as 'feel-good fiction'.[2]

I offer as one extended example the following passage from the 19th century novel, *Tom Brown's Schooldays,* by Thomas Hughes. The example may seem an odd one for the 21st century, but the 19th century school novel (there are many of them) is profoundly instructive about what can be valued in education without bringing the happiness of 'feeling good'. In the following extract, from Part 2, Chapter 5, 'The Fight', Tom's class are reading and translating from Homer's *Iliad*. There is a new master, who:

> ... looks round in despair at the boys on the top bench, to see if there is one out of whom he can strike a spark or two, and who will be too chivalrous to murder the most beautiful utterances of the most beautiful woman of the old world. His eye rests on Arthur, and he calls him up to finish construing Helen's speech. Whereupon all the other boys draw long breaths, and begin to stare about and take it easy. They are all safe: Arthur is the head of the form, and sure to be able to construe, and that will tide on safely till the hour strikes.
>
> Arthur proceeds to read out the passage in Greek before construing it, as the custom is. Tom, who isn't paying much attention, is suddenly caught by the falter in his voice as he reads the two lines—
>
> *alla su ton epeessi paraiphamenos katerukes*
> *sêi t'aganophrosunêi kai sois aganois epeessi*[3]
>
> He looks up at Arthur, 'Why, bless us,' thinks he, 'what can be the matter with the young un? He's never going to get floored. He's sure to have learnt to the end.' Next moment he is reassured by the spirited tone in which Arthur begins construing, and betakes himself to drawing dogs' heads in his notebook, while the master, evidently enjoying the change, turns his back on the middle bench and stands before Arthur, beating a sort of time with his hand and foot, and saying; 'Yes, yes,' 'Very well,' as Arthur goes on.
>
> But as he nears the fatal two lines, Tom catches that falter, and again looks up. He sees that there is something the matter; Arthur can hardly get on at all. What can it be?

Suddenly at this point Arthur breaks down altogether, and fairly bursts out crying, and dashes the cuff of his jacket across his eyes, blushing up to the roots of his hair, and feeling as if he should like to go down suddenly through the floor. The whole form are taken aback; most of them stare stupidly at him, while those who are gifted with presence of mind find their places and look steadily at their books, in hopes of not catching the master's eye and getting called up in Arthur's place.

The master looks puzzled for a moment, and then seeing, as the fact is, that the boy is really affected to tears by the most touching thing in Homer, perhaps in all profane poetry put together, steps up to him and lays his hand kindly on his shoulder, saying, 'Never mind, my little man, you've construed very well. Stop a minute; there's no hurry' (Hughes, 1857, Part 2, Chapter 5).

The plot now turns on the fact than one of the other boys, Williams, disgusted by what he sees as Arthur letting the class down by having prepared more than the conventional quota of lines to translate, calls attention to himself by mumbling threats and gets into trouble when he is asked to translate and cannot. After the class Williams turns on Arthur in revenge, and is stopped by Tom Brown, at the expense of having to take on Williams in a formal fight.

There is much here that repays study. Arthur is immensely moved by the lines from the *Iliad*, but is hardly made happy by them, since he bursts into tears. The whole business of translating Homer, and much else in these boys' curriculum, is grindingly hard work and is not valued simply for some kind of outcome, felicific or otherwise, that emerges from having done the work. The work itself is seen as valuable. It is worth noting too that there is something similar in the relationship—one of care and protection—between Arthur and Tom on the one hand and Helen and Hector on the other. The forces at play in Arthur's reading of the text—the reasons for his relishing it, we might say, are highly layered.

Thus we can value something that makes us cry. We can value things that puzzle us and daunt us. We value play, but are not always sure quite why: we talk, as I noted above, of how nice it is to see the children playing happily, or we fall back on instrumental talk of the development of fine and gross motor skills. We are in danger of losing subtleties of language as well as subtleties of thinking here, subtleties that come to be as remote to us as the world of Tom Brown and its ways of feeling and being.

My last example is of another language and way of life that are almost lost to us: that of craftsmanship. In his recent book *The Craftsman* Richard Sennett (2008) argues that the idea of craftsmanship has been 'hollowed out' by modern ways of working. A culture dominated by targets, the demand for efficiency and the requirement of the 'audit culture' that we sometimes seem to spend nearly as much time showing what we are doing as in actually doing it all work against the slow building of deftness that we associate with the kind of craftsman who made a violin or a cathedral.[4] Sennett argues that it is craftsmanship, dedication to good work for its own sake, which makes work seem worthwhile. The craftsman is attuned to his materials, whether this is a traditional context of carpentry or the modern one of Linux programming. He is willing to make mistakes, even to seek out challenges where he is bound to make them, because this is how skills become refined further. He 'feels fully and thinks deeply' about what he does, not least because his identity is bound up in his craft (it is no accident that many of us have names derived from craftsman ancestors: Baker, Archer, Thatcher, Mason). The mechanical routines typical of modern work militate against all this: against the proper development of skills, with its 'repetitions and slow revisions' (p. 291), partly because we democratically suppose that anyone can pick them up from a quick training course, and against the identification of self with craft because the insecurities of modern economies and the rapidity of change mean that it is both practically risky and emotionally dangerous to 'put yourself into' your job too much.

Craftsmanship, on Sennett's account, is at the root of human dignity and the individual's sense of his or her self-worth. A human being is, in Hannah Arendt's phrase, 'the creature that works', *animal laborans*,[5] whose life can be 'enriched by the skills and dignified by the spirit of craftsmanship' (p. 285). At the heart of craftsmanship lies pride in one's work 'as the reward for skill and commitment' (p. 294), the very 'slowness of craft time' (p. 295) being bound up with the kind of satisfaction that is involved. The harmony, then, of being attuned to tools and materials; pride in one's work and not, as the last sentence of the book reminds us, pride in oneself: yet again a distinctive kind of value, different from the other conditions and activities that we choose, relish, find satisfying, engaging or absorbing.

4 HAPPINESS BY THE WAY

As I have described it, the 'long slide to happiness' begins with the unexceptionable observation that an education system dominated by targets and testing is experienced as arid by both pupils and students on the one hand and those who teach them on the other. It proceeds, with the encouragement of 'positive psychology' and the kind of social science espoused by Richard Layard, to identify fulfilling education with teaching children, in Seldon's words, 'how to live and be happy'. In this, I have argued, it risks being seduced by over-simplified conceptions of happiness as a matter of 'feeling good'. At the end of this long slide it becomes harder for us to remember that there is a vast range of goods that we value and relish, not all of them by any means a matter of 'feeling good— enjoying life and feeling it is wonderful' (Layard's words again, quoted above). Seldon seems to know this well. In his *Guardian* debate with Furedi from which I have been quoting he writes of a 'wider vision' in which children, as well as being taught to pass exams, 'will also be prepared to embrace life in all its fullness'. This resonant phrase, 'life in all its fullness', captures much of what I have been urging here about the diversity of value. The problem is that the siren-call of 'happiness' lures us towards a false and one-sided vision of that fullness.

We have, as so often in these fundamental matters, been here before. In his *Autobiography*, John Stuart Mill wrote:

> I never, indeed, wavered in the conviction that happiness is the test of all rules of conduct, and the end of life. But I now thought that this end was only to be attained by not making it the direct end. Those only are happy (I thought) who have their minds fixed on some object other than their own happiness; on the happiness of others, on the improvement of mankind, even on some art or pursuit, followed not as a means, but as itself an ideal end. Aiming thus at something else, they find happiness by the way (Mill, 1873, Chapter 5).

Many of the dystopian novels of the 20th century explore the limitations of a civilisation dedicated to happiness. Aldous Huxley's *Brave New World* is perhaps the most famous of these, portraying a world where, as the Controller puts it, 'We prefer to do things comfortably', against which the 'Savage', the apostate from this anodyne vision, explicitly claims the right to be unhappy: 'But I don't want comfort. I want God, I want poetry, I want real danger, I want freedom, I want goodness. I want sin'. But the novel that we should most recall here is Ray Bradbury's *Fahrenheit 451*.[6] The firemen who are at the heart of this story have the job, not of putting out fires, but of burning books. Books are about good and evil, death and suffering, and they upset people. The fireman Montag is told by his captain: 'We are the Happiness Boys. We stand against the small tide of those who want to make everyone unhappy with conflicting theory and thought'. Montag however cannot help wondering just what is in these dangerous books. He steals a volume of poetry which includes Matthew Arnold's *Dover Beach,* with its devastating final lines:

> ... the world, which seems
> To lie before us like a land of dreams,
> So various, so beautiful, so new,
> Hath really neither joy, nor love, nor light,
> Nor certitude, nor peace, nor help for pain;
> And we are here as on a darkling plain
> Swept with confused alarms of struggle and flight,
> Where ignorant armies clash by night.

Montag senses that human life is here being accorded meaning and dignity even if (or because: 'the world, which seems . . .') our everyday certainties are here discomforted. At the end of the novel Montag joins other refugees from the world of reality television and tranquillisers. Each refugee learns a work of literature by heart and so keeps it alive: Montag learns *Ecclesiastes*. 'Vanity of vanities, saith the Preacher, all is vanity . . . For in much wisdom is much grief: and he that increaseth knowledge increaseth sorrow'. The connections between education and anything we might call happiness are stranger and more complex than recent attempts to chart them readily allow.

NOTES

1. Other reasons include the following:
   'It just happened'.
   'I wanted to give someone else a sexually transmitted disease (e.g. herpes, AIDS)'.
   'It was an initiation rite to a club or organization'.
   'I wanted to change the topic of conversation'
   'I wanted to gain access to that person's friend'.
   'I thought it would boost my social status'.
   'I wanted to feel young'.
   'I wanted to manipulate him/her into doing something for me'.
   'I felt sorry for the person'.
2. 'Do you ever want to curl up with a novel guaranteed to have a happy ending? There are several authors who create communities with recurring, quirky characters who become a family. Authors such as Jan Karon, Ann B. Ross, Joan Medlicott, J. Lynne Hinton and Philip Gulley write warm, witty books that provide a great escape from the real world'. See http://www.plcmc.org/readers_club/features/feature.asp?id=139
3. The lines come from *Iliad* 24. 771–2, where Helen is grieving over Hector, killed in combat by Achilles. In some editions of the novel they are translated: '[If anyone reproached me] you would reprove them, you would check them, with your gentle spirit and gentle words'. Some editions print the lines in the original and untransliterated Greek, in which Arthur would of course have read them.
4. It is important that in both cases, one more obvious than the other, the craftsman did not work alone but cooperatively as a member of a workshop or guild with shared practices and traditions.
5. Unfortunately this phrase becomes *animal laborens* throughout Sennett's book.
6. Fahrenheit 451, for those who do not know the novel or the Truffaut film based on it, is the temperature at which books burn. It is a pleasing touch that the novel, and its critique of happiness, takes its title from a *standard*. The paragraph above is adapted from my *Editorial* in *Journal of Philosophy of Education* 26.1, 1992. Hostility to 'theory and thought' takes different forms at different times.

REFERENCES

Bradbury, R. (1953) *Fahrenheit 451* (New York, Ballantine Books).
Furedi, F. and Seldon, A. (2008) Can We Teach People to be Happy?, *The Guardian*, 19 February. Available at: http://www.guardian.co.uk/education/2008/feb/19/highereducation.uk1
Hughes, T. (1857) *Tom Brown's Schooldays*. Available at: http://www.literature.org/authors/hughes-thomas/tom-browns-schooldays/chapter-14.html
Huxley, A. (1932) *Brave New World*. Available at: http://www.huxley.net/bnw/index.html
Layard, R. (2003) Happiness: Has Social Science a Clue? Available at: http://cep.lse.ac.uk/events/lectures/layard/RL030303.pdf
Layard, R. (2005) *Happiness: Lessons from a New Science* (London, Penguin).
MacIntyre, A. (1981) *After Virtue* (London, Duckworth).
Meston, C. M. and Buss, D. M. (2007) Why Humans Have Sex, *Archive of Sexual Behaviour*, 36, pp. 477–507.
Mill, J. S. (1863) *Utilitarianism*. Available at: http://www.gutenberg.org/ebooks/11224
Mill, J. S. (1873) *Autobiography*. Available at: ftp://ftp.mirrorservice.org/sites/ftp.ibiblio.org/pub/docs/books/gutenberg/1/0/3/7/10378/10378-8.txt
Sennett, R. (2008) *The Craftsman* (London, Allen Lane).
Smith, R. (2002) Self-Esteem: The Kindly Apocalypse, *Journal of Philosophy of Education*, 36.1, pp. 87–100.
Smith, R. (2006) Abstraction and Finitude: Education, Chance and Democracy, *Studies in Philosophy and Education*, 25.1–2, pp. 19–35.
Wittgenstein, L. (1972) *Philosophical Investigations* (Oxford, Blackwell).

4.4

Lessons from a New Science? On Teaching Happiness in Schools

JUDITH SUISSA

'The existence of the experimental method makes us think we have the means of solving the problems which trouble us ...' (Wittgenstein, Philosophical Investigations, Part II, section xiv).

The idea of teaching happiness has received considerable attention recently in Britain. Press reports draw attention to several reportedly successful attempts to introduce 'happiness lessons' in schools, such as those at Wellington College or South Tyneside (see for example *The Guardian*, 2008; *The Times*, 2008). Reference is often made, in the context of these pieces, to Richard Layard's influential report to the government in 2002 where, pointing out that the government spent more money on incapacity benefits for the mentally ill than it did on unemployment benefits, and declaring mental illness to be 'the major social problem facing our country today', he speaks enthusiastically about the new 'science of happiness' that ostensibly holds the secrets to solving these problems.

The term 'the science of happiness' is often used interchangeably with 'positive psychology' as an umbrella term to refer to the techniques of cognitive behavioural therapy (CBT), measurements of well-being, and research in social-science and economics based on such measurements. Those involved in the movement to teach happiness in schools are quite explicit about the fact that their intellectual roots lie in this approach. Prominent members of the positive psychology movement, for example Nick Baylis, are behind programmes such as the one adopted by Wellington College. Britain's leading academic centre for positive psychology, the University of Cambridge Well-Being Institute, has initiated and collaborated with several educational programmes, and makes prominent mention of education and children on its website (http://www.cambridgewellbeing. org/action_children.html). Martin Seligman, generally regarded as the founding father of positive psychology, remarked in a recent interview in The Times that 'nowhere else in the world have [my] ideas been so taken up by public policy as in the UK. There's a real buzz here about the politics of well-being' (The Times, 2008).

Attention to pupils' well-being is surely to be applauded. Many of the most vocal defenders of this approach, such as Anthony Seldon of Wellington College, the first headteacher in Britain to timetable happiness lessons, point out that the obsession with testing and assessing children has had detrimental effects on children's emotional and mental health and that we need to pay greater attention to their emotional well-being. This is a welcome and timely critique of our current education system. Likewise, research in the 'science of happiness' has yielded insights such as that 'extra income increases happiness less and less as people get richer' (Layard, 2005, p. 230), prompting influential theorists and advisors such as Layard to call for measures such as more equitable wealth-distribution through taxation, more flexible employment patterns, and a greater allocation of the budgets of developed countries to international aid. Layard's critique of the drive, in Western capitalist states, for ever-increasing wealth and consumption, alongside the emphasis on the importance of emotional well-being seems on the face of it, politically and morally laudable.

Yet there are serious problems involved with the 'science of happiness' and the educational programmes developed from it. I shall discuss these through an examination not of the experimental methods used in this research programme, but of the language in which this research is couched, what is implied by it, and what it leaves out.

MEASURING HAPPINESS

It has to be acknowledged that there are obvious questions one can ask about what exactly it is that positive psychologists are measuring when they report findings such as 'some 45% of the richest quarter of Americans are very happy, compared with only 33% of the poorest quarter' (Layard, 2005, p. 30). Layard defines happiness as simply 'feeling good', and is enthusiastic about neurological advances that measure activity in the brain that correspond to 'the feelings that people report'. Positive psychologists such as Seligman have devised various scales on which they map self-reported answers to various questions designed to elicit information about respondents' level of happiness or contentment. Of course, questions concerning the relationship between mental states, neurological functioning and ascriptions of moods or stable character traits are at the heart of the philosophical enquiry into the human mind, and I do not intend to revisit these debates. Yet it would be too easy to dismiss what is clearly an important body of empirical literature by simply accusing the authors of reductionism, or pointing out that one cannot offer a useful measurement of a phenomenon without an adequate understanding of what it is one is measuring. Most philosophers who have attempted to offer an account of happiness have acknowledged that individual levels of well-being, or contentment, have at least some role to play in our understanding of what we mean when we call someone 'happy'. Even bearing in mind the obvious problems involved in any experimental method that uses self-reporting as a measure, it would be odd to try to reach an understanding of people's happiness without taking their feelings or mental states into account.

The problem, in an educational context, is not so much that it is not clear what devices such as 'well-being indicators' are measuring or whether and in what way it constitutes 'happiness', but that the discourse around this research makes it impossible for us to talk of the things that cannot be measured. The founders of positive psychology are not unaware of the apparent oddness in claiming to measure happiness. As Peterson says, 'one cannot study happiness per se but only particular manifestations of it defined in specific ways and measured accordingly' (Peterson, 2006, p. 80). Yet having acknowledged this, researchers like Peterson then go on to devise measurements of something that they subsequently insist on referring to as 'happiness'. Furthermore, there are other serious problems with the implications of this statement. Firstly, it is only true if by 'study' we mean *empirically* study. One theme in my argument is that any rigorous understanding of happiness necessarily involves not just empirical study but conceptual philosophical enquiry. Connected to this point is the problem of assuming that whatever is being measured can be unproblematically described as a 'manifestation' of happiness. What does it mean to say that a neurologically identifiable phenomenon or a reported mood is a *manifestation* of happiness? Is it a necessary condition, a sufficient condition? These are not exclusively empirical questions, and answering them cannot be a purely empirical enquiry. To construe the relationship between particular measurable states and the concept of happiness as being one of 'manifestation' is itself to imply a particular picture of the meaning of happiness and of human life. To ignore the conceptual aspects of these questions and to approach the idea of happiness and its role in education solely on the basis of empirical research is thus inadequate. What it is more, as I shall argue below, it promotes a view that undermines central educational values.

It would be unfair to accuse positive psychologists of ignoring the philosophical tradition of work on happiness. Seligman, Baylis and other theorists often refer to the work of philosophers such as Aristotle. Yet while they acknowledge this work, they seem to simply side-step its significance in a way that has damaging educational implications. Thus Peterson notes, after surveying the philosophical tradition of work on happiness, starting from the time of the Ancient Greeks, that:

> ... happiness is a scientifically unwieldy term and that its serious study involves dissolving the term into at least three distinct and better-defined routes to happiness:
> a) positive emotion and pleasure,
> b) engagement (the engaged life)
> c) meaning (the meaningful life) (Peterson, 2006, p. 413).

This short passage in a sense encapsulates the serious problems at the heart of the project of 'teaching happiness' and the theoretical framework on which it is based.

First, the author could be accused of confusing two logically distinct questions: the question of what happiness is and the question of how individuals can achieve it. For a discussion of this point, see Barrow, 1980, although I shall suggest some problems with this distinction later. Second, he makes the bizarre assumption that the phrase 'a meaningful life' is somehow 'better defined' and less 'scientifically unwieldy' than the term 'happiness'. But most worrying of all, especially from an educational point of view, is the implication that we should aspire, when talking about and evaluating human experience, to eliminate from our vocabulary terms that are 'scientifically unwieldy' and to render our conceptual language as neat and scientifically tidy as possible.

While Peterson talks of 'the meaningful life', the sense in which this is used in the positive psychology literature is deeply problematic because of its failure to fully capture the role of normativity and questions of value in this area. Seligman, Peterson and other positive psychologists are well aware, as the above quote indicates, of the philosophical tradition of enquiry into happiness. Peterson, indeed, goes so far as to remark that the philosophers of ancient Greece were asking 'the same questions posed by contemporary positive psychologists'—What is the good life? Is virtue its own reward? What does it mean to be happy? And so on. Yet what Peterson seems to fail to realise is that the ancient Greeks were asking these questions as philosophical questions, not as empirical ones, and that this distinction is crucial.

THE ETHICAL LIFE

In asking what constituted a good or flourishing human life, Aristotle, for example, was not just looking for a descriptive, causal account of what made people happy, but was conducting a conceptual and normative enquiry into human life and values. In fact, if anything, Aristotle's form of enquiry and the line of thinking it inspired, rather than illustrating—as Barrow claims—a confusion between the logically distinct questions of what happiness is and how people reach it, demonstrates the impossibility of separating out these logically distinct strands in the context of a human life. For as Kenny and Kenny (2006) note, the Aristotelian concept of *eudaimonia* is probably more appropriately translated as 'worthwhile life'—thus capturing the normative and broader aspects of the term, alongside the insight that it always applies to the context of a human life. It is, indeed, by reading the term this way that one can make proper sense of the Aristotelian point that happiness is always sought for its own sake and never as a means to something else. For, on a narrow understanding of happiness as contentment or satisfaction it would be difficult to make sense of certain life-choices that involve, for example, sacrificing personal comfort or pleasure, as nevertheless constituting part of a life that is happy in the *eudaimonic* sense.

However, by adopting the language of positive psychology, Layard and other writers who have enthusiastically seized on this work as yielding important insights for education are ruling this broad normative dimension out of the discussion and relying on a far narrower—measurable—

definition of human contentment. Indeed, as Schoch points out, this is almost true by definition: 'Though the happiness scientists wisely promote "meaning and engagement" as the pinnacle of the good life, they consistently fall back upon a much weaker version of happiness—positive feelings, good moods—because that's the only kind they can measure. (How do you measure meaning?) And positive psychology is all about measuring happiness' (Schoch, 2008).

Yet to attempt to rule the realm of meaning out of education is highly problematic, as any coherent notion of education ought to involve meaning and values at all levels. Thus to espouse teaching happiness as an educational aim without acknowledging this is, in an important sense, anti-educational.

Let me give a concrete example of this point. The first item on the '10 point programme for developing well-being' developed at Wellington College by headteacher Anthony Seldon, in collaboration with Nick Baylis, co-director of the University of Cambridge's Well-Being Institute, is 'Relationships'. 'Productive relationships with other people', the programme sensibly advises, 'are utterly central to maintaining well-being . . . It is important that any partnership is constructive. Relationships that cause conflict should be resolved or avoided' (Wellington College, http://www.wellingtoncollege.org.uk/page.aspx?id=31). How would this pan out in practice? Well, Anna Karenina, for one, would have been well-advised to keep away from Count Vronsky. Yet anyone reading Tolstoy's novel may ask herself whether she could have really done so, and what this would have meant. The point of this thought-experiment is not to demonstrate the importance of thinking clearly about the consequences of one's actions, assessing the potential damage and weighing up the costs, but to illustrate how one cannot engage in such exercises without an appreciation of the values and meaning of particular events and experiences in the life of an individual. Of course, there are moral choices to be made here, and moral judgments one can make as a reader—or, indeed as Anna's peers in 19th century Russian aristocratic society—about Anna and Vronsky's choices. But the point is that one comes to make these choices as a moral agent through an appreciation of the texture of one's life, not through being given pre-packaged recipes like 'avoid conflict'. There are very many different types of conflict. Some people seem to thrive on conflict; others will do anything to avoid it. There are many ways in which relationships can be damaging to the individuals involved in them and many senses in which this may or may not cause apparent conflict. In order to fully understand what these different senses mean, what aspects of them have moral salience for particular individuals, and why, it is important to understand their meaning within the context of a human life. Neither the important empirical finding (although one can't help wondering whether we really needed this research) that people in stable, loving relationships are generally happier than others (Layard, 2005, p. 66), nor indeed the insight that conflict is generally damaging in relationships, is of any use whatsoever to me in assessing the significance of a particular kind of conflict in my relationship, how to resolve it, what cost this would entail, and whether I am willing to pay it.

The advice under point 10, 'Take Control': 'Don't live accidentally, live deliberately. Avoid being the kind of person who blames their misfortune on everything around them: take charge of the direction of your life and actively shape it by making positive choices . . .' raises similar questions. And this is not only because it may be somewhat easier for privileged children attending Wellington College to 'take charge' of their lives than for children struggling with the objective restrictions and lack of personal choice that result from socio-economic deprivation.

At the end of the novel, Anna Karenina, resolving to end once and for all her tortuous relationship with Vronsky and her inability to control the situation, reaches a clear-sighted conclusion: '"No, I will not let you torture me," she thought, addressing her threat not to him or to herself but to that which forced her to suffer' (Tolstoy, 1999, p. 757), as she heads towards the terrible resolution of her conflict. Can we understand her choice? Can we dismiss it as irrational, or as the inevitable result of a series of bad luck and bad choices? In what sense can Anna be said, in this awful act, to have taken charge of her life? I do not intend this as a glib rhetorical device, but as an illustration of how ethical judgment runs through this discussion at every level, and a warning against any recipes or one-size fits all formulae that seem to write this out of the picture. For education has a normative dimension built into it—not just in the sense that, as R. S. Peters famously argued, for something to coherently be described as 'educational', it must involve some notion of the good, but in the sense that a concern with values ought to be at the heart of any educational process. As Graham Haydon puts it, drawing on Blackburn's notion of the ethical environment, this goes beyond the realm of 'values education' in that education is inherently connected to our ethical environment in two interactive ways: 'education inescapably influences the ethical environment' (Haydon, 2006, p. 25) at the same time as 'the ethical environment has an important bearing on the nature and quality of education at a given time and place' (ibid.).

CORRELATIONS AND INDIVIDUALS

As my discussion of the above example suggests, it is highly problematic to draw normative educational conclusions from research findings in the field of positive psychology. Leaving aside the issues to do with what they are measuring and how accurate their measurements are, what the 'scientists of happiness' have done is to look for and establish patterns of correlations between these measurement scores, across a broad population sample, and the presence of some other measurable factors (such as average income or patterns of divorce). This has thrown up some interesting and important insights such as, for example, that general reported levels of happiness have not increased in line with the increase in economic prosperity in the West.

Yet it is one thing to establish a correlation between certain external factors and whatever reported internal state happiness surveys are purportedly measuring; quite another to import this into educational processes and curricula as a normative goal for the individual. A correlation cannot lead directly to normative conclusions for individuals, and education is not only about meaning and values, as described above, but also, crucially, about individuals. As such, it must address the meaning and role of values within the life of an individual. This involves grasping the significance of morally salient factors within the richly textured context of a particular human life.

Richard Layard, in enthusiastically reporting on the findings of neurologists and other scientists of happiness, states that 'we are programmed to seek happiness'. It may be that we are in some sense 'programmed' to seek pleasure or well-being, but to interpret the related observation that 'most if not all moral behaviour makes a person feel better' as somehow offering a reason to encourage children to 'do good deeds' is to completely sidestep the normative question about morality. As Korsgaard points out, the existence of a convincing account of the evolutionary role of morality, or, in Layard's case, its feel-good role, is not any use in answering the question, at the individual level, of 'why should I do this rather than that?'. Yet surely, for something to constitute education rather than mere conditioning or training, we want children to appreciate the normative aspect of certain types of moral behaviour, not just to accept that there may be sound evolutionary reasons for it. The moral agent, even for a thinker like Aristotle who put great emphasis on habituation as an essential early stage of moral education, is, crucially, someone who, as Korsgaard puts it, 'asks about ethical value from an ethical point of view' (Korsgaard, 1996, p. 77). In light of this point, the remark that 'most moral behaviour makes a person feel better' (Layard, 2005, p. 224), and the advice on the Wellington College programme that 'caring for others can be a valuable antidote to depression' seems not only misconceived but downright depressing.

Social policy may be able to make greater moral progress by looking at correlations to do with reported levels of individual well-being and investing in policies likely to maximise them. But education, to be worthy of the name, cannot be about such correlations. Layard's important suggestions, based on a wealth of social science research into human well-being, should indeed be seriously taken on board by policy makers. Indeed the very focus on personal well-being as a research agenda is a welcome shift from crude economic measures such as GDP, and from an assumption that the goal of economic policy is increasing wealth through growth. Yet while such critiques of economic policy are to be welcomed, they cannot serve as a normative guide for individuals and thus have nothing, really, to do with education.

In a sense, these problems with Layard's approach are the very same problems that lie at the heart of the political and moral doctrine that he so enthusiastically espouses: the 18th century utilitarianism of Jeremy Bentham. Layard, like other social theorists so impressed by this approach, seems oblivious to the point that, as Kenny and Kenny note, 'In introducing his Greatest Happiness principle, Bentham was less concerned to provide a criterion for individual moral choices than to offer guidance for rulers and legislators on the management of communities' (Kenny and Kenny, 2006, p. 29). Yet while the kind of social policy initiatives and economic reforms admirably proposed by Layard are to do with 'the management of communities', education, if it is to be something other than a form of social engineering, must be concerned with individuals and their ability to become agents capable of making moral choices. And addressing this concern must take into account not just descriptive, empirical findings, but conceptual and normative enquiry.

Our ethical thinking, in education as elsewhere, must be, as Richard Smith puts it, 'concerned with the shape of a life and its component parts' (Smith, 2005, p. 211). An appreciation of the idea of 'the shape of a life' and its meaning for ourselves and others cannot be reached through a pre-packaged list of techniques. Yet the well-being programmes adopted so enthusiastically by educationalists drawing on insights from positive psychology not only have the appearance of skills and techniques, but also are explicitly defined as such. Wellington College's 10 point plan is introduced in the following way: 'Well-being involves living skillfully as a human and it can be learnt. Here are 10 guidelines, or skills, that help to improve well-being dramatically' (Wellington College website). It may well be, as Layard and others discuss, that the techniques of meditation, or getting a good night's sleep (both of which also feature on the 10 point programme) can help us to achieve greater well-being or to deal with depressing or difficult situations. Yet in what sense can forming and sustaining 'productive relationships' or 'caring for others' be described as 'skills'? If happiness or well-being means something like 'living a worthwhile life'—or even 'living skillfully as a human'—then to achieve this, surely, one has to have some understanding of what it means to be human; what makes one's life worthwhile; what values one cherishes, and why. As the above examples demonstrate, such understanding is perhaps better achieved through the kind of rigorous and reflective engagement with the thick descriptions of 'the shape a life' reflected in works of literature. It may thus be better served by good teaching of literature and history, for example, than by 'happiness lessons' time-tabled onto the curriculum once every two weeks. Such a view is eloquently defended by moral philosophers such as Martha Nussbaum but also, I suspect, is something that many teachers have known for a long time.

The central question for Aristotle is 'how should a human being live?' and, as Nussbaum says, 'the general answer to this question suggested by Aristotle himself is "in accordance with all the forms of good functioning that make up a complete human life"'. In acting as moral agents in a variety of different situations, on this conception, part of our being and becoming fully moral means that we 'cannot get away with doing anything by rote; [we] must be actively aware and responsive at every moment, ready for surprises' (Nussbaum, 1990, pp. 94–95). Such a rich ethical approach seems to be shut down by an education that offers comprehensive lists of techniques. Crucially, what we bring to an educational encounter, as to other forms of ethical human interaction, is our 'evolving picture of the good and complete human life' (ibid.). Education should enable this picture to evolve, and offer children a range of possibilities with which to develop and inform it; not present them with a pre-packaged picture.

WHAT GOES RIGHT

I do not wish to sound overly cynical about the undoubtedly well-intentioned aims behind the project of positive psychology. Of course we would all rather have healthy relationships, and of course we should be open to learning from how people resolve conflicts and improve various aspects of their lives. This, indeed, is the motive behind the quite revolutionary shift in psychology heralded by the advent of positive psychology. As the founders of the movement put it, their aspiration, after decades of an overwhelming focus on psychopathology and the diagnosis, classification and treatment of various disorders, was to emphasise that 'human goodness and excellence are as authentic as disease, disorder and distress' (Peterson, 2006, p. 5) and to focus on 'what goes right with peoples' lives' (ibid.). This aspiration is evident in the almost evangelical statements of writers like Peterson, who describes positive psychology as 'a newly christened approach within psychology that takes seriously as a subject matter those things that make life most worth living' (ibid.).

Yet this shift in perspective does not resolve, but merely displaces the same normative and evaluative questions that have always lurked in the background of all psychological theory. As an illustration of the kind of shift in thinking that signalled the birth of the approach described as 'the scientific study of what goes right in life, from birth to death, and at all the steps in between', (Peterson, 2006, p. 4), Peterson cites an important study into the reported mental states of women who had been diagnosed with breast cancer. The authors of the study found that a significant proportion of women in this situation 'did not seem depressed, and dealt with their diagnosis by downward social comparison'—in other words, by drawing comparisons between their own state and that of 'people who are inferior or less fortunate' (Wood, Taylor and Lichtman, 1985, p. 1169). Commenting on these findings, Peterson remarks: 'A previous generation of psychologists might have concluded that these women were in denial, but they were clearly open-eyed, lucid, and sober. The only thing they denied was despair, and Taylor foreshadowed the premises of positive psychology concluding that this was an important aspect of human nature' (Peterson, 2006, p. 13).

But whether we describe the reported mental state of the women in question as 'denial' or 'hope' is a choice, not a straightforward description to be read off empirical facts (as illustrated by the story itself). A full account of this issue must confront questions such as what traits we consider normative and why; what values are prominent, socially and personally—precisely, in other words, the philosophical questions that

Aristotle and others were concerned to answer in their enquiry into the idea of a worthwhile life.

The task of positive psychology, its proponents claim, is 'to provide the most objective facts possible about the phenomena it studies so that every day people and society as a whole can make an informed decision about what goods to pursue in what circumstances' (Peterson, 2006, p. 16). Yet the story we tell about the 'objective facts' is part of our ongoing attempts to flourish as moral agents. Understanding the way certain psychological strategies, for example, have an adaptive role in allowing people to flourish in adverse circumstances cannot tell an individual what to do in similar circumstances. Such matters involve both individual choice and values. Thus if one wants to preserve the broad meaning of 'happiness' as 'the worthwhile life', it simply cannot be the case that 'the routes to the good life are an empirical matter' (p. 15).

Educationalists who have embraced positive psychology insist, however, on side-stepping this point, and thus offer an impoverished and distorted idea of education when they confidently declare that: 'since the development of the positive psychology movement under Martin Seligman and developments in neuroscience, we now know how to teach wellbeing, and have empirical evidence of its effectiveness' (Anthony Seldon, quoted in *The Guardian*, 2008).

HEADLESS FREEFALLS?

I am not suggesting that love and happiness are, as Peterson puts it, 'headless freefalls that just happen when gravity is on our side' (Peterson, 2006, p. 30), nor do I want to imply that we should abandon all attempts to understand what happiness is or to help individuals achieve it.

It may be helpful here to consider Kenny and Kenny's suggestion, in their attempt to integrate the insights of accounts of happiness from philosophical, psychological and economic work, that the notion involves three distinct elements: contentment—i.e. 'what is expressed by self-ascription of happiness; not so much a feeling or a sensation, but an attitude or state of mind'; welfare, construed basically as the satisfaction of needs; and 'psychological welfare', or what they describe as dignity, in the sense of 'the ability to live a life of one's choice'. As they note, although there may be correlations between these three elements, they act independently of each other and 'may vary independently' (Kenny and Kenny, 2006, p. 42). Thus we can make sense, for example, of the idea of someone being happy who has contentment and dignity, but not welfare—such as the undernourished, ascetic hermit living a life of religious devotion. The idea behind Kenny and Kenny's analysis is that the goal of achieving well-being or happiness is a complex one that cannot be measured by a single metric.

If we accept that even part of what it means to be happy involves an 'attitude or state of mind', and that we can, at least to a degree, intentionally do things that will have some effect on this, then some of the points on the 10 point programme indeed reflect fairly common sense ideas about the kinds of things that are likely to contribute to our well-being. Likewise, I would not dispute the evidence that many individuals have been helped by 'techniques of mental self-discipline' like cognitive behavioural therapy, that Layard and others enthusiastically cite as 'remarkably effective in treating major and minor depression' (Layard, 2005, p. 196). But the really important prior questions here are what depression is, and why, when and whether it is appropriate to treat it. Anecdotal experience of people suffering the debilitating depression that can often follow the loss of a loved one suggests that they do not want to be offered a form of therapy that will enable them to 'move on', and we can surely make sense of the idea that to do so would be, in an important sense, to fail to appreciate the enormity of their grief or to accord it its proper place in their lives.

'If happiness', Layard tells us 'depends on the gap between your perceived reality and your prior aspiration, cognitive therapy deals mainly with the perception of reality' (p. 197). This is all very well, but it is precisely our 'perception of reality' that is at the core of who we are as moral agents. To desire to change this, or to try to adapt our aspirations, may be a legitimate matter for individual choice, but to translate it into a general educational goal is not only to risk conflating education with therapy, but to undermine the value of autonomy that is regarded as a central educational aim by so many educators, including Seldon himself (see *The Guardian*, 2008).

While the techniques developed by positive psychologists may have a value, it is not just their role in educational programmes that is questionable, but their relative weight and significance in any programme designed to increase general levels of well-being. What, for example, if Layard's suggestions as to how to increase levels of well-being through progressive economic reforms such as higher taxation and limits to economic consumption are not heeded, and the distribution of scores on the happiness scale across the population remains more or less the same. Would we then want to argue that we should invest *more* money and effort in CBT programmes? Get children to do *more* meditation in school? Layard and the positive psychologists whose work he cites seem incapable of asking these questions, let alone of answering them. In the absence of any serious thought about these complex conceptual issues and the way they interact with moral values, it is hard to see how such an approach can constitute a coherent educational aim. However, phrasing these questions in this way should alert us to the possibility not that we have failed to offer any convincing answers to them; but, rather, that perhaps they are not the right questions to ask.

THE SEARCH FOR A SIMPLE FORMULA

While Kenny and Kenny's conceptual mapping of happiness as involving three separate elements goes some way towards untangling some strands of the debate, it is also, in my view, potentially dangerous as it obscures the point that although these strands may be conceptually separate, how they interconnect in practice is messy and unpredictable.

What, for instance, are we to make of the following description from Tolstoy:

... though he was a happy and healthy family man, Levin was several times so near to suicide that he hid a cord he had lest he should hang himself, and he feared to carry a gun lest he should shoot himself.

But he did not hang or shoot himself and went on living.

When Levin thought about what he was and why he lived, he could find no answer and was driven to despair; but when he left off asking himself those questions he seemed to know what he was and why he lived, so he acted unfalteringly and definitely—recently even more unfalteringly than before (Tolstoy, 1999, p. 778).

Levin does not appear to the reader as a psychologically imbalanced character, or an implausible caricature on Tolstoy's part. He is, rather, a totally believable, complex individual in whom we recognise subtle and rich reflections of core human experiences. Had he been given Seligman's 'Satisfaction with Life Scale', how would he have scored? It would probably have depended on what day he was given it. And what gives Tolstoy the right to decree that Levin is a happy and healthy man? Can someone really be described as happy if he occasionally has thoughts of his own death? Is Levin's dogged insistence to 'go on living' a kind of denial of the genuine problems facing him, or an admirable optimism? And is the fact that Levin's frequent attempts to ask himself probing questions about the meaning of his life end in disaster an indictment of the aims of positive psychology, or an indication that he is not doing it right—that he has not, perhaps, learned the right skills? Maybe with an informed use of CBT, Levin would have done a better job. But would this have been a good thing? What would it have meant for him, for his character, for those around him? Posing such questions only makes sense in the context of an individual life and the values it embodies.

Another way of looking at this issue is to say that while Layard is undoubtedly right in pointing out that 'happiness comes from within and without' (Layard, 2005, p. 184), the inescapable question at the heart of any enquiry into happiness is that of the connection between the 'within' and the 'without'. Conceptual and normative issues come into this question at every level: if someone is living in abject poverty and degradation, but claims to be happy, would we find this disturbing or inspiring, and why?

We cannot treat 'external' social reality, any more than we can treat 'internal' mental states or attitudes, as simply a given fact to be measured; nor can we ever devise a formula for calculating the relationship between them. The relationship between the 'within' and the 'without' in this context may be yet one more example of what Wittgenstein meant when he said: 'here we have two different language-games and a complicated relation between them.—If you try to reduce their relations to a *simple* formula you go wrong' (Wittgenstein, 1968, p. 180). Yet Layard and other social theorists, educationalists and popular writers apparently bewitched by the language (and the language game) of positive psychology, seem quite keen on simple formulae. Indeed, in dismissing the entire body of philosophical work critiquing utilitarianism, Layard declares: 'no one has proposed another ultimate principle that could arbitrate when one moral rule (like truth-telling) conflicts with another (like kindness)' (Layard, 2005, p. 225). The search for an 'ultimate' or 'overarching' principle (ibid.) is disturbing not just because it is often such aspirations that are behind some of the world's most oppressive and dangerous political regimes, but also because it is profoundly anti-educational. Education, as I argued above, is concerned with individual lives, and any notion of individual flourishing—not least the Aristotelian one to which positive psychologists purport to be indebted—has to acknowledge the sense in which 'the values that are constitutive of a good human life are plural and incommensurable' (Nussbaum, 2001, p. 294).

If, indeed, we could be fully confident that we had exhausted our enquiries into what makes people happy and could provide a foolproof recipe for how to maximise it, there would be little point—or at least little meaning—in education. How would education, in this case, be any different from therapy or social policy? Yet the fact that there cannot ever be such an exhaustive list should alert us not just to the inherent flaws in the attempt to make social science more 'scientific'—but to the fact that, perhaps, there is another way to think about happiness. Thus Robin Barrow's suggestion that 'happiness would seem to be or to involve seeing the world as one would like it to be' (Barrow, 1980, p. 74), rather than prompting us to think of ways to arrive at a state of happiness by bridging this gap, should, perhaps, be read as a hint that something else is at stake here.

This leads me to the final sense in which the educational programmes inspired by the discourse of positive psychology are anti-educational. I mentioned, above, the aspiration to expunge 'scientifically unwieldy concepts', and the danger of ruling out of our understanding the aspects of human life that cannot be measured. Yet that fact that something cannot be measured does not mean that it cannot be understood or that it cannot have an important meaning in our lives. Happiness may be 'a scientifically unwieldy term', yet it makes perfect sense for Tolstoy to write a sentence such as the following: 'that which for Anna had been an impossible, dreadful, but all the more bewitching dream of happiness, had come to pass' (Tolstoy, 1999, p. 146). To confront children with the idea that a dream of happiness can be at one and the same time dreadful, impossible, and bewitching, and to draw them into the full significance of Anna's predicament, may be unsettling and challenging. To imply that people who sometimes think of killing themselves can be happy, or that one can be both happy and miserable at the same time is, one may think, a fairly risky move. It would be far less unsettling and risky, surely, to simply advise children that 'conflictual relationships do not lead to happiness and should be avoided'. But a powerful and central part of all pictures of education since Plato involves the idea that for something to be truly educational, it must be challenging, unsettling; possibly liberating, but painfully so. To offer children straightforward, comfortable and unchallenging learning experiences is to deny them the excitement—and the risks—of a truly educational experience, and thus to deprive them of the encounter with what Nussbaum describes as 'the messy, unclear stuff of which our humanity is made' (Nussbaum, 2001, p. 260).

To understand Levin means precisely to understand the contradictions in his character and the choices he makes, or fails to make; to grasp the full tragedy of Anna's situation is to grasp precisely why her passion for Vronsky is both terrible and wonderful. Without an appreciation of the complexity and messiness of lived human lives, how can we hope to understand the meaning of emotions and values in our own lives, or to begin to make our own moral choices?

This suggests that part of our understanding of what happiness means and, thus, in what sense it can or should be an aim for us in our own lives, can perhaps be best reached through a consideration of such richly-textured examples. There is no need, then, to 'put happiness on the curriculum', for on any meaningful account of education as involving, centrally, challenge, disruption and an ability to appreciate complexity—it is already there (although whether or not this can be achieved is a matter for future work). I am not denying that getting children to do some meditation, play outside more and eat healthily would be a welcome addition to schools' objectives, or that paying attention to their emotional state should be part of all educators' concern. But to condense these common sense insights into a curricular programme, package them up for children and call them 'teaching happiness' is both misguided and redundant.

Aristotle's notion of happiness as flourishing is, as Kenny and Kenny say, more aptly described as 'a worthwhile life'. Towards the end of *Anna Karenina*, Levin eventually finds this—not through therapy, but through a bumpy and vaguely mystical process of his own. Some may find it in CBT. Others may find it through developing a passion for music, or mastering a craft. In a liberal democracy, it is not for economists, ministers of education or teachers to decide what our 'routes to happiness' are, but to allow schools to be the kinds of places that open up the questions and give children tools to answer them for themselves. I fully endorse Layard's recommendations that the government should take mental health far more seriously, and should invest more public funds in it. But education is not therapy and should not be confused with it.

CONCLUSION

I am not siding with those who Layard dismisses as believing that 'we are as we are and no mental practices can change us' (Layard, 2005, p. 202). I would be the first to agree that well-being can be at least partly influenced by factors within our control, and I have nothing against meditation or therapy. More importantly, I certainly think that we should acknowledge that there are objective factors, such as having enough to eat, having a decent job, and being able to form meaningful relationships, that are pretty basic conditions for any meaningful sense of well-being. There's no doubt that when you're feeling miserable, a brisk walk in the fresh air and a nice meal with friends will often do wonders to cheer you up. But often it will not. And sometimes no apparent explanation or useful exercise can help us to make sense of our subjective experiences. Remember David Lodge's character in the novel

Therapy who, asked by his therapist to make a list of all the bad things and all the good things in his life, comes up with two columns. The 'good' column contains about twenty items, such as 'well-off', 'professionally successful', 'stable marriage', 'good health', and so on. In the other column, there is just one item: 'feel unhappy most of the time' (Lodge, 1995, p. 23).

This example is not just telling us that, if everything on the 'outside' seems to be OK and someone nevertheless reports feeling miserable, they are clearly doing something wrong on the 'inside' and need some help, such as learning the Buddhist technique of how to 'eliminate negative thoughts and replace them with positive ones' (Layard, 2005, p. 188). I think, rather, it is telling us that the relationship between the outside and the inside, between what seems to be going right in our lives and what we feel about our lives, between what we care about and what we think we should care about, between our aspirations and our perception of reality— is neither straightforward nor controllable.

Between the inner and the outer is a realm of interpretation, meaning and value, and it is in this realm that education should operate. Although there may be some correlation between the various strands in human happiness, and some control can be exercised over part of them, we have to resign ourselves to the fact that this will always be imprecise and scientifically unwieldy. Not just because we do not yet understand the complex empirical story as to how one part of our life influences the other, but because this is not just an empirical story. Perhaps, indeed, as Jonathan Lear suggests, 'it is constitutive of human life—life influenced by fantasy, life in society, ethical life—that there is an experience that there is something more to life, something left out' (Lear, 2000, p. 163). Acknowledging this, in its full wonder, horror and richness, may be more truly educational than trying to overcome it by means of dubiously conceived and simplistic packages of 'skills'.

Between the pessimistic view that nothing can change us and the view that we can find a formula or an 'overriding principle' for positive change is a huge and messy space. And it is here that the educational journeys of individuals are situated.

ACKNOWLEDGEMENT

I would like to thank Andrew Davis for his very helpful comments on an earlier version of this chapter.

REFERENCES

Barrow, R. (1980) *Happiness* (Oxford, Martin Robertson).
The Guardian (2008) Can We Teach People to be Happy?, 19 February.
Haydon, G. (2006) *Education, Philosophy and the Ethical Environment* (Oxford, Routledge).
Kenny, A. and Kenny, C. (2006) *Life, Liberty and the Pursuit of Utility: Happiness in Philosophical and Economic Thought* (Exeter, Imprint Academic).
Korsgaard, C. (1996) *The Sources of Normativity* (Cambridge, Cambridge University Press).
Layard, R. (2005) *Happiness; Lessons from a New Science* (London, Penguin).

Lodge, D. (1995) *Therapy* (London, Secker and Warburg).

Lear, J. (2000) *Happiness, Death and the Remainder of Life* (Cambridge, MA, Harvard University Press).

Nussbaum, M. (1990) *Love's Knowledge; Essays on Philosophy and Literature* (New York, Oxford University Press).

Nussbaum, M. (2001) *The Fragility of Goodness; Luck and Ethics in Greek Tragedy and Philosophy* (New York, Cambridge University Press).

Peterson, C. (2006) *A Primer in Positive Psychology* (Oxford, Oxford University Press).

Schoch, R. (2008), Think Positive, *The Guardian*, 28 February.

Smith, R. (2005) Paths of Judgement: the Revival of Practical Wisdom, in: W. Carr (ed.) *The Routledge Falmer Reader in Philosophy of Education* (Oxford, Routledge).

The Times (2008) Teaching Happiness: The Classes in Wellbeing that are Helping our Children, 18 February.

Tolstoy, L. (1999) *Anna Karenina* (Ware, Wordsworth Editions).

Wittgenstein, L. (1968) *Philosophical Investigations* (Oxford, Basil Blackwell).

Wood, J. V., Taylor, S. E. and Lichtman, R. R. (1985) Social Comparison in Adjustment to Breast Cancer, *Journal of Personality and Social Psychology*, 49, pp. 1169–1183.

4.5
A Critique of Positive Psychology— or 'The New Science of Happiness'

INTRODUCTION

It is easy to poke fun at positive psychology or 'the new science of happiness' for offering facile, naively simplistic answers to age-old questions concerning the meaning of life, paths to fulfilment and 'the good life'. Many critics in the media have pointed out, and with some justification, that it appears to be little more than 'self help' (with all its attendant deficiencies) repackaged and given the veneer of respectable science. More perceptive commentators have drawn a distinction between happiness as the hedonistic pursuit of pleasure (with which they equate positive psychology) and happiness as the pursuit of the good life, in which meaning and fulfilment result from transcending immediate desires and impulses, cultivating the virtues and striving for some ideal of what it is to be human. As Richard Schoch complains, 'Somewhere between Plato and Prozac, happiness stopped being a lofty achievement and became an entitlement' (Schoch, 2007, p. 1). The answers are more likely to lie in the wisdom of the ages, in religion and philosophy, not in the pat answers of positive psychology.

But there is a lot more to positive psychology than some of its critics perhaps allow. Even a cursory reading will reveal that it is not concerned with the hedonistic pursuit of pleasure, at least not in the sense of immediate sensual gratification; instead, it proposes that absorbing activities and engagements (including selfless, altruistic ones) are central to a happy, meaningful life, and it is through these that the traditional virtues can be cultivated. The scientific basis of its claims lies firmly in evolutionary psychology, which explains the ultimate motivations and values of people in terms of needs that have evolved through natural selection, and which explains the positive emotions people feel as having evolved to stimulate the behaviour that confers adaptive advantage. Its 'positive thinking' prescriptions are justified by reference to practised cognitive therapeutic techniques. And perhaps most significantly of all, it appears to offer a scientifically grounded recipe for personal fulfilment in a liberal, utilitarian, materialistic age. Old beliefs rooted in common social structures, culture and religion have atrophied (at least in the West) and it is to evolutionary science and psychology that we must now look for the answers.

The appeal of positive psychology, whether to corporate managers, economists, educationalists or managerially minded politicians in search of optimal solutions, should not be under-estimated. In his book *Happiness: Lessons from a New Science*, the eminent economist Richard Layard is sufficiently convinced to attempt 'a new evidence-based vision of how we can live better' founded on 'the new psychology of happiness' (Layard, 2006, p. ix). Hundreds of courses in positive psychology are now available in American colleges and both the University of East London and the City University now run courses in the UK. Anthony Seldon has pioneered classes in 'well-being' at Wellington College and in the autumn of 2007 it was announced that all state schools in England would teach 'social and emotional intelligence'—or, as the media reported it, 'happiness lessons'.

Positive psychology has particular appeal in education where, in common with its close relations 'emotional intelligence' and 'multiple intelligences', it seems to promise achievement and empowerment for all. The 'SEAL' programme for developing 'the social and emotional aspects of learning', already piloted in primary schools, might well prove to be the first step toward a re-crafting of the whole of the school curriculum to take account of the new psychology. Unlike its forerunner 'PSHE' (Personal, Social and Health Education), SEAL is directly inspired by the work of Daniel Goleman on emotional intelligence, a field that has much in common with positive psychology.[1] It argues that both behaviour and attitudes to learning will be improved if, amongst other things, pupils learn to manage their emotions, 'feel optimistic about themselves and their ability to learn', 'reflect on longer-term goals' and 'learn to feel good about themselves' (Banda Pilot Site, 2007, 2.3). Moreover, it argues that the learning and teaching approaches that foster these attitudes should be adopted across the curriculum: collaborative group challenges, group enquiry, 'experiential learning opportunities' etc (5.4). It would be a logical next step to re-craft the curriculum itself, as Goleman advocates, so that pupils' learning matches their 'profile of natural competencies' and they can thereby 'gain flow from learning' (Goleman, 1996, pp. 93–5). The much-vaunted idea of 'personalised learning' could then be realised. Whether this will eventually happen remains to be seen, but the consequences for education if it did would be profound.

Much of the debate about the merits of positive psychology has centred on the 'research evidence' i.e. does it work or not? Advocates of positive psychology claim that its assertions are proved by a vast amount of research; opponents point to research evidence to the contrary. So we can read on the very same day in the Sunday Times, in relation to the 'SEAL' classes, that on the one hand, 'research found that teaching the subject in 300 primary schools had boosted the children's concentration by helping them understand and deal with their emotions' (Griffiths, 2007), and on the other, 'there is little evidence that the classes . . . led to any long-term improvement in emotional well-being or academic success' (Waite, 2007). We are reduced to choosing between rival pieces of research evidence.

But 'research evidence' in education purporting to prove a causal relation between two posited variables is notoriously unreliable and fraught with methodological difficulties. The research evidence, however voluminous (and whether for or against), is only as good as the assumptions underlying the concepts, terms and relationships being tested. As Richard Smith argues, it is a problem endemic right across the social sciences that a narrow concern with 'scientific' research techniques has tended to displace the exercise of broader judgement and insight concerning the validity of the underlying concepts and ideas themselves (Smith, 2006, pp. 159–61). This chapter is concerned with the logical validity of the arguments and underlying concepts of positive psychology. What are these?

The positive psychology movement encompasses a broad research programme, but the central arguments advanced by Martin Seligman, the acknowledged founder of positive psychology, are the twin ones that happiness—'authentic happiness' and not merely pleasure—can be achieved if a person utilises and develops the positive personality or character traits they are endowed with (their 'signature strengths') in purposeful activity; and that a positive, optimistic attitude toward oneself and to events in general helps enable a person achieve his goals (Seligman, 2006 and 2007). Happiness itself comprises positive feelings or emotions about the past and future—satisfaction, contentment, pride, serenity, optimism, hope, confidence, trust and faith—along with the positive activities that generate these feelings and in which they find expression (Seligman, 2007, p. 261).

These arguments are, however, founded on a number of assertions that are highly questionable: first, that life can be conceived in terms of the setting and achieving of goals (an assumption of psychological models in general); second, that the traits, dispositions, emotions, feelings, desires, beliefs and values that together comprise a person's attitudes or personality (and which psychology conceives as explaining or causing people's behaviour) can be consciously managed or controlled; third, that people can broadly be categorised as pessimistic or optimistic (with the optimists having the ability to persevere, achieve their goals and attain happiness); and finally, that expressing one's 'signature strengths' or positive traits and virtues in absorbing activities is the key to well-being.

In this chapter I examine these assertions and the assumptions that underlie them.

GOALS, ATTITUDES, BEHAVIOUR AND THE FALLACY OF CONSCIOUS CONTROL

A marked characteristic of psychological explanations of behaviour in general is the idea that life can be conceived instrumentally as comprising a series of goals that one is in the process of trying to achieve. For psychology to be able to explain human behaviour at all, behaviour must be conceived as intentional, with actions determined by motives and goals (Taylor *et al.*, 1982, p. 584). Positive psychology simply takes this further and promises that all can achieve their goals, provided that attitudes are sufficiently positive: 'Optimism is a tool to help the individual achieve the goals he has set for himself' (Seligman, 2006, p. 291).

The idea that all can achieve their goals would appear to be an illusion, particularly when goals and achievement are conceived in terms of social status and recognition, and so the proviso is added that goals must be realistic and achievable. But this begs the following questions: first, if a realistic goal is defined as that which is attainable now (given all existing constraints including motivation and circumstances), how does it differ from plans and actions that would be undertaken anyway; and second, if a realistic goal is defined more ambitiously as that which could be achieved if current constraints on behaviour (motivation and circumstances) were altered, how could a person possibly know in advance whether or not their goals were realistic? In other words, if one is motivated to achieve something in life, there is no need for setting it up as a goal; and if one is not motivated to achieve that thing, there is no point in setting it up as a goal. Either way, extraneous goal setting would seem to be redundant.

The very ideas of conscious goal setting and goal achievement conjure up images of Gilbert Ryle's 'ghost in the machine' and of the 'homunculus' that bedevils computer theories of the mind.[2] Though it is perfectly legitimate to distinguish intelligent, purposeful behaviour from instinctive, unconscious behaviour, to speak of consciously controlling your own attitudes, motivation, thoughts or actions implies an infinite regress of controllers or managers sitting one inside the other. It is only because computers, machines and businesses do not have minds of their own that they need plans, goals, targets and programmes. As Ryle comments, 'motives and moods are not the sort of things which could be among the direct intimations of consciousness' (Ryle, 1990, p. 111). George Miller and Robert Buckhout make essentially the same point: 'It is the result of thinking, not the process of thinking, that appears spontaneously in consciousness' (Miller and Buckhout, 1973, p. 70).

Explanations of behaviour in terms of personality traits or dispositions, emotions, moods, feelings, beliefs and values are all perfectly legitimate. They help provide intelligible, rational explanations of people's actions and by the same token enable us to interpret these actions as purposeful or goal-driven. What is questionable is whether any of these explanatory factors can by their very nature be considered as being under conscious control. And though we can evidently reflect on our motives and attitudes, subject them to rational examination, even choose to reject them altogether, this very process of reflection must itself be motivated by some emotional impulse, unconscious need or end. In the language of evolutionary psychology, 'without a specification of a creature's goals, the very idea of intelligence is meaningless' (Pinker, 1999, p. 61).

For most people most of the time, interests, passions, dreams, plans, goals and purpose emerge out of life and circumstances as possibilities and opportunities arise; and they are determined by traits of personality, aptitudes, dispositions and inclinations, none of which are *consciously* chosen or managed as instrumental means to the achievement of goals. Of course people may choose to make promotion at work, for example, their overriding goal and make all behaviour instrumental to that end. But it takes a certain sort of person with a certain sort of personality in very particular circumstances to be inclined or motivated to do that in the first place—the sort of person for whom promotion and the status that comes with it are all-important.

It is a central contention of positive psychology that people can be re-crafted into goal achievers able to control their emotions and harness all their positive energies in the service of their goals. For example, in Andy Smith's '55 Ways to Increase Your Emotional Intelligence', the reader is urged to 'make a list of what's important to you', 'prioritise your values' and 'discover what you really want' (Smith, 2002, p. 9). But unless you already know exactly what you want, and are therefore by definition motivated to achieve it, these are impossible tasks. The passions, emotions, instincts, dispositions and aptitudes together with the learning and experience that go to make up a person's goals and values are *necessarily* the same passions, emotions, instincts, dispositions and aptitudes that will motivate his attitudes toward the achievement of those goals and the practice of those values. The two cannot be separated.

Instincts, values, attitudes and hence behaviour can, however, be controlled in a rather different sense. On the one hand, they can be learned or inculcated as part of a process of education or training; and on the other, they can be subject to the exercise of 'self-control'. 'Self-control' and 'self-discipline' are needed to choose the course of action that one believes is right or that one most values over behaviour that has more immediate, instinctive appeal. A person might or might not have the self-control or determination, the drive or perseverance (together with the skill, judgement and luck) necessary to achieve his goals or ambitions. But these very qualities of self-control, determination and perseverance are themselves part and parcel of his personality, his history, his circum-stances and so forth. They cannot be regarded as being consciously imposed or managed any more than a person's goals or ambitions; otherwise we are back in the situation of the ghost in the machine, the homunculus and an infinite regress. In other words, it is out of a person's life that his goals together with the motivation and the attitudes necessary to achieve them emerge and take form.

The problem or paradox inherent in the very notion of self-control is exemplified in *akrasia*, the situation in which a person having decided after due deliberation that they will or will not do something then unaccountably does the reverse and subsequently regrets their 'weakness of will'. The problem is that if a person acts in a particular way, how can the act not be regarded as rational in the sense of fulfilling some overriding need or interest of the person concerned? In *The Emotions: A Philosophical Exploration*, Peter Goldie argues that the notion of 'weakness of will' can only really make sense when considered ethically as a matter of harnessing or controlling the bodily appetites and desires in the name of 'a rationally conceived goal or end'; and this in turn takes us back to Aristotle's temperate person habituated through a process of moral education to restrain appetites and emotions in the name of rational desires, goods and ends (Goldie, 2002, p. 113). However, one could go even further and argue that rational behaviour can only ever be conceived in relation to norms and virtues that are socially and culturally validated. To exhibit weakness of will or irrational behaviour is simply to fail to conform to these norms or to live up to society's ideals of virtue and morality. The Aristotelian notions of virtue and temperance (or self-control) lead on in turn to the notion of a political community in which there is a shared conception of the good life and hence of 'happiness'—a theme I shall return to later.

A person might exhibit 'weakness of will' for a variety of reasons. Education and upbringing (or lack of it), personality, past history and current circumstances might all be factors. But to speak of choosing to behave (or not to behave) rationally, morally or intelligently as if one's thoughts, attitudes and emotional impulses could be consciously directed or willed is surely to lead us again into an infinite regress. It should be noted, however, that this is not necessarily to argue that thoughts and acts are fully determined by antecedent events i.e. that there cannot be free will in its 'deep' sense. It is simply to argue that however we conceive consciousness or the mechanics of the process of rational deliberation, the complex of personality traits, emotions, beliefs and values that go to make up a person (the attitudes, needs and desires of the very subject or self who is deliberating), though continually evolving, are by their nature largely determined by the past history of that person i.e. by what has gone before.

There is, however, another sense in which we can speak of self-control being exercised: the self-control of emotions and feelings. Indeed, civilised life depends on people learning how to restrain their immediate, instinctive impulses, appetites and desires. Goleman is right to emphasise the importance of being able to control one's emotions and to delay self-gratification (Goleman, Chapters 5 and 6). Courses in emotional intelligence that teach techniques for managing anger, for example, may well be of value in this respect. But it is the *expression* of these impulses, appetites and feelings in actions or in words that is being controlled, not the impulses, appetites and feelings themselves. Therapy may help develop strategies for mitigating the destructive and debilitating effects of negative emotions, as in the case of 'learned helplessness' (as we shall see later); but to infer that one's attitudes and motives can be stage managed is quite another matter.

But even for the sort of person naturally driven by the desire to achieve economic or social status, there are dangers to the instrumental, managerial approach to work and to life. For example, Smith suggests 'Every time you communicate with someone, have a desired outcome . . . That way, you can know when you've achieved what you want' (Smith, 2002, p. 15); and in Wellington College's 10-point programme for well-being, 'productive relationships' are defined in similar terms: a good partner is 'someone with whom you can achieve positive outcomes' (Wellington College, 2007). This approach might make perfect sense in certain situations—at work, for example. But it is also the antithesis of the sort of communication or conversation that would develop mutual understanding, self-understanding, true knowledge and practical judgement—the goals of liberal learning. Worthwhile encounters and experiences, even at work, involve engagement on a quite different level. On this level, one must be open to having one's perceptions and values changed. In short, one must be open to learning, and this attitude, which must be an attitude to life, is simply not compatible with the instrumental attitude of the goal-achiever. By turning life into a series of goals and people into functionaries, life itself is diminished.

It might therefore be better to give up altogether the dual psychological concepts of goal-setting and goal-achieving, and instead limit goals to practical everyday situations where planning and setting priorities are needed to get things done with reasonable efficiency—in managing a business, organising one's diary or physical training, for example. Psychology's goal-achievement model seems to rest on little more than the empty assertion that behaviour and achievement are explained by the motivation necessary to bring them about. The very concepts of motivation, goal setting and goal achievement are therefore of dubious explanatory value.

OPTIMISM, HAPPINESS AND CIRCULAR REASONING

In Seligman's 'Learned Optimism', the two pivotal concepts are 'learned helplessness' and 'explanatory style' (Seligman, 2006). Learned helplessness is 'the giving-up reaction, the quitting response that follows from the belief that whatever you do doesn't matter'; and explanatory style, which is categorised as either optimistic or pessimistic, is 'the manner in which you habitually explain to yourself why events happen' (p. 15). Learned helplessness, argues Seligman, is intimately related to a pessimistic explanatory style, a habitual way of explaining bad events that is defeatist, self blaming and produces hopelessness and helplessness (pp.15-16). Explanatory style is a habit of thought learned in childhood and adolescence and 'stems directly from your view of your place in the world—whether you think you are valuable and deserving, or worthless and hopeless'; it is 'the hallmark of whether you are an optimist or a pessimist' (p. 44).

It seems that the concept of learned helplessness does usefully describe or categorise a particular view of the self, a chronic condition that prevents a normal life from being led and actively contributes to unhappiness and depression; and there is evidence that it can be treated effectively by cognitive therapy that breaks the vicious circle of self doubt and negativity, allowing positive thoughts to come into play. Moreover, it is quite plausible that learned helplessness and the pessimistic explanatory style associated with it are strongly influenced by childhood experience: the explanatory style of parents, criticism that leads the child to have a negative view of himself, and early traumas (p. 135). It is well established in social psychology that 'self-efficacy' (a person's belief or confidence that they can successfully complete tasks or undertake challenges) and 'attachment style' as an adult are significantly influenced by the social environment that is experienced as a young child (Matthews *et al.*, 2003, Chapter 8).

Nevertheless, learned helplessness remains a chronic and debilitating condition, a form of mental illness or abnormality, and it requires treatment as such—much as an obsessive-compulsive disorder would require treatment. The problem is that Seligman goes on to equate learned helplessness (or the chronic lack of confidence and self-belief that it perhaps describes in other words) with 'pessimism'. For Seligman, 'the defining characteristic of pessimists is that they tend to believe bad events will last a long time, will undermine everything they do, and are their own fault' (p. 4). He goes on: 'literally hundreds of studies show that pessimists give up more easily and get depressed more often' (p. 5). Even 'tendencies toward pessimism', mere 'traces of pessimism' are debilitating.

Seligman himself is at times ambivalent about the value of pessimism. Though he argues the balance is strongly against it, and he explains it as a hangover from the days when a pessimistic attitude was essential to survival in a dangerous and hostile world, Seligman does grudgingly admit that some jobs would suit a natural pessimist better than an optimist and that 'mild pessimists' may be 'merely prudent and measured people' (p. 112). Pessimists see reality more accurately than optimists (p. 111) and 'depressed people [now virtually indistinguishable from pessimists in Seligman's analysis] though sadder, are wiser' (p. 109). But pessimism's 'single virtue' is more than outweighed by 'its pervasive, crippling consequences' (p. 115). Positive psychology's programme to turn pessimists into optimists, by developing 'learned optimism,' is therefore more than justified.[3]

But just because a person suffering from the chronic condition of learned helplessness is permanently pessimistic and liable to depression (almost by definition), it cannot be inferred that a person who is pessimistic *in certain circumstances* is therefore suffering from some form of this debilitating condition and is in need of treatment. Indeed, this is an absurd generalisation. In 'The Positive Power of Negative Thinking', Julie Norem explores the cases of people who are clearly natural pessimists but who are notably successful in their careers (i.e. who are 'high achievers') and satisfied with their lives (Norem, 2001). Two outstanding things emerge. First, and perhaps unsurprisingly, people are not *just* pessimists or optimists. They have complex personality structures and 'sometimes the same person will have both positive and negative characteristics' (p. 24). A person might even at times be 'both strongly optimistic *and* strongly pessimistic' (p. 25); it all depends on the circumstances. Secondly, there is a very big difference between the person who has a disposition to be pessimistic 'all the time or in every situation' (p. 26)—i.e. who has 'a pessimistic attributional style' (p. 110) or learned helplessness—and the person who though anxious about future events is not debilitated by negative interpretations of past events. The latter, termed by Norem the 'defensive pessimist', has neither a consistently positive nor a consistently negative attributional style (p. 109), and is neither helpless nor hopeless in the face of setbacks.

In 'What (and Why) Is Positive Psychology?', Shelly Gable and Jonathan Haidt acknowledge Norem's work, accept that defensive pessimists constitute a 'subgroup of people' who would not benefit from being taught to be more optimistic, and argue that positive psychology must recognise that 'what is positive or good is complex and multi-dimensional' (Gable and Haidt, 2005, p. 108). But much of the problem lies with the very terms 'pessimistic' and 'optimistic' (or 'positive and 'negative') as personality categories and descriptors. When associated merely with obstruction, hopelessness, defeatism and resignation (or with 'learned helplessness'), the term 'pessimism' has indeed very negative connotations; but when it is associated with justified criticism, realism, the fatalism born of experience, and foresight, it is far more positive. It all depends on how pessimism is defined and interpreted. It also depends on the context, the situation and the other character traits that are brought into play. One could draw up an equivalent balance sheet for the term 'optimistic'. Both optimism *and* pessimism, so far as they have descriptive or explanatory value, must surely be counted as traits or features of a healthy, mature, balanced outlook.

Tendencies toward 'optimism' or 'pessimism' (assuming that we can speak in these terms and identify such traits) are really aspects of a much more complex whole. In fact, learned helplessness apart, it is questionable whether the terms optimistic and pessimistic have any value at all as freestanding descriptors of personality. At best, they can only describe attitudes to particular future events in particular situations and circumstances. It is the mental health and integrity of the person as a whole that must be considered, the totality of his attitudes and motivations, not the degree of perceived negativity or positivity of free-floating personality traits and descriptors.

Peter Goldie makes this point forcefully. Not only do personality traits cohere as part of a complex, interactive and dynamic whole, but a particular trait that is positive for one person can be negative for another (Goldie, 2002, pp. 157–160). To be able to understand and interpret a person's thoughts and feelings (and by extension their actions) at any given time, these need to be seen in the context of the overall narrative that constitutes a person's life (or the relevant parts of it) and in which they are embedded (pp. 4–5, 44–5). Indeed it is this narrative, of which emotions and personality traits or dispositions form an integral part, which enables a person to conceive of his situation in a certain way at all (p. 158). This in turn explains why it is perhaps the novelist rather than the psychologist who has more to teach us about the human condition.

There is unquestionably a mass of evidence to support the validity of personality traits as predictors of behaviour across a range of situations and to support the dominant 'Five Factor Model' in particular: that there are five broad dimensions of personality—neuroticism, extraversion, openness, agreeableness and conscientiousness (with the first two the most universally accepted). People *do* have dispositions to behave predictably in particular ways across a wide range of situations. Moreover, there appears to be a strong hereditary influence at work and genetic research promises more discoveries relating particular traits (especially abnormal ones) to individual genes or genetic configurations (see Matthews *et al.*, 2003; Eysenck, 1998, p. 452).

It could be reasonably objected that to really understand or appreciate the complex of thoughts, feelings, attitudes and motives that go to make up a person is quite a different matter from the act of labelling a person with trait descriptors based on the results of standardised personality tests (or questionnaires) that do no more than identify a person's behaviour across a range of typical social and work situations. Nevertheless, personality descriptors such as 'extravert' and 'neurotic' tell us a great deal more about a person than the terms pessimist and optimist. Factor models do at least help provide frameworks in which diverse traits or dispositions of personality can be placed in the context of broad dimensions of personality rather than categorised as free-floating absolutes, as positive or negative, good or bad.

For example, the classic personality types in psychology are 'extravert' and 'introvert'. It is easy to see how in a certain situation the more sociable, outgoing, impulsive extravert might get to be labelled as optimistic (and hopeful, and a host of other 'positive' epithets) and an introvert as pessimistic—the sort of social situation in which the extravert typically feels more comfortable than the introvert. But in another situation, it is the introvert who will come into his own and appear to display a host of positive qualities, traits and attitudes—indeed sometimes the very same ones.[4] There is in the psychology of personality types no suggestion at all that one type is better, superior, preferable or even 'happier' than another. The personalities—their dispositions, inclinations, motivations and temperaments—are simply different. Anthony Storr argues that natural classifications of human beings into extraverts and introverts, divergers and convergers, dramatists and patterners, suggest not that one group is normal and the other abnormal or neurotic, but that people have by temperament different ways of finding meaning in their lives (Storr, 1989, Chapter 7). Whereas extraverts, divergers and dramatists tend to find meaning in their interactions and relationships with other people, introverts, convergers and patterners have a greater imaginative need to find or impose order on their experience, to find systems and patterns, and to make sense of their own lives. Storr further argues that this is true of many creative people, who, necessarily, have a greater need for solitude: 'The creative person is constantly seeking to discover himself, to remodel his own identity, and to find meaning in the universe through what he creates. He finds this a valuable integrating process that, like meditation or prayer, has little to do with other people, but which has its own separate validity' (p. xiv).

Unfortunately, the goal-setting, goal-achieving optimist that positive psychology adopts as its model of mental health and well-being seems to be little more than a caricature of the traditional extravert—a manifestation of what David Ausubel and Floyd Robinson termed 'the cult of extraversion', the groundless but prevalent association of mental health with a personality that is 'warm, outgoing, amiable, and extraverted' (Ausubel and Robinson, 1969, p. 411). It is perhaps revealing that the terms 'extravert' and 'introvert', the classic descriptors of personality types, are largely conspicuous by their absence from the literature of positive psychology. There is a brief reference in Haidt, who claims that 'extraverts are naturally happier and healthier' and 'when introverts are forced to be more outgoing, they usually enjoy it' (Haidt, 2006, p. 133). Haidt is probably right that the company of others, which all people need to a greater or lesser extent, *is* more enjoyable than solitude. One is more likely to emerge amused, cheerful, and happy—happy in the sense of being amused and cheerful or cheered up. But this is entirely to miss the point, which is that not everyone needs or wants continual amusement or cheering up in order to be happy—happy in the sense of being fulfilled. Ed Diener also makes reference to extraversion as a personality factor related to 'feeling more positive emotions'; but he contrasts it not with introversion but neuroticism (Ed Diener's Website, 2008). The problem is that by defining happiness to begin with as 'subjective well-being' and measuring it according to a person's reported feelings of satisfaction, positive mood, pleasant emotions and so forth, Diener almost guarantees that a certain sort of person—a person perhaps typified by the amiable, cheerful extravert—will serve as our model of mental health.

PERSISTENCE AND SUCCESS

In 'Learned Optimism', Seligman argues that a key ingredient of success is persistence, 'the ability to not give up in the face of failure'; without it, 'talent and passion will come to nothing'. Moreover, a person's ability (or lack of it) to persist when faced with challenges or difficulties is explained by his explanatory style: while optimists persist, pessimists give up (Seligman, 2006, p. 101). A pessimistic explanatory style is therefore debilitating because it prevents people from fulfilling their potential. In support of his case, Seligman cites the Princeton-Penn Longitudinal Study in which those students shown to have an optimistic explanatory style (according to an 'Attributional Style Questionnaire' or ASQ) prior to college went on to do much better at the end of the first semester than those diagnosed as having a pessimistic explanatory style in relation to their predicted performance based on past grades and aptitude tests (pp. 150–2).

It seems quite plausible that people who have a pessimistic explanatory style (to use Seligman's categorisation) are more likely to have difficulties in coping or adjusting when faced with new challenges, pressures and circumstances when we recognise that the person who is identified in the ASQ test as attributing the causes of good events to himself rather than to others or to circumstances (i.e. has an optimistic as opposed to pessimistic explanatory style) could be described in other terms: he is simply the sort of person who has confidence and belief in himself in social situations, who adjusts easily to new situations and challenges, who looks forward rather than back, and who does not worry unnecessarily but takes things as they come—i.e. a person with something of the qualities of a natural extravert and a high degree of intrinsic self-esteem. It is perhaps no surprise that such a person might initially adjust better to the new challenges, both emotional and academic, of college or university.

Moreover, there are as we have seen people who are liable to suffer a collapse of confidence or self-belief at the slightest set back. It may well be, as David Ausubel suggested forty years ago, that failure to develop the intrinsic self-esteem that flows from unconditional parental acceptance and validation produces a person more likely to develop neurotic anxiety when faced with novel situations and challenges (Ausubel, 1968, pp. 401–7). And in these extreme cases, some sort of counselling or therapy may help enable a person to lead a normal life.

However, by the same token, a person's self-esteem and self-belief (or self-efficacy) are not isolated attributes but form part of the whole complex of his personality. And a person's personality together with his aptitudes is necessarily formed by myriad genetic, social, cultural and environmental influences. So long as he is able to find fulfilment in life, which involves coming to terms with who he is and learning what he is capable of, there seems no justification at all for attributing failure in any given situation to a defective personality or to 'negative' attitudes stemming from that personality. It is after all because people *are* different (and they have different personalities) that they cope differently in any given situation.

Indeed, does it make sense to assert that people who fail do so *because* they lack perseverance and persistence? It is in the very nature of a problem that does not yield an immediate solution or of any worthwhile activity or learning experience that one has to apply oneself. But applying oneself does not just mean 'keeping on trying' or 'not giving up' whatever the circumstances; if one is banging one's head against a brick wall, giving up might well be the best strategy. It means on the one hand having the aptitude to tackle the problem or undertake the task, which includes having the requisite skills and techniques, knowledge and experience, and on the other hand having the interest, motivation and dedication (which of course includes not giving up at the first hurdle). We might for example speak of a person having the potential to be a fine violinist if only they practised. But the point is that they do not practise and they do not practise because for one reason or another they are not sufficiently motivated to practise. They therefore do not have what it takes to be fine violinist. But this is not necessarily a failure on their part—unless perhaps they fail to find outlets in other directions for their talents and energies, in which case their failure to dedicate themselves to the violin might result in lifelong regret and unhappiness.

To attempt to isolate the quality or trait of perseverance and designate it an attitude explained by optimistic explanatory style is once again to misunderstand that perseverance, application, motivation, aptitude and ability in a particular field or situation are inextricably intertwined. The point is not that a person cannot change his behaviour or wish to change it if he feels he is completely debilitated by it, but that a person's disposition to think and behave in a certain way is the result of a whole complex of circumstances—historical, social and personal. The failure to achieve something is *in itself* no more problematic and no more a sign of mental ill health than the inability (through lack of motivation, inclination, aptitude or opportunity) of a boxer to play the violin or a teacher to become prime minister.

VIRTUE IN ABSORBING ACTIVITY

If the categorisation of people as optimists or pessimists and the goal-achievement model are of dubious value, the other main tenet of positive psychology might seem on the face of it more promising, namely that meaning, purpose and a feeling of well-being are derived from expressing one's positive personality traits or virtues ('signature strengths') in absorbing activities. Since positive emotions and feelings of well-being are generated by engagement in absorbing activities (the state of total absorption which is labelled 'flow'), maximising the feelings of well-being that we can derive from such activities is the key to happiness. Here, there are no elusive goals to achieve; one merely has to play to one's strengths.

There is of course nothing new in the idea that one of the keys to a fulfilling life is to find absorbing interests, passions, callings and commitments—indeed, it would be hard to define 'fulfilling' in any meaningful sense except in these terms. The special insight of positive psychology is that it is the engagement and expression of a person's 'signature strengths' that specifically produces the 'authentic positive emotion' (Seligman, 2007, p.138). Seligman has identified 24 positive personality traits, character strengths or 'signature strengths' and has grouped these into six 'core virtues'—the virtues that most commonly and consistently characterise human cultures: wisdom, courage, humanity, justice, temperance and transcendence (Seligman, 2007, Chapters 8 and 9; Haidt, 2006, pp. 167–9). The 'recrafting' of work to enable people to better exploit and express these personal or 'signature' strengths—enthusiasm, valour, originality, social intelligence and leadership are examples cited—will result in both happier people and more effective workers.

But are these signature strengths any more identifiable than the goals that are supposed to motivate us? As we have seen, free-floating positive traits of personality are only of significance or value in particular contexts or situations in conjunction with other personality traits together with the values, beliefs, aptitudes and life experiences that go to form a whole person. It is hard to see how they can be identified or realised apart from life itself; and, as we have seen, it is questionable whether it makes any sense to designate personality traits in isolation as 'positive' to begin with. Moreover, the list of virtues and signature strengths identified by Seligman conflates personality traits (or natural dispositions), learned values and beliefs, and the self-control (or integrity of character or 'will') needed to put these values and beliefs into practice. Because one's signature strengths are the positive personality traits one is naturally endowed with, everything that is cultivated or inculcated through learning (i.e. the things needing self-discipline, effort and guidance)—values, beliefs, virtues, habits, dispositions and attitudes—therefore becomes somehow optional, relevant only to the minority whose particular natural signature strengths happen to include 'love of learning' and 'self-control'. As Haidt puts it, instead of trying 'to change any aspect of your personality by sheer force of will', which is difficult, you simply 'work on your strengths, not your weaknesses' (p. 169); and because the exercise of your strengths is intrinsically rewarding and generates 'flow', you are much less likely to give up (p. 170).

However, when Aristotle originally listed and categorised the virtues, he was careful to distinguish the moral virtues from the intellectual virtues, the latter comprising wisdom (objective, scientific knowledge or truth) and prudence (practical wisdom or judgement). Though Aristotle recognises that the virtues must perforce have some basis in our natural instincts or dispositions (Aristotle, 1976, pp. 223–4), they are not natural endowments; training and instruction are needed respectively to develop habits of right action (moral virtues) and the rational intellect (intellectual virtue): 'The moral virtues, then, are engendered in us neither *by* nor *contrary* to nature; we are constituted by nature to receive them, but their full development in us is due to habit' (p. 91). Moreover, to behave virtuously is not merely to act in conformity with the virtues but to choose to act in a particular way in the *knowledge* that one is doing the right thing (p. 97). Temperance (the observance of the mean) and self-restraint are needed to master the pleasures and the passions. True virtue must have both a moral and an intellectual dimension.

In his broad defence of Aristotle's account of the virtues in 'After Virtue', Alasdair MacIntyre highlights this role of intelligence, of practical judgement (*phronesis*), in transforming moral dispositions into virtues and relates it to Aristotle's doctrine of the mean: it is precisely because a virtue cannot adequately be distinguished from its corresponding vices independently of circumstances that practical judgement, the knowledge of how to exercise judgement in particular cases, is needed (MacIntyre, 1985, p. 154). Moreover, the virtues are intimately related to each other and this is reflected in the idea of a political community in which there is a shared recognition and pursuit of the good life—'the moral unity of Aristotelianism' (p. 156).

MacIntyre goes on to explore how a person's life can have the moral unity necessary for it to be meaningful and for its acts to be intelligible and accountable. For this to happen, the life of the self must be conceived as a quest for the good life: 'It is in the course of the quest ... that the good of the quest is finally to be understood. A quest is always an education both as to the character of that which is sought and in self-knowledge' (p. 219). But the quest needs both a starting point and some initial conception of a possible shared future or *telos*, and this is only possible if the life of the self is also conceived as an enacted historical narrative framed in a living tradition i.e. if a person has an adequate sense of shared traditions and practices, a historical and a social identity (p. 223). The possibilities of the future are inevitably constrained by the events of the past, just as a person's own actions are constrained by the actions of others (p. 215).

To 'realise' himself, a person needs to learn what he is capable of being or becoming; and this in turn necessitates learning values and developing the self-control and integrity needed to put these values into practice. Of course, what he becomes is in part determined by inherited aptitudes, inclinations, traits and dispositions, but these only have significance in their totality and in conjunction with what is learned and experienced in a life framed in a particular social and historical setting. Only then can we speak of a person's 'personality' and begin to identify its positive or negative aspects. And if, as Goldie argues, the complex of traits, emotions, beliefs and values that make up one's personality produce a disposition to conceive of one's situation in a certain way, then they must also colour one's personal conception of happiness and the good life.

Though Haidt claims that the traditional virtues have found a new lease of life in the form of Seligman's diagnostic manual of signature strengths, it is clear that the re-conception is only possible by the virtual elimination from the picture of the very things that, at least in the Aristotelian tradition, make the idea of virtue conceivable at all.

CONCLUDING REMARKS

There is more than an air of circular reasoning and tautologous assertion about the whole positive psychology project. There is, for example, a certain tautological inevitability in the assertion that a person categorised as 'pessimistic' to begin with, and therefore with a tendency always to look at the worst aspect of things, is more prone to depression; or that to achieve a particular goal you need the attitudes, inclinations and motivations that are needed to achieve that goal; or that people with a pessimistic explanatory style, which is characterised by a tendency to give up, are more likely to give up; or that people who are by nature optimistic, amiable and untroubled by worries or doubts are happiest, when happiness is defined as a state of being optimistic, amiable and untroubled by worries or doubts.

It would be difficult to question the assertion that a person with a positive, optimistic attitude is happier in the sense of being optimistic and enjoying uniformly positive feelings about the past, the future and him or herself. We have here simply a description of a particular personality type together with a particular definition (all be it, a commonly accepted one) of the word happiness. The problems begin when this particular account of happiness is held up as a model of mental-health that can be achieved with the necessary re-crafting of people's attitudes.

If, however, life is a quest in which people explore the purpose and meaning of their lives, and develop their own conception of what constitutes a good life—all within the frame of a shared tradition and a living community—there is no need to make this association at all. You are free to find and therefore to define your own happiness. Gable and Haidt talk of the quest of positive psychology to 'properly map the domain of human optimal functioning' (Gable and Haidt, 2005, p. 108). But there is no optimal solution.

The positive, optimistic attitude that Seligman associates with achievement, success and happiness (and which he exemplifies with a successful insurance salesman—see Seligman, 2006, Chapter 6) seems moreover to pre-suppose a very narrow range of emotional response. Indeed, one might argue that it is the mark of wisdom and maturity, of an appreciation of the mysteries, tragedies and ironies of life, *not* to respond unambiguously positively or negatively, optimistically or pessimistically, to any given situation. The model of mental health depicted by positive psychology turns out to be little more than a caricature of an extravert—a bland, shallow, goal-driven careerist whose positive attitudes, certainties and 'high self-esteem' mask the fact that he lacks the very qualities that would enable him to attain a degree of true self-knowledge or wisdom, and to really grow as a human being.

Are people who are depressed and unfulfilled by their lives therefore condemned to misery? The sort of cognitive behavioural therapy advocated by Seligman may well be effective (as indeed may various drug treatments) in the case of certain debilitating conditions and psychiatric disorders—in the treatment of the chronic lack of confidence and loss of self-esteem that Seligman categorises as learned helplessness, as in obsessive-compulsive type disorders. But the wider claims of positive psychology to be able to re-craft most people's lives are grounded on a quite unjustified generalisation of these extreme cases. In breaking the vicious cycle of negative thinking that characterises these debilitating conditions, people are not transformed into optimistic, goal-setting, goal-achieving extraverts. They are simply freed to lead normal lives and to discover what they are capable of making of themselves.

Advances in molecular biology and genetics, however, would seem to raise the prospect that even a 'normal' person can be re-engineered (or simply drugged) to be more relaxed, cheerful and optimistic. This utilitarian dream might necessarily be at the expense of the qualities of being critical, perceptive, realistic and perhaps creative (unless a new robotic being could be designed from scratch). But the sum total of human happiness could no doubt be increased. This naturally raises a host of profound philosophical and ethical questions revolving around what it is to be a human being. But it also begs a very straightforward question: what is happiness? And this is a question that I have argued in this chapter can only be explored by people engaged in the quest to make sense of their own lives in a wider social and cultural context.

The danger is that instead of fostering the true learning that develops self-knowledge and wisdom, and instead of considering the social and political measures that might really improve people's circumstances, positive psychology offers a substitute recipe for success, achievement and happiness that ultimately has no substance at all.

NOTES

1. Goleman's *Emotional Intelligence*, which is cited in the SEAL literature, appeared in 1996 and therefore slightly predates the emergence of the positive psychology movement. Though there

are differences in emphasis, the broad themes and conclusions are the same (see Seligman, 2007, p. 294, endnote to p. 144).

2. The dogma of the ghost in the machine, as Ryle terms it, is the Cartesian belief that there are two different levels of existence or status: the things and events that belong to the physical world and the internal workings of the mind (Ryle, 1990, pp. 13–17). See Edelman for an account of the homunculus problem (Edelman, 1994, pp. 79–80).

3. It surely takes only a moment's reflection to appreciate how extraordinary these claims are. In writing off the facility or skill of being able to see reality accurately in favour of 'optimistic illusions about reality' (Seligman, 2006, p. 108)—the spirit of raw, positive energy that Seligman sees as the source of creativity and progress—the whole of philosophy, humane learning and rationality, of everything that has traditionally contributed to self-knowledge, judgement and wisdom is eliminated from the picture. These things do re-appear in the guise of signature strengths that may be cultivated by those so inclined in pursuit of the virtue of wisdom, but 'love of learning' is only one of six strengths leading to the higher-level virtue of wisdom, and wisdom is only one of six higher-level virtues comprising 24 strengths altogether. If education were to be re-crafted according to the insights of positive psychology and centre round the identification and development of a child's 'natural competencies' or strengths, and of the pursuit of 'flow through learning' (Goleman, 1996, p. 95), it would cease altogether in the traditional formative sense.

4. In 'On the Psychology of the Unconscious', Jung provides us with the classic depiction of the introvert and the extravert coming into their own in his story of two youths rambling in the country and coming upon a fine castle (Jung, 1983, pp. 162–4). It is the extravert's optimism and initiative that get them into the castle, but the introvert's delight in the castle's contents that then predominates.

REFERENCES

Aristotle (1976) *The Nicomachean Ethics* (Harmondsworth, Penguin Books).

Ausubel, D. P. (1968) *Educational Psychology: A Cognitive View* (New York, Holt, Rinehart and Winston).

Ausubel, D. P. and Robinson, F. G. (1969) *School Learning: An Introduction to Educational Psychology* (New York, Holt, Rinehart and Winston).

Banda Pilot Site, Excellence and Enjoyment (2007) *Social and Emotional Aspects of Learning (SEAL)* ⟨http://bandapilot.org.uk/secondary/index.html⟩ (Accessed 21.1.2008).

Ed Diener's Website (2008) *Discoveries from the Diener Lab, Contributions of the Ed Diener Laboratory to The Scientific Understanding of Well-Being*. Available at: ⟨http://www.psych.uiuc.edu/~ediener/contributions_of_lab.htm⟩ (Accessed 21.1.2008).

Edelman, G. M. (1994) *Brilliant Air, Brilliant Fire* (London, Penguin Books).

Eysenck, M. (1998) Personality, in: M. Eysenck (ed.) *Psychology: An Integrated Approach* (Harlow, Pearson).

Gable, S. L. and Haidt, J. (2005) What (and Why) Is Positive Psychology?, *Review of General Psychology*, 9.2, pp. 103–110.

Goldie, P. (2002) *The Emotions: A Philosophical Exploration* (Oxford, Clarendon Press).

Goleman, D. (1996) *Emotional Intelligence* (London, Bloomsbury).

Griffiths, S. (2007) Children—The New Battleground *The Sunday Times*, 9 September.

Haidt, J. (2006) *The Happiness Hypothesis* (London, Arrow Books).

Jung, C. G. (1983) On the Psychology of the Unconscious, (extracts), in: A. S. Storr (ed.) *Jung: Selected Writings* (London, Fontana), pp. 147–168.

Layard, R. (2006) *Happiness: Lessons from a New Science* (London, Penguin Books).

MacIntyre, A. (1985) *After Virtue* (London, Duckworth).

Matthews, G., Deary, I. J. and Whiteman, M. C. (2003) *Personality Traits* (Cambridge, Cambridge University Press).

Miller, G. A. and Buckhout, R. (1973) *Psychology: The Science of Mental Life* (New York, Harperand Row).

Norem, J. K. (2001) *The Positive Power of Negative Thinking* (Cambridge, MA, Basic Books).

Pinker, S. (1999) *How The Mind Works* (London, Penguin Books).

Ryle, G. (1990) *The Concept of Mind* (London, Penguin Books).

Schoch, R. (2007) *The Secrets of Happiness* (London, Profile Books).

Seligman, M. E. P. (2006) *Learned Optimism* (New York, Vintage Books).

Seligman, M. E. P. (2007) *Authentic Happiness* (New York, Free Press).

Smith, A. (2002) *55 Ways to Increase Your Emotional Intelligence* (Glossop, Coaching Leaders Ltd).

Smith, R. (2006) As if by Machinery: The Levelling of Educational Research, *Journal of Philosophy of Education*, 40.2, pp. 157–168.

Storr, A. S. (1989) *Solitude* (London, Flamingo).

Taylor, A., Sluckin, W., Davies, D. R., Reason, J. T., Thomson, R. and Colman, A. M. (1982) *Introducing Psychology* (Harmondsworth, Penguin Books).

Waite, R. (2007) Happiness Classes 'Depress Pupils' *The Sunday Times*, 9 September.

Wellington College (2007) *The Wellington College Programme for Developing Well-Being* ⟨http://www.wellington-college.berks.sch.uk/resource.aspx?id=62217⟩ (Accessed 21.1.2008).

5
NON-COGNITIVE INTELLIGENCES

5.1
Introduction

RUTH CIGMAN AND ANDREW DAVIS

If there is to be a theory of multiple intelligences (MI theory), there must be a satisfactory way of identifying these, distinguishing one intelligence from another. 'Illusory Intelligences?' is an abridged version of a previously published paper, detailing John White's view of the theory's failure to do this. In the present version, White quotes Gardner's responses at some length, and responds to the responses. It therefore represents a dialogue that the interested reader may follow up.

White examines the 'general prerequisites' that, according to Gardner, must be satisfied for something to count as an intelligence. These include problem-solving skills, the potential for finding or creating new problems, and most importantly, the (candidate) intelligence must be valued by human cultures. Candidates which survive this initial test, according to Gardner, include linguistic, logical-mathematical, spatial, musical, bodily-kinaesthetic, interpersonal and intrapersonal competences.

White queries the list. How about food-providing skills, he asks? Or shelter-providing, medical or child-rearing skills? Why did *these* not get through the first round of requirements? He takes up the issue of culture. The theory of multiple intelligences, argues Gardner, must capture 'a reasonably complete gamut of the kinds of abilities valued by human cultures'. What does this mean, asks White? In order to qualify as 'an intelligence', must it be valued by all human cultures, most, or only some?

White proceeds to examine the specific criteria which a candidate intelligence that has survived the first round must meet if it is to join, as Gardner puts it, 'our charmed circle of intelligences'. First, and controversially, is 'potential isolation of the area by brain damage'. In other words multiple intelligences, according to Gardner, are brain-based and innate, which means that they can in principle be assessed 'quite early in life, perhaps even in infancy' (Gardner, 1983). (As such, Gardner's theory has much in common with those discussed in Section 2 of this volume.) The intelligences are also susceptible to 'encoding in a symbol system' (a further criterion of an intelligence), which means that they have a crucial social dimension. Here is the crux of the disagreement between Gardner and White. Gardner (2006) wrote: 'I have always held that an approach through symbol analysis allows one to look toward a biological basis, on the one hand, and a cultural analysis, on the other.' White comments tersely: 'So intelligences both are and are not social constructions. That's where the unintelligibility resides.'

A key issue is the application of the theory, and here White has two major quarrels. First, MI theory, with its emphasis on biology, encourages selective policies and practices, exactly like IQ theory. Second, it is commonly used in schools to boost the self-esteem of children who excel in untraditional ways, and as such (given that, in his view, MI theory is untrue), children are habitually lied to. 'How much does truth matter?' asks White. Without defending moral purism, he suggests that it matters quite a bit.

In her chapter on emotional intelligence theory (EI), Rietti goes straight for the ethical jugular. EI, she argues, is not only a conceptual muddle; it smuggles in 'a particular picture of what the world, including the human psyche within it, is like, as well as what is good and bad about it, and of what people ought to do'. Tracing several versions of the theory, but concentrating mainly on the phenomenally successful version of Daniel Goleman, Rietti focuses on EI as an 'ability-cluster that can be taught and learned', rather than EI as non-cognitive variant on IQ, akin to Gardner's intelligences. As an ability-cluster, it is endowed with panacea-like qualities, like those ascribed to happiness, well-being, self-esteem (see Section 4, The Enhancement Agenda). Rietti registers deep unease about the idea, which she finds implicit in EI theory, of 'indoctrination, and of a particularly invasive kind at that, reaching right into the affected individuals' inner lives and dispositions.' What is needed, she argues, is critical discussion of a straightforwardly ethical kind. This argument has echoes throughout the book.

5.2
Illusory Intelligences?

JOHN WHITE

1 CAN GARDNER'S MULTIPLE INTELLIGENCES BE JUSTIFIED?

The theory of multiple intelligences has been influential in school reform across the world. In England, for instance, it is widely used to back the idea that pupils have preferred 'learning styles': some make better progress if they can involve their musical or interpersonal or other strengths in their learning than if they have to be dependent on language ability alone.

But does MI theory hold water?

Everything turns on the claim that there are a few relatively discrete intelligences: linguistic, musical, logico-mathematical, spatial, bodily-kinaesthetic, intrapersonal and interpersonal, to which have now been added naturalist and possibly existential intelligences. One reason for the popularity of MI theory is its rejection of the unitary general intelligence associated with IQ testing. Children who have been seen, or have seen themselves, as dim are recognised to have other strengths. This is an important thought. But it could be true and MI theory false. Long ago Gilbert Ryle reminded us that 'the boxer, the surgeon, the poet and the salesman' engage in their own kinds of intelligent operation, applying 'their special criteria to the performance of their special tasks' (Ryle, 1949, p. 48). On his view, intelligent action has to do with flexible adaptation of means in pursuit of one's goals. This means that there are as many types of human intelligence as there are types of human goal. Gardner has corralled this variety into a small number of categories. Is this justified?

How does Gardner identify his intelligences? The basic text here is Chapter 4 of *Frames of Mind: The Theory of Multiple Intelligences*. He writes:

> First of all, what are the prerequisites for an intelligence: that is, what are the general desiderata to which a set of intellectual skills ought to conform before that set is worth consideration in the master list of intellectual competences? Second, what are the actual criteria by which we can judge whether a candidate competence, which has passed the 'first cut', ought to be invited to join our charmed circle of intelligences? (Gardner, 1983, p. 60).

Identifying an intelligence is thus a two-stage process. It has to satisfy the prerequisites; and it has to meet the criteria.

1.1 Prerequisites

The first of these is crucial. If a candidate fails here, it stands no chance. Gardner tells us that: 'A human intellectual competence must entail a set of skills of problem-solving ... and must also entail the potential for finding or creating problems—thereby laying the groundwork for the acquisition of new knowledge. These prerequisites represent my effort to focus on those intellectual strengths that prove of some importance within a cultural context' (pp. 60–1). He adds that: 'a prerequisite for a theory of multiple intelligences, as a whole, is that it captures a reasonably complete gamut of the kinds of abilities valued by human cultures' (p. 62).

1.1.1 Failing Candidates Which candidates fail and which pass the test? Among failures, Gardner includes the 'ability to recognize faces' (p. 61). This is because it 'does not seem highly valued by cultures'. Is it true that the ability to recognise faces is not valued by cultures? This seems counterintuitive. For if most of us could not recognise the faces of our relatives, friends, colleagues, or political leaders, it is hard to see how social life would be possible. How can one tell, in any case, whether an ability is culturally important? Gardner writes as if there are clear tests at this first of the two filters. Yet his very first example of a failure is disputable.

1.1.2 Successful Candidates The candidates passing the first test obviously include Gardner's intelligences. They must have all been picked out for the high value that human cultures have placed on them.

Are we talking about all human cultures, most, or only some? Gardner is not clear on this. On the one hand, he says: 'The prerequisites are a way of ensuring that a human intelligence must be genuinely useful and important, at least in certain cultural settings' (p. 61). This looks like *some* cultures. On the other, a later work tells us: 'The theory is an account of human cognition in its fullness—I put forth the intelligences as a new definition of human nature, cognitively speaking' (Gardner, 1999a, p. 44). This looks like *all*. Whichever of these answers it is, how would we find out what human societies have valued? We have historical evidence stretching back a few millennia; and patchy archaeological evidence taking us back another few. Beyond that there are only commonsense hunches. Food-providing skills, for instance, must surely always have been highly prized.

The 'first cut' selection of the seven original intelligences must have been based on something other than a scientific study of skills that all or nearly all human societies have valued. I will come back to this later. In addition, there are other skills, not included among the intelligences, which have as much prima facie plausibility for this title as those included. I have mentioned food-providing skills, but we might also add shelter-providing skills, medical skills, child-rearing skills. Why did Gardner not discuss *these*?

As we have seen, he does not approach his prerequisites via a comprehensive consideration of what the valued problem-solving skills in any human society might have been, drawing on whatever empirical data is available. His decisions must rest on something more subjective. I will say more about this later.

1.2 Criteria

Once a candidate intelligence has satisfied the prerequisites, it has to meet various criteria. These comprise:

- potential isolation of the area by brain damage;
- the existence in it of idiots savants, prodigies and other exceptional individuals;
- an identifiable core operation/set of operations;
- a distinctive developmental history, along with a definable set of expert 'end-state' performances;
- an evolutionary history and evolutionary plausibility;
- support from experimental psychological tasks;
- support from psychometric findings;
- susceptibility to encoding in a symbol system (Gardner, 1983, pp. 62–9).

1.2.1. Problems with specific criteria There are specific problems about several of these items, as well as problems about the criteria in general. I begin with specific items. For convenience, I begin with two of them taken together.

- *an identifiable core operation/set of operations*
- *a distinctive developmental history, along with a 'definable set of expert "end-state" performances'*

The interconnectedness of these two can be illustrated by reference to linguistic intelligence. This has as its 'core operations' a sensitivity to the meaning of words, to order among words, to the sounds and rhythms of words, and to the different functions of language (p. 77). These core operations are seen at work 'with special clarity' in the work of the poet.

Linguistic intelligence also possesses a distinctive developmental history, culminating in expert 'end-state' performances like those of the poet. Syntactical and phonological processes lie close to the core, since they unfold 'with relatively scant need for support from environmental factors' (pp. 80–1). Other intelligences illustrate the same point. Musical intelligence involves, as core operations, pitch, rhythm and timbre (pp. 104–5). It begins in infancy with rudimentary singing (p. 108) and develops towards end-states exemplified this time by proficient composers. Spatial intelligence develops from such core abilities as perceiving the visual world accurately, performing transformations on one's visual experience, and recreating aspects of the latter (p. 173). The expert end-state performances are painting, sculpture and the sciences. Similar claims are made about the remaining intelligences.

Gardner's theory of intelligence is developmentalist. Developmentalism is the theory that the biological unfolding between two poles from seed through to mature specimen that we find in the physical world—e.g. of plants, or human bodies—is also found in the mental world. In his criteria, Gardner acknowledges the two poles in the mental case. At one end, there are allegedly genetically given capacities common to human beings like visual perception, innate knowledge of the rules of language (following Chomsky—see Gardner, 1983, p. 80), the ability to move our bodies in different ways etc. At the other end is the mature state, the 'definable set of expert "end-state" performances' mentioned among the criteria. We have already seen examples in the highest flights of poetry, music, painting, sculpture and science. Intrapersonal intelligence, whose core capacity or mental seed is 'access to one's own feeling life', finds its full development in the work of a novelist like Proust or the patient or therapist 'who comes to attain a deep knowledge of his feeling life' (p. 239). Interpersonal intelligence, arising out of the primitive 'ability to notice and make distinctions among other individuals' generates its 'highly developed forms ... in political and religious leaders (a Mahatma Gandhi or a Lyndon Johnson), in skilled parents and teachers' etc. (ibid.).

1.2.2 Problems in Developmentalism Gardner's theory faces an objection besetting all forms of developmentalism. The latter is based on the assumption that the unfolding familiar in the biological realm from seed to mature state is also found in the mental. The assumption is often taken as read in psychological and educational circles, but is deeply problematic. I shall now summarise its chief difficulties as illustrated in Gardner's own writings, a fuller account being available in my paper 'Multiple Invalidities' (2006).

1.2.2.1 Biological seeds, including the union of sperm and egg, *have within them the power to unfold* into more complex stages, given appropriate environmental conditions. To locate a mental equivalent it is not enough to pick out innate capacities. We are all born with the power to see and hear things, to move our bodies, to desire food and drink, to feel pain and pleasurable sensations. But these abilities do not have within them the power to *unfold* into more complex forms. Toothaches one has in the course of one's life do not grow into more advanced forms of the same thing. Many of the powers just mentioned can *change* into more sophisticated versions: the desire for food, for instance, becomes differentiated into desires for hamburgers and ice-cream. But this kind of change—driven by social expectations—is not an unfolding.

1.2.2.2 The second problem concerns the other pole, the mature state—Gardner's 'end-state'. We understand this notion well enough in physical contexts like fully-grown hollyhocks or human bodies. A fully-grown human body is one that can grow no further: it has reached the limits of its development. It can certainly go on *changing*, but the changes are to do with maintenance and deterioration, not further growth. If we apply these ideas to the mind, do we want to say that all human beings have mental ceilings—e.g. in each of Gardner's intelligences—beyond which they cannot progress? This goes against the grain for many of us. We like to think of our intellectual life as expandable and deepenable, in principle, in all sorts of directions. True, psychologists like Cyril Burt have built the notion of mental ceilings into their notion of intelligence, but their views have been rightly criticised. The claim that we all have individually differing intellectual limits is both unverifiable and unfalsifiable. It is not a scientific claim (see White, 1998a, pp. 29–32).

One answer to this might be that the development of intelligence is unlike physical development in that here there are no ceilings, simply the potential for endless growth. Grounds would have to be provided for this claim—which is tantamount to saying that mental development fails to manifest a feature found in biological development. But if we leave this on one side, the claim still includes the idea of growth towards states of relative maturity, even if ceilings are not to be found. It is not clear whether Gardner would embrace this claim. On the one hand he writes of 'end-state' performances (Gardner, 1983, p. 64), which suggests finality; on the other, he describes the process of development as leading to 'exceedingly high levels of competence', which does not.

Whichever view he takes, he still has to say *what counts* as maturity in the case of the intelligences. With the oak tree and the human body, we know through the use of our senses when maturity has occurred: over time we can *see* that a person is fully grown, physically speaking, or that an oak tree has reached its full dimensions. What equivalent is there in the mental realm? How do we know either that people have reached their mental ceiling or, on the ceiling-less view, that they are more mentally mature than they were?

We do not just use our senses. We cannot see a person's intellectual maturity as we can see that he or she is physically fully grown. So how *do* we tell? In ordinary life we make all sorts of judgments about people's intellectual maturity. These judgments tend to be controversial. Some people would understand intellectual maturity in quiz show terms; others would emphasise depth of understanding; yet others a synoptic grasp of connections between different fields; and so on. Judgments of mental maturity lack the consensus found in judgments about fully-grown pine trees or badgers. This is because different people apply their own value judgments.

Gardner's examples of high levels of development in the intelligences seem to reflect his own value judgments about what kinds of qualities are important. He starts—in his 'prerequisites'—from problem-solving skills important within cultures. He has in mind the achievements of outstanding poets, composers, religious leaders, politicians, scientists, novelists. So 'end states' are identified not by observation of what happens in nature, as with plants or bodies, but by what Gardner sees as socially valuable. His value judgments, not any empirical discoveries as a scientist, are his starting point. True, in his introduction to the second edition of *Frames of Mind*, Gardner backs off from using only ethically acceptable persons as illustrations: 'intelligences by themselves are neither pro-social nor antisocial. Goethe used his linguistic intelligence for positive ends, Goebbels his for destructive ones; Stalin and Gandhi both understood other individuals, but put their interpersonal intelligences to diverse uses' (Gardner, 1993, p. xxvi). But this casts doubt on whether 'end-states' are always achievements valued within a culture—and so negates what he says about 'prerequisites'. Whether we look towards the seed or towards the full flowering, we find insuperable problems in identifying mental counterparts to physical growth. Since developmentalist assumptions are central to Gardner's theory, this seriously undermines it.

- *'susceptibility to encoding in a symbol system'*

Gardner writes: 'following my mentor Nelson Goodman and other authorities, I conceive of a symbol as any entity (material or abstract) that can denote or refer to any other entity. On this definition, words, pictures, diagrams, numbers, and a host of other entities are readily considered symbols' (Goodman, 1968, p. 301). It is important to see how wide the range of Gardner's symbols is. They include not only obvious ones like words and mathematical symbols, but also paintings, symphonies, plays, dances and poems. It is because works of art are symbols in his view that he can connect many of his intelligences with their own kind of symbolic entities. For instance, words are not the only symbols associated with linguistic intelligence: also associated with this are such symbols as poems.

Gardner writes: 'In addition to denoting or representing, symbols convey meanings in another equally important but less often appreciated way. A symbol can convey some mood, feeling or tone ... Thus a painting, whether abstract or representational, can convey moods of sadness, triumph, anger, or 'blueness' (even if the painting itself is red!) (Gardner, 1983, p. 301). Gardner, following Goodman, is saying that some things—works of art—are symbols in that they convey or express feelings or moods. But just because works of art can be expressive of emotion, it is hard to see why they should be called 'symbols' for that reason. What are they symbolising? One can understand the notion readily enough when talking about words, flags or communion wine. In each of these cases one can draw a distinction between the symbol and what it is a symbol of: cats, America, the blood of Christ. If a song is a symbol in the same way, what is the thing symbolised?

The use of the term 'symbol' in Gardner's work is obscure. If in an artistic context 'symbolising' means no more than 'expressing feeling', the term is redundant. In addition, 'symbol' now comes to have a different meaning in the arts from what it has in language and in mathematical thinking. Without going through all the other criteria, a word about two of them.

- *'the potential isolation of the area by brain damage'*

The criteria to do with development and with symbol are central items on Gardner's list. This can be seen if one tries to imagine their absence. I shall come back to the centrality of the symbol criterion later. Meanwhile let us imagine the exclusion of the development criterion. Suppose we take what appears to be the weightiest of the other criteria: 'the potential isolation of the area by brain damage'. And let us take it that there are localised areas of function within the brain. If one part of the brain is damaged, one's sight is impaired, if another, one's ability to move one's left hand, or feel pain, or talk, or understand speech. What this shows is that certain physiological necessary conditions of exercising these capacities are absent. It does not help to indicate the existence of separate 'intelligences'. It is well known that language ability is impaired through brain injury to parts of the left hemisphere of the cerebral cortex. But the injury could in principle impair wired-in abilities implicated not only in language use but in all sorts of other things as well; and there does indeed seem to be empirical evidence that this is the case (Richardson, 1999, pp. 85–8). The capacities in question are not those of a language module but of 'much more general and lower-grade functions' (Gardner, 1983, p. 87).

Given his developmentalism, one can understand why Gardner should look to brain localisation in order to identify intelligences, for he has to provide an account of the 'seed' that is to unfold into its mature form, and this seed has to be part of our original, biologically given, constitution. But the kinds of function picked out by brain localisation research do not have the power, as far as I can see, to grow into more developed forms. I am indeed born with the power of vision or the power to move my thumbs, but although various forms of socialisation are built on these abilities, the latter do not *unfold* into maturer versions of themselves.

- *'the existence, in an area, of idiots savants, prodigies and other exceptional individuals'*

Gardner invokes the existence of *idiots savants* to support his theory, but what I know of them does not lead me to think of them as intelligent. Well known recent examples include an 11-year-old London boy who can draw complicated buildings perfectly having just seen them; a 23-year-old man who can play piano pieces perfectly having heard them only three times; and a young man who can tell you the day of the week of any date presented to him. All these cases are of subnormal mental ability. What they all have in common is a *mechanical* facility, one that lacks the flexibility of adapting means to ends found in intelligent behaviour.

Prodigies only support Gardner's case if there is good evidence that their talents are innate. But the evidence seems to point to acquired abilities (Howe, 1997, pp. 131–2)

1.2.3 Concluding Comments about Specific Criteria It would be natural to think that the 'criteria' against which one measures candidate intelligences that have survived the 'prerequisites' requirement are all straightforwardly applicable—in the sense that it is an empirical task to look at the relevant facts and come to a judgment. But this is not so, as the critique of five of the more important of the eight criteria has shown. In addition, the criteria to do with development and with symbols presuppose the truth of dubious *theories*—one in psychology, the other Goodman's theory of aesthetics. This undermines the validity of MI theory as a whole. Just as the discussion of the 'prerequisites' showed that the theory rests ultimately on value-judgements rather than empirical evidence, this discussion of particular criteria provides further evidence of its non-scientific nature. Yet more grounds for this conclusion are given in the sections 1.2.4 and 1.2.5 below.

1.2.4 How Are the Criteria to be Applied? How does one use the criteria to pick out intelligences? If they are all necessary conditions, each has to be met before we can say that an intelligence exists. Although some of them seem to be necessary—to judge by remarks like 'an intelligence must also be susceptible to encoding in a symbol system' (Gardner, 1990, p. 933), in his original work Gardner makes it clear that not all have to be satisfied (Gardner, 1983, p. 62). In places, the demand is more stringent. In his 1990 discussion of how he came to pick out his intelligences, he writes that 'only those candidate intelligences that satisfied all or a majority of the criteria were selected as *bona fide* intelligences' (Gardner, 1990, p. 932). If this is to be taken literally, then if five or more of the eight criteria listed are met, a candidate automatically passes the test. But *Frames of Mind* states that there is no 'algorithm for the selection of an intelligence, such that any trained researcher could determine whether a candidate intelligence met the appropriate criteria' (p. 63). Rather, Gardner goes on: 'At present, however, it must be admitted that the selection (or rejection) of a candidate intelligence is reminiscent more of an artistic judgment than of a scientific assessment' (p. 63).

The identification of intelligences appears, then to be a subjective matter, depending on the particular weightings that Gardner gives to different criteria in different cases. It is worth dwelling on this point. Gardner sees it as a special virtue of his theory, which differentiates it from rival ways of classifying basic intellectual abilities—like Paul Hirst's account of the 'forms of knowledge', for instance—that it is *scientifically* based and not derived *a priori* (Gardner, 1983, pp. 61–2). In saying that selecting intelligences is more like making an artistic judgment than a scientific assessment, Gardner thus seems to be contradicting himself. The subjective, non-empirical nature of his theory has also been shown above. We have seen how the 'prerequisites' are not based on empirical investigation of what different societies have held to be valuable; and that the 'criteria' depend on theories in psychology and aesthetics that themselves are not empirically founded. But it is in his above remark on how the intelligences are identified via the criteria, that the subjectivity is most striking. The issue of identification is crucial. If we have no objective way of identifying them, we have no reason to think that the multiple intelligences exist.

Gardner has replied to the charge I made originally in my 'Intelligence Guru on a Sticky Wicket' (White, 1998b), based on this same quotation, that his choice of intelligences is subjective. He wrote: 'White correctly notes that my original list depended on the judgment of a single analyst, who made his data available to others. However, White is naïve if he believes that science begins in any other way' (Gardner, 1998). What he may have in mind is the Popperian point that science begins with conjectures. But not all conjectures eventuate in science. Some may prove empirically untestable. A fundamental question about MI theory is whether it is empirically testable. Because it is not clear when a candidate intelligence passes or does not pass the 'criteria' test, it is uncertain under what conditions it may be empirically refuted.

1.2.5 Why These Criteria? A further question is: how does Gardner justify using these particular criteria? I have not been able to find any answer in his writings. Whenever he introduces the criteria, they are each spelt out in some detail, but there is no account of why these ones have been employed and not others. This is, if anything, an even more striking blow to the theory than the admission that the way the criteria are to be applied is more artistic than scientific. If we are given no good grounds for using these eight criteria, why should we take MI theory seriously?

2 CAN GARDNER'S MULTIPLE INTELLIGENCES BE EXPLAINED?

When justification falters, explanation may shed light. A philosophical critique of Gardner's theory has failed to find a rationale for it. This leaves us in an intellectually unsatisfying position. We still feel the need to understand the theory, even if we cannot make logical sense of it. At points like this, one has to turn from philosophy to history. In another context, this is true of the credentials of the traditional subject-based school curriculum, embodied, for instance, in the English National Curriculum of 1988. Having detected no defensible justification of it, I have found it profitable to explore its origins in Victorian educational policy and before. The pieces of the jigsaw have all then fallen—more or less—into place.

The curriculum story, which I hope soon to publish, led me back finally to the mid-16th century. Fortunately, the explanation of MI theory goes back only forty years. It concerns Gardner's own intellectual biography. Much of this has to do with the two major criteria examined above—about development and symbol systems.

2.1 Origins

The historical story runs like this. In the 1960s Gardner began his career as a developmental psychologist, profoundly influenced by Piaget as well as by structuralist thinkers in other fields, notably Claude Lévi-Strauss in anthropology: 'The structuralists are distinguished first and foremost by their ardent, powerfully held conviction that there is a structure underlying all human behaviour and mental functioning' (Gardner, 1972, p. 10). The young Gardner was also enthusiastically involved with music and other arts (Gardner, 2003, p. 1). As he was dissatisfied by the rationalism of the Piagetian approach, his first research was on a developmental psychology of the arts (Gardner, 1982, p. xii). He found the structuralist view that the direction of human thinking is preordained problematic. It could not account for innovation and creation, not least in the arts. Gardner found the key to understanding creativeness in the notion of symbol systems: 'These symbol systems—these codes of meaning—are the vehicles through which thought takes place: by their very nature they are creative, open systems. Through the use of symbols the human mind, operating according to structuralist principles, can revise, transform and re-create wholly fresh products, systems, and even worlds of meaning' (pp. 4–5). All this shows the centrality of theories of development and of symbol systems in Gardner's pre-1983 thinking. Much of his published work in this period was about the application of developmental psychology to the arts. He describes his 1973 book *The Arts and Human Development* as 'fleshing out the picture of development proposed by Piaget' (Gardner, 1973, p. vii).

Pivotal to this extension of Piagetian ideas to the arts is the notion of a 'symbol'. Here Gardner was influenced by the aesthetician Nelson Goodman, his colleague at Harvard in the 1960s. Goodman saw works of art as a whole as symbols and also as containing symbols within themselves. Different arts, he held, have their own symbol schemes—hence the title of his *Languages of Art* (Goodman, 1968). Some artistic symbols have a denotating function, as words do, in that they stand for something outside themselves. Others 'exemplify' rather than denote. A sad piece of music exemplifies sadness generally. Understanding a work of art is a matter of interpreting correctly what and how it symbolises. The arts, for Goodman, are forms of knowledge.

Gardner's early intellectual biography throws light on MI theory, especially the first five intelligences: linguistic, musical, logico-mathe-matical, spatial and bodily-kinaesthetic. Of these, logico-mathematical intelligence is related particularly to mathematics and science and its treatment follows Piaget's scheme quite closely. The other four reflect Gardner's work in extending Piagetian developmentalism into the arts: poetry is prominent in the chapter on linguistic intelligence, music in that the musical chapter, the visual arts in the spatial, mime and dance in the bodily-kinaesthetic. Piaget's and Goodman's theories are examples of developmentalism and the symbol theory of art respectively, both of which were criticised above. In addition, there are further conceptual problems damaging to these two theories taken specifically. These have been explored by David Hamlyn in the case of Piaget (Hamlyn, 1967, 1978) and Roger Scruton in the case of Goodman (Scruton, 1974).

2.2 The van Leer Project

A crucial turning point for Gardner came in 1979, when he moved from his long-standing project on the development of artistic competences to a wider, now all–embracing, theory of intellectual development. This came about through his involvement in the Harvard Project on Human Potential funded by the Bernard van Leer Foundation. The Foundation 'asked the Harvard Graduate School of Education to assess the state of scientific knowledge concerning human potential and its realization and to summarize the findings in a form that would assist educational policy and practice throughout the world' (Gardner, 1983, p. x). Gardner was the psychologist in an interdisciplinary team that also contained philosophical and anthropological expertise. *Frames of Mind* (1983) was the first publication from the team.

The first five intelligences in the book drew, as we have seen, on Gardner's pre-1979 work in the Piagetian and Goodmanian traditions and areas of interest. The other two were the personal intelligences—which have to do with understanding oneself and understanding other people. It is understandable that Gardner should wish to include other areas of interest than mathematics, science and the arts. The van Leer remit wanted something more comprehensive. In answer to his own question 'why have I incorporated personal intelligences in my survey?', Gardner wrote: 'Chiefly because I feel that these forms of knowledge are of tremendous importance in many, if not all, societies in the world (Gardner, 1983, p. 241). This is revealing—and not only for its use of the expression 'forms of knowledge', about which I say more below. It shows again how MI theory is built on value judgments. The personal intelligences pass the 'prerequisites' test because of their huge social importance in Gardner's view.

He then sees how far they pass the second, 'criteria' test. They do not meet these, in my view, very well. His section on 'the development of the personal intelligences' from infancy through to maturity (pp. 243–253) gives evidence of increasingly sophisticated *changes* in understanding, but not of *unfolding*. As Gardner for the most part treats 'the development of personal knowledge as a relatively natural process' (p. 253), he radically underplays the role of young children's mentors, especially their parents, in inducting them into this kind of understanding. The symbol test does no better. Gardner admits that there are no symbols unique to this area, only those of language in general (p. 242). In addition, what he says about brain lesion evidence points to changes in *mood and emotion*, e.g. depression, following injury to the frontal lobes, but not to changes in *understanding*. He himself says that positive evidence is sparse with regard to the criteria to do with evolutionary evidence, exceptional individuals, experimental psychology and psychological testing (ibid.). Despite all this discouraging news, the two intelligences somehow get their diplomas.

To come back to Gardner's use of the phrase 'forms of knowledge'. It is not coincidental that the expression is also closely associated with Paul Hirst's early theory of a liberal education. Gardner has always said that nothing has turned for him on the use of the term 'intelligences' (Gardner, 2003, p. 4) He has written: 'I would be satisfied to substitute such phrases as "intellectual competences", "thought processes", "cognitive capacities", "cognitive skills", "forms of knowledge", or any other cognate mentalistic terminology' (p. 284). The crucial issue for

Gardner has been not what words to use, but how far these various intelligences/forms of knowledge can be shown to exist by scientific evidence rather than by *a priori* reasoning. If his own empirical approach to demarcating intelligences should fail, 'then we may have to rely once more on *a priori* schemes, such as Hirst's' (pp. 61–2).

This raises a key question. If Gardner's intelligences are in the same ballpark as Hirst's forms of knowledge—and indeed as 'the medieval trivium and quadrivium' (ibid.), can they still be equated with abilities or talents? From the former point of view, they come out as ways of categorising the realm of intellectual phenomena; from the latter, as ways of categorising individuals' intellectual competences. For Gardner at this time the two ways of classifying were linked. He saw his theory as bridging the (bio-psychological) world of individual nervous systems and the (epistemological or anthropological) world of social forms. Symbols have a central role in this: 'The domain of symbols . . . is ideally suited to help span the gap between the aforementioned entities' (Gardner, 1983, p. 300). Outside Gardner's theory, the two classifications can be kept apart. Hirst, for instance, saw himself as doing epistemology, not psychology. His theory is about how knowledge is to be logically carved up, not about individuals' abilities. For Gardner, the two spheres are inseparably connected. This is implicit in his developmentalism and his symbol theory: abilities unfold from seeds within the nervous system towards mature end-states found in different intellectual activities; and it is through the acquisition of symbols that these end-states are those of the highest flights of creative activity. Because of this inseparable connection, studying one pole of the process throws light on steps leading to the other. The bio-psychological study of individuals is a key to the social/epistemological world of the disciplines; and vice-versa.

The requirements of the van Leer project allowed Gardner to expand from the limited theory of artistic development on which he had previously concentrated to a fuller account of the development of human intellectual competences as a whole. In doing so, he was able to retain the master-ambition that had motivated his work from his earliest days as a structuralist, bringing Piagetian insights into harmony with those of Lévi-Strauss: the desire to link biology and anthropology, to show that they are part of the same system.

3 FURTHER COMMENTS ON MI THEORY
3.1 MI Since 1983

Since 1983 there have been two important modifications of MI theory.

3.1.1 The original seven intelligences have now been extended to include 'the naturalist intelligence' and—possibly—'existential intelligence' (1999a, Chapter 4). Naturalist intelligence is picked out by reference to a valued social role found across many cultures: people expert in recognising and classifying the varieties of plants and animals in their environment. Gardner tells us that 'those valued human cognitions that I previously had to ignore or smuggle in under spatial or logico-mathematical intelligence deserve to be gathered under a single, recognized rubric' (Gardner, 1999a, p. 52). This seems to imply that, having reviewed the full gamut of intellectual activities, he realised that the taxonomic aspects of biology had been given short shrift in his original scheme.

This thought is reinforced by what he says in the same chapter on possible forms of spiritual intelligence and of existential intelligence—to do with 'big questions' about one's place in the cosmos, the significance of life and death, the experience of personal love and of artistic experience—as the strongest candidate among these (pp. 53–65). Religious and philosophical thinking are also parts of the intellectual world; and these, too, were ill-represented in the 1983 scheme.

All this lends strength to the suggestion that what powers MI theory is the drive to identify all major divisions of the intellectual life (taking the arts as always to be forms of knowledge). As should now be abundantly clear, the identification comes at the 'prerequisites' stage. Empirical evidence is not part of this story.

3.1.2 A second departure since 1983 has been Gardner's distinction between 'intelligence' and 'domain' (Gardner, 1999a, p. 82). The former is 'a biopsychological potential that is ours by virtue of our species membership'. The latter is a 'socially constructed human endeavor', for example 'physics, cooking, chess, constitutional law, and rap music'. It is 'characterized by a specific symbol system'. Gardner says he could have made this distinction more carefully in 1983. Readers would then have seen more clearly that several intelligences could be applied in the same domain, and the same intelligence in many domains.

This move detaches from each other the two dimensions, biological and social, that Gardner tried to hold together through his career. It makes MI theory unintelligible. For it has always been part of the concept of an intelligence that it is an ability that develops from a physiological origin towards an end-state belonging to a valued social activity. Poetry, music, the visual arts, dance, mathematics, logic, sport—the loci of the 1983 end-states—are all social constructions. Similarly, the idea of an intelligence was originally founded partly on the thought that symbols are bridges between the biological and the social. The 1999 version separates the previously inseparable and puts symbols and end-states firmly on the side of the social—as attached to *domains* rather than intelligences. At the same time, the 'criteria', which remain unchanged from 1983, include reference to both symbols and end-states among the distinguishing features of *intelligences*. This is why the 1999 version of MI theory is unintelligible.

3.2 MI and Education

Until the van Leer project Gardner was a psychologist, not an educationalist. But he had to adhere to the van Leer request that the

Harvard research should 'assist educational policy and practice' (Gardner, 1983, p. x). In *Frames of Mind* Gardner 'touched on some educational implications of the theory in the concluding chapters. This decision turned out to be another crucial point because it was educators, rather than psychologists, who found the theory of most interest' (Gardner, 2003, p. 4). Since 1983 MI theory has had a huge influence on educational reform, especially school improvement, across the world. It has affected perspectives on pupils and their aptitudes, methods of learning and teaching, and curriculum content. If the argument of this essay is correct, all this has been built on flaky theory.

3.2.1 Gardner holds that while nearly all children possess all the intelligences to some degree, some of them have particular aptitudes in one or more of them. 'My own belief is that one could assess an individual's intellectual potentials quite early in life, perhaps even in infancy' (1983, p. 385).

It is not surprising that ideas like these have—not intentionally— encouraged educational policies and practices to do with selection, specialisation, individualisation of learning, and assessment. But if the intelligences are not part of human nature but wobbly constructions on the part of their author, educators should treat them with caution. There may or may not be good grounds for personalised learning and other policies, but if they exist they must come from elsewhere. That teachers often need to vary the way they teach according to what best motivates particular pupils has been part of pedagogy for centuries; there is no good reason for confining this notion within the 'intelligences' framework.

3.2.2 There is abundant evidence that MI theory has been influential in reducing the low self-esteem of pupils who see themselves as stupid or thick, where this kind of judgment derives from conventional ideas of general intelligence based on IQ. The idea that intelligence is not necessarily tied to prowess in logical, mathematical and linguistic tasks but can be displayed across a variety of fields is true—as our opening quotation from Gilbert Ryle illustrates. But the idea is not by any means original to MI theory (White, 1998a, pp. 3–4).

3.2.3 One reason why MI theory has been so influential may be its basis in supposedly discrete forms of intellectual activity—in Gardner's broad use of the term to embrace not only disciplines based on the pursuit of truth like biology and mathematics, but also the arts and athletics. With some exceptions, the areas it covers are close to those in a traditional so-called 'liberal education' based mainly on initiation into all the main areas of knowledge, to be pursued largely for their own sake. The addition of naturalist intelligence and (possibly) existential intelligence have made the fit even closer, seeing the affinities of these areas with biology and with work of a philosophical/religious sort.

On the whole, Gardner has refrained from deriving curricular consequences from MI theory. His writings on what the content of education should be show that the type of schooling he favours is in the 'liberal education' tradition: 'Education in our time should provide the basis for enhanced understanding of our several worlds—the physical world, the biological world, the world of human beings, the world of human artifacts, and the world of the self' (Gardner, 1999b, p. 158). He also thinks this understanding should be largely for intrinsic ends. He writes: 'I favor . . . the pursuit of knowledge for its own sake over the obeisance to utility' (p. 39). This locates him firmly within the 'liberal education' camp, along with—in Britain—(the early) Paul Hirst, Richard Peters, Roger Scruton and others.

It is not surprising that Gardner's curricular ideas dovetail with his ideas of the intelligences, even if this was not his original intention. For the 'liberal education' tradition and MI theory share the same starting point. They both assume the importance in human life of intellectual activities pursued largely for their own sake. It is not surprising that educators reacting against recent utilitarian tendencies in schooling and looking for a more humane alternative have been attracted by MI theory, given its closeness to traditional 'liberal education'. But the latter idea is not necessarily tied to MI. Hirst, Peters and others have argued for it on quite other grounds (Hirst, 1974; Peters, 1966, Chapter 5). What is more, 'liberal education'—in this sense of intellectual learning for its own sake—itself needs justification. I have argued that this view does not hold water (White, 1982, Chapter 2; 2007). There is a danger that in basing children's schooling on it we are imposing a life ideal on them that *we*, as intellectually inclined people, may find personally appealing, but that, after all, is only one of many possible life ideals.

4 RESPONSE TO GARDNER'S CRITIQUE

The argument presented above is a streamlined, amended version of White, 2006, in which further refinements of it can be found. That book is a collection of papers on Gardner's work in general (not only in MI) and contains a chapter in which he replies to each author. In this final section, I outline Gardner's criticisms of my own paper (Gardner, 2006, pp. 295–7) and try to answer them. They nearly all apply to my arguments in this chapter and I make clear where they do not.

4.1 Incommensurate Paradigms?

Gardner's first point is a general one:

Taking on a perspective which has its origins in Wittgenstein and has reverberation in more recent writings . . . White questions my whole effort: it is hopeless, in his view, to try to place on a scientific basis distinctions and categories that essentially grow out of our language, our ways of talking and conceptualizating (*sic*). If I am right in my characterization of White, there is no way that I could satisfy him. In the phrase made famous by Thomas Kuhn (1970), we are proceeding from 'incommensurate paradigms' (Gardner, 2006, p. 295).

Gardner concludes 'that there is no bridge between us'. But I think he is wrong about this. It is not that he works with one paradigm—empirical science—and I work with an incommensurate one—'linguistic philosophy' perhaps. I am quite comfortable with treating intelligence as a topic for scientific investigation. Other animals besides human beings can act intelligently, and it is a matter of empirical enquiry to examine such behaviour, for instance, in different species. There can also be scientific investigations of intelligence—or, if you prefer, intellectual abilities—in human beings. One might compare, for instance, the mathematical competences of girls and boys of the same age and social background. In my paper, although sceptical from the start, I have been prepared to go along with the suggestion that there is a scientific way of categorising intellectual abilities. I have taken seriously Gardner's attempt to do this and examined the main stages of his argument in some detail. My conclusion is that he has failed to make his case. It is not that Gardner is working within science and I am rejecting science. It is questionable, indeed, as I have shown in some detail above, whether at the crucial turning points of his system—e.g. in the 'prerequisites', and in how the 'criteria' are to be applied—Gardner operates as a scientist at all. Gardner himself casts doubt on the scientific nature of his procedure in his admission, worth quoting again here, that 'At present, however, it must be admitted that the selection (or rejection) of a candidate intelligence is reminiscent more of an artistic judgment than of a scientific assessment' (Gardner, 1983, p. 63).

4.2 Gardner's Four Specific Responses

After this first comment of a general sort, Gardner goes on to make four specific responses.

4.2.1 End State (p. 295) Gardner says that 'as a developmentalist, I believe that one cannot study an area without having some sense of what it is like in its full-blown form', but that 'this delineation of an end-state need not at all be fixed or frozen' (ibid.) This is a useful elucidation of his position, but I do not see it as at odds with what I wrote, since I agreed in my discussion of developmentalism that some people may argue that the development of intelligence does not necessitate intellectual ceilings.

4.2.2 Criteria for Criteria (p. 296) Gardner makes several points about criteria for criteria.

4.2.2.1 He writes:

White asks, with reference to my criteria for an intelligence, from what source do they emanate? As I explained above, they represent my effort to incorporate the principal disciplinary strands that are relevant to any examination of human cognition. My response to White: The search for criteria for an investigation opens up the possibility of an infinite regress. If he puts forth criteria, I can simply respond by asking him for the criteria for those criteria. I see my list as an entirely reasonable first pass; the proper response would be to suggest an alternative set of criteria, and to show that they are better motivated or less problematic for the task at hand.

I suppose the point about an infinite regress is that if one asks for good reasons for something, one can ask for good reasons for relying on those good reasons, and so on. I don't see an infinite regress necessarily opening up here. In any intellectual dispute some things are going to be taken for granted, otherwise no discussion would get off the ground. But Gardner's main response to my request for a justification for these particular eight criteria is that they 'incorporate the principal disciplinary strands that are relevant to any examination of human cognition'. I do not think they do. There is no philosophical or historical criterion, for instance. 'Susceptibility to encoding in a symbol system' hardly indicates a 'principal disciplinary strand': it is so obviously tied to a particular, and not widely accepted, approach to aesthetics associated with Goodman and behind him Cassirer and Langer. The criterion to do with development, likewise, is tied to a highly controversial perspective on the acquisition of competencies.

These two examples—and I could adduce others—reinforce the point I made in the paper, that the only way of understanding why Gardner proceeds as he does is via the contingencies of his biography (perhaps Goodman's happening to be at Harvard at the same time as Gardner, for instance?). Gardner himself in the above quotation talks of the 'sources' from which the criteria emanate. But explanation is different from justification, and it is lack of justification that I was criticising in the paper, not provenance.

4.2.2.2 Gardner takes exception to my claim that 'mathematical abilities are, to a large extent, a specialized kind of linguistic ability'. I claimed this in the original paper (p. 47)—but not in this version—as a challenge to Gardner's view that the intelligences are 'relatively autonomous competences' (1983, p. 8). In his reply, Gardner says that 'the statement is not one that can be established by authority; it is an empirical issue'. But these are not the only two possible kinds of backing. There is also *a priori* argument. I have in mind the definability of many if not all mathematical terms, 'prime number', for instance, 'x', 'π', etc. in simpler terms familiar, ultimately, in ordinary language. Someone with a deep understanding of mathematical concepts has a deep understanding of a certain sort of language.

4.2.2.3 With regard to the criterion to do with *idiots savants* (etc.), Gardner objects to my describing the architectural drawing of autistic artist Stephen Wiltshire as 'subnormal mental facility'. Gardner replies that many knowledgeable observers hold his gift in high esteem. I do not doubt that people marvel at it. I called it 'subnormal' because—if I'm right—it 'is a *mechanical* facility, one that lacks the flexibility of adapting means to ends found in intelligent behaviour'.

4.2.3 Domains and Intelligences (p. 296) Gardner says that I 'completely misconstrue' this distinction. 'Far from making my theory "unintelligible", this terminological shift has clarified what I have always sought to do'. But I cleave to the charge of unintelligibility. For something to be an intelligence, it must pass the 'prerequisites' test. That is, it has to be a valued social activity of some sort. But according to Gardner's distinction, it is *domains*, not intelligences, that are social constructions, while intelligences are biopsychological potentials. So intelligences both are and are not social constructions. That's where the unintelligibility resides.

4.2.4 Educational Implications (p. 297) Gardner dismisses my suggestion 'that MI-inspired classroom practices are necessarily ill-advised'. Many practitioners do feel the theory is helpful; and there is empirical evidence that MI-inspired practices can be productive.

Suppose both these latter things are the case, would it matter if the theory behind the practices were shown to be untenable? And would it matter if practitioners rightly believed it to be untenable? Some people, e.g. Phil Beadle, would say no. Writing about my critique of MI theory, Beadle balks 'at any suggestion that schools should throw out effective practice because it is built on sand' (*Education Guardian*, January 17, 2006). This raises the question 'How much does truth matter?' Sometimes in life, saying or acting on what one knows to be untrue may be justifiable. Truth may be of less high a priority than, say, concern for another's welfare—as in the often-cited case of lying to someone intent on murder about the whereabouts of the victim. A consideration here is that it is a teacher's professional duty, among other things, to steer learners away from what is false and ill-founded to what is true and well-founded. I did not in fact write that MI-inspired practices are 'necessarily ill-advised', but that educators should treat the intelligences 'with caution'. Maybe there *are* circumstances when teachers are justified in lying. Maybe it is all right to tell a child that she comes up high on spatial intelligence, even though one thinks there's no such thing: perhaps this gives her a lasting motivational boost. But at the very least, the teacher should make the truth clear to the student at some later point. It would be even better to give her the boost in a way not dependent on MI theory but on what is true. 'That's brilliant, Caitlin. I really like your plan (for a house). And you always tell me you're thick! It just brings home, doesn't it, that there are so many different ways in which people can be clever. You're a star!'.

ACKNOWLEDGEMENTS

This chapter is a much shortened, amended version of my essay 'Multiple Invalidities' (White, 2006). My 'Response to Gardner's comments' was also absent, of course, from the original paper. I am most grateful to Jeffrey Schaler for allowing me to publish this new version in the present volume. I am also indebted to the following UK teachers for information about how MI theory has been applied in their schools: Margaret Grant, Deputy Headteacher of Broughton Hall School, Liverpool; and James McAleese, of Richard Hale School, Hertford.

REFERENCES

Beadle, P. (2006) Mixed Abilities: It Ain't What You Think, It's The Way That You Think It, *Education Guardian*, 17th January.
Gardner, H. (1972) *The Quest for Mind* (London, Coventure).
Gardner, H. (1973) *The Arts and Human Development* (New York, John Wiley).
Gardner, H. (1982) *Art, Mind and Brain* (New York, Basic Books).
Gardner, H. (1983) *Frames of Mind: The Theory of Multiple Intelligences* (London, Heinemann).
Gardner, H. (1990) The Theory of Multiple Intelligences, in: N. Entwistle (ed.) *Handbook of Educational Ideas and Practices* (London, Routledge).
Gardner, H. (1993) *Frames of Mind: The Theory of Multiple Intelligences*, 2nd edn. (London, Heinemann).
Gardner, H. (1998) An Intelligent Way to Progress, *The Independent*, 19 March.
Gardner, H. (1999a) *Intelligence Reframed: Multiple Intelligences for the 21st Century* (New York, Basic Books).
Gardner, H. (1999b) *The Disciplined Mind* (New York, Simon and Shuster).
Gardner, H. (2003) Multiple Intelligences after Twenty Years. Paper presented at the American Educational Research Association, Chicago, Illinois, April 21 2003. Available at: http://www.pz.harvard.edu/PIs/HG_MI_after_20_years.pdf
Gardner, H. (2006) Replies to my Critics, in: J. A. Schaler (ed.) *Howard Gardner under Fire: the Rebel Psychologist Faces his Critics* (Chicago, Open Court).
Goodman, N. (1968) *Languages of Art* (Indianapolis, IN, Hackett).
Hamlyn, D. (1967) Logical and Psychological Aspects of Learning, in: R. S. Peters (ed) *The Concept of Education* (London, Routledge and Kegan Paul).
Hamlyn, D. (1978) *Experience and the Growth of Understanding* (London, Routledge and Kegan Paul).
Hirst, P. H. (1974) Liberal Education and the Nature of Knowledge, in: *Knowledge and the Curriculum* (London, Routledge and Kegan Paul).
Howe, M. J. A. (1997) *The IQ in Question* (London, Sage).
Kuhn, T. S. (1970) *The Structure of Scientific Revolutions*, 2nd edn. (Chicago, IL, University of Chicago Press).
Peters, R. S. (1966) *Ethics and Education* (London, Allen and Unwin).
Richardson, K. (1999) *The Making of Intelligence* (London, Weidenfeld and Nicolson).
Ryle, G. (1949) *The Concept of Mind* (London, Hutchinson).
Scruton, R. (1974) *Art and Imagination* (London, Methuen).
White, J. (1982) *The Aims of Education Restated* (London, Routledge and Kegan Paul).
White, J. (1986) On Reconstructing the Notion of Human Potential, *Journal of Philosophy of Education*, 20.1, pp. 133–142.
White, J. (1998a) *Do Howard Gardner's Multiple Intelligences Add Up?* (London, Institute of Education, University of London).
White, J. (1998b) Intelligence Guru on a Sticky Wicket, *The Independent*, 19 February.
White, J. (2006) Multiple Invalidities, in: J. A. Schaler (ed.) *Howard Gardner under Fire: the Rebel Psychologist Faces his Critics* (Chicago, Open Court).
White, J. (2007) *What Schools Are For and Why*. Impact Paper No 14 (The Philosophy of Education Society of Great Britain).

5.3

Emotional Intelligence as Educational Goal: A Case for Caution

SOPHIE RIETTI

1 INTRODUCTION

The concept of emotional intelligence (EI) currently popular among educators and educational policy makers draws its original inspiration, and its name, from the early 1990s work of psychologists John D. Mayer and Peter Salovey (1990, 1993). But its success, in education theory as in other areas such as business administration and professional training, especially in the care professions, is primarily due to the phenomenal success of Daniel Goleman's 1995 best-selling popularisation (Goleman, 1995). Goleman's account of EI, however, differs from Mayer and Salovey's in important ways that are also broadly shared by a third major model of EI, that of Reuven Bar-On. While these three models do not exhaust current thinking on EI[1] they, and in particular Goleman's, will be the main focus here. Given that the aspects of Goleman's (and Bar-On's) concept of EI that have led to its adoption as a goal of educators tend to be the ones that diverge from Mayer and Salovey's conception, however,differences between the accounts will also be important throughout, and the fact that Goleman's is not the only one to diverge from Mayer and Salovey in this way is itself significant.

Mayer and Salovey's aim, notably, was to model a form of intelligence that, while concerned with a different domain of information than 'traditional' verbal, mathematical and logical intelligence(s), would in other respects resemble them (Mayer et al., 1999). That is, it would not be a (mere) matter of possessing a particular form of information or knowledge, or of having been taught skills for processing this knowledge. For EI as for IQ, the question of whether the relevant intelligence itself could be affected or acquired by nurture, and the practical difficulties of measuring the intelligence itself rather than information-possession and taught skills, would be difficult and contentious matters. Qua intelligence, EI was also not intended as a measure of personality or character, and Mayer and Salovey have aimed, as far as possible, to define it in value-neutral terms—an aim that may in any case not be fully viable.

Goleman and Bar-On, by contrast, define EI in part in terms of an ability-cluster that can be taught and learned—albeit Bar-On qualifies this somewhat more than Goleman (Bar-On, 2007). Moreover, both of them include character and personality traits, and often value-laden and culture-bound ones at that, in their concepts of emotional intelligence. Thus, for instance, Bar-On's definition of EI (cf. Bar-On, 1997) includes traits such as assertiveness, independence, optimism, adaptability and sense of social responsibility. EI, here, is not only strongly correlated to, but even identified with and constituted by, traits and skills likely to promote the bearer's success at their life goals, pro-social dispositions such as empathy and altruism, and even—most explicitly in Goleman's case—moral and civic virtues. Mayer and Salovey had suggested—and cautiously explored—correlations between EI and such other features, but they do not identify EI with any of them, and have expressed misgivings (Paul, 1999) about the conflation of EI with them, and the claims made for EI as a near-panacea for both individual and social troubles. Goleman's concepts of a good life, pro-sociality and moral and civic virtues are also highly coloured by a specific value-pluralistic liberal democrat outlook, tempered by internally rather heterogeneous influences from both humanistic psychology and some more old-fashioned forms of moral-ism—but neither the particularity, eclecticism nor justification of this value-system are addressed by Goleman in any depth.

Insofar as what has fired the imagination of educators and educational policy makers tends to be features specific to Goleman's and Bar-On's concepts of EI, there are real conceptual problems at stake here, even before empirical, moral and political issues are raised, though the conceptual problems themselves give rise to a number of these. For it tends to look, on closer inspection, as if what is meant by teaching people to become more emotionally intelligent is that the EI-promoters in question would like their 'students' (literal or figurative) to understand and manage their own and other people's emotions according to a particular system of values and beliefs—a particular picture of what the world, including the human psyche within it, is like, as well as what is good and bad about it, and of what people ought to do—and to internalise this into their emotional and behavioural dispositions. Insofar as EI, in these cases, is also often understood as including character traits, the goal is also to make people *be* the EI-promoter's preferred kind(s) of people. Goleman's own preferences have been outlined above: this will be examined in some more depth in the next two sections.1

Insofar as any socialisation will involve a degree of such conditioning (or at least determined aiming for it on the part of the socialisers) such a goal is hardly avoidable, and depending on the system of values and beliefs in question may even be highly laudable. But such a goal should be seen, and held, for what it is, and the values in question assessed and defended as what they are, also in terms of their place in education. This is not possible if they are conflated with, or semi-disguised as, elements of an applied science whose descriptive distinctions—for instance between abilities, including intelligences, and personality traits—have not even been fully kept clear. And insofar as EI can be defined in a more value-neutral way—and even Mayer and Salovey's version does not entirely achieve this goal—what we should expect from education in it, if and insofar as it can be taught, need not amount to life success and prosocial attitudes, let alone virtue. Nor need these three latter converge as smoothly as Goleman's account, especially, seems to assume. The empirical evidence for correlations between these various desired outcomes and EI itself is also at a more exploratory stage, even now, than the claims that motivated its adoption as an educational policy goal would suggest.

While this may sound largely negative, there is in fact a good deal left to be excited about in the concept of emotional intelligence itself, and in its applications to education, including moral education. But to gain these benefits, we need to distinguish those things EI (of a reasonably conceptualised and operationalised kind) can deliver, and those it cannot. Examining reasons to be cautious will be helpful in making these distinctions. I will begin, in what follows, with a closer look at the concepts of EI introduced here, and some of the reasons why EI caught on as an educational goal. In view of the concerns raised, I will also argue for caution in trying to inculcate 'emotional intelligence' into what effectively amounts to captive audiences, especially ones that are at impressionable developmental stages. Imposing on people a particular concept of what they ought to feel is an invasive procedure, and may come at some cost to those against whom it is enforced. This is not to say that the EI-concept is without merit, or that the goals for which it has been applied are without merit, but to urge due care.

2 EMOTIONAL INTELLIGENCE: DEFINITIONS, AGAIN

As indicated above, Goleman in his 1995 book gives as his definition of EI the one proposed by Peter Salovey and John D. Mayer in their 1990 article. In this early version (also cited in Goleman, 1995, pp. 43–4), EI is divided into five domains:

(1) *knowing/recognizing one's emotions*: Goleman's preferred term for this is 'self-awareness';
(2) *managing emotions*: Goleman emphasizes 'self-soothing' and 'shaking off negative emotions';
(3) *motivating oneself*: Goleman refers to this as 'emotional self-control', emphasizing capacities for optimism, delayed gratification and impulse control in 'enhancing productivity';
(4) *recognizing emotions in others*: Goleman refers to this primarily in terms of empathy, though other ways of becoming aware of and understanding others' emotions are also included;
(5) *handling relationships*: Goleman understands this primarily in terms of managing others' emotions in what he terms a 'prosocial' manner, adding that '[t]hese are the abilities that undergird popularity, leadership, and interpersonal effectiveness' (Goleman, 1995, p. 43).

To the borrowed definition, Goleman also adds, towards the end of the book: 'There is an old-fashioned word for the body of skills that emotional intelligence represents: *character*' (Goleman, 1995, p. 285). Character development, he argues, 'is a foundation of democratic societies' and '[t]he bedrock of character is self-discipline; the virtuous life, as philosophers since Aristotle have observed, is based on self-control. A related keystone of character is being able to motivate and guide oneself . . . the ability to defer gratification and to control and channel one's urges to act is a basic emotional skill, one that in a former day was called will'. Moreover: 'Being able to put aside one's self-centered focus and impulses has social benefits: it opens the way to empathy'. And: 'Empathy, as we have seen, leads to caring, altruism and compassion. Seeing things from another's perspective breaks down biased stereotypes, and so breeds tolerance and acceptance of differences. These capacities are ever more called on in our increasingly pluralistic society, allowing people to live together in mutual respect and creating the possibility of productive public discourse' (p. 285).

Schools, Goleman argues, need to inculcate into their students 'self-discipline and empathy, which in turn enable true commitment to civic and moral values' not just by formal instruction but by practice and provision of examples: 'In this sense, emotional literacy goes hand in hand with education for character, for moral development and for citizenship' (p. 286).

Leaving aside for the moment the number of ways in which Goleman, explicit invocations of Aristotle notwithstanding, diverges from Aristotle on points of descriptive psychology, meta-ethics *and* politics,[2] it will be instructive, more immediately, to compare his fleshing out of Mayer and Salovey's original account with their own subsequent refinement of the EI-concept. Mayer and Salovey, at this point, view EI as a capacity with four 'branches':

(1) *perceiving emotion* (in self and others);
(2) *facilitating thinking through emotions* (using affective states to promote good reasoning);
(3) *understanding emotional meaning* (communicative and behavioural implications of emotions, and the ways in which emotions blend into each other and change over time);
(4) and *managing emotions in self and others* so as to promote own/others'/joint goals.

The development of the concept has been driven, for Mayer, Salovey and associates,[3] by successive refinements of the psychometric tools used to measure the abilities involved in EI. By notable contrast with both Goleman and Bar-On, whose tests measure EI by self-report, Mayer and Salovey assign EI-scores based on task-performance. The test-taker, for instance, is asked to identify the emotion expressed by a person on a photograph (branch 1), and select the emotion most conducive to facilitating, for example, the planning of a birthday party (branch 2) or successfully managing a first encounter with prospective in-laws (branch 4). Scores are assigned by comparing the taker's answer (from multiple choice options throughout) with those selected by a 'consensus' group and an 'expert' group.

For immediate purposes, the crucial points are that Mayer and Salovey's approach aims to operationalise EI only *qua* emotion-related intelligence. Traits, such as being self-motivating or optimistic, are not part of the test, or of the concept. The test also aims to be neutral about value-related issues. The assessment of emotion-management, for instance, aims as far as possible to test only the test-taker's grasp of facts (for instance about which facial expression in another indicates joy as opposed to fear) and means-ends relations relative to a given goal, not to judge the value (the 'intelligence') of the goal itself. Except, that is, insofar as the achievement of a given goal is itself liable not to actually produce the satisfaction imagined, in itself or by interfering with other goals the person has (Mayer and Salovey, 1995)—as when, for instance, the short-term satisfaction of venting anger damages longer-term good regarding relationships with others that the person also desires.

A further important point here, however, is that this attempted value-neutrality does not, and arguably cannot, entirely succeed. What behaviours and emotional expressions are most conducive to sustaining good relationships with others, for instance, will be relative to what those others value and disvalue, and to the definitions of the people involved as to what constitute good relationships, a point on which there is ample room for individual and cultural divergence in views. For instance, a child taught to manage emotional expressiveness around authority figures according to fairly mainstream current Western ideals such as assertiveness, open self-expression, and background egalitarian assumptions, may well strike someone with more authoritarian ideals of child-raising as bordering on rudeness. And we do not need to place the child in question into a particularly culturally diverse setting to get such contrasting reactions: it will often be enough that parents or teachers, or both, hold more left-liberal views than the child's grandparents. Mayer and Salovey, while they sometimes concede such points, also argue that reasonable 'convergent' views of what is emotionally intelligent (or not) can be derived from a consideration of 'biosocial' features of human nature that can be expected to be pan-culturally present, given our shared evolutionary history (Mayer *et al.*, 2001). From the point of view of moral philosophy, of course, these assumptions seem questionable: I shall return to these points in more depth shortly.

3 EMOTIONAL INTELLIGENCE AS AN EDUCATIONAL GOAL: THE HISTORICAL BACKGROUND

Given the concerns raised so far, it may be helpful to look also at some of the reasons why EI became such a phenomenon. In part, the inspirations for the EI-concept are empirical, for instance based on discoveries about the effects on agency, reasoning capacities and social adaptability of conditions whose most striking initial effects were on the subject's emotions. This covers both cases of neurological damage from accidents and conditions such as alexithymia and autism, whose aetiologies are more contentious.[4] These kinds of empirical data in turn helped prompt a rethinking of emotions—Mayer and Salovey (1990, 1993) talk about a shift from seeing emotions as 'disorganized responses' and 'irruptive states' to seeing them as 'organized responses' with important positive contributions to make to successful agency. Similar views have also gained widespread attention outside of the direct field of emotional intelligence discussion in the work of authors such as Antonio Damasio (1994).

Another main source of inspiration was theories of 'multiple intelligences', such as Howard Gardner's (1983), which reconceptualised the notion of intelligence itself in ways that went beyond the verbal, mathematical and logical skills standard IQ-testing aims to measure. Those who approached emotions in this seemingly new way could also draw both on a philosophical tradition going back at least to the ancient Greeks (Goleman, as indicated, frequently and explicitly draws on Aristotle) and on empirical approaches going back to the beginnings of modern science, for instance in Darwin's studies of emotion in humans and animals. The success of 'EQ', the popular term for emotional intelligence quotient, as an analogue of IQ is also attributed by a number of commentators to unease about the more traditional intelligence concepts in the wake of the *Bell Curve* controversies. Claims that EQ was a significantly better predictor of life success than IQ abounded when Goleman's book first hit the bestseller lists, in large part coming directly from Goleman himself.

In educational theory, the EQ-concept also struck chords with other existing ideas, such as focusing on 'the whole child' rather than purely on academic factors—and of focusing on the whole child in order to facilitate academic achievement, too. Goleman's promise that EQ also aligns in important ways with character and moral skills, as well as with plain getting along better with others and long-term success in one's life goals, also no doubt helped make for a warm reception for the concept among educators, particularly given its resonance with a revived, often neo-Aristotelian, 'character education' movement, as well as with theories about the importance of 'socioemotional learning' influenced by humanistic psychology.[5]

That Goleman's version of the concept was also supposed to be one that could to some significant extent be acquired, or at least helped to develop, through a child's learning context (broadly understood to take in a number of factors other than just formal instruction) would of course make it additionally attractive to educators with aims to instil such capacities. And, of course, to those, whether they are themselves educators or not, who think that educators ought to instil such capacities—policy makers, parents, and so on. Goleman's book also drew, explicitly, on a sense of social crisis about (perceived) rising levels of violence and anti-social behaviours, especially among the young, and offered EI as a major part of the solution to this situation.

Mayer and Salovey's account, by contrast, offers less direct reason to expect that emotional intelligence need yield such benefits. *Values* children can certainly be taught, and they can also be taught that particular emotional reactions and habits, and ways of managing their own and others' emotions, will be met with approval and others not. Mayer and Salovey also hold that what they call emotional knowledge (EK), that is, the body of information to which EI applies, can be taught: so one might teach children how to put words to their feelings, read facial and other expressions in others, how different emotions relate to each other, and techniques for managing emotions in oneself or others. But this is in principle no different from saying that children can be taught maths, reading and writing, and for that matter logic (formal or informal), which does not amount to saying that one can instil in them, by teaching, the relevant forms of intelligence involved. That difficulties, empirical and conceptual, arise here about the extent to which the relevant intelligence can be assessed in isolation from the relevant body of knowledge and information-processing methods, makes EI in this sense more like conventional intelligences, not less. Mayer and Cobb (2000), assessing educational policies on EI, also offer the hopes held for self-esteem as a cautionary analogue of the current hopes for EI, including what they consider to be preemptive enthusiasm *and* resource allocation (financial and other) to a goal whose expected efficacy has yet to be adequately empirically supported. They argue, also, that there are in both cases good logical and conceptual reasons to question the necessary connection between either EI or self-esteem and the individual, social and moral benefits claimed. (On the self-esteem debate, see Ruth Cigman's chapter 'Enhancing Children' in this volume.)

4 EMOTIONAL INTELLIGENCE AS AN EDUCATIONAL GOAL: REASONS TO BE CAUTIOUS

As indicated above, the most immediate reasons for concern about EI as an educational goal may be conceptual, though a number of these directly point to moral and political reasons for concern. I shall have rather less to say here about the empirical issues, partly because they raise issues of scientific methodology that fall outside the concerns of the present chapter, but also because they are further complicated by the very issues of contentious definition and blurring between descriptive and evaluative claims that have already been indicated, and that will be the main focus here.

Where EI just stands in for already existing concepts or measures, such as personality traits, there are issues of conceptual redundancy, and also of whether the EI-label is a misnomer. Given the concerns about the teachability of EI raised above, there are also real conceptual worries about its viability as an educational goal. If what can be taught is not EI itself, it seems a vocabulary change is at the least in order, and a more consistent use of terms such as 'emotional literacy' or 'emotion-management skills' rather than 'emotional intelligence', where it is in fact the two former and not the latter that is meant.

If EI-concepts are informed by particular evaluative stances, as it seems they must be if EI is to be so clearly conducive to life success, prosocial attitude and virtue as claimed by Goleman, those stances warrant examination in their own right: what is it about these abilities and traits that makes them conducive to having a life that is not only beneficial, but morally beneficial, to oneself and others? If EI is conceived as in itself value-neutral, however, it is not clear that it would necessarily confer the benefits claimed for it by Goleman and Bar-On. In this case, education aimed at emotional literacy and skill in emotion-management, if undertaken, would need to be supplemented by explicitly value-informed goals in order also to count as moral education or morally valuable education.

In Goleman's and Bar-On's accounts, then, there is also the worry of conceptual conflation of EI, *qua* ability to i) reason about emotions, ii) reason using emotions, iii) manage emotions in self and others, and iv) use and acquire EK, with three kinds of other goods that in turn are conflated with each other. That is, notions of (1) moral and civic virtues, (2) prosocial attitudes and (3) life success skills tend to be run together, often without any of them being clearly defined or such definition as they are given being argued for, and then all in turn included in EI.

However, morally good character would only also be prosocial, and vice versa, if what serves the society or particular others in question is also morally good: empathising with bad people, and aiming to promote their goals, even if done from good (if deluded) intentions, will not tend to promote morally good outcomes. If serving the interests of the society, or particular other individuals, in question is viewed as inherently morally worthy, this still needs to be argued for in its own right. Similarly, moral goodness need not lend itself to life success: the virtuous man need not be happy on the rack, or be guaranteed not to end up on it in the first place. Nor need prosocial tendencies such as empathy and conscientiousness guarantee life success for the prosocial individual him- or herself: they might just get them taken advantage of. A number of things that could be counted as life success indicators (fame, riches, political office) may well be possible without, even helped by the absence of, prosocial tendencies, let alone moral and civic virtue.

What counts as life success could also use more clarification, elaboration and justification—adaptability is cited by both Bar-On and Goleman, but this could be understood in a primarily reactive sense, as a *capacity to adjust to external* circumstances whose moral and other goodness may be in serious question. Both authors, however, also seem to have something more proactive in mind—the ability to produce positive changes in external circumstances, in other people, in oneself, and in one's relationships.

The standards by which something counts as positive in any of these areas—life success, being prosocial, possessing moral or civic virtue—are however left largely undefined and unexamined. Where particular values are specified, there tends to be little discussion of what *makes* them values, and neither Bar-On nor Goleman, nor for that matter Mayer and Salovey, really address the issue of justifying these particular values against possible criticisms and competitors, taking the goodness of for instance self-actualisation, independence, and respect for value-pluralism, largely as read. Mayer and Cobb (2000), in addressing the lists of traits adduced by Bar-On and Goleman, do however notably suggest that some of the traits may be in potential tension with each other: traits that serve the individual who possesses them in particular, such as independence and initiative, may be in some tension, logically and psychologically, with empathetic and other-responsive tendencies also listed as part of (the benefits of) EI.

These concerns also point, more generally, towards a tendency to ignore both fact/value distinctions and relevant distinctions between different ways in which traits and abilities can be valuable and valued. Notably, we might want clearer distinctions between goods valued in themselves and instrumentally: skill in managing and understanding one's own and others' emotions might well be used for bad ends, and to achieve those bad ends more effectively. There is also a distinction to be made between the benefits a trait or ability confers on its bearer as opposed to on others or society in general—a distinction that would also, for completeness, require an understanding of the intervening variables that might modify whether or not benefits of either kind actually materialise. Some more thought to issues of value-relativism, in particular, would also be helpful: are the standards we measure EI by informed by views and practices, especially on issues of value, that can legitimately vary between groups or between individuals? If yes, how do we handle such diversity without losing clear standards? If not, which values, if any, should we apply, and why? That a particular value system commands current widespread consensus does not by itself prove it right, nor would even universal agreement on a value system by itself prove it right: the *reasons* for the agreement are crucial. And this also points to the problematic nature of Mayer and Salovey's tendency to implicit appeals to a kind of meta-ethical naturalism: even if certain evaluative inclinations could be shown to be in us by nature, *and* were pan-cultural, this would not by itself prove them right. As even cursory familiarity with moral philosophy debates indicates, moreover, the notion of proving *any* value system definitively right is problematic. But then to draw on any value system without properly addressing the question of how it *might* be justifiable, or at least preferable over others, is also a troubling move.

A related worry, also with moral and political implications, is that EI may be a measure of conformity: a person might qualify as emotionally intelligent simply because they have more or less uncritically internalised, or innately tended towards, the same values and beliefs that those who measure EI would prefer them to have—and this worry has been raised about Mayer and Salovey's account (Roberts *et al.*, 2001). It is worth noting that this concern applies even if the values to which the conformist conforms are good ones—for we may want that people should hold the right values reflectively and even critically, not just as a matter of (natural or nurture-given) course. *Qua* educational goal, this also raises the worry that teaching emotional intelligence is largely about indoctrination, and of a particularly invasive kind at that, reaching right into the affected individuals' inner lives and dispositions. Such concerns might be alleviated to some extent by introducing encouragements to critical reflection and discussion into the relevant curriculum—but in order to really reach the root of the concern, this would need to include encouraging critical reflection and discussion about the content of the notion of emotional intelligence itself, especially where it comes with the tacit assumption that the rightness of certain values are a given (should everyone necessarily want to be 'self-actualized', for instance?).

If EI is defined in more value-neutral terms, however, the worry again arises that it may be a measure of purely instrumental capacities that may not be used for good: the abilities listed in the four-branch model do not seem as though they would necessarily have to be used for morally good purposes, or for the benefit of others than their possessor more generally. Understanding one's own and others' emotions, being able to use emotions to enhance reasoning, understanding emotional meaning and being skilled at managing emotions in oneself and others: none of these are inherently skills that could only be used for morally good purposes. In order to direct them to good uses, we would need to reintroduce values into the picture. That doing so would, in this case, have to be explicit, might however be beneficial from the point of view of wanting also to encourage critical reflection and discussion.

A somewhat less frequently focused worry, but one implicit in the discussion above about EI and its connection to life success, is whether EI is necessarily good for the person who has it: to be better than most around you at understanding and managing your own and others' feelings could be a mixed blessing, at least if it means you have to do most of the emotional 'heavy lifting' to promote the good of all involved. Here, the worry is not so much the emotionally intelligent person's being a sheep-like conformist, or a wolf in sheep's clothing, as that they might end up, especially if they are both prosocially disposed and concerned to be morally good, being emotional beasts of burden, at considerable potential detriment to success at their more individual life goals. (Worries on these lines also apply to the issue of whose interests 'emotionally intelligent' habits advocated by educational institutions or workplaces serve—the student/employee's, or the institution's: these can come apart.)

That these contrasting kinds of concerns can all apply to the idea of an emotionally intelligent person also indicates, again, the extent to which the various putative benefits of EI can come apart, and the extent to which the concept, in itself, lacks determinate moral import. Insofar as the latter issue arises in part because EI is used in different senses, this also points to a number of further reasons for caution in adopting it as an educational goal. For one thing, in the absence of clear definition, it is harder still to say what would count as empirical evidence for the claims made on behalf of EI, even if the empirical work on it had not otherwise been, as in fact it is, in quite early stages, and considered by many to be inconclusive. For another, the definitional issues, and the value-related issues, point to ways in which EI might be difficult to defend as an educational goal even if the empirical evidence were clearer. For instance, even if we had clearer evidence that EI, whether as defined by Goleman or by others, did correlate to outcomes that would, on some particular definition, count as life success, or socially benefit, or moral and civic virtue, or all of these, there would still be an issue of whether this particular way of defining life success, social benefit, or virtues, would be the right ones, let alone whether they should be taught in schools, and if so, in what way.

Insofar as what is taught in 'teaching emotional intelligence' is values, the issue of how these values are to be justified, particularly in the face of competing value systems, needs to be tackled more directly. Insofar as what we can expect from emotional literacy and management skills need not straightforwardly contribute to moral education, there is also the interesting, and so far largely neglected, issue of what such emotional learning might be worth apart from the goals of moral education, or education for life success. Conversely, Mayer and Cobb suggest that the renewed interest in emotions might provide new ways of validating parts of the curriculum, such as arts and literature classes, whose 'usefulness' in themselves are often queried. Since the arts may help promote emotional literacy, the ability to reason about emotions and reason drawing on emotions (as when a novel, film, painting or piece of music helps release new ideas and give access to new perspectives through the emotions it evokes), promoting such emotion-related skills could help keep these subjects on the curriculum.

The debates around EI as an educational goal also put the focus on aspects of learning that are not purely academic, and might in that way help deepen and broaden our understanding of education—though this can cut both ways: focus on topics like EI may also serve as a distraction from academic issues, and even as an excuse to put less resources into more traditional academic learning. Becoming more aware of the ways in which EI as an educational goal is problematic might also not be a bad thing for teaching efforts aimed at promoting emotional learning—'teaching the controversy', in this context, would help alleviate concerns about EI-teaching as a mode of social control. While this will of course be difficult to do with children at early developmental stages, as they grow, it will be useful to introduce a degree of critical reflection on the curriculum itself.

CONCLUSION

A major part of what motivates educational policy on EI appears to be more or less covert moves towards value education and emotional habituation of students according to the value system in question, rather than simply increasing emotional literacy and emotion-management skills among students. This need not be illegitimate—though the question of how deeply the educational system should attempt to reach into a student, and according to which values, does rather uneasily pose itself here. It is important, though, that the value aspect of this should be clearly identified and justified as such, and be introduced in such a way as to leave room for critical examination and discussion, at least once the students are sufficiently developed to engage on this level, and certainly by the society at large. And this is not a goal best achieved by blurring the lines between value systems and applied science.

NOTES

1. For a comprehensive survey article on EI concepts and issues of definition, measurement and correlation with other psychometric measures, see Mayer *et al.*, 2008; this also summarises research on attempts to improve EI by educational means.
2. For a more in-depth comparison of Aristotelian views on emotion-education with Goleman's approach, see also Kristjánsson, 2006. Some points that may be worth mentioning briefly here: Aristotle, unlike Goleman, has a rather derisory opinion of the value of self-control: his picture of a virtuous person is of someone whose emotions are aligned and well integrated with their reason, not having to be continually forced under its control. Will does not appear in Aristotle's account of human psychology, let alone as a 'skill', nor does it feature in his account of the education of the emotions. Aristotle also distinguishes fairly sharply, in *The Politics*, between civic and moral virtues, and to interpret him as a respecter of cultural diversity and related forms of value pluralism is on the face of that same work rather a challenge. Kristjansson also argues, in some depth, that Goleman's notion of emotional intelligence is closer to what Aristotle calls 'cleverness' than to virtue with respect to the emotions.
3. Notably David R. Caruso, with whom they developed their current EI-test (Mayer *et al.*, 2002). I shall tend to use 'Mayer and Salovey' as shorthand for 'Mayer, Salovey and associates' throughout, when not referring directly to specific works, where full author lists are given in the bibliography.
4. For discussion of ways in which these kinds of considerations have influenced thinking on EI, see, for example, Bechara *et al.*, 2007.
5. For more detailed discussion of these two educational movements (both internally rather heterogeneous) and their relation to educational policies on EI, see also Mayer and Cobb, 2000); on criteria for assessing EI learning programs, see also Zins (2000). For examples of instruction methods for EI teaching, see also e.g. Saarni (2007).

REFERENCES

Bar-On, R. (1997) *Bar-On Emotional Quotient Inventory: Technical Manual* (Toronto, Multi-Health Systems).

Bar-On, R. (2007) How Important is it to Educate People to be Emotionally Intelligent, and Can it be Done?, in: Bar-On *et al.*, 2007, pp. 1–14.

Bar-On, R., Maree, J. G. and Elias, M. J. (eds) (2007) *Educating People to be Emotionally Intelligent* (London/Westport, CT, Praeger).

Bechara, A., Damasio, A. R. and Bar-On, R. (2007) The Anatomy of Emotional Intelligence and Implications for Educating People to be Emotionally Intelligent, in: Bar-On *et al.*, 2007, pp. 291–298.

Damasio, A. (1994) *Descartes' Error: Emotion, Reason and the Human Brain* (New York, Grosset/Putnam).

Gardner, H. (1983) *Frames of Mind: The Theory of Multiple Intelligences* (New York, Basic Books).

Goleman, D. (1995) *Emotional Intelligence: Why it Can Matter More Than IQ* (New York, Bantam Books).

Kristjánsson, K (2006) 'Emotional Intelligence' in the Classroom? An Aristotelian Critique, *Educational Theory*, 56, pp. 36–56.

Mayer, J. D. and Cobb, C. D. (2000) Educational Policy on Emotional Intelligence: Does It Make Sense?, *Educational Psychology*, 12, pp. 163–183.

Mayer, J. D. and Salovey, P. (1990) Emotional Intelligence, *Imagination, Cognition, and Personality*, 9, pp. 185–211.

Mayer, J. D. and Salovey, P. (1993) The Intelligence of Emotional Intelligence, *Intelligence*, 17, pp. 433–442.

Mayer, J. D. and Salovey, P. (1995) Emotional Intelligence and the Construction and Regulation of Feelings, *Applied and Preventive Psychology*, 4, pp. 197–208.

Mayer, J. D., Salovey, P. and Caruso, D. R. (1999) Emotional Intelligence Meets Traditional Standards for an Intelligence, *Intelligence*, 27, pp. 267–298.

Mayer, J. D., Salovey, P. and Caruso, D. R. (2002) *Mayer-Salovey-Caruso Emotional Intelligence Test (MSCEIT)*, Version 2.0 (Toronto, Multi-Health Systems).

Mayer, J. D., Roberts, R. D. and Barsade, S. G. (2008) Human Abilities: Emotional Intelligence, *Annual Review of Psychology*, 59, pp. 507–36.

Mayer, J. D., Salovey, P., Caruso, D. R. and Sitarenios, G. (2001) Emotional Intelligence as a Standard Intelligence, *Emotion*, 1, pp. 232–242.

Paul, A. M. (1999) Promotional Intelligence, originally published by *Salon.com* June 28, 1999. Available at: http://www.salon.com/books/it/1999/06/28/emotional/

Roberts, R. D., Zeidner, M. and Matthews, G. (2001) Does Emotional Intelligence Meet Traditional Standards for an Intelligence? Some New Data and Conclusions, *Emotion*, 1, pp. 196–231.

Saarni, C. (2007) The Development of Emotional Competence: Pathways for Helping Children to Become Emotionally Intelligent, in: Bar-On *et al.*, 2007, pp. 15–36.

Zins, J. E. (2000) Criteria for Evaluating the Quality of School-Based Social and Emotional Learning Programs, in: R. Bar-On and J. D. A. Parker (eds) *The Handbook of Emotional Intelligence: Theory, Development, Assessment, and Appreciation of Home, School, and in the Workplace* (San Francisco, CA, Jossey-Bass), pp. 391–410.

5.4
Commentary

RUTH CIGMAN AND ANDREW DAVIS

IQ theory has exercised a great influence on educational policy. It has also been largely discredited by the discovery that IQ can be 'improved' by the right kind of training. Out of this tension between influence and validity emerges the debate about non-cognitive intelligences.

Both multiple and emotional intelligence theories—represented principally by Gardner and Goleman, respectively—have been hugely influential on educators. There are many reasons for this influence, but we shall concentrate on one here: the problem of conceptualising difference. This is an abiding preoccupation of contemporary educators, though it extends far wider than the field of education. It is particularly crucial in special education, where the post-war distinction between so-called normal and abnormal ('handicapped') children was challenged by Mary Warnock's concept of a special educational need. 'Handicaps' are attributed to a minority of the population. However, everyone has needs, and this concept was intended to blur the distinction between 'normal' and 'abnormal' children.

Why was this so important? The normal/abnormal distinction was supplemented by another, between 'intelligent' and 'unintelligent' children, as measured by an IQ test. As with normal/abnormal, the categories intelligent/unintelligent were the basis for mandatory, differential provision. It gradually became apparent to many that *both* kinds of differentiation are disrespectful and unjust. Children were stigmatised by being cast as 'abnormal' or 'unintelligent', and in many cases deprived of an adequate education.

The need to re-conceptualise difference, attempted by Warnock on behalf of so-called handicapped children, came to be seen as an ethical and political imperative. Like the 'handicapped', the 'unintelligent' needed to be released from a conceptual imprisonment that could scupper educational chances. Both categories were regarded as grounded in biology, if not in genetics, and a particularly pernicious aspect of IQ theory was the idea that everyone has an intelligence 'ceiling'. Ability was innate and immutable; children who were endowed with very little had better get used to the idea.

This situation seemed to demand both a scientific and an ethical response, and Gardner's theory has been perceived as providing a scientific foundation for the latter. There are no longer intelligent and unintelligent children. There are children who exemplify a variety of intelligences, and it is unacceptable to denigrate a child because she fails to demonstrate the kind of intelligence that has traditionally been valued. Instead, it is appropriate—according to teachers who use MI theory in their classrooms—to draw attention to some other intelligence: spatial, intrapersonal, musical or whatever. Implicit in this approach is the idea that everyone can ('by nature') do *something* well; no one need suffer from low self-esteem on account of their alleged inabilities.

However, this is hardly a scientific, or indeed logical, inference from MI theory. If there are seven or more intelligences, the odds may seem better that a particular individual will prove 'intelligent' in some sphere than if there was only one. But this is not inevitable; it depends on the statistical distribution of the intelligences. MI theory does not avert the possibility that some children will turn out to be 'unintelligent'.

This fairly obvious point tends to be ignored, and MI theory has caught on, we suggest, because people see it as potentially humane, rather than because they are convinced of its scientific validity. The theory supports our everyday sense that human beings are not identical in their abilities, but have different strengths, aptitudes and proclivities. However it is one thing to recognise such differences informally, as teachers and parents do. It is another to formalise them into an account of human differences without fully considering the implications of so doing.

How should we conceptualise differences between children? If, as seems likely, MI theory is a theory of human 'interactive kinds' (see Andrew Davis' discussion of Ian Hacking in Section 2 of this volume), what are the likely effects of saying to a child: 'you may not have much linguistic intelligence but you have plenty of spatial intelligence'? 'Interactive kinds', to recall, 'are moving targets because our investigations interact with the targets themselves, and change them ...' (this volume, p. 86). Does MI theory 'make up children'? If so, how does it affect them? Is it motivated, in part, by a spurious attempt to keep self-esteem safely above a certain level (see Ruth Cigman's 'Enhancing Children' in Section 4)? Is this at the cost—as White suggests—of spinning an elaborate web of lies?

6
LEARNERS, TEACHERS AND REFLECTION

6.1
Introduction

RUTH CIGMAN AND ANDREW DAVIS

The National Workplace Learning Network (NWLN) runs a Campaign for Learning (see http://www.campaign-for-learning.org.uk/cfl/learningin schools), based on the premise that: '"learning to learn" [is] a process of discovery about learning. It involves a set of principles and skills which, if understood and used, help learners learn more effectively and so become learners for life. At its heart is the belief that learning is learnable' (NWLN, 2008). This section focuses directly on 'philosophies of learning', and is introduced by Christopher Winch's chapter on 'Learning how to learn'. The concept is not new—R. F. Dearden used it in 1976—but it permeates current educational policy, though its meaning is far from clear. There is something seductive about the idea that, instead of merely *teaching* children, teachers might teach them 'how to learn', and indeed how to be *proficient* at learning, so that they become independent learners for life. A perennial difficulty experienced by teachers is how to make learning stick. 'Learning how to learn' (or as Winch calls it, lh2l) sounds like a formula for doing this—and indeed 'lifelong learning' is one of its promised benefits.

Is lh2l a capacity? An ability? A set of personal qualities or virtues? Winch examines and rejects the first two options, having investigated the possibility that certain transferable abilities might satisfy the description 'learning how to learn'. His tentative answer to the question 'what sense can be made of lh2l?' is that 'aretetic (virtue-based) and personal qualities rather than cognitive ones may be most decisive for developing independent learning in a range of subject matters'. Take confidence, for example. 'Other things being equal,' he writes, 'someone who is confident that they will succeed in achieving something if they attempt it, is more likely to attempt and succeed than someone who is not.'

This raises interesting philosophical questions, and it contrasts in a subtle way with the theme of the chapter that follows, Karin Murris' 'Philosophy with Children, the Stingray and the Educative Value of Disequilibrium'. Disequilibrium, argues Murris, is an essential component of Philosophy for Children (P4C); it should be actively sought and welcomed by teachers. It is a 'paralysis that usefully undermines confidence', and readers may at this point experience some disequilibrium themselves, asking: should we promote or undermine the confidence of children? We would suggest, indeed, that this question usefully illustrates Murris' call for enquiry that expresses ambiguity and provokes puzzlement.

Although she is talking primarily about the teaching of philosophy, Murris' chapter includes a hearty critique of current assumptions about education as a field 'that prioritises transmission (by an adult) and acquisition (by a young learner) of pre-determined knowledge' (this volume, p. 106). Even thinking skills as currently taught, she argues, confers on teachers 'epistemological authority with the children sitting silently in rows doing paper and pencil tests'. Some readers may wonder at this (it does not describe this editor's experience of the teaching of thinking skills), but the important point here is the one about epistemological authority, which Murris proposes that teachers should forego. In its place is a 'community of enquiry', in which the balance of power between educator and learner reflects a new ontology of 'child'.

In the third chapter of this section, Simons and Masschelein offer a Foucauldian analysis of the postmodern 'learning environment', which marks a paradigm shift from a historical to an environmental understanding: a shift in the understanding of space and time. According to the historical (or traditional) understanding, individuals are bound by a notion of time that is 'serial, orientated and cumulative'. Children, in this context, are organised, controlled, viewed as 'cases' for instruction; their 'progress' is assessed in a linear way according to norms that are common to all. Here 'comparisons and averages primarily hold the risk of being regarded as a comforting norm', and it is implied that they may also tyrannise individuals.

Within an environmental understanding, children compete only with themselves. They are in a new way *agents* of their own learning, that is, individuals who seek to better themselves by 'appropriating' knowledge, using (one could almost say requisitioning) feedback from their teachers. The latter, as Simons and Masschelein say in their abstract: 'are redefined as instructors, designers of (powerful) learning environments and facilitators or coaches of learning processes'. However, this environmental understanding has a 'dark side', and readers may enjoy the sense of anticipation about how the authors will characterise this in the final section. Until this point, the tone is subtly descriptive, inspired by the notion of 'Foucauldian curiosity'. This attitude, which is possibly the most fascinating aspect of the paper, involves: 'a willingness to become a stranger in the familiar present . . . and to regard who we are and what we do . . . as no longer obvious'. From this perspective, the chapter is not only about 'them': schools, teachers, parents and so on, from whom we might (in some respects) want to distance ourselves. It is also, and crucially, about 'us', and it involves articulating understandings and exposing tensions of which we were presumably unaware. The chapter ends with a kind of challenge, akin, perhaps, to those faced by postmodern learners, according to the argument of the paper. Is another pedagogic attitude possible? ask the authors. Is it possible, in other words, to avoid the 'dark sides' of *both* the historical and environmental understandings, in favour of a 'new' attitude, or perhaps a 'third way'?

6.2
Learning How to Learn: A Critique

CHRISTOPHER WINCH

So much is written about 'learnacy' or 'learning how to learn' (lh2l for short) and so little argued about what it actually consists in (if indeed the term lh2l does refer to anything distinct), that it is appropriate to examine the claim that one of the central aims of education should be the development of the ability to learn how to learn. Robert Dearden had already used this term in 1976 and in this chapter, especially in the conclusion, I follow up some of his suggestions. The claim is essentially this; that if one learns how to learn then one can be an independent learner who can not only learn well at school but throughout life. Not surprisingly, lh2l is thought by some to be the central curricular aim of formal education. But do we really understand what is being claimed about this putative ability?

THE CLAIM THAT WE ARE 'BORN TO LEARN' AND THE CONFUSION BETWEEN CAPACITIES AND ABILITIES

It is sometimes claimed that we are born with an innate drive to learn (Rousseau, 1762; Chomsky, 1988). The implication is that if we can harness that drive then we will become successful learners for life. But the claim itself is exceedingly vague. Is it a *conative* claim? Does it mean that we have a desire or *impulse* to learn? If so, then this might not be sufficient for learning, for wanting something is not the same as knowing how to get it. Is it a *cognitive* claim? Does it mean that we have an ability to learn? If so, then this also might not be sufficient for learning, for knowing how to do something is not the same as wanting to do it. In developmental theory, from Rousseau to Chomsky, the impulse to learn is understood as a biologically-based mixture of the conative and the cognitive, so educational progress should be guaranteed through our biological development if it takes place in appropriate conditions. In what immediately follows I will be discussing the cognitive rather than the conative claim.

It makes little sense to say that we are born with a generalised ability to learn, since it is far from clear what this would amount to. We could, however, be possessed of a *capacity* to learn, meaning an ability to acquire an ability (a distinction made in Kenny, 1968, for example). Having a capacity to learn would be a necessary but not sufficient condition for having such an ability, which would, presumably, be acquired rather than innate. Indeed, it is difficult to see how we could have an ability to learn if we did not already have a capacity to learn. But if we had such a capacity, why would we also need an ability to learn? Although the capacity to learn would be innate, the ability would be acquired. However, why should we need an ability to do x if we already had a capacity to do x? If a human baby has an innate capacity to learn to speak, then surely it does not need an acquired ability to do so in addition.

These reflections should serve only to heighten our puzzlement about the claim that we should be encouraged to learn how to learn. The problem is that if we do indeed have a cognitive and a conative capacity to learn generally, then that should be sufficient for learning to take place given the right environmental conditions. If I can and want to learn, then I should learn in the right conditions. But then either a general capacity or a general ability to learn how to learn is apparently quite superfluous, since if I can learn, then *a fortiori* I must be able to learn how to learn. But if I can learn, why should I need to learn how to learn? On the other hand, if I don't have a capacity to learn, then *a fortiori* I will never acquire an ability to learn how to learn and all efforts in that direction will be in vain. It looks as if it is difficult to attach a clear sense to the claim that it is a key aim of education to enable children to learn how to learn. Why then has the claim become so influential?

The distinction between a capacity and an ability also makes it clear that the claim that the ability to learn how to learn is incoherent because it leads to a vicious regress, is a false one. The claim is this. If I can learn how to learn then I must be able to learn. So in order to learn how to learn I need to be able to learn how to learn how to learn. I can learn how to learn how to learn. But if I am able to learn how to learn how to learn then I need to be able to learn. But then I will need to learn how to learn how to learn how to learn. An infinite regress of abilities threatens, which makes the lh2l claim incoherent. But the objection proves far too much, for the argument works on the simple case of learning as well. Thus, if I can learn, then I must be able to learn how to learn. But then I must be able to learn how to learn how to learn etc. and we are back to the same problem. The capacity/ability distinction stops this regress in its tracks. If I can learn, then I must have a capacity to learn. But I do not need a capacity to learn how to learn, since the capacity to learn is innate and encompasses the capacity to learn how to learn. But although the distinction rescues learning as a capacity, it cannot do anything for learning how to learn as an ability, since if I do have a capacity for learning, I won't need an ability to learn, let alone an ability to learn how to learn.

In order to understand this, we need to look more closely at our capacity to learn. Possession of a capacity to learn is, tautologically, the necessary condition of learning. However, it is far from being sufficient. The capacity to learn in a human being must be a general one, a capacity to learn all the kinds of things that a human can learn. But in order to be realised, that capacity must be accompanied by a will to learn and the right conditions for learning, such as exposure to spoken language in the case of learning to speak, or of firm surfaces for learning to walk. In addition, there is very often a sensitive period in which the capacity operates in certain areas, for example, one cannot readily learn to speak after a certain age (Lieberman, 1990). For learning to speak one's mother tongue a capacity to learn, together with the right environmental conditions, ought to be sufficient to acquire that ability. But the capacity for learning languages will not enable one to go on learning other languages in the same way; later learning of different languages will be slower and more difficult. Thus the capacity to learn may manifest itself in different ways (see also Adey and Shayer, 1994).

Given these considerations, can it make any sense to speak of an *ability* to learn as opposed to a *capacity* to do so? It seems that it can. A may be better able than B to learn carpentry, for example. In this sense, A and B both know how to learn carpentry and the ability is properly described as a skill or as know-how, to distinguish it from capacities like breathing that cannot be so described (cf. Snowdon, 2003).[1] Both have the capacity to learn carpentry, but A also has knowledge and technique that enable her to learn it more effectively than B. Thus A may have a good understanding of the property of wood, of the powers and functions of woodworking tools, a firm but subtle grip, good hand-eye co-ordination and an ability to visualise, all of which B possesses to a lesser or non-existent degree. Thus A has specific abilities that enable her to learn how to do carpentry. The capacity to learn must, in many cases, it seems, be supplemented by *specific abilities* to do certain things if it is be effective.

Does this support the claim that there is an ability to learn how to learn that educators should strive to develop? Here we encounter a further problem, for abilities are domain-specific. We cannot just be able; we must be able *at* something or other. And even if we claim that there are abilities of a general nature, then we must be able to give an account of the *range* of those abilities. But the lh2l claim seems to be that such an ability is a general one, to be applied across the full range of subject matter. Can that make sense?

Let us review the situation so far. For the claim that we need an ability to learn how to learn to be plausible, the following must be true.

1. We have a capacity to learn. If we did not we could not learn anything.
2. We do not therefore have a distinct capacity to learn how to learn, since this would be superfluous, being part of our capacity to learn.
3. We need to acquire the ability to learn how to learn, since the *capacity* to learn is a necessary but not sufficient condition for acquiring the ability to learn how to learn.

But 3 is puzzling. It is simply not clear why, given that the capacity to learn is a necessary condition for learning (and, *a fortiori*, for learning how to learn), the ability to learn how to learn should constitute a prima facie sufficient condition for learning. One obvious *riposte* would be that one needs, in addition to the capacity to learn, certain highly specific abilities that are necessary to acquire further knowledge or abilities. Whether these highly specific abilities are themselves singly, or in conjunction with other abilities, sufficient to acquire a range of further abilities, will require further conceptual and empirical investigation. What is clear as a matter of logical grammar is that the verb 'is able to' and its cognates 'knows how to', 'can' etc. are transitive, that is, they take an object phrase like swim or play the piano, which signifies an ability, skill or disposition. This does not mean, of course, that such abilities, skills and dispositions do not have a range of situations in which they can obtain, which might be narrow or broad, but it does mean that they do need to be completed with an object specification.

One reply could be that one could complete 'A is able to ...' with 'learn' (referring to an ability), to yield 'A is able to learn' that would specify the outcome of 'A has learned how to learn'. Reflection shows that this will not do. The problem is that the verb 'learn' is, in this respect, similar to 'is able to'. Whether as an indicative as in 'A is learning ...' or coupled with a modal auxiliary as in 'A can learn ...', the verb is also transitive. In order to understand a sentence containing the verb in whatever form, we need it to be completed with an object phrase that sets out the range of abilities, skills, theories or propositions that A is learning or is capable of learning. This object phrase may signify a more or less broad range of such things, but it must be present. However, the following is not remotely plausible in characterising an ability: 'For any ability, skill, knowledge, theory, proposition that a human being could reasonably be expected to possess, A is able to learn that ability, skill, theory or proposition'.[2] Why is this so? Because the range of such things is so diverse that we would not know how to identify such an ability. Consider:

    i. A can control his breathing;
    ii. A can ride a bike;
    iii. A can repair an electrical circuit;
    iv. A can throw a pot;
    v. A can read;
    vi. A knows the main sequence of events in the First World War;
    vii. A knows whether it is time to go home;
    viii. A knows the theoretical basis of quantum mechanics;

and one can see that it would be very hard to specify such an ability. i seems to require specific muscular and neural capacity, ii co-ordination and balance, iii both theoretical and specific knowledge and manual ability, iv practical knowledge of the properties of clay, an aesthetic sense and manual ability, v co-ordination of knowledge of properties of spoken and written language, vi knowledge of a series of interconnected propositions and how they relate to each other, vii the ability to read a clock or otherwise judge the time, and or a sense of what it is appropriate to do, viii knowledge of a physical theory expressed in mathematical language.

To talk of an underlying ability, as opposed to a capacity, to acquire all these accomplishments seems absurd. Even the characterisation of the diversity in this brief list underestimates the complexity of what we are talking about. For example, i-iv seem to involve, in some way, bodily strength. Yet, as Ryle (1974) pointed out, physical strength is not one, but many (albeit overlapping) things: the punching power of a boxer, the stamina of a runner, the pull and grip of an archer, the musculature of a jumper, that of a weightlifter and so on. These abilities are so diverse that to talk of an ability to acquire them requires it to be a unique ability, since all the others have a range that can be specified with reasonable accuracy. It seems, therefore, that we have not yet succeeded in attaching a clear sense to the verb 'to learn how to learn'. Let us now look at the most plausible candidates.

TRYING TO ATTACH SENSE TO 'LEARNING HOW TO LEARN'

(a) Forming and Testing Hypotheses

One very popular candidate for the highly general ability of learning how to learn is the ability to form and test hypotheses. It is an idea that we find, for example, in the work of Dewey and in a range of neo-Cartesian thought about learning. The efficiency of learning, and, in particular of learning our mother tongue, is attributed to our abilities to match the sounds we hear to hypothesised grammatical structures and meanings and to test them against subsequent input, thus building up an accurate theoretical picture of the structure and meaning of our native language (cf. Chomsky, 1988; Fodor, 1975). Now there are reasons for doubting that we learn language by forming and testing hypotheses, for reasons connected with Wittgenstein's private language argument (see Wittgenstein, 1953), but let us concede the point to Chomsky and Fodor for a moment.

Their claim is that the ability to form and test hypotheses is innate, part of our neurological wiring and operates automatically. In other words, it is, as we saw, a capacity rather than an ability. In fact, it is a way of characterising our capacity to learn the range of things that a human being is capable of learning. If this characterisation of the capacity to learn is correct, then it should be superfluous to claim, in addition, that we need to have an acquired ability to form and test hypotheses, for such a capacity would preclude the need for an ability to learn how to learn.

But of course, humans do acquire abilities to form and test hypotheses. There are two points to be made about these abilities. First of all, it is a moot point whether the method of forming and testing hypotheses is the only or even the most efficient way to learn something in particular areas of activity. Fodor's (1975) claim that it is difficult to see what other ways there are of learning is simply false. One can learn through being drilled, trained, instructed, by memorising, by practice, through indoctrination, through intuition and so on. There are also good reasons to think that the hypothetico-deductive approach may not be the best way of characterising our inferential and explanatory (and hence some of our learning) abilities (Lipton, 2004). Humans learn many different things and do so in many different ways; this is part of what Wittgenstein called our 'natural history' and it cannot be reduced to hypothesis formation and testing without some pretty convincing evidence and argumentation, which has not, so far, been forthcoming.

Second, it is far more plausible to suggest that the hypothetico-deductive method is more appropriate in some areas than others. The nature and extent of its use in science is, for example, a matter of longstanding and continually lively debate (Kuhn, 1962; Lakatos, 1970; Newton-Smith, 1990; Okasha, 2002; Lipton, 2004; Popper, 1936). But, where it is used, it is an ability grounded in detailed subject knowledge and rigorous techniques, which only an expert in a specific area can use to acquire significant new knowledge. Even where the hypothetico-deductive method is appropriate, it presupposes *training* in technique and *instruction* in theory and specific facts. Even if the learning *capacity* were best characterised as hypothetico-deductive, it would constitute a necessary condition of learning hypothetico-deductively rather than a sufficient one, since otherwise babies might carry out work in quantum mechanics through the exercise of that capacity. For these reasons, although a hypothetico-deductive capacity is a plausible candidate for a general power of the mind, it is not going to work as characterisation of a general *ability* of the mind underlying learning how to learn.

(b) Modularity and Connectionism

One of the continuing themes of the debate about general powers of the mind is the attraction of the computer model as a way of understanding such powers. In one way, this is not difficult to understand, since computers are structured in such a way as to permit identification of distinct functions. These functions are integral to the machine and constitute its basic 'architecture'. Connectionist models, on the other hand, dispense with architecture and allow connections to build up with the impact of experience. But connectionism is unlikely to yield an overall strategic direction for learning since, as in empiricist epistemology, the connections are experience-dependent and thus, to a certain extent, *ad hoc*.

But if an innatist computer-based model of the acquisition and integration of knowledge is more suitable to the project of identifying a generalised learning ability than a connectionist model, it brings significant problems of its own. Not the least of these is the fact that, if the learning capacity is *innate*, it cannot play the role of an acquired *ability* to learn how to learn. On the other hand, if it is an acquired ability, then we are owed a story concerning why we need this, since, according to the conventional computer architecture story, we already have a hypothetico-deductive module embodying the capacity, innately. But there is a further problem with the modular thesis. It claims that the human mind is organised into discrete functional parts that each carry out an element of mental activity autonomously. There is thus a language module, a visual one, a hypothetico-deductive one, a mathematical one, and so on. Fodor (2001) has argued, however, that the modularity thesis has enormous problems in making sense of the *global* or *abductive* nature of human cognition, the fact that all relevant faculties are brought to bear in decision making, for example, not just particular modules. One particular problem may apparently be suitable for solution by a particular module. But a decision needs to be made concerning which module should solve the problem. There is no general rule concerning what this should be, because decision-making is context-dependent. Circumstances, rather than general principles, determine how one goes about making decisions or, in our case, how one goes about learning or indeed, making decisions whether one should learn in particular circumstances (Fodor, 2001, Chapter 3). Fodor also argues that connectionist models are no better, since the relevance of any piece of information to a network is determined by the relationship of junctions (nodes) on the network. But since these are invariant once established, since they are neurological junctions that by their nature are permanent, the relevance of a piece of information within the network to other nodes in the network will also be invariant. But a key point about abductive processes is that they make considerations of relevance context-dependent. Whether or not the state of my bank balance is relevant to my decision-making will depend on what kind of decision I am making and particular circumstances relevant to the decision. Connectionism, since it requires that the relevance of information is invariant, is unable to account for this (Fodor, 2001, pp. 50–51). All of this is particularly relevant to the learning how to learn thesis, since if it is to be a practical ability, learning how to learn will involve decision-making about the relevance of certain information to the learner's projects, circumstances and background. It appears, then, that learning how to learn is difficult to explain in terms of both the modularity and connectionist theses.

(c) Abduction and Integration

Human beings have the ability to bring to bear on a decision or judgment those considerations that are relevant, or at least enough considerations that are relevant to the making of that decision or judgment. What these considerations are will depend on the issue being faced. Clearly we must have an innate *capacity* to do this. However, our *ability* to do so is not available at birth. There is plenty of evidence that it grows gradually over a long period (Wood, 1990). It is a sign of intellectual maturity that one can judge in this way. So it looks at last if we have an acquired ability— the ability to abduct—with the requisite generality to serve as the candidate general mental power that we need in order to account for learning how to learn.

Unfortunately, however, this is a false promise. The abductive faculty, although acquired and of general application, is a mark of mature human rationality as such: it is not an optional desirable feature. Those who cannot bring together relevant considerations in their judgments are not able to make rational judgments, since that is part of what we mean by rational judgment. The making of rational judgments does not require the acquisition of an *ability* to learn how to learn, but an ability to bring to bear relevant considerations on judgment making. This means learning to make a very wide range of contextual judgements, using existing knowledge and experience of different kinds of circumstances. This involves a great deal of learning, but not learning how to learn as an ability. The abductive ability is acquired, often painfully and over a long period, but is a property of every rational human being, not just of those who are good at learning. If it could be identified with the ability to learn how to learn, then we would not need to advocate it, since everyone who is rational would have it.

We have now looked at two candidate general powers of the mind that could be what learning how to learn is: the hypothetico-deductive faculty and the integrative one. The hypothetico-deductive faculty will not do, either because it is innate or, if it is not, it is context- and knowledge-dependent. The integrative faculty will not either, since although it is acquired, it is a general property of all rational humans and not a desirable option such as learning how to learn is said to be. We have run out of options for *general* powers of the mind that could elucidate the notion of learning how to learn. It is now time to look elsewhere.

(d) Generality and Transfer

If lh2l is not a general power of the mind, could it be something else? The other kind of candidate would be a skill or skills that were relatively specific in kind, but that were *transferable;* that is, they could be learned in one context and then used in others. A skill is a kind of ability that has a more or less specifiable range, but that can also possibly be employed in a variety of situations. A skill is, more precisely, a form of *knowing how to do something*, which is itself learned. To make the point clearer with an example, digesting is a capacity that I have, but it is not a skill since I can either digest normally or abnormally, but I cannot digest well or badly in the way that I can, for example, ride a bike correctly or incorrectly and, if correctly, well or badly (Snowdon, 2003). Skills are attributes that I have to learn before I can be said to have acquired them and, as with knowing how to do things generally, they are normative, that is, they must be done correctly if someone can be truly said to possess them.

In order to make sense of lh2l in this way, we require abilities that have to be learned but that can be put to work in a variety of contexts in order to assist further learning. Are there such abilities? It seems that there are and the two of greatest interest in our enquiry are called *literacy* and *numeracy*. One might add, of course, that equally important are the skills of speaking and listening. But these are abilities, of broad range and applicable in a wide variety of situations, which most of us acquire independently of formal education. There are some aspects of these abilities that need to be learned through the right kind of experience or even through some formal learning, but on the whole, they are not, outside deficit models such as that of Bernstein, considered to be the proper province of education, or at least if speaking is, listening, which would be the medium of learning, is generally not.

(e) Literacy

Reading is an ability that has a number of different dimensions, the most simple of which many children never acquire. Approximately 20% of 11-year-olds fail to reach Level 4 in the English National Curriculum, which requires that they should: 'show understanding of significant ideas, themes, events and characters, beginning to use inference and deduction. They should refer to the text when explaining their views. They locate and use ideas and information'.³ As can be seen by an inspection of the different dimensions of reading, described below, these are criteria for fairly basic functional literacy, not for the sophisticated use of text as a learning tool. We may safely assume that anyone who fails to reach level 4 in reading will not be able to make use of it in significantly furthering their education without help in achieving higher levels of reading ability.

The first of these dimensions of reading is *literal comprehension*, which allows the reader to understand the primary meanings (as opposed to secondary or metaphorical meanings) of sentences in the text. But the ability to *reorganise* material, to understand at a supra-sentential level, for example, the structure of an argument or arguments within a more extended section of text, is vitally important for the proper use of non-narrative prose. It is also the case that even simple narrative, because it uses supra-sentential forms of textual organisation, requires acquaintance with such structures before narratives can be understood.

The ability to understand textual organisation is also vital for the ability to locate information through the use of *supra-sentential* structural features of text in order to eliminate the literal reading of material superfluous to the reader's immediate purpose. Beard (2000) has enumerated these different techniques that depend on the use of large-scale structural features of texts, such as contents, indexes, abstracts, headings and subheadings, to the use of *skimming* (rapid, superficial reading of text to obtain the general drift of a passage), *scanning* (looking for words or phrases related to one's purpose) and *search reading* (looking for particular words or phrases). These are all skills that only become apparent at level 5 of the National Curriculum. In addition, there are *meta-structural* aspects of text that need to be understood. These include: *inference* beyond the literal (for example, the detection of enthymematic arguments and the use of implicature), *evaluation* (for example, the appraisal of a text as fit for stated or implicit purpose) and *appreciation* (for example, the appraisal of a text according to aesthetic criteria). These last would include, not just the appreciation of a poem or novel as something to be enjoyed, but more generally the use of style and other effects in a pleasing way. None of these skills are accessible below level 5 and some of them, such as appreciation, only fully at level 8.

Not only is there evidence that the more basic aspects of reading fail to be achieved by many young people, but there is also evidence that supra-sentential and meta-structural comprehension is generally weak. For example, level 5 in English requires that pupils:

... show understanding of a range of texts, selecting essential points and using inference and deduction where appropriate. In their responses, they identify key features, themes and characters and select sentences, phrases and relevant information to support their views. They retrieve and collate information from a range of sources (QCA, 2008).

The achievement figures for these abilities for 2005 are as follows: 68% overall (75% girls, 61% boys). These are levels of achievement that an able 11-year-old should be able to reach and are figures for the achievement of 14-year-olds.

At least since the HMI report on primary education published in 1978, it has been a persistent complaint that these 'higher reading skills' are poorly taught and inadequately learned (HMSO, 1978). It may be doubted whether a significant number of postgraduate students ever fully attain some of these skills. Personal experience of postgraduate teaching at M and D level at a variety of institutions suggests this to be the case, together with the fact that study skills texts are used in ESRC training programmes, not to mention the popularity of study skill material at undergraduate level. These problems, remarkable in a country that prides itself on having aspirations to take part in the 'knowledge economy' are odd, and attest to a deep-seated failure to successfully teach, not only basic literacy, but also those literary abilities that allow for the understanding of supra-sentential and meta-structural features of text in a range of non-narrative, non-fictional genres and that involve, in particular, the identification and evaluation of structures of argumentation in the most general sense of transitions from premise to conclusion ('pc structures' in Levi's (2000) terms). Such failures are quite fundamental whatever position one takes on the question of whether 'thinking skills' are context-dependent or context-independent, since it is a presupposition of either position that one has the ability to identify and evaluate a pc structure (Toulmin, 1957; Fisher, 2001).

It might be argued that these higher order reading skills are, in fact, a form of thinking skill and so misnamed as reading skills. The PISA study of 2006 appears to take the view that reasoning skills are at the heart of problem solving ability and that such abilities can be cross-disciplinary (p. 6). We can assume, then, that the generic ability to solve problems and to reason are in fact dealt with under the misleading heading of reading ability at level 5 and above. This, however, is a serious misunderstanding of what is involved in solving the problems in PISA-type tests. No-one would seriously expect a pupil to be competent to solve the 'real-life' problems set up in the tests, such as prescribing drugs, simply because they would have neither the detailed knowledge of pharmacy, biochemistry or general practice, nor the professional experience to do anything of the sort. These problems are not generic but, in this example, specific medical problems. One can only *simulate* the solution of such problems through these tests. They are essentially tests of comprehension, using specially prepared texts as a basis, of *extracting* and *organising* relevant information from text or tables and *reorganising* it into a form prescribed by the test. They also involve the organisation of the material so that correct inferences are drawn from the information given. They are the kind of ability that an advanced reader should display; they are *not* an ability to solve complex real-life professional problems, and it is highly misleading to suggest that they are anything of the sort.

Such abilities are also a form of *know how* rather than merely being forms of capacity, since they need to be learned and can be normatively appraised. They also have an identifiable *range of application*, relating to certain kinds of text. In this sense, such know-how is *transferable*, since it can be applied to more than one text, or indeed, more than one kind of text. This does not, of course, mean that having such know how in one subject area is sufficient to transfer such abilities, since if the context-dependent school has it right, one would need to have sufficient subject knowledge to identify characteristic argument forms, enthymematic structures and implicatures within text of a certain type. Adey and Shayer's (1994) work on science teaching had the greatest impact on GCSE English scores, suggesting that the development of higher literacy skills may have been one of the significant effects of their approach to science teaching. PISA-type tests avoid this problem by providing all necessary information within a text prepared in such a way as to render unnecessary the search for enthymeme and implicature. But this is not at all how real life problem-solving works, depending as it does on background knowledge, situational awareness, contextual inference and personal contact.[4] What is less in dispute, however, is that such higher level literacy skills may well, in the hands of skilful teachers, be applied to text in particular subjects as a very useful foundation on which to build subject-specific analytical skills. We can conclude, then, that the ability to read (and associated auxiliary writing abilities relating to the reorganisation of text) is a form of know how, is an identifiable type of skill and is, although not without further teaching, *transferable* to cognate activity within a range of disciplines. In this sense the ability to read, broadly conceived, is a specific transferable skill or form of know how and a plausible candidate for one of the attributes to be acquired if one is to learn how to learn. Furthermore, there is good evidence that it is a form of know how lacked by many people. Here then, is ample grist for the mill of learning how to learn and a considerable pedagogic challenge.

It should be noted that literacy, as a transferable ability that assists learning, would need to be acquired prior to learning how to learn as a general ability. If one had to learn how to learn before one could learn to read and write, then it is not clear how one would become literate. On the other hand, if learning how to learn requires literacy, it is not at all clear what this hypothesised general ability would add to an extremely useful transferable ability of wide application.

(f) Numeracy[5]

Similar considerations and arguments apply to the range of skills that go under the 'numeracy' heading. In fact, in many respects they are closely related to the higher level reading skills discussed in the previous section. There is little doubt that ability to handle numerical operations, geometrical, algebraic and statistical techniques can, in principle, be applied across a range of subject matters. There is also compelling evidence of the limited range of such abilities within the school population and beyond. Recent government statistics on the achievement of Level 6 in Key Stage 3 assessment of Mathematics, which is below the basic level of simple algebraic competence, is 52% for all pupils at age 14 (53% teacher assessment, 51% test assessment) (DfES, 2005).

The analogy with literacy goes further however. First, there is good reason to think that although, in principle, mathematical abilities are transferable from one context to another, the mere possession of such abilities in one context is by no means sufficient for their successful use in other contexts. This applies both to the transfer of relatively decontextualised mathematical abilities to practical contexts such as commerce or engineering (Hoyles, Noss and Pozzi, 1999), or the transfer of such abilities from practical to abstract contexts and *vice versa* (Nunes, Schliemann and Carraher, 1993; Lave 1988).

Second, there is the issue of the representation of mathematical structures. This can be done in various ways that involve: lateral and columnar organisation of numeric and algebraic structures, geometric proof in formal deductive mode, tabular and graphic representation of information in numeric form and mathematical display and argumentation within non-mathematical texts (for example, in situating mathematical problems in practical contexts). *Post hoc* at least, mathematical structures are, in many cases, of pc form, that is, they represent more or less formal, ordered transitions from premise to conclusion. There are a number of characteristic forms employed in mathematics: arithmetical, geometrical and algebraic deduction, which belong to the larger family of deductive inference, since they are all truth-preserving forms of argumentation, although the principles involved in each differ somewhat (e.g. specific axioms in geometry, specific rules of inference in arithmetic), mathematical induction (a form of deductive reasoning used in higher order reasoning in mathematics and formal logic), and various forms of inductive argument employed in statistical reasoning. Like the case of reading and writing, however, the practical knowledge involved, although necessarily learned in certain contexts, is in principle applicable across a range of contexts, even if applicability is often difficult in practice. Finally, as in the case of literacy, there is good evidence that such know-how is (a) poorly distributed amongst the population (DfES, 2003; Cockcroft, 1982) and (b) where it does exist, the evidence of ability to transfer is also limited (Hoyles *et al.*, 1999; Boaler, 2002. The latter draws attention to significant differences between school and operational conditions).

We thus have two very plausible examples of specific transferable skills, whose applicability, at least in theory, to a very wide range of subject matter is enormous. There is ample evidence that these have not been acquired even at a basic level by vast numbers of the population and, where they have, they have not always been acquired to the degree of depth and confidence that makes them transferable. Here, then, is ample evidence both of the need for learning how to learn and of its failure to be met. This constitutes a major educational challenge that, in the UK at least, has yet to be addressed.

(g) Character, Disposition and Virtue

I have concentrated on the cognitive aspects of lh2l as these are the ones most often emphasised. To leave out other features would, however, give a misleading picture. The *conative* aspects were mentioned at the outset and it was noted that one cannot assume that a general desire to learn is innate, as was assumed by Rousseau and many although not all developmentalists up to and including contemporary figures like Chomsky (1988). The desire to learn can, however, be acquired and maintained and it is a matter of no little interest to consider how that can happen. One key point is that success in an activity tends, other things being equal, to bring confidence that future attempts will lead to success. Confidence in doing something is a motivational factor since, again, other things being equal, someone who is confident that they will succeed in achieving something if they attempt it, is more likely to attempt and succeed than someone who is not. So those who succeed in mastering the crucial specific transferable abilities discussed in the previous section have a very significant advantage in this respect, and we can reasonably infer that early educational success in these areas is crucial to establishing confident attitudes towards the kinds of learning that presuppose these abilities. The confidence gained in one area is not automatically transferable to another; confidence in reading does not equate to confidence in doing long division, for example. However, if we assume that reading and numeracy are specific transferable abilities then it is reasonable to assume that there will be some positive transfer of confidence from using one of these abilities in one context to using them in another, *ceteris paribus*.

However, we also know that learning is not always easy. Often it requires patience, persistence, diligence, attention to detail, the ability not to be too discouraged by initial failure, and so on. These attributes are given various names: they are Nietzsche's petty virtues, they are sometimes called self-regarding as opposed to other-regarding virtues, and Kerschensteiner (1964) called them the 'bourgeois' as opposed to the 'civic' virtues (see also Gramsci, 1975). Despite these somewhat disparaging references, however, they are of enormous importance for our enquiry. Learning is difficult and is often literally a character-forming experience (see Polya, 1954, for the case of mathematics). Educators often have to strike a delicate balance between engendering confidence and encouraging students to overcome the inevitable difficulties that come in the path of learning. Too few difficulties encountered and the student becomes over-confident and never acquires the bourgeois virtues needed for difficult learning; too many and for the opposite reason the bourgeois virtues never get developed, and confidence is undermined. This is why it is important to identify and to successfully teach those abilities whose transfer value is high.

One of the key attributes associated with successful learning is that of *independence* (sometimes referred to as 'autonomy'). Independence is partly attitudinal and is connected with self-confidence. It is thus related to the virtues; however, it presupposes certain skills that allow tasks to be performed without supervision, these include the ability to plan, regulate and assess one's own activity and to work collaboratively with others. Black *et al.* draw attention to a number of projects that suggest that qualities of independence are important in making learning more effective. As they point out, Robert Dearden had already, in 1976, drawn attention to the importance, not of a unitary second-order ability that could be characterised as 'learning to learn' but to the possibility of clusters of skills, attitudes and dispositions that, taken together, might perceptibly improve the ability of individuals to learn in a variety of contexts, which he preferred to characterise as 'learning how to learn' (Black *et al.*, 2006, p. 3).

There is a case for maintaining that the virtues are themselves transferable. This claim needs to be made carefully as there are different aspects of important and complex virtues such as courage and justice that make them difficult to describe as unitary. However, it is a general characteristic of the virtues that they can be practised in a variety of contexts. Indeed, if the claim that they can only be fully acquired if they are prefiguratively exercised in a large variety of different situations is correct, then we would expect this to be the case almost as a quasi-tautology. This conceptual point has enormous relevance for curriculum design and pedagogy since it suggests that one will not become patient, self-disciplined etc. if one is not given a chance to fully practice these virtues. It suggests, in the first instance, that particular attention be paid to those transferable abilities whose early mastery is likely to breed success in a variety of areas and the confidence to work independently. In the second instance, it suggests that a broadly based curriculum that gives students the opportunity to achieve in diverse kinds of activity that involve music, sport or physical activity, technical skill and so on, is likely to assist in the development of such virtues. It does not require, of course, that they become experts in these areas, but that they learn and achieve enough to gain some appreciation of what excellence would look like and to acquire the confidence to go towards a significant degree of mastery should they so wish. Confining them to subjects that are particularly suited to certain 'learning styles' is not likely to allow them to do this (see Coffield *et al.*, 2004).

CONCLUSION

There is no general ability to learn how to learn. There are, however, skills, dispositions and virtues whose acquisition and exercise may well make attempts to learn more effective. However, there is nothing about these skills and virtues that is startling or new. The teaching of literacy and numeracy is one of the most ancient aims of formal education, and the development of appropriate attitudes and virtues is one of the most ancient aims of both formal and informal education. It is, perhaps, a measure of our failure to educate our population adequately that we cast around for such desperate remedies as an ability that has never been recognised before and cannot be intelligibly described, despite many attempts to do so. We need, rather, to take a fresh look at what we are currently doing and to see if it cannot be improved.

However, if the argument is correct, the aretaic aspects of lh2l will not be adequately addressed by a narrowly constrained literacy and numeracy curriculum that does not focus on the application, and hence the transferability, of such skills, although attention to these areas is of enormous importance. This is one of the central challenges for curriculum design and is nothing new. As Alexander (1984) pointed out, it is the axis around which competing conceptions of the primary curriculum have long revolved.

NOTES

1. Somewhat confusingly, the literature on knowing how often calls these innate capacities 'abilities' in contrast to examples of knowing how. I shall use the term 'capacity' for these innate phenomena.
2. One may be able to do something (e.g. digest food or breathe) without knowing how to do so, and in this sense, one could be able to learn, rather than know how to. Note, though, that one may learn to know how to control some aspects of such a capacity, e.g. to hold one's breath.
3. http://www.nc.uk.net/webdav/servlet/XRM?Page/@id=6001&Session/@id=D_yis3e4CTrL-s7ag596PwI&POS[@stateId_eq_main]/@id=6048&POS[@stateId_eq_at]/@id=6048)
4. There is an associated problem of thinking that a fallacious kind of reasoning in one area is always such in another. An example can be found in Halpern (1998, p. 457), when she claims that the notion of 'sunk costs' in economics and accountancy has application across a range of contexts, and that sunk costs arguments can be identified in other areas. It is doubtful, for example, that someone who wants to marry his girlfriend because they have spent many years together is using a sunk cost argument. More likely he is inferring future happiness from past and wishes to take steps to secure it more firmly.
5. I am grateful to Jeremy Hodgen for suggestions in this section.

REFERENCES

Adey, P. S. and Shayer, M. (1994) *Really Raising Standards* (London, Routledge).

Alexander, R. (1984) *Primary Teaching* (London, Holt).

Beard, R. (2000) *Developing Reading 3–13* (London, Hodder Arnold).

Black, P., McCormick, R., James, M. and Pedder, R. (2006) Learning how to Learn and Assessment for Learning: A Theoretical Inquiry, *Research Papers in Education*, 21.2, pp. 119–132.

Boaler, J. (2002) *Experiencing School Mathematics: Traditional and Reform Approaches to Teaching and their Impact on Student Learning*, 2nd edn. (Mahwah, NJ, Lawrence Erlbaum Associates).

Chomsky, N. (1988) *Language and Problems of Knowledge* (Cambridge, MA, MIT Press).

Cockcroft, W. H. (1982) The Mathematical Needs of Adult Life, in: W. H. Cockcroft (ed.) *Mathematics Counts* (London, HMSO), pp. 5–11.

Coffield, F., Mosely, D., Hall, E. and Ecclestone, K. (2004) *Learning Styles and Pedagogy in Post-16 Learning*. Available at: http://www.lsda.org.uk/files/PDF/1543.pdf

Dearden, R. (1976) *Problems of Primary Education* (London, Routledge).

DfES (2003) *The Skills for Life survey: A National Needs and Impact Survey of Literacy, Numeracy and ICT Skills* (Norwich, HMSO).

DfES (2005) National Statistics: National Curriculum Assessments of 14 Year Olds in England, 2005 (Provisional) http://www.dfes.gov.uk/rsgateway/DB/SFR/s000599/SFR32-2005v7.pdf, p. 10, (Accessed 10.05.06).

Fisher, A. (2001) *The Logic of Real Arguments* (Cambridge, Cambridge University Press).

Fodor, J. (1975) *The Language of Thought* (Cambridge, MA, Harvard University Press).

Fodor, J. (2001) *The Mind Doesn't Work That Way: The Scope and Limits of Computational Psychology* (Cambridge, MA, MIT Press).

Gramsci, A. (1975) *The Prison Notebooks* (section on Education) (London, Lawrence and Wishart).

Halpern, D. (1998) Teaching Critical Thinking for Transfer Across Domains: Dispositions, Skills, Structure Training and Metacognitive Monitoring, *American Psychologist*, 53.4, pp. 449–455.

HMSO (1978) *Primary Education Survey* (London, HMSO).

Hoyles, C., Noss, R. and Pozzi, S. (1999) Mathematizing in Practice, in: C. Hoyles, C. Morgan and G. Woodhouse (eds) *Rethinking the Mathematics Curriculum* (London, Falmer Press), pp. 48–62.

Kenny, A. (1968) *Descartes* (New York, Random House).

Kerschensteiner, G. (1964) *Ausgewählter Pädagogische Texte*, Band 1 (Paderborn, Schöningh).

Kuhn, T. (1962) *The Structure of Scientific Revolutions* (Chicago, University of Chicago Press).

Lakatos, I. (1970) Criticism and the Growth of Knowledge: Volume 4: *Proceedings of the International Colloquium in the Philosophy of Science* (held in London, 1965) I. Lakatos and A. Musgrave, eds (Cambridge, Cambridge University Press).

Lave, J. (1988) *Cognition in Practice: Mind, Mathematics and Culture in Everyday Life* (Cambridge, Cambridge University Press).

Levi, D. (2000) *In Defence of Informal Logic* (Dordrecht, Kluwer).

Lieberman, D. (1990) *Learning* (California, Wadsworth).

Lipton, P. (2004) *Inference to the Best Explanation* (London, Routledge).

Newton-Smith, W. H. (1990) *The Rationality of Science* (London, Routledge).

Nunes, T., Schliemann, A. D. and Carraher, D. W. (1993) *Street Mathematics and School Mathematics* (Cambridge, Cambridge University Press).

Okasha, S. (2002) *The Philosophy of Science* (Oxford, Oxford University Press).

PISA (2006) *OECD Programme for International Student Assessment*. Available at: http://www.pisa.oecd.org/pages/0,2987,en_32252351_32235731_1_1_1_1_1,00.html

Polya, G. (1954) *Induction and Analogy in Mathematics: Mathematics and Plausible Reasoning, Volume 1*, 2nd edn. (Princeton, NJ, Princeton University Press).

Popper, K. (1936) *The Logic of Scientific Discovery* (London, Routledge).

QCA (2008) The National Curriculum: English Key Stage 2. Available at: http://curriculum.qca.org.uk/key-stages-1-and-2/subjects/english/attainmenttargets/index.aspx?return=/key-stages-1-and-2/subjects/english/keystage2/index.aspx%3Freturn%3D/key-stages-1-and-2/subjects/english/index.aspx

Rousseau, J-J. (1762) (1968) *Emile ou l'Education* (Paris, Flammarion).

Ryle, G. (1974) Intelligence and the Logic of the Nature-Nurture Debate, *Proceedings of the Philosophy of Education Society of Great Britain*, 8.1, pp. 52–60.

Snowdon, P. (2003) Knowing How and Knowing That: A Distinction Reconsidered, address delivered to the Aristotelian Society, 13th October, 2003, pp. 1–29.

Toulmin, S. (1957) *The Uses of Argument* (Cambridge, Cambridge University Press).

Wittgenstein, L. (1953) *Philosophical Investigations* (Oxford, Blackwell).

Wood, D. (1990) *How Children Think and Learn* (Oxford, Blackwell).

6.3
Philosophy with Children, the Stingray and the Educative Value of Disequilibrium

KARIN SASKIA MURRIS

THE ORIGIN OF PHILOSOPHY WITH CHILDREN

> Meno: Socrates, even before I met you they told me that in plain truth you are a perplexed man yourself and reduce others to perplexity. If I may be flippant, I think that not only in outward appearance but in other respects as well you are exactly like the flat stingray that one meets in the sea. Whenever anyone comes into contact with it, it numbs him, and that is the sort of thing that you seem to be doing to me now . . .

> Socrates: . . . if the stingray paralyses others only through being paralysed itself, then the comparison is just, but not otherwise. It isn't that knowing the answers myself, I perplex other people. The truth is rather that I infect them also with the perplexity I feel myself (*Meno*, 80a–c; in Guthrie, 1956).

Inspired by the philosophies of Plato and John Dewey, Matthew Lipman pioneered the teaching of philosophy to children as a response to his concerns that children do not think as well as they are capable of, or as is necessary for a well functioning truly democratic society. He speculated that early intervention through a logically, not empirically,[1] sequenced specially-written curriculum would tap into children's original curiosity, sense of wonder and enthusiasm for intellectual enquiry, and strengthen their philosophical thinking. In collaboration with colleagues at the Institute for the Advancement of Philosophy for Children (IAPC) at Montclair State University (USA), he developed the Philosophy for Children (P4C)[2] Program consisting of seven philosophical novels and accompanying teacher manuals specially designed for primary and secondary education.[3] The fictional novels model children and adults engaged in philosophical enquiries.

The programme is the most widely used resource,[4] and has also inspired others to create a variety of alternative resources and approaches to support teachers in their innovative work, either for practical reasons (e.g. shorter, cheaper), or for philosophical and pedagogical reasons.[5]

Lipman's pioneering work reaches beyond the mere introduction of just another subject in the curriculum—philosophy. It profoundly questions how schools regard knowledge and how subjects are taught. For Lipman, the statements of which human knowledge is said to be composed are, in fact, answers to long forgotten questions (Lipman and Sharp, 1985, p. 158). What we now call factual knowledge is the generally accepted outcome of previous enquiries.

One of philosophy's educational aims is that every student should become, or continue to remain, an enquirer. For Lipman we cannot 'educate *for* inquiry unless we have education *as* inquiry—unless, that is, the qualitative character we desire to have in the end is loaded into the means' (Lipman, 1991, pp. 15, 245, fn 3). Learning philosophy is best achieved through engagement in philosophical practice as a form of life 'that gives expression to the deepest purposes of education' (Cam, 2000, p 10) and includes 'the strengths of thinking, often linked to children's forms of life and capacity for play' (Haynes, 2008, p. 59).

For Philip Cam the implications are that P4C cannot be regarded as an additional subject to the curriculum, on a par with the others. Lipman shares with Cam the view that the task of philosophy is to encourage children to think for themselves *in*, *about* and *among* the disciplines, which involves an induction into higher-order thinking and critical reflection upon the methodology of each discipline, its assumptions, criteria, procedures and modes of reasoning (Lipman, 1991, pp. 263, 4). This reaches far beyond teaching a set of generic thinking skills. Thinking skills, he insists, should always be taught in the context of a humanistic discipline, such as philosophy—a discipline that is 'representative of the heritage of human thought' (Lipman, 1988, p. 40; 1991, pp. 29, 30). *How* we think is as important as *what* we think about. Sensitivity to concrete, unique context in philosophical enquiry is paramount.[6]

Philosophers have different ideas about what makes their practice philosophical, and there is a risk when concentrating teacher education on a particular P4C training package or programme. If one of the main objectives of P4C is to teach children to think for themselves, it is imperative that *educators* too think for themselves about the philosophical dimensions of their own practice. Adults are badly prepared for pedagogical engagement that is unpredictable and, on the whole, are unfamiliar with philosophy as a subject, or with philosophical reflection as such. The line between materials that offer *support* to teachers and those that *prescribe* is a thin one, especially in an educational system that is hierarchical and celebrates the notion of 'experts' who tell others what to do and what to think on the basis of their perceived authority.

DIALOGUE AND META-DIALOGUE IN THE COMMUNITY OF ENQUIRY

P4C practitioners differ in their choice of educational resource material, but on the whole there is consensus about the 'community of enquiry' as the P4C pedagogy. American pragmatist Charles Sanders Peirce (1839–1914) was the first to fuse together the terms 'community' and 'enquiry' in the domain of scientific inquiry, but it was Lipman who introduced the phrase to describe the pedagogy for teaching philosophy in schools (Lipman *et al.*, 1977, Chapter 7). It is now used in all subject areas, with all age groups and also includes informal education.[7] Laurance Splitter and Ann Margaret Sharp, who have written extensively on the subject, prefer not to give a definition of a community of enquiry,[8] because it is one of those key concepts, they say, that 'takes on new aspects and dimensions as teachers and students apply it and modify it to their purposes. A community of enquiry is at once immanent and transcendent: it provides a framework which pervades the everyday life of its participants and it serves as an ideal to strive for' (Splitter and Sharp, 1995, pp. 17, 18). The pedagogy is inspired by Socrates with the prevailing metaphor of thinking as 'inner speech'. In the dialogue *Theaetetus*, Socrates says:

> ... when the mind is thinking, it is simply talking to itself, asking questions and answering them, and saying Yes or No. When it reaches a decision—which may come slowly or in a sudden rush—when doubt is over and the two voices affirm the same thing, then we call that its 'judgement'. So I should describe thinking as discourse, and judgement as a statement pronounced, not aloud to someone else, but silently to oneself (Plato quoted in Matthews, 1980, p. 42).

It has been claimed, that the pedagogy of a community of enquiry is based on the Vygotskyan assumption that children will learn to think for themselves if they engage in the social practice of thinking together (Cam, 1995, p. 17). Dialogue can be understood as the externalisation of thinking, and thinking as the internalisation of dialogue (Jenkins, 1988). Therefore members of a community of language-users are 'present' in an enquiry as they give language (and therefore thinking) its meaning. The idea is that the internalisation of the 'voices' that build on each other's ideas in a community of enquiry will lead to a richer, more varied 'inner' dialogue, and as a result a better, more reasonable thinking, through 'self-correction'. It is because we define ourselves as persons through the dialogues and conversations we engage in, that the notion of reason in a community of enquiry has ethical, social and ontological aspects (Splitter and Sharp, 1995, pp. 32, 33). Importantly, in dialogue we also address the 'child within'—the child the adult once 'was' and still 'is' (Kennedy, 2006, p 159).

   Through language we address not only our manifold selves in inner dialogue (and others in outer dialogue), but in a community of *philosophical* enquiry we also use language to reflect on the dialogue itself at *meta-dialogical* level; its procedures, its values, its thinking strategies and its truth value. At this level, questions are addressed such as 'Is it fair to always choose the question for enquiry that gets most votes?', 'Can we talk about *anything* we want?', or 'Are some questions better than others for enquiry?'. It is this thinking *about* thinking in an enquiry that is necessary for the practice to be philosophical, and also democratic when children's decisions and ideas shape the 'direction' of the enquiry. The role of the educator is that of a 'guide', a 'guardian' and a 'co-enquirer', who in a spirit of open ended enquiry helps to map out the territory of the dialogue, but does not manipulate or steer the course of the enquiry (Murris and Haynes, 2000a). Some authors emphasise the radically democratic nature of the practice. The concept of 'democracy' is understood to include moral principles such as freedom and equality of opportunity and implies that schools make space for children to actively participate as citizens in contexts that are meaningful to them. Joanna Haynes sketches the possible consequences when children's rights as citizens are promoted and exercised: 'this could well include direct challenges to ways in which the authority of the school is deployed' (Haynes, 2008, p. 58). Regard for children's rights also involves an acknowledgment and acceptance that children have the right to have knowledge presented to them as fallible, problematic and therefore always open to revision (Lipman, 1991; Murris, 1997b). The teacher models such a stance towards knowledge and the meaning of abstract concepts is routinely problematised. Gareth Matthews aptly describes a philosophy teacher as a stingray—a metaphor used by Socrates in the *Meno*.[9] In the sea, a stingray stings not only its victims, but also itself. Similarly, through Socratic questioning, the P4C facilitator is as 'numb' and perplexed as the other members of the community of enquiry (Matthews, 1999, pp. 87–91). It is a paralysis that usefully undermines confidence. It can start to shake the habitual certainty with which people take for granted the meaning of everyday abstract concepts, such as 'respect' or 'space'.

For the teaching of an arguably critical pedagogy that allows thinking to be expressed and challenged, and for new thoughts to be collaboratively constructed, it is crucial that meta-dialogues (dialogues about dialogues) take place not only in classrooms and staffrooms, but also in the physical and metaphorical spaces where teacher educators 'meet'. The facilitator of such meta-dialogues is again like a stingray: actively seeking opportunities to be perplexed, numbed and open to change through reflection and self-reflection. As a pedagogy that responds to the thoughts of its members, genuinely open-ended, critical and self-reflective communities of enquiry are necessary requirements for the practice to continuously renew, transform or diverge. Although there is disagreement in P4C literature about the need for practitioners to have a background in academic philosophy to enable them to generate philosophical questions when facilitating enquiries, not much attention is paid to the various values and epistemological assumptions educators unwittingly bring to their practice. Joanna Haynes points to the constructive role philosophy should play here in 'rearranging, shifting, displacing and reframing ideas and beliefs' as philosophy attempts 'to exist in places of uncertainty, exploration, possibility and imagination (Haynes, 2008, p. 51).

P4C assumes a pedagogy that fosters communicative virtues such as tolerance and respect across differences. Differences between people are regarded as rich educational opportunities for the construction of new ideas collaboratively, and learning is seen as a process that involves making connections between what people (think they) know and what is new. The diversity among P4C practitioners *itself* requires dialogue about their differences. What *is* clear is that this meta-dialogue needs to be philosophical; what is less clear is what the goal of such an exploration among colleagues might be. If such a dialogue were guided by the idea that a philosophy of education could provide a once and for all 'sorting out' of P4C's philosophical 'underpinning', this would already bring a particular rationalist bias to the exercise. Teachers bring their prior knowledge and experiences to their practices, and, as Joseph Dunne eloquently puts it,

> Reason has no absolute standpoint from which it could make all its assumptions transparent, and to accept one's boundedness within tradition, therefore, far from being an abdication of reason, is simply to resign oneself to the only kind of reasonableness that is available to a finite creature (Dunne, 1993, p. 39).

Contextual contingency is characteristic not only of classroom dialogue, but also of dialogue among P4C teacher educators. Such meta-dialogues would inform the *theory* of this new approach to learning; and good *practice* depends upon it. It is the reflective activity of such philosophical engagement itself, not the instrumental desire for the one right answer, that should be their guide. Borrowing a simile from Joseph Dunne, the concrete situatedness[10] of each P4Cer affects one's interpretations and response that 'has its roots in a subsoil of the mind which can never be fully turned over for inspection' (Dunne, 1993, p. 40).

A 'FAMILY' OF PRACTITIONERS

In the current positivist educational climate it comes as no surprise that many advocates justify introduction of P4C by highlighting its compatibility with a number of current agenda items for education—raising standards, teaching thinking skills, creativity, citizenship, inclusion and emotional literacy—justifications that are often motivated by accountability, or the need to secure funding. Understandably, such an instrumental approach has been criticised (Vansiegelheim, 2005; Long, 2005). P4C can be the home of a complex mixture of educational ideas and philosophical traditions as practitioners situate the approach in their own cultural context and infuse the practice with their own identity and philosophical beliefs. In a profound sense, what P4C *is*,[11] can be experienced only in practice, and it embraces a wide range of practices worldwide. In a Wittgensteinian sense, they are united in the way members of a family share certain resemblances—any generalisations about P4C fail to do justice to what is unique about each family member.

P4C has been endorsed by an increasing number of academic philosophers, teachers and teacher educators, as well as policy-makers. But, to continue the simile, with the inclusion of P4C in a nation's curriculum, there is a danger that the patriarch will be tempted to clone, rather than to tolerate real diversity in his family. The question as to what extent P4C can also remain a critical, politically acute and moral activity when part of mainstream education has become an urgent one. The obstacles to adopting it as a critical and self-critical pedagogy are huge when it is increasingly under pressure from an educational system that values individual achievement over collaborative enquiry. As a practice P4C challenges much received wisdom about classroom size, epistemological expertise, the limits of scientific knowledge and who should ask the questions in class (see e.g. Benjamin and Eccheverria, 1992). It questions what it means to be child and what it means to be treated as a citizen, rather than a *citizen-to-be* (Haynes, 2008, Chapter 2). Depending on one's practice, P4C can nibble away at the undemocratic foundations of modern education itself.

WHAT IS A 'CHILD'?

Some authors emphasise the need to regard children as able and resilient thinkers, as equal partners in dialogue, and as *subjects*. Curriculum and assessment frameworks, on the other hand, assume developmental constructs that turn children into *objects* of study (Walkerdine, 1984). Everyday language in schools is saturated by metaphors that objectify children's minds; this gives a false picture of objectivity, certainty and control. Even P4Cers are sometimes tempted to succumb to the prevailing discourse of describing children as 'mature' or 'immature' thinkers, with their 'shallow' or 'deep' contributions, and their need to be taught by an expert adult to move them from 'simple', 'concrete' thoughts to more 'complex' and 'abstract' ones.[12] This deficiency model of childhood is an expression of a discourse saturated with deep dualistic[13] metaphors we teach by, using a language that inadvertently hides the crucial role of dialogue when teaching for better thinking (Murris, 1997a). Our educational language is far from neutral or innocent. Essentialist notions of childhood deny children the possibility of being listened to philosophically and respected as individuals (see e.g. Haynes, 2007b). Children are a marginalised minority; the implicit language of developmental stage theory confirms established hierarchies and encourages a 'distancing' by the adult from (even its own) child (see Matthews, 1994; Kennedy, 2006). Joanna Haynes urges for a re-orientation in teacher education towards the 'being of children, rather than concentrating exclusively on their becoming, their future and their leaving of childhood'. She concludes that:

> At the heart of a community of philosophical enquiry is the commitment to listen in a radically open way and to learn collaboratively: a commitment that has to be worked out in the current culture of child, schools and learning. Such an ethics of listening in education must be pursued with a sensitive political will on the part of adults: through relinquishing authority and unlearning assumptions routinely made about children (Haynes, 2007b).

Although perhaps attractive to curriculum planners, thinking can not be taught mechanically, in contrast to a thinking skills approach, in which the teacher can remain the epistemological authority with the children sitting silently in rows doing paper and pencil tests (Lipman, 1991, pp. 41, 42). Martin Heidegger insists that the teacher-student relationship should be like that between master and apprentice in the medieval guilds—to let 'learning occur'. The mind is not thinking *about* the world, but is always already 'there', *in* the world, thinking, and thinking about its own thinking (Heidegger, 1979). Thinking is understood as an *activity* not a *thing*, and can therefore become neither an *object* for either scientific study (e.g. to be broken down into skills), or philosophical speculation (e.g. to determine its 'essence') as this would assume the possibility of taking a spectator view of thinking; as if humans were able to think about thinking from the 'outside' as it were. Gert Biesta reiterates the epistemological impossibility of humans being the *source* of all knowledge and at the same time the *object* of that knowledge (Biesta, 2006, p. 4). Philosopher of education Michael Bonnett is also critical of an instrumental approach to ;the teaching of thinking that is motivated by 'a desire to turn the environment (including the world of meanings) into a resource' (Bonnett, 1995, p. 304). It is an example of 'deep dualism', or, what Bonnett calls 'a certain *disconnection* between thinker and world, thinker and truth', and expresses 'thinking as a form of mastery, domination' and 'manipulation of a content' (p. 303). Some P4Cers also emphasise the need for educators to focus on thinking *persons*, rather than lists of skills and dispositions, and understand the teaching of thinking as a mode of 'being', rather than a 'doing to' (Haynes, 2008, p. 51; Splitter and Sharp, 1995, p. 8). An example from Heidegger may clarify. When something is 'thought-provoking' it *gives* itself to thought, but also we can only learn to think by '*giving* our mind to what there is to think about' (Heidegger, 1968, p. 4; my emphasis). Inspired by Heidegger, Bonnett argues for 'real' thinking, i.e. 'an open engagement imbued with a sense of the unknown' with the role of the educator as a guide to support 'the *experience* of thinking' and that includes all 'affective-cognitive responses' when fully engaged with content (Bonnett, 1995, p. 306).

Walter Kohan and David Kennedy, in particular, emphasise the emancipatory role of philosophy with children. They agree that—as Kohan puts it—children are confined to the 'space of otherness': systematically undervalued, excluded and objectified through science (Kohan, 1998, 2002). He sees the role of philosophy as problematising ideas, including beliefs and values in what is taken for granted as 'normal' or 'natural' concerning childhood.

As Gareth Matthews observes, 'the concept of childhood is philosophically problematic in that genuinely philosophical difficulties stand in the way of saying just what *kind* of difference between children and adult human beings is' (Matthews, 1994, p. 8). How this difference should be valued has given rise to disagreement amongst P4C practitioners. Kohan, for example, is critical of Matthews' efforts to include children in the rational world of adults as it legitimises the current dominant form of rationality—its knowledge, values and practices (Kohan 1995, 1998). Showing that children can think like adults (for example, by focusing on the *similarities* between the thinking of adults and children), he says, 'would be yet another way of silencing them'. The encounter between philosophy and childhood opens up the challenge for adults 'to listen to a different voice—to a different form of reason, a different theory of knowledge, a different ethics amid a different politics' resulting in different philosophies that children may bring to academic philosophy itself (Kohan, 1998).

Philosophy is more than conversation. It is what David Kennedy describes as a 'multivocal and interactive story about the world, and about persons thinking about the world' (Kennedy, 1998). The oral character of P4C opens up the possibility for inclusion of the excluded non-literate child. Inevitably the creative challenges that emerge for the P4C teacher are experienced as dangerous in a social world that regards children as 'too natural for comfort' and responds by strictly controlling public expression of emotions and other behaviour that challenges the unspoken rules (Kennedy, 2006, p. 84).

David Kennedy's radical conceptualisation is an open invitation to reflect on whether P4C is even possible within compulsory state education. He argues that the implicit goals of schooling are in 'direct contradiction with a major conditional requirement for dialogue—that it is possible only in a context of non-instrumental relations' (Kennedy, 2006, p. 166). He is critical of the sentimentality and instrumentalism of educational rhetoric, which he regards as 'chillingly grotesque' and 'hypocritical', reducing education to the calculated manufacturing of 'citizens', 'workers', and 'consumers' (p. 166). In P4C such instrumentalism can also be at work when the goals that guide facilitation are predetermined—e.g. the P4C child needs to become a 'responsible citizen', a 'critical thinker' and a 'reasonable person in control of its emotions'—fixed and defined by the adult world. To avoid collaboration with such systematic and structurally oppressive political practice, it is imperative to listen philosophically to *individual* children and to resist their objectification through science or everyday educational language (Murris, 1997; Haynes, 2008). Dialogical engagements with children do have outcomes, but they are unexpected, provisional and creative. P4C can open up a space in which adult and child both juggle to 'think otherwise' (Fiumara, 1990, 1995; see also Haynes and Murris, 2000b) about what it means, for example, to be a 'citizen', a 'worker' or a 'consumer'. This will have consequences for the governance of educational institutions, as well as their architecture (Kennedy, 2006, Chapter 5).

'PRODUCTS' OF PHILOSOPHICAL ENQUIRY

Lipman compares progress in a community of enquiry with the movement of a boat tacking into the wind (Lipman, 1991, pp. 15, 16). The teacher as facilitator supports the sailors of the boat in their effort to construct new knowledge by building (and helping others to build) on each other's ideas. Facilitation of philosophical enquiries involves many intuitive decisions, and reaches far beyond the mechanical application of a philosophical toolbox. It requires complex, practical judgments balancing critical, creative, caring and collaborative thinking as well as exercising social intellectual virtues, such as courage, modesty, honesty, respect, patience, awareness and constructiveness in giving and receiving critical challenge (Quinn, 1997, Chapter 9). Without interventions from a facilitator the boat will float like driftwood, especially in the beginning. Lipman and others insist that academic philosophy is crucial for progress to be made (Lipman *et al.*, 1977, pp. 60; Gardner, 1995). Philip Cam, on the other hand, points out that 'freedom' as a guiding ideal for P4C is often overlooked. Drawing on Dewey, he emphasises how 'manifold associations with others' in a community of enquiry enable individuals to fulfil certain 'personal potentialities' (Cam, 2000, pp. 12, 13). Although the focus on truth, insight and meaning is important for progress, each community of enquiry is self-regulating. Cam stresses a kind of rationality that is neither individual—as opposed to social—but transcends this opposition by regarding a reflective community as a means for participants to nurture their own skills and abilities.

Some P4Cers insist that members of a community of enquiry do not learn *about* philosophy, but learn to *philosophise* better. The strict separation of the two (by some) has fuelled many discussions in the field. For example, Ekkehard Martens argues that the two cannot be separated out and that knowledge of academic philosophy is a necessary condition for the activity of philosophising, although he admits that it is difficult to say how much exactly is necessary (Martens, 2008, p. 32). Teachers receive mixed messages from P4C educators about the need for a background in philosophy as taught at universities.

The link between 'community' and 'enquiry' opens up a space in which practitioners are challenged to make their philosophy of education explicit. Laurance Splitter claims the relationship between the two is asymmetrical and interdependent: 'a community is not necessarily a community of inquiry, but inquiry necessarily presupposes an element of community' (Splitter, 2000, p. 12). Communities may have powerful bonds, he explains, of trust, collaboration, risk-taking and a sense of common purpose, but they lack necessary features of enquiry, such as reflection, dialogue, and acknowledging alternative perspectives. Splitter insists that a community is a necessary condition for the teaching of enquiry, because as a mode of thinking, enquiry has a dialogical structure and as such is 'problem-focused, self-correcting, empathetic and multi-perspectival' (p. 13). For enquiry to be *philosophical*, members think not only about a particular question or problem, but they enquire about the *procedures* of this thinking about a subject matter. This meta-thinking by the community, or what Lipman calls 'complex thinking' (Lipman, 1991, pp. 23, 24) needs educators who can meta-think about methodology, assumptions, points of view, bias and prejudice. It is here that acquaintance with philosophers' dialogues that constitute the subject of philosophy is particularly helpful, and for some judged to be necessary.[14]

Difference in P4C practice depends for a large degree on the interpretation of both 'community' and 'enquiry' and the balance of the two.[15] What it means to learn to 'think for yourself' through 'thinking with others' can easily become social conformity, especially with the current political correctness agenda (Browne, 2006). Teachers often take to the P4C community dimension as 'ducks to water'. It is a particular strength teachers bring to the practice—often providing good models for philosophers. However, the rigour that accompanies philosophically building on ideas through argument and democratic enquiry can cause great anxiety. Teachers are unfamiliar with teaching enquiry, let alone philosophical enquiry. A 'diluted' form of P4C—one that focuses primarily on community building[16]—is good enough to satisfy curriculum objectives, such as better speaking and listening skills, questioning and thinking skills, or even education for global citizenship. If P4C becomes a part of mainstream education, the danger is that it may be at risk of losing its philosophical rigour, and critical educational and political agenda.

One's epistemology and ontology (e.g. what is a 'child'?) alter what counts as progress or what is valuable in P4C, and therefore directly influence pedagogical interventions. Often without being aware of it, educators bring their epistemological assumptions and political views to their practice, and the pedagogy gives rise to uncertainty, and therefore insecurity, in the facilitation process (Haynes, 2005, 2007b). Disequilibrium regularly emerges in my own practice, often deliberately provoked, as it exposes educators' struggle with the changed teacher/pupil relationships and their different role as educator. These situated pedagogical tensions offer creative opportunities for P4C educators as they open up a transient space to reflect on the values and beliefs about learning and teaching that educators bring to their practice. The transformative power of such philosophical reflections goes beyond the teaching of a subject, and invites educators to rethink education, and their role in it, afresh. The following examples occur regularly and illustrate a profound and welcome clash of educational paradigms provoked by dialogical learning and teaching, philosophy as a form of life, democratic practice and a different ontology of child. P4C practice profoundly questions educational practice that implicitly claims knowledge about 'child' (as 'object') handing over control to adults and affirming their position of power. When introduced to P4C, educators' insecurities can cause resistance or other responses that aim to restore equilibrium as soon as possible. To help educators feel comfortable with the uncertainties that are tied up with P4C practice—and to enjoy them—is a real challenge for P4C teacher education. One way forward is to have meta-dialogues with colleagues about the specific role philosophy of education could and should play in this process.[17] It is the commonality between the examples that gives the list below its force— each tension is merely outlined. Answers to the questions they raise cannot be provided. In teacher education the educational value of disequilibrium is that each community of enquiry needs to map the territory when disequilibrium occurs and construct their own answers collaboratively— supported by the teacher educator. 'Educators' means here: P4C 'teachers' and 'teacher educators' as well as the 'teachers and mentors of teacher educators'.

RECURRING MOMENTS OF DISEQUILIBRIUM

A. Selecting Starting Points for Enquiry

When educators choose materials that give the right 'message', raise the 'right' theme or 'fit in' with current educational concerns.

In line with the pedagogy, starting points for enquiry need to be selected carefully for their power to express ambiguity, to produce puzzlement, or to evoke deep responses. The questions they provoke cannot be answered by set methods or by 'doing' something, e.g. observation or research. Each member of the community needs to do the thinking for themselves (with the help of the thinking of others). Despite this, much specially written P4C material is didactic, prescriptive and sometimes even moralising (see e.g. Cleghorn and Baudet, 2002). Even complex and open-ended narratives are often used by educators to fit in with curriculum objectives, or their own moral and political agenda, for example, emotional literacy. Unfamiliar with *philosophical* approaches to emotions (Nussbaum, 2001, 2004; Murris, 2008), educators tend to use *psychological* frameworks even when they do P4C as they are more familiar with it. Through the careful selection of certain starting points P4C teacher education can make explicit the dominance of psychological approaches to education and put it forward for discussion.

B. Translation

When educators have difficulty in making sense of what members of a community of enquiry are saying.

The extent to which philosophical enquiries are meaningful depends on the connections and links made by the community between abstract concepts or ideas, and the interests and personal experiences of its members. A willingness to experiment and play with new ideas demands philosophical steps from the known to the unknown in which the educator needs to resist the urge to 'translate' what is being said into the more familiar public knowledge embodied in the curriculum (Haynes and Murris, 2006). If not, children will simply conform to educators' efforts to control. Interpreting transcripts of enquiries with children is profoundly complex (Haynes, 2007b; Murris, 2000). Reading transcripts and analysing tapes of enquiries in P4C teacher education makes adults not only aware of assumptions they bring to their readings, but also raises the question about the extent to which enquiries with adults sufficiently prepare teachers for facilitating enquiries with children.

C. Finding the 'Right' Question

When educators learn to identify philosophical questions by looking at word use (e.g. 'why') or strategies that focus on the analysis of abstract concepts.

The challenge here for teacher education is huge. Educators are quick to learn to identify abstract philosophical concepts and to generate philosophical questions with a *'what is. . .?'* structure.[18] However, this new found knowledge can easily become a technique, giving educators what looks like a tool, to help tell the difference between 'good' and 'bad' philosophical questions. But embedding abstract philosophical questions in concrete experiences or narratives cannot be reduced to a *technique*; it requires not only practical wisdom (Dunne, 1993; Murris, 2008), but also engagement with the history of philosophical ideas.

D. Psychological and Philosophical Investigations

When educators ask 'what are the author's intentions', or 'how does this make you feel?'.

On the whole, educators struggle with the difference between psychological and philosophical responses to abstract questions (see e.g. Gardner, 1995). What counts as an explanation in science, psychology or literacy is different in philosophy as the answers to philosophical questions remain contestable. Even when a procedure has been agreed upon to answer these questions (e.g. conceptual analysis), this procedure itself can also be questioned on its sufficiency or validity (Splitter, 2000, p. 3). Again, the disequilibrium caused by the tension between philosophical and psychological questions can offer invaluable educational opportunities as the distinction between the two is far from straightforward.

E. Lack of Progress

When educators are troubled by a lack of linear direction in the dialogue, and express their uncertainty with remarks such as 'They are going round in circles', or 'They keep going off on a tangent'.

Unlike ordinary conversation, a community of enquiry aims at a *disequilibrium*. Lipman compares the movement of an enquiry with walking. When you walk you constantly shift your weight from your left foot to your right and so on; in the process throwing yourself off balance (Lipman, 1991, p. 229). The movement in a community of enquiry is not linear, nor circular, but that of a spiral that generates thinking (Murris and Haynes, 2000a). The 'products' of an enquiry are 'reasonable judgments' and as such are never set in stone, but are 'temporary resting places' (Lipman, 1991, pp. 17, 65). Various metaphors have structured our adult beliefs that arguments should have a goal, a beginning, and should proceed in a linear fashion (Murris, 1997a). However, enquiries do often seem to go round in circles. The various ways in which progress can be assessed and what counts as the products of an enquiry in P4C, need to be explored dialogically in teacher education.

F. Conceptual Enquiry

When educators comment that we should start with the definition of a concept ('to get it over and done with'), and urge this to be 'sorted' before the 'proper' discussion can begin.

Philosophy with children is concerned with the interactional properties of a concept, that is, how people use the concept in a variety of human contexts. Progress is made in an enquiry when the meanings of central concepts are illuminated and new understandings constructed collaboratively by locating a concept, an activity or a story in a framework that is connected to something in our own experience (Splitter and Sharp, 1995, p 71). A community of enquiry proceeds on the basis that each and every assumption, statement or argument can be questioned, including the community's own assumptions and procedures, and therefore requires an attitude of tentativeness, open-mindedness, non-dogmatism and humility towards knowledge. The implications for teacher education are that P4C itself cannot be introduced by telling or explaining to educators what P4C is—with the help of a definition—but requires critical engagement with the process and the literature.

G. Peace-Keeping

When educators are fearful of the possibility that teachers or children might get upset and therefore try and avoid certain topics for enquiry.

In P4C, children's personal opinions and questions shape the content and direction of an enquiry, and the children are also co-responsible for its procedures, its rules and its identity. Adult taboo topics such as 'death', 'sex' or 'religion'—even when children have chosen to talk about them—can trigger censorial reactions in educators (Haynes, 2005, 2007b; Haynes and Murris, 2006). Emotional disturbance can offer rich opportunities for the community to explore its values and procedures at meta-level, and to strengthen its practice. But there are no easy answers when balancing the core-values of autonomy and protection in education. Difference, which results in cognitive and emotional conflict, is the dialogical engine that urges participants to explore the conceptual framework of their own thinking.

H. Preparing for the Unexpected

When educators seek explicit guidance with P4C lesson planning and preparation.

Educators are used to a culture of schooling that prioritises transmission (by an adult) and acquisition (by a young learner) of pre-determined knowledge. It is telling that the idea of children's rights to academic freedom (a pursuit of knowledge for its own sake) does not emerge in primary and secondary education (Haynes, 2007a). When philosophy is regarded as an academic subject, rather than as a school subject, possibilities open up for authentic enquiries in communities that create, share, challenge, validate and apply ideas (Kelly, 2002). The pedagogical responsiveness and good questioning such practice requires cannot be planned in advance, and in order to avoid the insecurity it brings about in educators, there is a temptation to focus instead on skills, pre-planned activities, exercises and 'warm-up' activities.

Teacher educators (or the institutions they work for or with) can also fall prey to the idea that knowledge about P4C can be standardised and transmitted through ready-made packages. Such course programmes and the prescribed 'ground that needs to covered' can stifle any dialogical and philosophical responses that might have been important to the community, but that may not have been planned for.[19]

I. Right and Wrong Answers, Freedom to Speak

When educators inform others that there are no right or wrong answers in P4C.

Such a reassurance can indeed be liberating for teachers and children and may have psychological benefits. P4C does aim to give equal opportunities, where every participant is a potential source of insight and worthy of listening to responsively. But it is not the case that 'anything goes' or is accepted uncritically: some contributions can still be treated as invalid, incorrect or irrelevant by the community. However, as seen earlier, the balance between 'progress towards truth', freedom and the needs of the community is far from straightforward and a philosophical exploration of the issues involved should be part of P4C teacher education.

CONCLUSION

Recurring moments of disequilibrium show the considerable challenges P4C teacher education faces, but also how these tensions can create rich opportunities for the P4C facilitator who practises like a stingray. Through actively seeking disequilibrium, these issues can be raised not only in classrooms, staffrooms and by teacher educators, but also can include children who are significant stakeholders in the difficult decisions the practice throws up.

P4C cannot be learned from books. An experiential base is essential. Learning about the 'community of enquiry' is possible only through active participation in such communities. But practice alone is not sufficient: the language educators bring to their practice and how it shapes it, is informed and continuously renewed and changed by rigorous and challenging philosophical reflection. If not, the philosophical dimensions of P4C remain dormant and (non-philosophical) pragmatism prevails.

ACKNOWLEDGEMENTS

I would like to thank in particular Dr Joanna Haynes and Simon Geschwindt for their invaluable critical comments and substantial editorial advice, as well as the children, students, teachers and colleagues who have helped me to develop my thinking and practice, especially through our disagreements.

NOTES

1. An empirical sequence would involve a correspondence 'to already existing stages of cognitive development derived from descriptions of children's behavior in non-educational contexts' (Lipman, 1988, p. 147).
2. 'P4C' is now the most widely used abbreviation for the diverse movements involved in philosophy with children.
3. For a diagrammatical overview of the P4C Program see Fisher, 1998, p. 28.
4. With Britain one of the notable exceptions with, arguably, picturebooks the most popular P4C resource in primary schools.
5. For an analysis of the P4C Program's internal inconsistency, see Murris, 1997a. For its Anglo-American philosophy bias, see Martens, 1999 and 2008.
6. Stephen Johnson also powerfully critiques the current popular interest in thinking skills as transferable 'tools' that can be taught independently from any specific context. These skills are supposedly simple, quantifiable and objective, but he rejects regarding thinking as a 'thing' as we cannot initiate, nor control it. Philosophical thinking in particular will lead to further questioning and deeper perplexity. It is sensitive to and derives its energy from content and involves a variety of virtues and dispositions (see Johnson, 2001).
7. See e.g. the *Thinking Village* project in a small village near York. Through P4C, the objectives of the project are to promote intergenerational understanding and dialogue, and to engage the whole community. See: http://www.jrht.org.uk/New+projects/Innovative+new+projects/Community+philosophy+project+(CPP).htm
8. Rather than giving a definition, Laurance Splitter and Ann Margaret Sharp invite their readers to visualise a P4C classroom. They describe it as: 'We would see a physical configuration which maximises opportunities for participants—notably, students and teachers—to communicate with one another; a round table format or perhaps a collection of smaller groups ... We would see participants building on, shaping and modifying one another's ideas, bound by their interest in the subject matter to keep a unified focus and to follow the enquiry wherever it may lead, rather than wander off in individual directions. We would hear, from students and from teachers, the kinds of questions, answers, hypotheses, ponderings and explanations which reflect the nature of inquiry as open-ended, yet shaped by a logic which has features which are both general and specific to each discipline or subject. We would detect a persistence to get to the bottom of things, balanced by a realisation that the bottom is a long way down. This means, for example, that the members of a community of enquiry are not afraid to modify their point of view or correct any reasoning—their own or that of their fellow members—which seems faulty; and they are willing to give up an idea or an answer which is found wanting' (Splitter and Sharp, 1995, pp. 18, 19). For practical advice on the establishment of a community of enquiry— physical arrangements, length of sessions, how to set the agenda, and how to conduct philosophical enquiries—see, for example, Murris and Haynes, 2000a.
9. See the quotation at the beginning of this chapter.
10. The difficulty for many P4C educators is their specific professional context in which they are seen as 'trainers', not 'educators', and are asked to 'deliver' a course in accordance with pre-determined learning outcomes and objectives.
11. See Endnote 4.
12. See e.g. the thinking skills framework of the revised curriculum in Wales, 2008: http://wales.gov.uk/topics/educationandskills/curriculum_and_assessment/arevisedcurriculumfor-wales/skillsdevelopment/?lang=en
13. Fernando Leal and Patricia Shipley call this dualism in our inner dialogue 'deep dualism' as it is not merely a theoretical stance, but it has *practical* consequences for how we treat people (see Leal and Shipley, 1992, Vol. VII, p. 34). This dualism is an expression of territorial instincts, according to George Lakoff and Mark Johnson. They are a consequence of the fact that human beings have bodies and are separated from the rest of the world by the surface of their skin. Psychologically we experience the world 'outside' us and ourselves as containers with an in-out orientation. This orientation we project not only onto other physical objects, but also onto concepts such as 'mind'. Even the very idea of Socratic teaching is conceptually structured through metaphors—including the core belief that the teacher as facilitator works as a midwife (see Lakoff and Johnson, 1980, pp. 29, 74).

14. During a meeting in June 2008, organised by the European P4C network, SOPHIA, members present identified an in depth acquaintance of, and engagement with, a wide range of philosophical traditions as a necessary condition for philosophical practice.
15. See e.g. Dr Catherine McCall's C.O.P.I. method (http://www.cll.strath.ac.uk/cpd/cpdcem.htm).
16. See for example the DVD *Thinking Allowed* (2007) with unedited whole-class enquiries in Gallions Primary School, London (orders@gallions.newham.sch.uk). The teachers show an unusual ability to listen to the children and have created a culture in the school where ideas are taken seriously and collaboratively explored. The lessons are examples of excellent practice, with the teachers engaged in respectful and skilful discussions using the procedures of P4C, but there is little evidence of meta-thinking (e.g. challenging of assumptions, asking for criteria), or what Marie-France Daniel calls 'critical dialogue': 'explicit interdependence between interventions, process of inquiry is established, search centered on the construction of meaning (vs. truth), search for divergence, uncertainty does not create uneasiness, evaluation of statements and criteria, open-mindedness towards new alternatives, spontaneous and complete justifications, moral preoccupations, statements in the form of hypotheses to be verified (vs. closed conclusions), modification of the initial idea' (Daniel, nd, p. 5).
17. Suitable platforms for such meta-dialogues could be: the British charity S.A.P.E.R.E. (www.sapere.org.uk), the European network SOPHIA (www.sophia.eu.org) and the international organisation I.C.P.I.C (www.icpic.org).
18. Abstract concepts with a social or personal theme are particularly popular: e.g. *'what is friendship?'*, *'what is happiness?'*. By contrast, questions such as *'what is time?'* or *'what is infinity?'* are usually not followed up—even when children raise them.
19. In the past couple of years, Britain's national body for P4C is under pressure to take that route although there is a healthy diversity of views among its members.

REFERENCES

Benjamin, M. and Echeverria, E. (1992) Knowledge in the Classroom, in: A. M. Sharp and R. Reed (eds) *Studies in Philosophy for Children* (Philadelphia, PA, Temple University Press), pp. 64–79.

Biesta, G. (2006) *Beyond Learning: Democratic Education for a Human Future* (Boulder, CO, Paradigm Publishers).

Bonnett, M. (1995) Teaching Thinking and the Sanctity of Content, *Journal of Philosophy of Education*, 29.3, pp. 295–311.

Browne, A. (2006) *The Retreat of Reason: Political Correctness and the Corruption of Public Debate in Modern Britain* (London, Civitas, Institute for the Study of Civil Society).

Cam, P. (1995) *Thinking Together: Philosophical Inquiry for the Classroom* (Sydney, Primary English Teaching Association and Hale and Iremonger).

Cam, P. (2000) Philosophy and Freedom, *Thinking: The Journal of Philosophy for Children*, 15.1, pp. 10–13.

Cleghorn, P. and Baudet, S. (2002) *Let's Think: Philosophical Stories to Stimulate Thinking* (Blackburn, Educational Printing Services Ltd).

Daniel, M-F. (nd) Learning to Dialogue in Kindergarten. A Case Study, *e-Analytic Teaching*, 25.3, pp. 23–52.

Dunne, J. (1993) *Back to the Rough Ground: Practical Judgment and the Lure of Technique* (Notre Dame, IN, University of Notre Dame Press).

Fisher, R. (1998) *Teaching Thinking: Philosophical Enquiry in the Classroom* (London, Cassell).

Fiumara, G. C. (1990) *The Other Side of Language: A Philosophy of Listening* (London and New York, Routledge).

Fiumara, G. C. (1995) *The Metaphoric Process: Connections between Language and Life* (London and New York, Routledge).

Gardner, S. T. (1995) Inquiry is no Mere Conversation (or Discussion or Dialogue): Facilitation is Hard Work!, *Creative and Critical Thinking*, 3.2, pp. 38–49.

Guthrie, W. K. C. (1956) *Plato: Protagoras and Meno* (London, Penguin).

Haynes, J. (2005) The Costs of Thinking, *Teaching Thinking and Creativity*, 17 (Birmingham, Imaginative Minds).

Haynes, J. (2007a) Freedom and the Urge to Think in Philosophy with Children, *Gifted Education and International*, 22.2/3, pp. 229–38.

Haynes, J. (2007b) *Listening as a Critical Practice: Learning from Philosophy with Children*, PhD thesis submitted for examination to University of Exeter.

Haynes, J. (2008) *Children as Philosophers. Learning through Enquiry and Dialogue in the Primary School*, 2nd edn. (London, RoutledgeFalmer).

Haynes, J. and Murris, K. (2000) Listening, Juggling and Travelling in Philosophical Space, *Critical and Creative Thinking, Australasian Journal of Philosophy for Children*, 8.1, pp. 23–32.

Haynes, J and Murris, K. (2006) The 'Wrong Message': Risk, Censorship and The Struggle for Democracy in the Primary School (presented at Philosophy of Education Society Conference, Oxford, 31 March-2 April 2006), to be published in *Thinking: The Journal of Philosophy for Children* (forthcoming).

Heidegger, M. (1968) *What is called Thinking?*, J. G. Gray, trans. and intro. (New York, Harper and Row).

Heidegger, M. (1979) *Sein und Zeit* (Tübingen, Max Niemeyer Verlag).

Jenkins, T. J. O. (1988) Philosophy for Children, *Values*, 2.3.

Johnson, S. (2001) *Teaching Thinking Skills*. Impact Paper No 8 in a series of policy discussions, C. Winch and R. Smith, eds (The Philosophy of Education Society of Great Britain).

Kelly, P. (2002) Authentic Enquiry in the Classroom, *Teaching Thinking and Creativity*, 7, pp. 38–42.

Kennedy, D. (1998) Reconstructing Childhood, *Thinking. The Journal of Philosophy for Children*, 14.1, pp. 29–37.

Kennedy, D. (2006) *The Well of Being: Childhood, Subjectivity and Education* (Albany, State University of New York Press).

Kohan, W. O. (1995) The Origin, Nature and Aim of Philosophy in relation to Philosophy for Children, *Thinking: The Journal of Philosophy for Children*, 12.2, pp. 25–31.

Kohan, W. O. (1998) What Can Philosophy and Children Offer Each Other?, *Thinking. The Journal of Philosophy for Children*, 14.4, pp. 2–8.

Kohan, W. O. (2002) Education, Philosophy and Childhood: The Need to Think an Encounter, *Thinking: The Journal of Philosophy for Children*, 16.1, pp 4–11.

Lakoff, G. and Johnson, M. (1980) *Metaphors We Live By* (London, University of Chicago Press).

Leal, F. and Shipley, P. (1992) Deep Dualism, *International Journal of Applied Philosophy*, VII, pp. 33–44.

Lipman, M. (1988) *Philosophy Goes to School* (Philadelphia, PA, Temple University Press).

Lipman, M. (1991) *Thinking in Education* (Cambridge, MA, Cambridge University Press).

Lipman, M. and Sharp, A. M. (1985) *Ethical Inquiry: Instructional Manual to Accompany Lisa* (Montclair, NJ, Institute for the Advancement of Philosophy for Children with University Press of America).

Lipman, M., Sharp, A. M. and Oscanyan, F. S. (1977) *Philosophy in the Classroom* (Philadelphia, PA, Temple University Press).

Long, F (2005) Thomas Reid and Philosophy with Children, *Journal of Philosophy of Education*, 39.4, pp. 599–615.

Martens, E. (1999) *Spelen met denken: Over Filosoferen met Kinderen* (Rotterdam, Lemniscaat).

Martens, E. (2008) 'Can Animals Think?' The Five Most Important Methods of Philosophizing with Children, *Thinking: The Journal of Philosophy for Children*, 18.4, pp. 32–35.

Matthews, G. (1980) *Philosophy and the Young Child* (Cambridge, MA, Harvard University Press).

Matthews, G. (1994) *The Philosophy of Childhood* (Cambridge, MA, Harvard University Press).

Matthews, G. (1999) *Socratic Perplexity and the Nature of Philosophy* (Oxford, Oxford University Press).

Murris, K. (1997a) *Metaphors of the Child's Mind: Teaching Philosophy to Young Children*. Phd Thesis, University of Hull.

Murris, K. (1997b) Philosophy with Children: More Basic than the Basics, *Curriculum*, 18.3, pp. 129–140.

Murris, K. (1999) Philosophy with Preliterate Children, *Thinking: The Journal of Philosophy for Children*, 14.4, pp. 23–34.

Murris, K. (2000) The Role of the Facilitator in Philosophical Enquiry, *Thinking*, 15.2, pp. 40–47.

Murris, K. (2008) Autonomous and Authentic Thinking through Philosophy with Picturebooks, in: M. Hand and C. Winstanley (eds) *Philosophy in Schools* (London, Continuum).

Murris, K. and Haynes, J. (2000a) *Storywise: Thinking through Stories* (Newport, Dialogueworks).

Murris, K. and Haynes, J. (2000b) Listening, Juggling and Travelling in Philosophical Space, *Critical and Creative Thinking*, 8.1, pp. 23–32.

Nussbaum, M. (2001) *Upheavals of Thought: the Intelligence of Emotions* (Cambridge, Cambridge University Press).

Nussbaum, M. (2004) Emotions as Judgments of Value and Importance, in: R. C. Solomon (ed.) *Thinking about Feeling: Contemporary Philosophers on Emotions* (Oxford, Oxford University Press).

Quinn, V. (1997) *Critical Thinking in Young Minds* (London, David Fulton).

Splitter, L. (2000) Concepts, Communities and the Tools for Good Thinking, *Inquiry: Critical Thinking Across the Disciplines*, 19.2, pp 11–26.

Splitter, L. and Sharp, A. M. (1995) *Teaching for Better Thinking; The Classroom Community of Enquiry* (Melbourne, Acer).

Thinking Allowed (2007) DVD; published by Gallions Primary School, London (orders@gal lions.newham.sch.uk).

Vansiegelheim, N. (2005) Philosophy for Children as the Wind of Thinking, *Journal of Philosophy of Education*, 39.1, pp. 19–37.

Walkerdine, V. (1984) Developmental Psychology and the Child-centred Pedagogy, in: J. Henriques, W. Holloway, C. Unwin, C. Venn and V. Walkerdine (eds), *Changing the Subject: Psychology, Social Regulation and Subjectivity* (London and New York, Routledge).

6.4
From Schools to Learning Environments: The Dark Side of Being Exceptional

MAARTEN SIMONS AND JAN MASSCHELEIN

1 INTRODUCTION

In contemporary discourse the family and school no longer appear as *institutions* for child rearing and education. The leading (reform) discourse in academic contexts as well as in the popular media prefers the concept of the 'learning *environment*'. The use of this concept is endemic. Schools and classrooms, as well as the work place and the Internet, are considered today as learning environments. Furthermore, people today are regarded as learners and one main target of school education has become 'learning' pupils and students how to learn. The roles of teachers and lecturers are consequently redefined as instructors, designers of (powerful) learning environments, and facilitators or coaches of learning processes.

It is not an exaggeration to consider this new vocabulary as already being part of our collective experience or current self-understanding as teachers, lecturers or researchers, or at least, as guiding the reform of educational practices. The chapter, however, will not focus on the consequences of these reforms for teachers and the effects on the practice of teaching. Instead, the chapter takes these (reform) discourses, and the current way of speaking about and looking at 'learning', as a point of departure to analyse the new mode of understanding ourselves and the world that is implied. The aim of this chapter is to argue that the current self-understanding in terms of learning environments is not merely about a renewal of our vocabulary, but an indication of a far more general transformation of the world of education. In short, we want to argue that the current self-understanding in terms of 'learning environments' and 'learners' indicates a shift in our experience of time and place; a shift from what is called further on in this chapter a 'historical self-understanding' to a 'environmental self-understanding'. In order to clarify the precise scope of this chapter, two preliminary remarks have to be made: on the 'curiosity' underlying this research and on the understanding of the terms 'space and time'.

In order to fully explore and describe current transformations, we want to apply a kind of 'curiosity' that, according to Foucault, includes an attitude of *care* for the present (Foucault, (1980, p. 108; cf. Rajchman, 1991, p. 141). The aim of this attitude of care is not to 'understand' the present, but to 'cut' into the present or to 'introduce a discontinuity' in our current self-understanding (Foucault, 1984a, p. 88). This Foucauldian curiosity is motivated by a willingness to become a stranger in the familiar present (of 'learning environments') and to regard who we are and what we do ('facilitating learning processes') as no longer obvious. As such, curiosity combines both vigilance or attention and distance (towards oneself in the present) (Gros, 2001, p. 512). Hence, the first aim of this essay is to try to cut into our current understanding of the world of education in terms of 'learning environments'. It can be read as a careful attempt to modify our mode of being in the present, an attempt to 'live the present otherwise' (Foucault, 1979, p. 790), to open up spaces in the present in order to think otherwise about pedagogy—beyond the current ideas on instruction in learning environments.

Second, in this essay special attention will be given to the issues of space and time in educational settings. The concern for space and time should be located at two levels. First, and in line with the 'spatial turn' in social science, it is important to acknowledge the 'spatial context in which particular identities develop and are sustained' (Paechter, 2004, p. 307; cf. Giddens, 1990). Therefore, we want to focus on how past and present modes of self-understanding (of pupils, teachers, parents) are connected with a particular spatial (as well as temporal) *organisation* of educational infrastructures and places (cf. Nespor, 1994; Edwards and Usher, 2000, 2003; Paechter *et al.*, 2001; Mulcahy, 2006). Second, and on a different level, we want to focus on the past and present *experience* of space and time (of pupils, teachers, parents) as such, that is, how time and space are being objectified within different modes of self-understanding (cf. Foucault, 1967/1984; Castells, 1996). The term 'experience' (like related terms such as 'self-understanding' and 'consciousness') is used here in a specific, Foucauldian sense (Foucault, 1984b, p. 13). It refers to a mode of seeing and a way of speaking (about ourselves, others and the world) that emerges in a particular moment and context, and that gradually becomes the (evident) horizon of what we do and think. (Foucault described the emergence of 'sexuality' and 'madness' as such an experience.)

At this level, we want to develop the thesis about a shift from *historical* self-understanding towards *environmental* self-understanding, that is, re-garding oneself as pupils, teachers and parents as part of an 'environment'. The shift from 'the historical' to 'the environmental' is our attempt to explore and describe what is called in more familiar terms the transition from modernity to post-modernity (Lyotard, 1979). Historical self-understanding refers to an experience that privileges time (objectified as 'historical development/progress/accumulation') over space (regarding space in terms of 'location and extension'). Environmental self-under-standing refers to an experience that privileges space (objectified as 'environment') over time (regarding time as the 'here and now' in an environment).

In sum, the first part of this essay will draw upon Foucauldian concepts in order to map the modern organisation of time and space in schools (section 2). In the next section, this past organisation will be confronted with the current organisation of time and space in learning environments (section 3). Contrasting both maps will help to focus further on the main characteristics of the current experience of time and space (discussed in sections 4 and 5), in order to explore, finally, the 'dark side' of this environmental understanding of education (section 6).

2 THE MODERN ORGANISATION OF TIME AND SPACE IN SCHOOLS

Although often discussed elsewhere, we want to start with a schematic Foucauldian (1977) characterisation of the modern organisation of schools (see for example: Pongratz, 1989; Ball, 1990; Popkewitz and Brennan, 1998). Without claiming to produce an exhaustive description, we will focus in particular on the organisation of time and space and the self-understanding (of pupils, teachers and parents) that emerges here (see also Masschelein and Simons, 2007).

The modern school is an organisation that positions and classifies people spatially in view of controlling their behaviour and purposefully organising individual development. This classification is regarded as indispensable for a detailed surveillance and examination of pupils' development over a period of time. Or to put it more precisely: this spatial organisation is the condition needed to regard pupils' individuality in evolutionary terms and to view the pupil as an object or 'case' for adequate classroom instruction and judgement. Foucault stressed that this arrangement and comparison in classrooms does not deprive pupils of a kind of 'natural' individuality or identity. On the contrary, without this spatial and temporal organisation in schools the modern experience of pupils' individuality or identity (in evolutionary terms) would not be possible at all. It is important indeed to underline in more detail the specificity of this evolutionary individuality.

Foucault elaborated in detail how disciplinary practices from the 18th century onwards produced a specific experience of space and time, which was also related to the establishment of scientific disciplines and practices in the human sciences. He clarified how the spatial and temporal organisation of schools divided duration into successive or parallel segments, where they add up in a cumulative series of temporal stages, towards a terminable stable point. This organisation allowed for the discovery of time as an 'evolutive', linear process that is characterised as 'progress'. In Foucault's words: 'The disciplinary methods reveal a linear time whose moments are integrated, one upon another, and which is orientated towards a terminal, stable point, in short, an "evolutive" time ... at the same moment, the administrative and economic techniques of control reveal a social time of a serial, orientated, cumulative time: the discovery of an evolution in terms of "progress". The disciplinary techniques reveal individual series: the discovery of an evolution in terms of "genesis"' (Foucault, 1977, p. 160). Time is thus administered by making it useful, by segmentation, seriation, synthesis and totalisation.

These disciplining practices lead to a specific problematisation (and consciousness), and allow for specific scientific disciplines to emerge, like an 'analytic pedagogy'. This is a type of pedagogy that establishes educative procedures dividing the process of learning into several levels, and hierarchising each step of development into small cumulative steps. In this context, questions related to 'goals' or 'ends' (that is, the terminal state) and 'means' appear as elements of the general concern to organise 'development'. By bending behaviours towards a terminal state (a fixed norm), disciplinary exercises make possible 'a perpetual characterization of the individual, either in relation to this term [state], in relation to other individuals or in relation to a type of itinerary' (p. 161). This short account helps to clarify how the modern school and classroom arrangement normalises pupils.

Normalisation involves specific activities such as: homogenisation on the basis of age (groups), differentiation with regard to the subject material of teaching, definition of aptitude and abilities of each pupil, regular measurement/assessment of the development of individuals on the basis of examinations (and grades or ranks), noting gaps and hierarchising qualities, skills and aptitudes in order to reward or punish pupils (Foucault, 1977). The allocation of a normalised position in this arrangement of time or space makes it possible for the pupil to know herself in relation to other pupils based on norms. It leads to 'scholastic' knowledge about the self as pupil or 'normalised' self-knowledge. In short, the pupils' relation of the self to the self is a relation mediated by ranks, marks, or averages (in relation to schoolmates of roughly the same age).

In this arrangement, the writing of a report based on marks and ranks is a kind of instrument for positioning a pupil (and oneself as pupil), and this reported knowledge supports educational intervention or correction and further disciplinary surveillance. In short, this 'scholastic' knowledge and self-knowledge is the directory for a successful, gradual and programmed school career. In the modern school and classroom, the pupil is therefore someone who can and should orient herself (or who is being oriented) by marks and averages. Based on these marks and ranks, and in the name of aptitudes and abilities, it is an orientation with a particular destiny and towards a clearly defined future within the school system and finally within society. We will later clarify the way in which the orientation within learning environments is different. However, it is important first to discuss the modern relationship between school life and family life.

Indeed, the organisation of time and space in schools and classrooms, as well as the circulation of 'scholastic' knowledge and self-knowledge, penetrate the family and redefine it as a milieu of education or an extension of school-life (Donzelot, 1977). Parents, for instance, come to know their children in comparison to classmates and in relation to what is average or normal. Through these orientations towards the normal at school parents become involved in the school career of their children, i.e.

as parents they can re-orient their pedagogic behaviour and their way of behaving in the family receives a 'scholastic' dimension and relevance. Hence, school reports on pupils correlate with new parental responsibilities and, as a result, with parental feelings of pride ('look at my child ...') and experiences of (im)perfection ('it is my fault that my child ...'). In modern society, parents' views of their children become coloured by 'scholastic' lenses, from the time children get up in the morning until they go to bed at night, at work and at play, and children become as closely observed and monitored by parents as they are within the rhythm of the school life.

3 THE CURRENT ORGANISATION OF TIME AND SPACE IN LEARNING ENVIRONMENTS

The current organisation of time and space in many schools (and elsewhere) is different (see also Nespor, 1994; Edwards, 2002). As mentioned earlier, the aim of this essay however is not to focus in detail on subtle historical developments, but to highlight discontinuities through confronting the modern organisation (and experience) of time and space described earlier with its current organisation in learning environments. For the description of current learning environments, we will rely mainly on discourses and practices of influential reform initiatives in Flanders (Belgium) (Bossaerts *et al.*, 2002; Ministry of the Flemish Community (MFC), 2006), the Netherlands (Dutch Ministry of Education, Culture and Science (DMECS), 2004) and the UK (Pollard and James, 2004), supported by discourses and reform initiatives of international organisations such as OECD and UNESCO.

In all these discourses, a shift can be detected from talking about normalised school careers to looking at individual learning trajectories and 'personalised learning' (Bossaerts *et al.*, 2002; Pollard and James, 2004). Additionally, these discourses claim that pupils should be regarded today as the subjects of learning and no longer as merely objects of teaching (methods): '... the learning of pupils, not teaching, must be the main priority.' (DMECS, 2004, p. 13) Learning is the central term here, and is defined as a 'process of change and development'—at the level of knowledge, skills and attitudes, or competencies. 'Learning to learn' is about becoming a (mature, independent) 'learner', that is, someone who has learned to manage or steer this ongoing process of change or accumulation of competencies by oneself (MFC, 2006). From this perspective, pupils' individuality and identity is no longer conceived in evolutionary terms (with a clear destination). As learners involved in an ongoing process of learning or accumulation, pupils' individuality and identity is seen as always provisional. It is a momentary phase in a trajectory or lifelong process. As such, individuality and identity are considered as snapshots of realised opportunities at a certain moment (e.g. acquired competencies), on the one hand, and of the remaining learning needs (to continue the learning process), on the other.

Accordingly, what is suggested in these reform initiatives is that the learning environment in schools (and in other organisations) should be designed with a view to stimulating processes of learning (to learn) and in particular offering learning resources and learning opportunities. The teacher is regarded as a main actor in this design: 'It is essential for a teacher to be able to create learning environments ... that lead to a maximum of profit of the learning process. The management activities of the teacher are focused on creating the condition for learning' (MFC, 1999, p. 11). In order to be effectively offering 'stimuli' for learning, learning environments should function furthermore as an environment of simulation. The challenge according to current school reformers is to simulate real-life stimuli (e.g. problems) in order to enable effective learning (e.g. problem-solving) (MFC, 2006). Resources and stimuli from the societal environment, the labour environment, the cultural and political environment can be simulated within learning environments and used as learning resources (to train one's ability to learn). As such, these discourses on reform argue that adult life and challenges in the adult environment should be virtually present in the school environment. Society is a resource for the determination of realistic learning goals or real-life problems (useful competencies); it is a yardstick for assessing the functionality of what has been learned (practical relevancy), or a resource for converting knowledge into competencies (internship).

It is important to notice that, according to this discourse, neither age nor subject material, nor time of 'scholastic' evolution, determine someone's position as learner: 'Choosing for the pupil is choosing to deal with differences. Each pupil is different, each learns differently. It is the task of the school to provide each pupil with an education that addresses his particular talents, learning style, baggage and background' (DMECS, 2004, p. 16; Bossaerts *et al.*, 2002). In a strict sense, within a learning environment the idea of a (normal) 'position' no longer makes sense. Instead, a learner is in continuous movement or involved in an ongoing process to accumulate competencies in order to satisfy learning needs. These learning needs correlate with the chosen learning trajectory, the phase in the learning trajectory, prior learning outcomes and personal preferences, disabilities, etc. Hence, in contemporary discourse pupils are regarded as all having unique needs and foremost (stimulated and simulated) learning needs, and the reforms stress again and again that 'the average pupil does not exist' (*Klasse voor Ouders*, 1997, p. 2). Individual needs appear as normative and these needs are variable and relative. Consequently, what is required today is a 'tailored curriculum', 'pupil choice for study and learning' and 'flexibility leading to qualifications for all' (Pollard and James, 2004, p. 4; Bossaerts *et al.*, 2002).

In the learning environments suggested by the reformers, continuous assessment and feedback become indispensable. These technologies offer a snapshot image of someone who is in movement and they accompany someone who is involved in an ongoing process. As such, in her unique trajectory the learner is no longer in need of surveillance and normalising instruction, but is in need of permanent monitoring, coaching and feedback. What is needed in 'personalised learning' is 'setting personal targets', giving 'effective feedback to the learner' and 'effective use of data to plan learning' (Pollard and James, 2004, p. 4). For the pupil who is steering her own learning process, self-knowledge is about information: information on the required competencies that will give access to a learning environment, on the expected learning outcomes, on the required time investment; information manuals or instructions on how to (learn to) manage the learning process; information on the added value of competencies obtained elsewhere and information on the supply of learning environments. Also necessary for this pupil is information on model or successful trajectories, on the average time investment required and on the market value of (combinations of) modules. All this information helps the learner to be an effective 'autonomous chooser' (see also Marshall, 1996).

As a result, the arrangement of the school as an environment of 'continual learning lines' correlates with the need for what the DMECS calls 'permanent information for permanent orientation' (DMECS, 2004, p. 14). What is required in an environment where one has to know everyone's movements and needs at any moment is a concentration of this kind of information in a system of permanent monitoring or positioning (Vrije Centra voor Leerlingenbegeleiding/Centres for Pupil Monitoring, 2002). This 'environmental' monitoring has a particular aim. Permanent monitoring helps to connect different learning environments and protect the continuity of the learning trajectory, from the point of view of the learner: 'It is the shared responsibility of primary and secondary schools to exchange the knowledge and data on the pupil in such a way that the pupil can continue the path he has chosen as much as possible. Continual pupil-monitoring systems and digital portfolios could be important instruments for accomplishing this' (DMECS, 2004, p. 14). The aim is no longer to know oneself as a pupil in relation to a particular standard, in view of a societal destiny and based on a normalising judgement. Instead, self-knowledge is about the endless accumulation of learning outcomes in one's personalised learning trajectory, and about the in-between 'trade balance' of learning investments.

The reference level for this kind of learning balance is no longer an average as in the modern school organisation. A child's reference level in today's learning environments is the previous phase in her own individual learning process. Therefore, each pupil is for herself the biggest competitor and, being the norm for oneself, everything can always be better or different. The good learner in this context is someone who knows her strengths and weaknesses, and is aware of remaining learning needs. Averages and marks can still be useful in today's learning environments, but they have a particular function. Information on averages functions as a 'benchmark', and can inspire and motivate pupils in their self-competition: 'where do I stand in comparison to others?' This is where the competitive notion of 'excellence' enters the scene of current school reform (see also Readings, 1996). From the viewpoint of 'excellence', comparisons and averages primarily hold the risk of being regarded as a comforting norm and, as a result, for interrupting the ongoing process of accumulation and competitions with oneself. Excellent learners compete foremost with themselves. Before focusing more abstractly on the changed experience of time and space in learning environments, it is important to focus briefly on the redefinition of family life (among other spheres of life) within contemporary educational discourse.

In this context, the family too is conceived as a learning environment; families are more or less powerful or effective, with small or large learning opportunities/resources and more or less adequately simulating (for children) the broader societal environment or the learning environment within schools. Due to this organisation of time and space in terms of learning environments, parents and teachers become partners or 'stakeholders'—among other partners in the broader environment of the school. As stakeholders they have to 'exchange knowledge' in view of optimally coaching the personal learning process of the child (Pollard and James, 2004, p. 14; see also OECD, 1997). All stakeholders must take into account the diversity of learning opportunities and must recognise the added value of each environment: '. . . the pupil can achieve more and at a higher level and can use his talents better if we are successful at integrating learning inside and outside of schools, as well as formal and informal learning, into the regular course programme better and recognise different learning experiences via, for instance, portfolio' (DMECS, 2004, p. 19). Hence, the reform discourses stress constantly that the labour division between both partners is not stable. It is the topic of ongoing bargaining— who is responsible for what? who coaches what?—and decisions on labour division depend upon the needs and interests within the societal environment. As such, bargaining about the division of labour—in view of optimally 'co-ordinated services in/out of schools to support the whole child' (Pollard and James, 2004, p. 4)—is a permanent concern and is part of the design of today's learning environments.

4 THE EMERGENCE OF AN 'ENVIRONMENTAL' SELF-UNDERSTANDING

Based on the previous map of the present organisation of time and space, and in contrast with some features of the modern (school) organisation, we want to clarify that the concept of '(learning) environment' (combined with the many reform initiatives and monitoring tools for learners used today) indicates the emergence of a new experience of time and space, a new self-understanding. Regarding the world as (learning) environment, and regarding oneself as learner in this world, has the following implications.

Primarily, what is being stressed when referring to an environment is the 'here and now': an environment creates challenges and needs here and now, and offers opportunities or resources here and now (Donzelot, 1991, p. 276). This kind of environmental self-understanding is a-temporal and leading to an experience of a 'timeless time', an 'ever-present' or 'eternal ephemerality' (Castells, 1996, pp. 433, 467). To regard oneself as inhabiting an environment implies that one's self-understanding is focused on present capacities and opportunities to meet present challenges and needs. Of paramount importance are the capacities and resources that one has at one's disposal and therefore it is indispensable to have transparent and up-to-date information on what is available here and now. This environmental self-understanding implies a particular conception of the past and the future.

From this viewpoint, someone's past is no longer regarded as a hidden history, as what is partially revealed; and it is not conceived of as determining one's present, and (if not 'therapeutically re-worked') also one's future actions. The new self-understanding's relation to the past is captured very well in recent sociological accounts of the 'individualized society'. Beck, for example, notices that perceptions have become 'private' and 'ahistorical': 'the temporal horizons of perception narrow more and more, until finally in the limiting case *history* shrinks *to the (eternal) present*, and everything revolves around the axis of one's personal ego and personal life' (Beck, 1992, p. 135). The past thus is judged in terms of the opportunities (and resources) it offers today to face present challenges. Therefore the past is something that can and should be used or forgotten in view of these challenges and the future they open up. What is at stake in an environment is the preparedness to clean one's past and memory in view of present usefulness, potential and benefit and thus to safeguard one's opportunities 'here and now'. As a result, the human subject is no longer regarded as that which is foundational or underlying—always already there, more or less transparent—but as a snapshot of realised opportunities.

For this environmental self-understanding, not just the past but also the future is conceived in terms of the opportunities and limits of the 'here and now'. The future is what could be realised or constructed in view of the opportunities and resources that one has at one's disposal. Hence, the world is no longer something 'outside', as Arendt stated, and something that has its own durability (Arendt, 1994). Neither is the world, as modern (techno-) scientists assumed, that which can and should be deciphered in order to change or master it through the application of knowledge and understanding. In environmental terms, the world is what offers here and now opportunities and resources to construct a future. The future of the world therefore is a calculation on the basis of what is available here and now, in a particular environment.

It is this *environmental* self-understanding that we would like to outline in more detail by focusing in particular on the experience of human finitude that emerges here: how do we (as learners) experience our finitude while moving around in environments? Drawing upon Deleuze (1986), the specificity of the present experience of finitude in (learning) environments can be depicted when juxtaposing it schematically with pre-modern and modern experiences of finitude.

In pre-modern times, people experience their finitude in confrontation with an infinite (God) outside of the world. In relation to God, people acknowledge infinitude and learn to know themselves as finite beings. Yet people also come to understand themselves as able to appropriate this finitude and to find their destiny in this appropriation (for example, in living according to a divine order and its moral law). According to Deleuze, this relation between God and human finitude transmutes in modernity to become a secular relation between infinite processes within the world and within humanity. Hence, modern humanity experiences a finitude again but in a quite different way. In modern times, language, labour processes and processes of life (but also culture, nationality, rationality and reason) are regarded as autonomous processes having their own history and development (Foucault, 1966). Division of labour and capitalism, for example, as well as the evolution of life and natural selection, are regarded as occurring independently from singular persons. In relation to the infinitude of these (inner-world) processes, mankind experiences finitude in a new way, but also attempts to appropriate this finitude and to give life a particular, human destiny. Examples of these appropriations are the (teleological) stories on emancipation and progress both at the individual and collective level. These are the stories on the glorious future of (German, French, English) cultures and nations and on the cultivation and emancipation of each and all (see also Lyotard, 1979). These stories, with their distinctive political and educational dimension, hold the promise of a human destiny, i.e. a future reconciliation of mankind with its true nature. Hence, these modern stories assume a kind of *historical* self-understanding, i.e. an understanding of the self as being part of a historical process, as having a historical mission and heading towards a glorious future.

What we want to argue, and drawing on Deleuze, is that exactly the modern experience of finitude and the appropriation in projects of emancipation is no longer ours—despite all nostalgia. There is a shift from this *historical* self-understanding to our present *environmental* self-understanding. In addition, what emerges is a new experience of finitude, and a new way to appropriate this finitude.

5 THE EXPERIENCE OF FINITUDE WITHIN (LEARNING) ENVIRONMENTS

To regard oneself as being part of an environment leads to a particular experience of finitude: *the experience of being permanently in a condition with limited resources* (Deleuze, 1986). Finitude here has a spatial dimension (the environment) and this spatiality generates a particular temporal dimension (the 'here and now', 'the future that is virtually present', 'the benefits from the past that are available'). This is different from the modern experience of finitude, for modern consciousness first of all had a temporal dimension (a historical consciousness and a historical project of emancipation) and in addition a spatial dimension (for example a 'scholastic', disciplinary arrangement of a teleological emancipation) (Foucault, 1966). But not just the temporal and spatial dimension of the experience of finitude has changed. Also the appropriation of this finitude has a different meaning.

Appropriation is no longer something that people have lost and that they have to gain back, as in Marxism, humanism, liberalism, etc. That is a typical modern story of appropriation of one's past and future. Appropriation of finitude nowadays is instead a permanent dedication. Being confronted permanently with limited resources, what people have to appropriate is the force to combine in an unlimited way the limited resources that one has here and now at one's disposal. It is the capacity to make original combinations and to create or construct what is needed, here and now, within an environment. Appropriation thus is about 'sampling' and 'recycling' linguistic, social, cultural, natural resources and being 'innovative'.

It is important to stress again that for this environmental self-understanding the modern idea of progress and emancipation, and its historical assumption, no longer makes sense. Instead, the word 'empowerment' becomes part of our vocabulary of daily struggle (Cruikshank, 1996; Donzelot *et al.*, 2003). It is about empowering people instead of emancipating classes, races and cultures. Of course, it is still possible indeed to qualify a single, creative act, here and now, in terms of emancipation and progress. Yet this essentially temporal qualification then merely refers to the success of an (empowerment) initiative within a particular environment and at a particular moment. What is really at stake is seeking to be empowered or to have the power and authority to face challenges in one's environment. Thus, if one wants to stick to the term 'emancipation', one should keep in mind that environmental emancipation first of all has a spatial dimension; the qualification in terms of emancipation expires when there is a new, more successful combination and when there are new environmental needs.

The shift from emancipation to empowerment does not imply that there are no longer reliable stories to orient ourselves in the world or that people (states, cultures, communities, etc.) are lost without destiny. There are still stories—even 'meta-narratives'—yet these are focused on empowerment or environmental emancipation. An example is the story of the empowerment of Europe as told in the Lisbon Declaration: to become the strongest and most dynamic knowledge society and economy in the world (Lisbon European Council, 2000). It is a story about Europe's lack of competitiveness in comparison to that of the United States and Asia. The story pictures a snapshot of realised opportunities and mobilised resources and summons European countries to combine in a creative and successful way the (reserve of) resources and opportunities in our European environment. It is a story about a Europe that wants to compete with itself and that benchmarks and monitors its performance. Part of the story is to recall Europe's history—i.e. the historical importance of Europe as knowledge society *avant la lettre*—in order to remind us of the potential that is available. In short, it is a story about a future—some prefer to use to word 'survival'—of a Europe that is virtually present.

This shift from a historical to an environmental self-understanding helps to explain the overwhelming use of the word 'learning' today (Simons and Masschelein, 2008). Learning is regarded as the fundamental force or capacity for appropriation. Through learning, mankind is regarded as able to face challenges within an environment. As a consequence, learning needs are translations of limits and opportunities in an environment, and their detection is a first step in the ongoing, strategic appropriation of one's finitude. The societal norm today is the ability to use autonomously one's learning force, determine carefully one's learning goals and manage efficiently and effectively the learning process. The norm is having a permanent dedication to find or 'construct' one's destiny, to make 'projects' and to learn. Therefore, optimal learning today presupposes, as a kind of environmental virtue, 'strategic reasoning' or the ability to read the environment, to judge potentialities in terms of usefulness, to foresee needs, to dare to take risks in order to become excellent, etc.

Environmental self-understanding, and the strategy of appropriation through learning, also explains the emergence of new tensions (and political attitudes). The tension between being conservative and being progressive belongs to a modern, historical self-understanding, for both poles presuppose a temporal, historical dimension. Within an environmental self-understanding, a tension between being pro-active and being re-active begins to emerge. Both poles can be regarded as possible attitudes or strategies towards challenges and opportunities in an environment. Similarly with regard to the concept of emancipation in the ongoing struggle of empowerment, the concept 'tradition' may still be part of present (political) vocabularies. However, 'tradition' today refers to a kind of resource or an 'added value' to face current challenges. It refers to a remainder from the past that becomes (again) a useful resource and should be conserved for that reason.

Finally, it is within this space of thought that societal as well as individual problems can be unmasked as learning problems, or as difficulties with regard to empowerment and the appropriation of one's finitude. Unemployment, for example, can be explained as an unsuccessful combination of human resources within the present environment, and (re)training can be regarded as a solution. Stress can be explained by a lack of pro-activity, and limited social skills can be regarded as the cause of solitude (cf. Rose, 1990). These problems are all to be considered as being caused by an unsuccessful appropriation of one's finitude and, as a result, learning is suggested to be a solution. In sum, learning and 'mobilising the lifelong learner' are regarded as conditions for well-being and welfare, and ultimately for life as such (Edwards, 2002).

Drawing upon this outline of the present arrangement of time and space, and the emergence of an environmental self-understanding, the following section explores the dark side of this self-understanding: the explosion of systems of monitoring and assessment (in order to position oneself permanently).

6 THE DARK SIDE OF 'ENVIRONMENTAL' SELF-UNDERSTANDING: BEING A-BAN-DONED

To experience oneself as being part of an environment implies that the appropriation of one's finitude (through learning) and finding a destination (in empowerment) are permanent dedications. The emergence of environmental self-understanding, however, cannot be disconnected from an explosion of monitoring and assessments systems.

As discussed earlier, the project of steering one's learning process means that the learner is permanently in need of a particular kind of information, that is, information about her performance. She needs to know how to improve or change her performance in order to meet more optimally her needs within an environment. This kind of evaluative information is described in cybernetics as 'feedback', and its function is to control the operation of a system 'by inserting into it the results of past performance' (Wiener in van Peursen *et al.*, 1968, p. 57; cf. McKenzie, 2001, p. 70). Feedback information, and detailed self-assessment based on the feedback that is available ('what are my strengths? what are my weaknesses? what are my learning needs?'), allows the learner to 'govern' herself within an environment. Feedback is the kind of information that is indispensable to orient one's learning force and therefore to orient one's empowerment through learning. In other words, while moving around in environments feedback functions as a kind of permanent 'global positioning', for one who is seeking to be permanently 'empowered'. Hence, feedback and self-assessment becomes a powerful steering mechanism in today's learning environment (cf. Bröckling, 2006).

At this point, it is important to stress the difference from the position within a modern (disciplinary) organisation (such as the school and classroom). The modern school and classroom, as we explained in the second section of the chapter, works according to fixed norms and standards and with experts observing and judging pupils on a regular basis and according to these norms and standards. The learner in contemporary discourses, however, is no longer in need of regular surveillance and normalising instruction by experts, but is in need of permanent feedback in order to permanently know one's own position (Deleuze, 1990). What emerges is the permanent need for feedback: How was my performance? Where aim I standing? Please, evaluate me (See also McKenzie, 2001). In other words, feedback and self-assessment function as a kind of permanent 'global positioning'—permanent feedback information for permanent orientation. Regarding oneself as part of an environment correlates with the experiences of wanting to know one's position at each moment. The ideal situation is the situation where one disposes of what is called 'concurrent feedback', that is, feedback that one receives during (and not after) one's performance.

This ideal of self-government and self-control based on permanent environmental positioning (and feedback information) does not imply, however, there is no (longer) external control. The type of control has changed, and the learner is confronted with new figures entering the scene of surveillance and judgment. For instance, personae enter the scene and tribunals are installed in order to measure, judge and develop the degree of 'capitalizing oneself through learning' (e.g. counsellors), to guard the access to environments (e.g. to new learning environments and their trajectories, to labour environments . . .) and to judge one's potential (e.g.

professional assessors). It seems as if each environment has its own assessment mechanisms, organises its own commissions of assessment, judgement and selection, and defines its own criteria to judge whether access can be provided. This becomes clearly visible in the school environment. Qualifications obtained at school, for instance, are no longer a sufficient condition to enter the labour market. They are at best a necessary condition. Pupils instead are asked to regard themselves as learners and to focus on lifetime employability. Each labour organisation decides itself whether additional learning trajectories are needed in order to grant learners access and to employ them (provisionally). It is important to stress here that the criteria by which to judge someone (that is, to assess someone and to give someone access to an environment) are not fixed and decided in advance. What today is sufficient or a requirement to have access to an environment may no longer be sufficient or required tomorrow.

What we want to highlight here is that the act of determining and fixing criteria, rules and norms no longer precede the acts of judgement. In today's environments, both acts are confused or coincide. Increasingly, decisions are made ad hoc and one learns to know the criteria during the verdict. Information on the criteria used to decide on admission of access is often communicated together with the information on the decision itself: 'Your application is rejected for you do not meet these particular requirements.' But this information on criteria is always too late in order to be useful. In this context, the act of decreeing and judging is often the mandate of the same character, the same commission, or the same board. In a sense, judiciary power and legislative power are being mixed up. Consequently, and drawing upon the ideas of Agamben (1997), within an environmental arrangement of time and space one is increasingly handed over to or at the mercy of sovereign power. This type of power does not make judgements based on criteria or rules that were formulated earlier on, but establishes these criteria and rules in the very act of judgement.

From here we can conclude that perhaps the concept 'being abandoned' characterises most adequately the experience of being part of an environmental condition, that is, the experience of being free from any normalising framework yet at the same time running the risk of being given up. The term 'abandoned' should be understood here in its double meaning: being wholly free from restraint, but at the same time being given up or forsaken (Agamben, 1997). Thus, it is not just about being 'abandoned', but at the same time about being 'banned', which implies being expelled from regular or normal life, and thus being free, yet at the same time no longer being protected by rules, norms etc. An environment like a learning environment at school or a labour environment no longer offers a normalising and collective framework in order to position and to orient oneself as a pupil, teacher or labourer (in relation to fellow pupils, teachers or labourers). Within an environment, trajectories are defined and pursued following the rhythm of one's own needs (and therefore experienced as being within one's own self-control), but at the same time one is always in a position where one could be handed over to or be at the mercy of external judgements or decisions.

Perhaps the term 'exception' grasps even better the specificity of the experience of being part of an environment. To feel oneself abandoned comes close to feeling oneself an exception or feeling like someone to whom the rule or norm does not apply (ibid.). Yet, experiencing oneself as an exception means that one experiences oneself in relation to a norm or rule that is suspended (and thus, the experience of freedom), yet this experience implies at the same time the possible 'execution' of whatever decision on new rules or norms (and thus, the experience of being handed over to sovereign decisions). In short, this condition is about being in a 'state of exception'. Indeed, on the one hand, within a learning environment all learners are 'exceptional' with their individual needs and learning trajectories (not falling under any norm or rule), but on the other hand, each and all may become the victim, or the chosen one, of sovereign decisions. These sovereign decisions are not based on pre-existing norms or rules, but they make or enact rules and norms in the act of deciding.

Hence, environmental self-understanding seems to include a very specific experience; an experience of being exceptional, as not falling under a particular rule or norm, but at the same time experiencing oneself as being at the mercy of ad hoc criteria and judgements. One is thrown back on oneself (given the opportunity to control oneself), but at the same time always already in a position of being at the mercy of (or of being delivered to) someone or something. In short, the experience of being normative for oneself and of having to find over and over again a destiny (through learning and empowerment) can always suddenly transform into an experience of being handed over (and being judged as inappropriate).

Being at the mercy of sovereign decisions is the dark or shady side of environmental self-understanding. Perhaps foremost children and pupils are 'suffering' from this experience because they are told over and over again they all have unique needs and each of them is exceptional. Today indeed, each pupil or learner is regarded as exceptional; each pupil has special educational needs, and each pupil may choose her own trajectory in view of what she sees as her own destiny. This sounds indeed like a present-day, educational liberation—'*zum kinde aus*'. However, it is important to keep in mind that this liberation is in fact an environmental strategy of 'empowerment' with its particular seamy side; the emergence of systems of monitoring, feedback and assessment, as well as the exposure to sovereign decisions. Indeed, each pupil is asked to experience herself as unique and exceptional, but this positioning and self-understanding exposes her permanently to sovereign decisions.

The current organisation of learning environments can hardly be regarded as leading to the 'liberation of the child/pupil'—something that most present day reforms nevertheless have in mind. Of course, the normalising judgement on the bases of fixed norms seems to be something of the past. Yet new mechanisms of both self-control and control have entered the (lifelong) learning scene, combined with ad hoc judgements. They transformed pedagogic concerns into matters of monitoring and feedback. A pressing question, therefore, is this: is another pedagogic attitude possible, beyond the permanent control attitudes and ad hoc judgements that are part of environmental self-understanding, yet without restoring (normalising) judgements and pedagogic attitudes belonging to historical self-understanding?

REFERENCES

Agamben, G. (1997) *Homo Sacer. Le pouvouir souverain et la vie nue*, M. Raiola, trans. (Paris, Seuil).

Arendt, H. (1994) *Vita activa. De mens: bestaan en bestemming*, C. Houwaard, trans. (Amsterdam, Boom).

Ball, S. J. (ed.) (1990) *Foucault and Education. Disciplines and Knowledge* (London, Routledge).

Beck, U. (1992) *Risk Society. Towards a New Modernity* (London, Sage).

Bossaerts, B., Denys, J. and Tegenbos, G. (eds) (2002) *Accent op talent: een geïntegreerde visie op leren en werken (Koning Boudewijnstichting)* (Antwerpen, Garant).

Bröckling, U. (2006) Und ... wie war ich? Über feedback, *Mittelweg*, 36.2, pp. 26–43.

Castells, M. (1996) *The Information Age: Economy, Society and Culture. Volume 1: The Rise of the Network Society* (Oxford, Blackwell).

Cruikshank, B. (1996) Revolutions Within: Self-Government and Self-Esteem, in: A. Barry, T. Osborne and N. Rose (eds) *Foucault and the Political Reason: Liberalism, Neo-Liberalism and Rationalities of Government* (London, UCL Press), pp. 231–251.

Deleuze, G. (1986) *Foucault* (Paris, Les Éditions de Minuit).

Deleuze, G. (1990) *Pourparlers* (Paris, Les Editions de Minuit).

Donzelot, J. (1977) *La police des familles* (Paris, Les Éditions de Minuit).

Donzelot, J. (1991) Pleasure in Work, in: G. Burchell, C. Gordon and P. Miller (eds) *The Foucault Effect: Studies in Governmentality* (London, Harvester Wheatsheaf), pp. 251–278.

Donzelot, J. (with C. Mével and A. Wyvekens) (2003) *Faire Société : La Polique de la Ville aux Etats-Unis et en France* (Paris, Seuil).

Dutch Ministry of Education, Culture and Science (DMECS) (2004) Secondary Education in the Netherlands: Agenda for 2010, 'The Pupil Captivated, the School Unfettered'. The Hague: Government of the Netherlands. [Retrieved 13 April, from http://www.minocw.nl/documenten/koersvo-doc-koersvo_agenda2010_en.pdf]

Edwards, R. (2002) Mobilizing Lifelong Learning: Governmentality in Educational Practices, *Journal of Education Policy*, 17.3, pp. 353–365.

Edwards, R. and Usher, R. (2000) *Globalisation and Pedagogy: Space, Place and Identity* (London, Routledge).

Edwards, R. and Usher, R. (eds) (2003) *Space, Curriculum, and Learning* (Greenwich, CT, Information Age Publishing Inc).

Foucault, M. (1966) *Les mots et les choses* (Paris, Gallimard).

Foucault, M. (1967/1984) Des espaces autres, in: D. Defert, F. Ewald and J. Lagrange (eds) *Dits et écrits IV 1980–1988* (Paris, Gallimard), pp. 752–762.

Foucault, M. (1977) *Discipline and Punish: The Birth of the Prison* (Harmondsworth , Penguin).

Foucault, M. (1979) Vivre autrement le temps, in: D. Defert, F. Ewald and J. Lagrange (eds) *Dits et écrits III 1976–1979* (Paris, Gallimard), pp. 788–790.

Foucault, M. (1980) Entretien avec Michel Foucault, in: D. Defert, F. Ewald and J. Lagrange (eds) *Dits et écrits IV 1980–1988* (Paris, Gallimard), pp. 104–110.

Foucault, M. (1984a) Nietzsche, Genealogy, History, in: P. Rabinow (ed.) *The Foucault Reader* (New York, Pantheon), pp. 76–100.

Foucault, M. (1984b) *Histoire de la sexualité 2. L'usage des plaisirs* (Paris, Gallimard).

Giddens, A. (1990) *The Consequences of Modernity* (Cambridge, Polity Press).

Gros, F. (2001) Situation du cours, in: M. Foucault, *L'Herméneutique du sujet. Cours au Collège de France (1981–1982)* (Paris, Gallimard), pp. 488–526.

Klasse voor Ouders (1997) De gemiddelde leerling bestaat niet [The Average Pupil Does Not Exist], *Klasse voor Ouders*, 7, pp. 2–3.

Lisbon European Council (2000) *Presidency Conclusions*, Lisbon 23–24 March 2006. Available at: http://consilium.europa.eu/ueDocs/cms_Data/docs/pressData/en/ec/00100-r1.en0.htm

Lyotard, J-F. (1979) *La condition postmoderne* (Paris, Les Éditions de Minuit).

McKenzie, J. (2001) *Perform or Else: From Discipline to Performance* (London, Routledge).

Marshall, J. D. (1996) The Autonomous Chooser and 'Reforms' in Education, *Studies in Philosophy and Education*, 15, pp. 89–96.

Masschelein, J. and Simons, M. (2007) The Architecture of the Learning Environment/A 'School' Without a 'Soul'? De architectuur van de leeromgeving/Een 'school' zonder 'ziel'?, *Oase, Journal for Architecture/Tijdschrift voor architectuur*, 72, pp. 6–13.

Ministry of the Flemish Community (MFC) (1999), Departement Onderwijs. *Beroepsprofielen en Basiscompetenties van de leraren*. Decretale Tekst en memorie van toelichting (Brussels, MFC).

Ministry of the Flemish Community (MFC) (2006) Attainment Targets Primary Education: Learning to Learn. Retrieved on January 4 2008, from: http://www.ond.vlaanderen.be/dvo/basisonderwijs/lager/uitgangspunten/lerenleren.htm

Mulcahy, D. (2006) The Salience of Space for Pedagogy and Identity: Problem Based Learning as a Case in Point, *Pedagogy, Culture and Society*, 14.1, pp. 55–69.

Nespor, J. (1994) *Knowledge in motion: Space, Time, and Curriculum in Undergraduate Physics and Management* (London; Washington, DC, Falmer Press).

OECD (1997) *Parents as Partners in Schooling* (Paris, OECD).

Paechter, C. (2004) Editorial: Space, Identity and Education, *Pedagogy, Culture and Society*, 12.3, pp. 307–308.

Paechter, C., Edwards, R., Harrison, R. and Twining, P. (2001) *Learning, Space, Identity* (London, Paul Chapman).

Pollard, A. and James, M. (eds) (2004) *Personalised Learning: A Commentary by the Teaching and Learning Research Programme* (London, Economic and Social Research Council).

Pongratz, L. A. (1989) *Pädagogik im Prozess der Moderne. Studien zur Sozial- und Theoriegeschichte der Schule* (Weinheim, Deutscher Studien Verlag).

Popkewitz, T. and Brennan, M. (eds) (1998) *Foucault's Challenge: Discourse, Knowledge and Political Projects of Schooling* (New York, Teachers College Press).

Rajchman, J. (1991) *Truth and Eros: Foucault, Lacan and the Question of Ethics* (London, Routledge).

Readings, B. (1996) *The University in Ruins* (Cambridge, MA, Harvard University Press).

Rose, N. (1990) *Governing the Soul. The Shaping of the Private Self* (London, Routledge).

Simons, M. and Masschelein, J. (2008) Our 'Will to Learn' and the Assemblage of a Learning Apparatus, in: A. Fejes and K. Nicoll (eds), *Foucault and Adult Education* (London, Routledge).

Van Peursen, C., Bertels, C. and Nauta, D. (1968) *Informatie: een interdisciplinarie studie* (Utrecht, Het Spectrum).

Vrije Centra voor Leerlingenbegeleiding [Centers for Pupil Monitoring] (2002) LVS-draaiboek voor leraars (Kim du Pont) [Pupil Monitoring System]. Available at: http://www.vclb-koepel.be/lvs/lvs/dwnld/draaiboek_leraars.doc

6.5
Commentary

RUTH CIGMAN AND ANDREW DAVIS

Winch's enquiry into the concept of 'learning how to learn' includes an investigation into the notion of a transferable ability. He writes: 'In order to make sense of lh2l in this way, we require abilities that have to be learned but which can be put to work in a variety of contexts in order to assist further learning. Are there such abilities? It seems that there are and the two of greatest interest in our enquiry are called *literacy* and *numeracy*.' This way of expressing matters arguably begs a few questions. Many psychologists and philosophers have come to believe that the metaphor of transfer is radically misleading in the context of learning. It is assumed that we know what counts as a specific ability which can be 'put to work in a variety of contexts'. Rather like a suit of clothes or a hairstyle, it is presented as an individual asset that a person can acquire, keep over a period of time and 'take' (transfer) from one context to another. But what is 'it'? 'Ability' is a transitive concept, which is to say that it is intelligible insofar as it relates to a specific act or performance (reading, counting, swimming etc.) in some way. Do we understand the notion of a 'specific ability' which is not *simply* an ability to x or y, but is transferable *from* x *to* y? What reason do we have to say (or indeed deny) that the ability that now manifests as an ability to y is the *same ability* as that which formerly manifested as an ability to x?

These are sticky philosophical questions, and although it is true that we often talk as though abilities are 'transferable' in the way Winch suggests, it is arguable that everyday ability language treats abilities rather as though they resembled the capacities and dispositions of natural substances. The concern about human abilities is that they reflect shifting and complex aspects of social conventions and practices. What an agent is now doing is *conceptually* linked to her social/cultural context. On this point, see the Commentary to the section on Brain-based Learning, where the Wittgensteinian development in philosophy of mind called 'externalism' is discussed (see also Davis, 1998 and 2005).

In Murris' discussion of Philosophy for Children (P4C), we are again confronted with challenging questions about the *identity* of the alleged capacities that P4C fosters. Instead of describing these as cognitive abilities, it might be better to explore the possibility that high quality P4C promotes some important intellectual (and other) virtues, both individual and social. The theory attributes to children, as a class of individuals, some substantial—and arguably questionable—virtues and attributes. These belong to the 'ontology of the child' that lies at the heart of P4C, according to which children should be regarded as 'able and resilient thinkers, as equal partners in dialogue, and as *subjects*'. The 'deficiency model of childhood' should be given up, and replaced by one in which children are 'listened to philosophically and respected as individuals'. It is crucial that P4C teachers are willing to 'relinquish authority', particularly the epistemological authority that claims knowledge of right and wrong.

One may be forgiven for asking how the new 'ontology' differs from bog-standard child-centred education. The crucial question, however, is how a theory of childhood brings us into the fresh, immediate contact with children that is implied by Heidegger's expression (quoted approvingly by Murris) '*giving* our mind to what there is to think about'. Children should be regarded as 'able and resilient thinkers'; but are all children this way? They should be regarded as 'equal partners in dialogue'; but is this appropriate for each and every child? Is there not a tension between the idea of respecting children as individuals, and having a theory of children in general? The notion of a 'deficiency model of childhood' is rightly found alarming; but might there be uncertainties and insecurities that are experienced by some children *by virtue of being children*, and not by virtue of being patronised by adults? In short, salutary as it may be to emphasise the disequilibrium of teachers, do we also need to remind ourselves who is the educator and who is the educated in a community of enquiry? One does not have to be a hardened developmentalist to see the distinction between childhood and adulthood as somehow irreducible in the context of a human life.

From communities of enquiry, we proceed to learning environments, and questions about why learning is such a prominent and ubiquitous concept in contemporary education. What is the meaning of this preoccupation? ask Simons and Masschelein. What purposes does it fulfil? They write:

[the] shift from a historical to an environmental self-understanding helps to explain the overwhelming use of the word 'learning' today (Simons and Masschelein, 2008). Learning is regarded as the fundamental force or capacity for appropriation. Through learning, mankind is regarded as able to face challenges within an environment.

The postmodern individual, according to this picture, occupies an environment which is permanently, even threateningly, challenging. The proper response to this is to 'appropriate' (if not seize) the means whereby one can respond to these challenges. Indeed we need to do this if we are to survive in the postmodern world (the Darwinian connotations are unmistakable), and in this sense *all* children (and by implication all adults too) have 'special educational needs'. We are inescapably exceptional, and exceptionally challenged, and we need to respond to this by competing with ourselves, using norms which are exclusively our own, referring to nothing but the previous phase in our own former learning process.

However there is a tension here. The imperative to overcome challenges cannot be as solipsistic as this picture suggests, for success in the workplace is an inescapably competitive matter, in an inter-personal as well as personal sense. My survival in the 'real' world *is* unfortunately the 'survival of the fittest', for with jobs as with medical and other resources, there are not enough to go round. This tension between individual and community runs through Simons and Masschelein's account. They write that 'what is being stressed when referring to an environment is the "here and now"', and talk about the 'timelessness' of the environmental understanding. However, a child's 'reference level in today's learning environments is the previous phase in her own individual learning process', which is an unmistakably timely notion. A similar tension exists in the idea that 'averages' inspire children to ask 'where do I stand in comparison to others?' and that this is a form of '*self*-competition'. Children apparently *enquire* about how they compare with others without taking the further step of *competing* with others. It seems natural to ask how far this 'ideal' is or could ever be realised in the 'real' environment of schools.

Simons and Masschelein talk about the 'dark side' of the learning environment idea, but we would go further and suggest that it is horrifying. 'Dark side' suggests that there is also a 'light side', but the more one unpicks the concept of a learning environment, the more the light side fades into shadow. The environments into which we deliver children when we send them to school have nothing of Winnicott's maternal, facilitating quality. Yes, there are teachers whose responsibility it is to 'facilitate' learning processes, but their human faces are veiled by their functional identity. Fascinating as Simons and Masschelein's account undoubtedly is, from our perspective it fails to capture this terrifying inhumanity. They discuss our vulnerability to 'sovereign powers' which, in the absence of common norms, establish new ones (it is implied whimsically) 'in the very act of judgement'. But they do not discuss our vulnerability to paradigms or 'pedagogical attitudes', and indeed the chapter ends with a call to find a 'new attitude' that overcomes the limitations of the historical and environmental paradigms. To us, this sounds a warning bell, and although we are certain the authors had no such intention, there is a possible tension with Nigel Tubbs' (2005) 'philosophy of the teacher' which 'refuses to identify learning as a generality'. Foucauldian curiosity takes us into deep into the currents of generalities, but does it take us into the lives of teachers and children which are, as Tubbs says, 'specific and actual'? Does it overcome the perennial tendency of philosophically-minded people to use language that 'idles' rather than engages with the machinery of everyday life?

REFERENCES

Davis, A. (1998) *The Limits of Educational Assessment* (Oxford, Blackwell).
Davis, A. (2005) Learning and the Social Nature of Mental Powers, *Educational Philosophy and Theory*, 37.5, pp. 635–647.
Tubbs, N. (2005) *Philosophy of the Teacher* (Oxford, Blackwell).

Index

9 781405 195645